KU-344-516

Marrakesh Fez Rabat

Cadogan Guides
West End House, 11 Hills Place,
London W1R 1AG, UK
becky.kendall@morrispub.co.uk

The Globe Pequot Press
246 Goose Lane, PO Box 480, Guilford,
Connecticut 06437–0480

Book and cover design by Animage
Cover photographs by Kicca Tommasi
Maps © Cadogan Guides, drawn by Map Creation Ltd

Editorial Director: Vicki Ingle
Series Editor: Linda McQueen
Editor: Claudia Martin
Indexing: Isobel McLean
Production: Book Production Services

A catalogue record for this book is available from the British Library
ISBN 1-86011-973-5

The author and publishers have made every effort to ensure the accuracy of the information in this book
at the time of going to press. However, they cannot accept any responsibility for any loss, injury or
inconvenience resulting from the use of information contained in this guide.

Please help us to keep this guide up to date

We have done our best to ensure that the information in this guide is correct at the time of going to
press. But places and facilities are constantly changing, and standards and prices in hotels and
restaurants fluctuate. We would be delighted to receive any comments concerning existing entries
or omissions. Authors of the best letters will receive a copy of the Cadogan Guide of their choice.

Printed and bound in Great Britain by Cambridge University Press

For Commander and Mrs K.F. Rogerson and a shared passion for misadventures in Morocco.

About the Author

Barnaby Rogerson first fell in love with the idea of Morocco aged nine, standing before Delacroix's *Arab Tax* in Washington D.C.'s National Gallery. He first visited Morocco when he was 16, on an errand from Gibraltar to buy fresh vegetables in the souk in Tetouan. He has been going back ever since, but over the last two decades has also found time to lay pebble floors in grottoes and write a history of North Africa.

Acknowledgements

One of the joys of putting together a guide is to put various friends to work. In particular I would like to thank Fi Lowry for improving the section on birds, Johnny Bell for that on flora, David Flower on music, Annie Bell on cooking, Rose Baring on language and Vanessa Harley on the geology of Morocco. Sir Bernard Fielden has also provided invaluable information on earth-built buildings and Joel Zack on Jewish Morocco.

The most informative of the letters received from travellers include those of Andrew Gold and Dori Katz from Hartford, Connecticut; Richard Bergman from New York; Robin Rown-Clarke from Maryland; John Stack from Carnforth, Lancashire; Count Clanderwood from Tangier; and William Bickerdike of the British Council at Rabat. They will, I hope, see that their hotel and restaurant recommendations, after suitable testing, have gone into print. The best-letter prize goes to David Lass (Founder-member of the Science Fiction Society and Hon Librarian of the Bram Stoker Society), who kindly sent me a passionate 14-page summary of his misadventures with a hire-car.

Many thanks also to Mary Miers, John Kasmin, Kate Hubbard, Hannah Brookfield, Ros O'Shaugnessy, Hannah Rogerson, Molly Rogerson, Rose Baring, Peter and Lucy Neil and my parents.

As always I depend heavily on the advice of real experts of Moroccan travel, particularly Chris and Max Lawrence of Best of Morocco and Annie Austin of CLM. For past hospitality in Morocco I would like to thank Christopher Gibbs, Jonathan Dawson, Billy Willis, Elisabeth Bouchet-Bouhlal, Jamai Atbir Eddine, Barry Stern, Madame Gunnel Nejar and all at the Riad Enija dream factory.

An even greater debt is owed to Mohammed Jebbour, with whom I have now travelled across the length and breadth of his country with a shared interest in history and an indifference to football. He has helped me to meet a new generation of guides as well as such scholars and dedicated museum curators as Mohammed Choukri of the centre for Alaouite research in Rissani, Hassan Cheradi of the Dar Jamaï museum at Meknès, Si Mohammed, archaeologist-teacher and director of the Tangier museum, Mohammed Chadli of the Fondouq Nejjarine, Thor Kuniholm of the Old American Legation and Hassan Limane, curator of the site of Volubilis.

A final word of thanks goes to the team at Cadogan and to Claudia Martin for pushing this new book into print.

Contents

Contents   v

Morocco has been likened both to an island and a palm tree. For it is all but surrounded by three seas—the Atlantic, the Mediterranean and the sand sea of the Sahara—and like the desert palm, though it is rooted in Africa, it is watered by Islam and rustled by the winds of Europe. The country has an exoticism all its own, created by these conflicting influences washing against its shore.

Whatever your experience of the latin temper of southern Europeans, the heady lifestyle of Morocco is more dramatic. From the moment you land, adventure

Introduction

assails you. In simple transactions, such as buying a kilo of oranges, there is unexpected drama, humour and competitive gamesmanship. The sun is always shining somewhere in Morocco, and from March to October it is difficult to avoid. Travelling is cheap and easy. You can fly, drive, take the train, or share the tempo of local life by packing into a communal taxi or bus.

It is not only the sites of Morocco but also the everyday way of life that lingers in the memory: breakfasts of aromatic coffee, croissants and freshly squeezed orange juice, the heady odour of virgin olive oil. And in the markets stand shiny pyramids of fruit, vegetables, olives, dates and nuts which are so fresh and pure they seem like a new species altogether.

This guide concentrates on the chief glory of Morocco—the vast storehouse of architecture, culture, history, cuisine and craftsmanship preserved in the Imperial Cities.

The sunbaked walls, gardens, covered markets and magical open square of **Marrakesh** have become a worldwide icon of exotic elegance. The city, fringed with palm, orange and olive groves, sits beneath the snow-capped peaks of the High Atlas. At its heart lies a complex spider's web of narrow alleys, through which this book will guide you to track down hidden markets, museums and palatial restaurants. Immediately south of the city half a dozen valleys allow access into the mountains, either for a cool lunch or a visit to an ancient mosque or kasbah.

Fez, just a day's drive north across the Tadla Plain, is bewitchingly different. While Marrakesh is a recognizably African city, particularly in terms of space and colour, Fez is a triumphant citadel of Arabic and Islamic culture. It is one of the world's miraculous survivals, an almost complete medieval city which still maintains its ancient guild system of craftsmen. To walk its narrow streets, to smell, to taste and feel your way through the tanneries, shrines, theological courtyards and bazaars is as close to time travel as a mortal can get. Cupped in a bowl of low hills, this labyrinthine city has been likened to an ossified prayer. **Meknès**, which sits on the western side of the fertile plain of Saiss, just an hour away from Fez, was turned into an Imperial capital in the 17th century. Though not so famous, rich or ancient as its neighbour, the scale of the Imperial City, its vast gates, cisterns, stables and walls, seems to exceed the imagination even of Piranesi. To the north-east of Meknès lie the extensive ruins of Volubulis, the inland capital of Morocco during the Roman Empire, with its intact mosaic floors.

Rabat lies on the coast overlooking the Bou Regreg river. It is a city of multiple identi-ties—12th-century gates and towers, an elegant 17th-century old town, a modern political capital—not to mention its medieval walled neighbour, Salé, on the other bank of the river. The tempo of life in Rabat is calmer than in the other, frenetic Imperial Cities, though it is just as rich in cultural monuments as Fez, Meknès and Marrakesh. The great commercial 20th-century city of **Casablanca**, an hour's journey from Rabat, has never been a cultural centre, though the late king did his best to reverse this with the construc-tion of the monumental Grand Mosque of Hassan II. This, one of the eight wonders of the modern world, combines with the logistics of Casablanca's international airport to attract visitors to the city.

Although the history, environment and architecture of Morocco's great cities are extra-ordinarily diverse, ultimately it is their people that prove most fascinating. In any one Moroccan there may lurk a turbulent and diverse ancestry: of slaves brought across the Saharan wastes to serve as concubines or warriors, of Andalucían refugees from the ancient Moorish cities of southern Spain, and of bedouin Arabs from the tribes that fought their way west along the North African shore. All these people have mingled with the indigenous Berbers, who have continuously occupied the land since the Stone Age. The new young ruler of Morocco, King Mohammed VI, shares these influences, as well as being a direct descendant of the Prophet Mohammed.

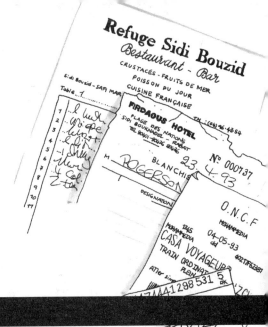

Travel

By Air

From Britain on a Scheduled Flight

The most comfortable and efficient way to travel between Britain and Morocco is with one of the scheduled flights to Marrakesh or Casablanca. There are two companies that run regular, year-round flights between Britain and Morocco: **Royal Air Maroc (RAM)** and **GB Airways**. Prices can vary from around £250 to £350 return, depending on the season. Peak periods for prices are around Christmas or New Year and during the Easter school holidays.

The airlines do not like to sell tickets at discount themselves but will shed blocks of seats to selected travel agents. This process is entirely controlled by supply and demand, but the timing is unpredictable. One day you may find no seats available, at any price, while the next day there are bargains aplenty. The internet has made more information available (especially about flights from other European cities) but is unlikely to rationalize the anarchic pricing.

RAM fly from Heathrow (from Terminal Two, using the Air France lobby at the far right end from the main entrance). There are flights to Casablanca every day of the week. There are no direct flights to Marrakesh, but it is easy to make a connection at Casablanca's Mohammed V airport, the hub of RAM internal services to regional airports such as Fez and Marrakesh.

To make a reservation use a local travel agent or inquire directly from **RAM**, 205 Regent St, London W1R 7DE, ✆ (020) 7439 4361/✆ (020) 7439 8854, ✆ (020) 7287 0127.

GB/British Airways have daily flights to Casablanca leaving Gatwick at 16.55 and arriving 21.35 local time. There are also twice-weekly flights to Marrakesh (*Tues and Fri*).

For **GB/British Airways** information on departures and arrivals, call ✆ (0990) 444 000 (a 24-hour, part-automated answering service), or ✆ (0345) 222 111, for a direct sales line (also partly automated).

From Britain on a Chartered Flight

Seats on charter flights are supposed to be sold as part of an inclusive package holiday, but unbooked seats are routinely sold at a discount. Flights can sometimes be picked up very cheaply, although you will need to fit in with whatever a company has to offer in terms of availability, destinations, fixed return dates, departure times and unfashionable departure airports. In recent years, political events (the Gulf War and Algerian insurrection) have had an adverse effect on the British package-holiday market to Morocco, though a number of companies have returned to Agadir and the Rif coast. Check prices and availability from any of the independent bucket-shop ads in the back pages of *Time Out, Private Eye,* the *Sunday Times* and the *Observer*, or ring the Air Travel Advisory Bureau, ✆ (020) 7636 5000, which can give you a short list of some of the most competitive bucket shops to ring for prices.

At busy times, when there is not a seat to be found, it can also be useful to pick up one of the many cheap charter flights to Málaga or Almería in southern Spain. You can then catch one of the ferries (detailed below) or the three-times-a-week RAM Málaga–Casablanca flight.

From Ireland

There are no direct scheduled flights from Ireland, but **Sunway Travel**, Blackrock, Dublin 6, ✆ (01) 288 6828, arranges direct charter flights from Dublin to Agadir throughout the year. An off-season flight can usually be picked up for around IR£200, or around IR£300 with accommodation.

From France

When direct flights are all sold out remember that Paris has by far the best air connections with Morocco of anywhere in Europe. The routes are shared equally between Air France and Royal Air Maroc. There are 30 flights a week to Casablanca, 12 to Marrakesh and half a dozen each to Fez and Rabat. From provincial cities such as Toulouse, Strasbourg, Nice, Marseille, Lyon and Bordeaux there are at least twice-weekly flights direct to Casablanca.

To check timetables and prices in Britain call **Air France**, ✆ (020) 8759 2311, for recorded information, or visit or call their London office at Colet Court, Hammersmith Rd, London W6, ✆ (020) 8742 6600.

From Other European Countries

Royal Air Maroc and the reciprocal national airlines run regular services to the principal Moroccan airports (including Casablanca and Marrakesh) from Brussels, Amsterdam, Dusseldorf, Frankfurt, Geneva and Madrid. There are also direct weekly flights to and from Copenhagen, Lisbon, Strasbourg, Stockholm, Vienna, Zurich, Milan and Munich.

From North America

There is a variety of ways of crossing the Atlantic to Morocco. The easiest is to book yourself on to the direct twice-weekly **Royal Air Maroc** (**RAM**) flight from JFK airport in New York to Casablanca, or the weekly flight from Montreal to Casablanca. Check availability well in advance, as not all the advertised flights actually run. In New York enquire from the RAM office, ✆ (212) 750 6071, ✇ (212) 980 7924; in Montreal from the RAM office, ✆ 285 1937/✆ 285 1435. Both flights currently depart around 8.30pm and arrive in Morocco just after 7am. An APEX return costs around US$1,000, depending on the season. If you are under 24 you can get a 10 per cent reduction by buying directly from these offices.

The second option is to make a two-stage flight with one of the national European airlines with services to Morocco. They have the advantage of a wide variety of North American departure points, if you don't live near New York or Montreal. The disadvantage is having to change planes and wait in a European transit lounge for the connection to Morocco. APEX returns from the East Coast can usually be picked up for around US$650–US$800; from the West for around US$900–US$1,100.

The third option is to hunt for a bargain flight across the Atlantic to London or Paris (return ticket prices can be anything from US$200 to US$800) and then pick up on the cheap travel offers available in these European cities. Financially this only works well if you have friends or family to stay with, or want a few days in Europe. A London or Paris hotel bill could distort this route into a false economy. There are hundreds of transatlantic flight options—ring around budget travel agents that advertise in Sunday papers, especially the *New York Times*.

The following airlines have toll-free numbers: British Airways: ✆ 1 800 247 2747; Air France: ✆ 1 800 237 2747; Iberia: ✆ 1 800 722 4642; RAM: ✆ 1 800 892 6726; and Virgin Atlantic: ✆ 1 800 862 8621.

From Australia and New Zealand

There are no direct flights from Australasia to Morocco. The nearest thing available is either the Singapore–Casablanca connection operated by Royal Jordanian Airways, or Royal Air Maroc's Dubai–Casablanca flight, but as this already involves one change you might as well visit those sad, grey-coloured cousins in London and pick up a connection from there. It usually works out cheaper.

By Sea

Travelling to Morocco by boat, gently shedding the shores of Europe for those of Africa, is undeniably appealing. There are no ferries to Morocco from Britain or northern Europe, but there is a good choice of routes once you reach the shores of the western Mediterranean. Outside of the peak six weeks from late July to early September, it is usually possible to pick up tickets for a vehicle crossing at ferry ports without too much of a wait. If you wish to make a firm booking in advance there is an efficient British travel agent, **Southern Ferries**, 179 Piccadilly, London W1V 9DB, ✆ (020) 7491 4968, ✉ (020) 7491 3502, who can make all the arrangements necessary, or just advise you as to the times, prices and frequency of this year's sailings.

From France

The car ferry *Marrakesh* sails from Sète, near Montpellier, three times a week in summer and once a week over the winter, and takes 39hrs to arrive in Tangier. This is a popular passage from France but an odd route to take from Britain. Tickets (a return adult fare costs around US$400/£270) are available from the SNCM offices, 4 Quai d'Alger, in Sète, or through their British agents, Southern Ferries (*see* above).

From Spain

The 10hr trip from Almería to Melilla is covered by five sailings a week in the summer and three in winter. Boats depart at 1pm from Almería and at 11pm from Melilla. Tickets can be bought from the port gates or their British agents, Southern Ferries (*see* above).

Ferries run daily throughout the summer for the 8hr trip from Málaga to Melilla, and in the winter there are five sailings a week. Boats depart from Málaga at 1pm and at 11pm from Melilla. Two boats a week travel throughout the year from Málaga to Tangier, a 5hr sail. In Málaga buy tickets from **Limadet**, Muelle Heredia 8, or **Transmediterranea**, Calle Juan Diaz 4, or book ahead through Southern Ferries (*see* above).

From Gibraltar

by ferry

The Gibraltar to Tangier route has flickered on and off over the last two decades. At the time of writing it is running three times a week (*Mon, Wed and Fri*). Book through Southern Ferries (*see* above) or **Bland Travel**, Cloister Building, Irish Town, ✆ (350) 76 155, when in Gibraltar (*c. £20* per passenger, *£50* per car).

The ferries from Algeciras to Tangier or the Spanish enclave of Ceuta offer by far the quickest, cheapest and most popular connection to Morocco. Of the two choices of destination, the sailing to Ceuta is temptingly cheaper and quicker, but the lack of public transport and delays at the border crossing can sometimes make this a false economy. Unless you want to visit Ceuta it is better, even with a car, to go to Tangier. All ferry tickets can be bought at the port gates at Recinto del Puerto in Algeciras, or in advance from Southern Ferries (*see* above). In high season there are 12 one-and-a-half-hour crossings to Ceuta a day, and three or four crossings to Tangier (two and a half hours). The frequency drops to eight (Ceuta) and one or two (Tangier) in the winter.

by hydrofoil

Hydrofoils offer quick, noisy, passenger-only crossings. There is not much view, and no passing breeze, as you are usually confined inside the aircraft-like interior. They do not run in rough weather and do not operate on Sundays, but the tickets (which are all around US$30/£20 for a single) are only about a third more expensive than for a conventional ferry.

Transtour of Algeciras, ✆ (350) 665 200, run at least four half-hour crossings daily to Ceuta throughout the year, the cheapest and most reliable hydrofoil crossing of the Straits of Gibraltar. They also run a daily 1hr service to Tangier from March to September. In high summer a service also sometimes runs to Mdiq, a port on the 'Côte du Rif'.

The celebrated steamer SS *Mons Calpe* which ran from Gibraltar to Tangier is no longer in operation. Its place has been taken by a twice-weekly hydrofoil, which takes an hour and a half. In the summer months there is also a weekly boat to Mdiq. Timetable details and tickets are obtained from **Seagle Ltd**, 9B St George's Lane, Gibraltar, ✆ (350) 76 763/71 415.

The route from Tarifa to Tangier—shortest of them all—is very liable to cancellation if the on-off situation of the last five years is anything to go by. At the time of writing, Transtour provides hydrofoil crossings five days a week.

By Rail

From Britain via France and Spain

The train remains the most civilized way to travel. As my great-grandmother was fond of declaring, if God had meant us to fly he would never have given us the railway. A conventional return ticket from London to Algeciras in Spain will cost about US$420/£280, with perhaps US$75/£50 extra to pay in supplements for couchettes and fast trains in Spain. If you decide to leave London after breakfast on a Thursday, a Eurostar train through the Channel Tunnel will have you in the Gare du Nord in Paris by early afternoon (or early evening, if you take the cheaper ferry train via Dover). You then need to cross Paris to the Gare d'Austerlitz for the 22.58 to Irun on the Spanish border. Arriving at 07.40, you leave at 08.15 to arrive in Madrid at 14.56. You can then have the afternoon and evening on the town before catching the 23.00 night train, which takes you into Algeciras by 9.30am on Saturday.

For information and reservations on all of these services in Britain call **International Travel**, Victoria Station, ✆ (0990) 848 848.

If you are over 26 the discount **InterRail Pass**, which provides unlimited rail travel for a variable period of between 15 days and three months (but is only available to European citizens) is a waste of money for this trip, as it excludes France, Spain and Morocco. If you are under 26, it works for these vital countries, but you will still have to pay extra supplements for ferries and sleepers. The similar **Eurail Pass** is designed for the use of non-European citizens who are not resident in Europe for more than six months. It offers unlimited rail travel in 17 European nations, but again excludes Morocco. There are also supplements to pay for ferries, sleepers and the first and last leg of travel. A two-month pass for someone under 26 costs around US$930/£620, and would not be of any use for a Moroccan-based trip. They are available from many travel agents.

By Bus

From **Britain** there is a regular thrice-weekly service (*Mon, Tues and Wed at 10pm*) from London's Victoria Coach Station for the two-day journey to Tangier. A return ticket from Eurolines, 52 Grosvenor Gardens, London SW1W 0AU, ✆ (020) 7730 8235, currently costs just US$255/£170, a single US$135/£90. From **France**, if you make your own way to Paris, there is a Euroline coach that leaves from Porte de la Villette station for Tangier (*Mon, Wed, Fri and Sat*), from where the same route continues down through Rabat, Casablanca and Marrakesh. For reservations call Eurolines, Porte de la Villette, ✆ (33) 01 40 38 93 93, ✉ 01 42 05 12 10.

By Car

It is possible with two drivers and very little rest to get from England to Tangier in two days, although four or five days would allow you to enjoy something other than fast driving. To effect a smooth entrance into Morocco with a car, it is best to have your paperwork well organized, with documents under one name and one address. You should have **Green Card Insurance** for the journey through Europe, your **Vehicle Registration Document** and your **Driving Licence**. The pink EU driving licence is recognized in Morocco, although the more impressive International Driving Licence (available from the RAC or AA, or the AAA in the USA), with its seal, passport photograph and French translation, is preferred. At the customs post you must buy **Moroccan Frontier Insurance**, which is about US$75/£50 for the maximum permitted visit of three months. This is a bureaucratic 'third party' requirement which, whatever the paper might actually claim, is unlikely to provide any reimbursement in the event of an accident; for working insurance you will need to take out separate cover. In the UK, fire and theft insurance can be arranged with the Norwich Union for a month but no British company is yet prepared to give comprehensive cover for any longer period. If you are bringing a **caravan** (trailer), you will need an International Customs Carnet.

There is a full range of ferries connecting the various channel ports of France and England. The most useful are the night crossings to Le Havre, Caen or Cherbourg. Arriving in these ports in the early morning, you can cross France during that day, to stay in the Pyrenean foothills that night. Crossing Spain can be done at a more leisurely pace, perhaps with a stop at Segovia before concentrating on the splendours of Moorish Andalucía in Granada, Córdoba or Sevilla. There is a twice-weekly ferry from Plymouth to Santander (no sailings in January), but it is an expensive and tedious voyage. Ferry cafés compare badly in expense, entertainment and quality with the roadside restaurants of France and Spain.

Travel Agents and Specialist Holidays

Travel Agents

Creative Leisure Management (CLM), 1st Floor, 69 Knightsbridge, London SW1X 7RA, ✆ (020) 7235 0123/7235 2110, ✉ (020) 7235 3851. Annie Austin has presided over CLM for 23 years and has an exhaustive and intimate knowledge of the country, in part learnt in the seven years when she ran a hotel in Salé.

Best of Morocco, Seend Park, Seend, Wiltshire SN12 6NZ, ✆ (01380) 828 533, ✉ (01380) 828 630; and an office in Marrakesh. This has been managed by Chris Lawrence since 1967. His son Max works full time in Morocco, but has branched out of general travel to take advantage of Morocco's growing popularity as a film and photo-shoot location.

Both Creative Leisure Management and Best of Morocco specialize in arranging holidays for the independent traveller. They can arrange flexible flight plans (flying into one city and out of another), fix good rates for a hire car, organize riding, walking, fishing or shooting holidays and drivers, as well as recommend restaurants or the hire of a villa. The first step in any planned holiday is to look through their annual brochures. These companies also act as agents for **Atlas Sahara Trek** (AST), a well-established Moroccan–French agency that is run by Bernard Fabry and based in Marrakesh. AST run week-long hiking, rafting and camel-riding trips anywhere that you wish to go in the Moroccan south.

STA Travel, 74 and 86 Old Brompton Rd, SW7 3LQ, and 117 Euston Rd, London NW1 2SX, ✆ (020) 7937 9921 (for European enquiries), ✆ (020) 7465 0486 (for Africa); 10 High St, Auckland, ✆ (09) 309 9723; 256 Flinders St, Melbourne, ✆ (03) 347 4711; 1 Lee St, Sydney, ✆ (02) 281 9866; 7204 Melrose Avenue, Los Angeles, CA 90046, ✆ (213) 934 8722; 116 Geary St, Suite 702, San Francisco, CA 94108, ✆ (415) 391 8407; 273 Newbury St, Boston, MA 02116, ✆ (617) 266 6014; 48 East 11th St, New York, NY 10003, ✆ (212) 477 7166. They are an experienced firm well placed to give advice on connecting flights and can also book you in with one of the British-based specialist operators detailed in this section.

Even if you are travelling from North America or Australasia, it may be worth making any special arrangements you require via a specialist agent in the UK, since there are more of them there. Or the Moroccan Tourist Board will send you their current list of approved travel agents, which at the moment includes **Les Soleil**, ✆ (212) 308 4249, **Marsans**, ✆ (212) 239 3880, and **RAM tours**, ✆ 1 800 344 6726, in New York; **Morocco Travel**, ✆ 1 800 428 5550 (toll-free) in Virginia; **Maupintour**, ✆ 1 800 255 6162 (toll-free) in the Mid-West; and **ATC**, ✆ 1 800 227 9747 (toll-free) on the West Coast.

Specialist-Interest Tour Operators

Aardvark Safaris Ltd, RBL House, Ordnance Rd, Tidworth, Hants SP9 7QD, ✆ (01980) 849 160, 🖷 (01980) 849 161, offers safaris and treks, including one trip to the Imperial Cities.

Andante, ✆ (01980) 610 555, 🖷 (01980) 610 002, is a Wiltshire-based agency specializing in historical and archaeological tours. They organize a week-long tour of Roman Morocco, Fez, Rabat and Meknès.

Encounter Overland, 267 Old Brompton Rd, London SW5 9JA, ✆ (020) 7370 6845, 🖷 (020) 7244 9737, arranges 15-day tours of Morocco from May to September, starting from Málaga.

Explore Worldwide, 1 Frederick St, Aldershot, Hampshire GU11 1LQ, ✆ (01252) 319 448, arranges small-group walking treks, including an Imperial City tour and a desert trip.

Golf International, International House, Priestley Way, Staples Corner, London NW2 7AW, ✆ (020) 8450 6671, arranges golfing holidays based around the courses at Tangier, Rabat and Mohammedia.

Guerba Expeditions, 101 Eden Vale Rd, Westbury, Wiltshire BA13 3QX, ✆ (01373) 858 956, arranges two-week jeep tours in the Anti-Atlas, or High Atlas mountains and oasis valleys, as well as cultural tours of the country.

Marrakesh Express, 133 Hill St, Glasgow G3 6JA, ✆ (0141) 332 1991, 🖷 (0141) 332 1881, offers golfing, cycling, trekking and specialist-interest holidays throughout Morocco.

Martin Randall, 10 Barley Mow Passage, Chiswick, London W4 4PH, ✆ (020) 8742 3355, 🖷 (020) 8742 1066, arranges an annual trip in late October, with a strong architectural and historical bias, that follows the old caravan route of the Saharan gold trade from Tangier to Sijilmassa and back to Marrakesh.

Morocco Made to Measure, 1st Floor, 69 Knightsbridge, London SW1X 7RA, ✆ (020) 7235 0123, 🖷 (020) 7235 3851, offers specialist-interest tours throughout Morocco, including archaeology, painting, photography, golf, gardens, horse-riding and camel-riding.

Nomadic Expeditions, 263 Barkham Rd, Wokingham, Berkshire RG41 4BY, ✆ (0118) 978 0800, ✉ (0118) 978 2344, offers three- and five-week expeditions that include the Imperial Cities.

Ramblers Holidays, Box 34, Welwyn Garden City, Hertfordshire AL8 6PQ, ✆ (01707) 331 133, arranges walking holidays from Marrakesh into the foothills of the High Atlas, as well as trips to the Imperial Cities.

Saga Holidays, Middleburg Square, Folkestone, Kent CT20 1AZ, ✆ 0800 300 500, organizes holidays for the over-60s in Marrakesh and Agadir.

Sherpa Expeditions, 131A Heston Rd, Hounslow, Middlesex TW5 0RD, ✆ (020) 8577 2717, arranges week- and two-week-long treks from Marrakesh.

Steppes East, Castle Eaton, Cricklade, Swindon, Wiltshire SN6 6JU, ✆ (01285) 810 267, ✉ (01285) 810 693, offers tailor-made travel and natural-history tours, as well as an escorted textiles-of-Morocco tour.

The Imaginative Traveller, 14 Barley Mow Passage, Chiswick, London W4 4PH, ✆ (020) 8742 8612, ✉ (020) 8742 3045, offers camel treks, walking tours and jeep safaris, including visits to the Imperial Cities.

Topdeck, 131 Earl's Court Rd, London SW5 9RH, ✆ (020) 7244 8641, arranges five- or seven-week tours through Spain, Portugal, Morocco, Algeria, Tunisia and Italy, a whistle-stop cultural skirmish that is particularly popular with non-European students and Australians.

Tribes Travel, 7 The Business Centre, Earl Soham, Woodbridge, Suffolk IP13 7SA, ✆ (01728) 685 971, ✉ (01728) 685 973, organizes cultural, wildlife and trekking holidays, aimed at benefiting local people, including one to Marrakesh, Fez and the High Atlas.

Truck Africa Ltd, 6 Hurlingham Studios, Renelagh Gardens, Fulham, London SW6 3PA, ✆ (020) 7731 6142, ✉ (020) 7731 7445, organizes camping safaris, including a five-month Africa North–South trip that includes the Imperial Cities of Morocco.

General Tour Operators

Other tour operators or travel agencies that offer packages or will book tailor-made trips include such names as:

Abercrombie and Kent, Sloane Square House, Holbein Place, London SW1W 8NS, ✆ (020) 7730 9600, ✉ (020) 7730 9376, will arrange tailor-made tours and various packages.

Alecoss Travel, 3a Camden Rd, London NW1 9LG, ✆ (020) 7267 2092, ✉ (020) 7284 2891, arranges tailor-made packages and fly-drives.

Amoun Travel and Tours, 56 Kendal St, London W2 2BP, ✆ (020) 7402 3100, ✉ (020) 7402 3424, arranges tailor-made packages.

Archers Direct, Garrard House, 2–6 Homesdale Rd, Bromley, Kent BR2 9LZ, ✆ 0870 751 2000, 🖷 (020) 8313 1670, offers a nine-day highlights-of-Morocco tour.

British Airways Holidays, Astral Towers, Betts Way, London Rd, Crawley, West Sussex RH10 2XA, ✆ 0870 242 4243, 🖷 (01293) 722 803, runs a 15-day tour visiting the Imperial Cities and many other sites.

Cadogan Travel, Cadogan House, 9–10 Portland St, Southampton, Hampshire SO9 1ZP, ✆ (01703) 332 66, arranges tailor-made travel (the company has no connection with Cadogan Guides).

CV Travel, 43 Cadogan St, London SW3 2PR, ✆ (020) 7581 0851, 🖷 (020) 7584 5229, will arrange tailor-made journeys.

Hayes and Jarvis, 152 King St, London W6 0QU, ✆ (020) 8748 0088, 🖷 (020) 8741 0299, will arrange tailor-made trips and also offer a seven-night tour of the Imperial Cities.

Insight Vacations, Reservations Office, Gareloch House, Gareloch Rd, Port Glasgow PA14 5XH, ✆ 0870 514 3433, 🖷 (01475) 742 073, runs an escorted 17-day trip to Morocco, including Spain and Portugal.

Oasis Tours, 37 Market Place, Kingston-upon-Thames, Surrey KT1 1JQ, ✆ (020) 8296 8877, 🖷 (020) 8296 9911, arranges an eight-day Imperial City tour.

Sam Travel Services, 5 Baker St, London W1M 1AA, ✆ (020) 7487 4404, 🖷 (020) 7487 4232, will arrange tailor-made journeys.

Sunway Holidays, The Sunway Travel Group, PO Box 1680, Slough PDO SL1 7XX, ✆ (01628) 660 664, 🖷 (01628) 602 859, offer tailor-made itineraries, short breaks and escorted tours.

Trafalgar, 15 Grosvenor Place, London SW1X 7HH, ✆ (020) 7574 7444, 🖷 (020) 7873 8614, runs a 10-day grand tour of Morocco.

Travel Path, PO Box 32, Grantham, Linconshire NG31 7JA, ✆ (01476) 570 187, 🖷 (01476) 572 718, organizes tailor-made itineraries.

Travelscene, 11–15 St Ann's Rd, Harrow, Middlesex HA1 1LQ, ✆ 0870 777 4445, 🖷 (020) 8861 4154, offers short breaks in Marrakesh, Fez, Rabat and Casablanca.

Voyages Jules Verne, 21 Dorset Square, London NW1 6QG, ✆ (020) 7616 1000, 🖷 (020) 7723 8629, has an eight-day Imperial Cities tour, as well as a nine-day Andalucía to the High Atlas trip.

Entry Formalities

A valid Australian, British, Irish, Canadian, New Zealand or United States passport allows you to enter Morocco. A small 90-day entrance visa is then stamped into your passport. Temporary British Visitors passports are not accepted. As a retaliation for Benelux restrictions on Moroccan migrant workers, Dutch and Belgian passport holders have to apply for a visa in advance which is valid for only one month.

Whether arriving by air or sea you will need to have filled in a form (a *fiche*) with personal details as you approach the immigration desk. This is perfectly straightforward, providing you avoid any flowery prose beside 'purpose of visit' and humbly write 'tourism'. If you are a journalist or spy you should pretend to have another profession while on holiday in Morocco. If you are, or could be mistaken as, a hippy and are coming off the boat into Morocco it is worth tidying yourself up. If for some reason your hair, dress and jewellery has excited the enmity of an immigration officer, then in extremis there is nothing to stop you trying a different boat and/or port on another day.

Extending Your Stay

For extending a visit beyond 90 days you are officially required to report to a Gendarmerie headquarters. In practice even these officials counsel against entering the labyrinthine world of Moroccan bureaucracy and recommend a simple day trip across the border to either Ceuta, Gibraltar, Algeciras or Melilla in order to collect a fresh 90-day entrance stamp.

Currency

The Moroccan currency is the **dirham** (dh). It is not one of the world's hard currencies (those with rates of exchange fixed by the fast-dealing world of international markets). The dirham's exchange rate is fixed by the Moroccan government at an artificially high rate. In order to maintain this the exportation of currency is strictly forbidden, and so it is not possible to acquire dirhams outside the country. There is no black market, although shop-keepers are often happy enough to accept dollars and major European currencies.

There is usually an exchange booth open at seaports and airports on arrival. Should you arrive at night or outside conventional hours, you may find them closed and that it is impossible to cash travellers' cheques or Eurocheques at all until the next day, let alone use a credit card, so it's best to be armed with cash as well. Local taxi drivers, again, will be only too happy to accept dollars, francs, pounds and just about any other European currency, but try not to accept wildly excessive charging, even after a long flight (*see* 'By Taxi' under Getting Around later in this chapter).

Before leaving try to use up any Moroccan dirhams you may have already exchanged, as currency checks are carried out at passport and customs control at departure points. You will only be allowed to change back half of any amount you are carrying in excess of about 10dh, and the rest will be confiscated outright, with no compensation offered.

Customs

The usual duty-free allowances mean that many people start their trip with an extra bag, a shin-bruising thing in clanking, garish bright yellow. Unless you are a confirmed whisky drinker, forget all the duty-free hype and stick to Moroccan products while you're there.

Cars, sporting guns and expensive electronic equipment (which generally means professional still and video camera equipment) can be imported into the country duty-free for 90 days. The details will be entered into your passport on arrival and will be checked off as you leave. If you cannot produce evidence of their theft (police documentation) you will be presumed to have sold them and charged a punitive duty. There is no way around this; even if you have written your car off on some obscure mountain road you will eventually find yourself having to fetch the wreck and tow it on to the ferry.

Customs officers routinely check bags as you arrive and depart. They are generally courteous and correct with foreigners. Moroccan emigrant workers returning home are careful to include some tempting item at the top of their bag, a small bottle of scent or tin of tea that might take their fancy.

Getting Around

By Air

There are plenty of **Royal Air Maroc** (**RAM**) internal flights between Casablanca (handy for Rabat), Fez and Marrakesh, as well as the other principal cities of Morocco, although the timetables shift constantly. Contact the nearest RAM office for details. To give you a rough idea of prices, it currently costs about US$90/£60 to fly from Tangier to Agadir. All RAM return flights need to be confirmed three days before departure, and there is a 25 per cent discount if you are a student or under 26. However, to fly between the principal cities of Morocco would negate the very real pleasure of travelling through the countryside.

By Rail

Travel by train whenever possible. The Moroccan state railway, the **ONCF**, manages the difficult trick of being both colourful and efficient. It runs over 1,700km (1,000 miles) of line on two axes, from Tangier to Marrakesh (via Rabat and Casablanca) and Casablanca to Oujda (via Rabat, Meknès and Fez). Both of these long routes have a sleeper service, but otherwise daytime travel is divided between first, second and a very basic *économique* class. A second-class ticket is not much more than a bus fare, although the air-conditioning and less cramped seating of first class makes it especially attractive in summer. A bar and restaurant operate on the major connections and there are cafés, news-stands and left-luggage kiosks at most stations. Only lockable luggage is accepted, but nearby cafés can often be persuaded to look after shopping and backpacks. The railway stations are handsome colonial buildings, placed off a major avenue on the edge of the French-built new towns. The recent establishment of the elegant chain of Moussafir hotels beside many of the principal stations has also greatly improved the convenience of rail travel.

For details of daily departures (which are modified but not radically changed from year to year) look under 'Getting There' in the relevant sections of the guide.

If you are under 26 you can travel with InterRail cards in Morocco. Those of us over 26 but still passionate about rail travel can, however, buy a **Carte Fidelité** from the ONCF, which entitles you to a 50 per cent reduction on second-class tickets for 12 journeys. These can then be topped up with a supplement to allow you to travel first class.

By Bus

Morocco is well served by buses, which, apart from being a quick, cheap and convenient way across the country, are a pleasure in themselves. Musicians, beggars and vendors collect around bus stops throughout the country and often wander down the aisle before departure. There is an undoubted camaraderie of travel, and buses are one of the best places in which to meet some of the vast majority of unhustling Moroccans, and a relaxing place to gather unbiased information, exchange oranges or cigarettes, enjoy unusually frank discussions and perhaps collect an invitation to tea. All those who dismiss the internal combustion engine as an un-romantic form of travel cannot have taken a night bus in Morocco, stopped at a lone café for a bowl of soup under the stars, paused beside a smoking row of kebab stalls lit up by a chain of lights, or joined the queue that obediently follows the conductor to drink from a favourite hillside spring in the early-morning light.

There is a barrage of bus companies that all enjoy some level of state or provincial funding. Whenever possible (and it usually is), travel by **CTM**, which runs an efficient national network. They have a regular schedule of departures, numbered seats with sufficient leg-room, and a secure baggage check-in system that issues tallied receipts. They are only slightly more expensive than local firms. In some cities, such as Casablanca, they have their own depot; in others, such as Marrakesh, they share the central bus depot with a lively assortment of rival firms. Local bus firms tend to run older, slower buses that stop more frequently and leave only when they are full. This can add to your education and entertainment but drastically increase the presumed length of a journey.

The bus companies are increasingly being brought together in one terminal or neighbour-hood of each city. This makes buying tickets in advance for popular inter-city routes an easy and effortless procedure. Even if companies still run separate depots, check out the travel situation for yourself as soon as you have deposited your bags. Hotel porters, guides and tourist offices cannot ultimately be relied upon, while guidebooks can get out of date surprisingly quickly. It is customary to pay 1dh or 2dh for each item of baggage stored on the roof, but not for the use of the side lockers.

For details of daily departures, look under 'Getting There' in the relevant sections later in the guide.

By Taxi

Travelling by '*place*' in a **grand taxi**, usually a big, battered Mercedes, should work out only a few dirhams more than a bus ride. At specific collection spots, which are mentioned throughout the guide, taxi drivers shout out their destination; if there is none going in your direction ask around. However, as six passengers are packed into a white diesel Mercedes before the taxi will leave, this method of travel has the advantage of speed but not always of comfort. In this enforced proximity it is, however, quite easy to ape the bulk of the passengers and fall fast asleep for most of the trip. *Grands taxis* travel only on routes where they can be sure of picking up a full load, typically from one town to the next. For a long distance you will have to leapfrog along a chain of *grand taxi* routes.

For more **individual destinations** you will have to bargain a price for the journey or employ the taxi for the whole day. Though much more than a '*place*', when compared to hiring a car the cost appears reasonable enough.

Petits taxis are limited to three passengers and the city limits. Except in Fez, Casablanca and Rabat the meters seldom seem to function. The going rate for locals is around 3dh per person for a short city ride, but for tourists the sky can be the limit. Arabic, charm or conviction is required to get the price down to the reasonable level of 5–10dh per person for the usually quite short journey required from a bus/train station to a central hotel. Do not be afraid to ask for a price in advance, ideally with a door open before taking a seat, for pricing discussions at the end of a journey have a habit of becoming more vociferous and less successful.

Do not take up the offers of **unlicensed cars** operating as taxis, whatever the price. Even if they are perfectly honest with you, their manoeuvres to avoid the attention of the police on the main roads can make for an exasperatingly slow journey.

By Car

Driving on the near-empty Moroccan country roads is a treat in itself, provided you bear a few warnings in mind. Remember, of course, to drive on the right-hand side. Following the French system, vehicles coming from the right have priority, so give way to cars coming on to a roundabout. Watch out for trucks on narrow roads, as they will expect you to move out of the way. Beware of patches of gravel on the hairpin bends of mountain roads, which can have the same effect as ice. Though comparatively empty of cars, Moroccan roads seldom lack wayside fruit stalls, dogs, drifting livestock, cyclists and children. In the cool of the night there is also often quite a stream of quiet horsedrawn traffic, walkers and cyclists which requires especial vigilance. I saw two children killed on a bridge in the confused light of dusk by a careless lorry driver. The roadside was quickly filled with ululating village women, and angry farmers rushed in from the fields armed with hoes and forks to demand instant justice. Fortunately, the police were at hand. Be careful.

On the open roads there is a **speed limit** of 100km (62 miles) an hour, though few drivers seem to respect it. The usual urban speed limit of 40km (25 miles) an hour should be adhered to whenever there is the slightest evidence of inhabitation.

Driving in cities can become especially confusing, with constant streams of mopeds and cyclists weaving through the traffic. It is often much better to find a hotel, park your car and then forget it. Wherever you leave your car, always appoint a guardian. Hotels, restaurants and city streets often have their own *gardien de voiture,* identified by a brass badge, who will accept 2dh for each guarding session. In the countryside, try to appoint a child. Hire cars are very easy to break into (a well-directed backward thump will open the locked front window of any Renault 4), and batteries and spare wheels are mobile and useful trading items.

Petrol/gasoline is roughly the same price as in Britain (about twice as much as in the USA) and stations are reasonably well distributed. Not all the petrol gauges are totally reliable, so it is advisable to keep topping up the tank whenever possible, or buy a plastic canister to make an emergency reserve. Moroccan mechanics are among some of the more resourceful and innovative in the world. I have witnessed in stunned admiration a clutch plate being carved out of an old Bedford truck and fitted into an Alfa Romeo, although if you are driving a Renault, Peugeot or Land Rover there should be no lack of orthodox spare parts.

car hire

Buses, though admirably friendly, keep you on well-established routes. In practice, despite the best of intentions, you often end up whizzing from one tourist feature to another. By hiring a car you can picnic, find lone places to swim, and explore empty sites and the magnificent and hospitable Moroccan countryside.

Each city chapter of the guide includes a full list of car-hire firms. It is worth shopping around, and also finding out whether you can return the car to another depot. Even the big agencies are often prepared to drop prices or do deals in tune with the season and demand. The various offices are usually found in close proximity to each other on the major avenue of a city's New Town. The two specialist travel agents listed on p.7, CLM and Best of Morocco, can organize flexible car hire that often works out cheaper than anything you can arrange directly, and is certainly more convenient. They can have a car delivered to a hotel or awaiting you at an airport, which can be dropped off later somewhere else.

As a basic indication, a Renault 4 (which is the cheapest, most universal and often the most useful vehicle in Morocco) can be hired from a reputable dealer for around 3,400dh (US$360/£240) for four days, which includes all taxes, full insurance and unlimited mileage. At the top end of the rentals, a Land Rover can be hired from around 8,000dh (US$855/£570) a week, but book in advance to be certain of getting one. On receiving a car you should check the brakes, insurance documentation, and that it has a working jack and a spare tyre.

The minimum rental period is usually one day. You will need to be over 21 (usually 25 for Land Rovers) and to have held a full driving licence for a year. A deposit, usually around 2,500dh, is accepted by most agencies through credit cards. Hire includes third-party, fire and theft insurance, although the latter only applies for the total theft of the car and not for any missing parts. There are often optional personal insurance policies, and you might hire an extra spare tyre and accident coverage if you are planning on any dirt-track driving.

By Bicycle, Moped and Donkey

Moroccan enthusiasm for any sport extends to cyclists, who can expect a welcome and consistent interest wherever they go. If you are thinking of bringing your own bicycle to Morocco, the **Cyclists' Touring Club**, Cotterell House, 69 Meadrow, Godalming, Surrey GU7 3HS, ✆ (01483) 417 217, can provide invaluable information on flight transport and insurance, as well as suggesting some routes.

Ask for advice about bicycle, moped or donkey hire from hotel porters, who usually know much more about this shifting pattern of trade than the tourist offices. A day's bicycle hire will cost around 50dh. You can if you wish buy a donkey or mule for around 600dh, but rental works out at about 10dh an hour.

Disabled Travellers

Neither the pavements of the New Town boulevards of Moroccan cities nor the narrow, packed streets of medinas are particularly suitable for visitors in wheelchairs. To set against the many stairs, few ramps and virtually complete absence of adapted toilets there is, however, the very willing and unflappable attitude to be found in Morocco. You will seldom be short of a pair of extra hands in need, though—as with any Westerner—tips or at least cigarettes should be offered around. Do not let the difficulties put you off. Some of the most enthusiastic accounts of North Africa I have heard have come from friends who use wheelchairs. If you are in need of encouragement, read Quentin Crewe's *In Search of the Sahara*, a book full of possibilities and adventures.

Practical A–Z

Bargaining

This is a necessary art that is fully enjoyed and understood in Morocco. For a foreign traveller, transport, hotel and restaurant prices are all fixed. It is only in the purchase of local crafts (and the odd taxi ride) that your bargaining skills will be required. A visit to a museum to remind yourself of what quality you are aspiring to, and to a state-run Ensemble Artisanal for the maximum price, is a good start: you will be helpless unless you have a firm and confident idea of the price you should be paying.

It is good tactics, and in the highest order of gamesmanship, to greet the shopkeeper, shake his hand and praise his colourful display of goods before he does. Look at some items other than what you are actually interested in first, and have a friend act out the negative, mean and unenthusiastic role. Accept as many cups of tea as you are offered and delay for as long as possible the mention of your first price, praising the goods but looking sad, wistful and tearful in turn at the impossible prices. Once you have named your price be obstinate, and watch out for the skilfully deployed ratchet gambit by which he gradually drops his price in exchange for a gradual rise in yours.

There are **three rules**:

1. Never bargain for something you don't want.

2. Don't hurry.

3. Even if you think you have just made a great financial coup, praise your opponent for his ruthless hard bargaining and great skill.

Beggars and Alms

Keep and collect all loose change from cafés for alms and tips. A dirham is considered generous in a country where 3dh an hour is still a reasonable labouring wage. Any more than that and you will be presumed not to recognize the value of money and possibly be asked for more. On the giving of alms, the Koran gives the most excellent advice. The Prophet Mohammed was questioned: 'What shall we bestow in alms?' To which he replied, 'What you can spare—for thus God instructs that you might think more deeply. . . but if you turn away from them, while you yourself yet hope for help from God, at least speak to them in a kindly manner.'

Children

Children are much more of an advantage than an impediment to travelling in Morocco. Next to speaking Maghrebi Arabic or converting to Islam, they form the most enduring bridge between cultures. They cause a drastic reduction in hassle and can be relied upon to look effortlessly stoical during bargaining sessions and (unless they are absolute monsters) improve your relationship with the staff of a restaurant, café or hotel. Hotels are usually happy to provide extra mattresses or a cot in a room, usually without any extra charge.

Children's tastes should be taken into account when planning trips since they tend to be easily bored by architecture and museums but more than usually excited by snakes, minerals, working potteries, horse-drawn-carriage rides, camels, donkeys, mules and running water. The one thing you must always bear in mind, even on the most sheltered beach, is the strong undertow off the Atlantic coast.

Wide straw hats can be bought locally as necessary protection against the sun, and packets of nuts, raisins, sultanas, dates and other dried fruit can be carried around in a raffia bag for snacks. Sterilized Ecremé milk can be bought in litre cartons, but should be consumed quickly once opened. Throughout Morocco it is also possible to buy small plastic sacks of fresh milk which have their date stamped in one corner, for 2.5dh. However, no matter how attentive you are about mineral water and peeling fruit, it is very likely that your child will be hit by an attack of diarrhoea in the first week or two in Morocco. Try not to panic, and feed them lots of bananas.

Climate

The Tourist Board promises 350 days of sunshine a year and so, as hotels and restaurants remain open all year round, any month is a good time to visit Morocco. There are, however, seasonal variations to take into account when planning the shape of your holiday. Also, during the 1990s Morocco, like much of the world, has witnessed a more erratic climate.

Morocco has been called a cold country with a hot sun. The monthly averages given here hide an often dramatic range in temperatures through each day. Even in the mid-summer months a sweater may be useful against evening coastal breezes, the cool of the mountain peaks and the desert nights. At the very least it can be moulded into a pillow for long bus journeys.

average daily temperatures °C (°F)

	Jan	April	June	Aug	Oct	Dec
Fez	16 (61)	22 (72)	31 (88)	36 (97)	28 (82)	16 (61)
Marrakesh	19 (66)	26 (79)	33 (91)	38 (101)	28 (82)	16 (61)
Rabat	17 (63)	21 (70)	25 (77)	28 (82)	25 (77)	18 (64)

From **November** to **February** there is the possibility of rain, and you will find the beach resorts distinctly off-season. **March**, **April** and **May** are reliably but not cripplingly hot, and the countryside, with its fast-ripening harvest and busy rural souks, is at its most interesting. **June, July** and **August** are the hottest and busiest tourist months, but there is little activity in evidence on the part of the locals during the heat of the day. The farmland is baked dry, and most schools, offices and industries have stopped work. The nation is on holiday, if not at the beach. These months do have most of the *moussems* (religious festivals). The High Atlas mountains, south of Marrakesh, are at their most accessible and attractive now. **September** and **October** witness a slight but welcome reduction in temperature and in the crowds.

Electricity and Gas

The standard European current of 220 volts AC has now largely replaced the 110 volt AC system. You will need **two-pin flat plugs** to fit Moroccan sockets, and if you have any US or Canadian 110-volt appliances you will also need a current transformer. On or off the grid, cooking, heating and lighting is largely dependent on charcoal or gas. The ubiquitous blue gas bottles fitted with a ceramic hob are subsidized by the government as one of the principal necessities of the poor.

Embassies and Consulates

Casablanca: British Commercial Consulate, 60 Blvd d'Anfa, ✆ (02) 22 16 53;
US Consulate, 8 Blvd Moulay Youssef, ✆ (02) 36 15 88.

Rabat: British Embassy, 17 Blvd de la Tour Hassan, ✆ (07) 72 09 05;
Canadian Embassy, 13 Rue Joafar Assadik, Agdal, ✆ (07) 77 13 75;
US Embassy, 2 Av de Marrakesh, ✆ (07) 76 22 65.

Australia, Ireland and New Zealand have arrangements for their citizens to be represented in Morocco by British diplomatic staff.

Food and Drink

Morocco has a distinctive, varied and very attractive national cuisine, with dishes from simple to sophisticated that make great and imaginative use of Mediterranean produce. Whatever your budget, try to eat in a good Moroccan restaurant at least once during your stay, and accept any genuine invitation to share in a family meal. Eating, for all but the rich, French-influenced merchant class, is a home-based family affair. In a country of high unemployment the shared family meal of couscous, usually enlivened by a few chunks of steamed meat and vegetables, is the one great source of sustenance for the day.

traditional dishes

One of the most striking features of Moroccan cooking is the quality and freshness of the ingredients. Produce comes from a land without pesticides, chemicals, hormones or preservatives. Animals are slaughtered just hours before they are eaten. The meat you are offered will generally be mutton, not lamb. Market vegetables will have been gathered that morning. Spices, herbs, fresh fruit, nuts and dried fruit have an invigorating vitality completely removed from the packaged and imported products available in much of Europe and North America.

To encourage you, here are explanations of some of the most common and popular Moroccan traditional dishes (for details of Arab and French pronunciation, *see* **Language**, pp.270–71):

Brochettes: grilled kebabs of mutton, liver and fat.

Cornes de gazelle: croissant-like pastries filled with honey and almonds.

Couscous: made from flour that is half-baked then ground to form semolina-like grains. A perfectly prepared couscous is laboriously cooked in a succession of steamings and oilings that allow each grain to cook while retaining a distinct granular texture. Couscous served outside of a home or a good restaurant is unlikely to be found at its best. It is usually accompanied by *sept légumes,* seven steamed vegetables with the odd lump of mutton. It can also be served as a pudding with sugar, cinnamon and rich warmed goat's milk.

Harira: a thick soup of chick peas, lentils and haricot beans often flavoured with mutton or chicken, lemon and tarragon.

Kefta: spicy meatballs made of minced mutton and offal, often served in a rich egg sauce.

Mechoui: a lamb roasted whole on a spit or baked in a special oven. This delicate and fragrant meat, far removed from the usual mutton, is eaten with bread. It is, however, an elaborate luxury which is often only available if ordered well in advance.

Pastilla/Bastilla: a pie made up of multiple layers of flaky pastry filled with finely chopped pigeon meat, eggs, almonds and spices. Chicken or fish may be used instead of pigeon.

Tagine: a slowly simmered stew, cooked in its own juices in an earthenware bowl with a distinctive conical lid. The *tagine* provides a basis for a whole galaxy of ingredients, spices and styles. The most popular variants found on most menus are: *tagine de viande,* mutton stew cooked with vegetables, or served alone with prunes; *tagine de poisson,* usually bream or sardines, cooked with tomatoes and herbs; *tagine de lapin,* rabbit stew; and *tagine de poulet aux olives et citron,* a delicious dish of chicken cooked with lemon and olives, the lemon giving a delicious bitter touch to the meat.

Eating Out

Exceptions aside, there are four basic categories of public eating-places: the **café**, the **café-restaurant**, the **New Town restaurant** and the **Moorish palace**.

All the more conspicuous **cafés** are male social centres that might serve a cake or croissant with mint tea or coffee, but seldom anything more substantial. It is usually quite acceptable to consume something from a nearby pâtisserie at a café table. The smarter pâtisseries may have their own tables, and serve fruit juices, ice creams and delicious cakes. They are some of the few places where you will regularly see the two sexes happily mix in public. Rural cafés serve *tagines* on market days, and can usually be persuaded to run up an omelette and salad.

Café-restaurants serve the freshest and by far the cheapest food in town. There will usually be a choice of salads, vegetables, soups, grilled meats and cold puddings. Their clients are principally travellers and workers away from home who are deprived of their customary meal. Café-restaurants usually do not have a licence to serve alcoholic drinks and are fairly functional, and in short are not places to dawdle away an evening with wine and chatter. However, they are easy to sniff out and are excellent for a quickly consumed lunch or supper, eaten while perched on a shared bench. They are often clustered in a row along a street in such a way that it is useless to make distinctions, or suggest an exact address or telephone number.

New Town restaurants: for a neat tablecloth, wine, a menu and regular opening hours you will usually have to go to a French-, Spanish- or Italian-influenced restaurant in the modern port or New Town areas of a city. On the Atlantic coast of Morocco (where they attract the local business and adminstrative class and serve freshly caught seafood) these restaurants can be very good and yet remain reasonably priced. Inland, unless you go very expensive they tend to become increasingly dependent on the tourist trade and frequently suffer from a corresponding blandness.

Moorish palaces: there are a number of 19th-century merchant palaces in the medinas of Fez, Meknès and Marrakesh that have been converted into restaurants. Traditional Moroccan cooking is served in a sumptuous Moorish interior, and most have drinks licences. It is rare to have this kind of evening without hearing local music or suffering some belly-dancing entertainment, and you won't be surprised to find that such places are almost entirely filled by tourists. Nevertheless, even though they are often expensive and boisterous, they are some of the few places where you can sample the more sophisticated and opulent dishes of Moroccan cuisine. If you are saving up for one grand meal, make it in Marrakesh, which is where the best and most genuinely opulent examples of this kind of restaurant are to be found.

Restaurant Price Categories

The price categories used for restaurants throughout the book are per head for a full meal without drinks:

expensive	over 300dh (£20/$30)
moderate	between 300dh (£20/$30) and 150dh (£10/$15)
cheap	under 150dh (£10/$15)

The cost of a bottle of local wine in most restaurants is around 90dh.

Drink

The principal drink of Morocco is **mint tea**. This is green or gunpowder tea flavoured with a few sprigs of mint and saturated with sugar. It is almost repulsively sweet when you first taste it. You will be offered glasses of mint tea in every house or shop you visit, and it is expected that a guest drinks at least three glasses of tea before departing. Enjoying mint tea becomes a vital social grace and, with luck, before long you may begin to appreciate this invigorating and thirst-quenching drink. Before tea was brought to Morocco (it was first imported by British merchants in the 19th century; they also later created the distinctive Moroccan teapot, first manufactured in Manchester, by giving the Yemeni coffee pot a fat bottom), hot infusions of sweet mint, verbena and wormwood were popular. These are still occasionally added to green tea.

Morocco is a Muslim nation. There is a law that prohibits Moroccan Muslims from buying bottles of alcohol—though this is not strictly enforced outside of Ramadan. This ban does not apply to visitors and, curiously, it is in any case legal for Muslim Moroccans to drink at bars, which are found discreetly tucked behind closed doors in the New Town areas, never in the medinas, which are generally no-alcohol zones.

Owing to the actual wording of the Koran, which specifically mentions wine when counselling against alcohol abuse, Moroccans tend to consume **grain-based drinks** such as '*spéciale flag*' beer, *anis* or whisky, but seldom touch wine in public. Away from the big cities or principal tourist destinations, drinking is confined to the bars of just a few hotels. In all but a few of the very smartest hotels it is impossible to drink wine, either by the glass or the bottle, outside the structure of a meal. Order a plate of prawns or a *salade niçoise* as tapas, to justify the wine.

You can order Moroccan **wine** to drink with your meal in licensed restaurants. Wine for lunchtime picnics can be bought from a few selected grocery shops in larger towns and cities (mentioned in the guide). Despite Islamic prohibitions, wine is produced in Morocco in three regions: Berkane, Meknès and Boulâouane. You might find the Moroccan reds rather strong and heavy to drink without something to nibble at: they are at their best when accompanying a rich spiced meat *tagine.* Due to the problem of keeping a white or a rosé cool while travelling, reds are also much better suited for picnics, and don't seem to mind being shaken around in the boot of a car or bus for several hundred kilometres. The principal **reds** are Toulal, Rabbi Jacob, Beni Snassen, Père Antoine, Le Châtelain, Valpierre, Les Trois Domaines, Amazir Beni M'Tir and Cabernet Président. If you have a choice, you might try the last two.

The best of the Moroccan **whites** is Special Coquillages, and after that Valpierre Blanc de Blanc, which is dry and not too astringent. They are at their best when accompanying fish or a plate of shellfish at a meal on the coast. The **rosé** wines, Gris de Boulâouane and Oustalet, are delightful at any time of the day, especially when chilled, and provide one of the basic sensory backdrops to a Moroccan holiday.

The universal colas are naturally available throughout the country, but a recommended **non-alcoholic** choice is freshly squeezed orange juice (*orange pressé*), which is often served enlivened with a little grapefruit or lemon. This is available in hotels and cafés in most towns.

Guides

Official guides of the highest (national) grade can be hired from tourist offices for 150dh (£10/$15) for a half-day and 250dh for a full day. Local guides charge 120dh the half-day, 150dh the full day. They are all well trained in history and anecdotes, fluent in most languages, and trustworthy.

Alternatively, if you have just arrived in a city and not yet found your way to your hotel, let alone the tourist office, you will not find it difficult to find yourself an unofficial guide. In fact, there will most probably be a profusion of them offering their services and asking where you want to go as soon as you appear on the street.

Dealing with the attention of unwanted urban guides is one of the recurring problems of travelling in Morocco, although in recent years the deployment of plain-clothes policemen has cut down the aggressive hustling of foreigners in such key tourist destinations as Fez and Marrakesh. The discordant cries of hustlers just as you arrive fresh in a town or at the medina gates can be irritating. Accept this, though, as a facet of Moroccan life. There is certainly no easy way to avoid it, short of jumping in a taxi and hiding in a hotel. Use your energy not to avoid these guides, but to select the most appealing.

A little humility is also an asset. On your first visit to a large and strange town, some help in finding your hotel or a taxi will very probably actually be useful. The aggression with which many visitors cold-shoulder themselves through potential helpers and then later bemusedly consult their imported maps and guidebooks is faintly ridiculous, but a curious and revealing insight into Western attitudes. Meet the problem in a Moroccan manner, and deploy qualities of charm and enthusiasm. Enjoy the human skills required in choosing the friendliest character from a group. As in all situations of life the eyes are the true mirror of the soul, and there is no point in having a conversation with anybody while they wear dark glasses. Greet your chosen guide with a *salaam* and a handshake, praise the weather and his town and tell him how delighted you are at last to be here. If need be, check out your character judgement over a cup of tea. Tell him exactly where you want to go and what you intend to give, which, however rich you are, should never be more than 10dh.

A guide's natural interest lies in directing you to the medina. For in the confusing labyrinth of medina avenues you become more dependent on him, and this is also where lurk the bazaars, where he can earn commissions (fixed at a traditional five per cent, which can win your guide a comparative fortune) and additional kudos with his neighbours. Be aware of this and, if need be, hold out a visit to a bazaar as a carrot at the end of the day. You will soon find out that the habitat of the hustling guide is almost entirely confined to bus stops and medina gates. Marrakesh and Fez have hustling reputations. But even in these cities, when you know your way around (and show an increasing lack of interest in bazaars) you will find yourself increasingly left alone.

When you feel annoyed, run over a few relevant facts. An unskilled labouring wage in Morocco is 3dh an hour. The chances of getting even that in a country of 25 per cent employment, with over half the population under 21 years old, is low, and competition is heavy. Even a European unemployment dole converts into an enviable quantity of dirhams. Under those conditions might you not try your luck at skimming off a few dirhams from often arrogant and unfriendly foreigners?

Hammams

A *hammam* is a public steam bath which, before the advent of showers and private bathrooms, was one of the great urban centres of Moroccan life. Some of them are a little bit run-down from their days of glory at the turn of the 20th century, but they survive throughout this arid country as a working institution. Apart from in those in tourist hotels, male nudity is taboo and the sexes are strictly divided, either by different opening hours (usually for women in the daylight hours, with men in the evening) or by a completely different set of chambers. The *hammams* of Morocco are rarely as elaborate as the great domed, multi-chambered, marble-clad structures of Ottoman Turkey, though they will usually have an entrance lobby, a changing room and a double set of doors into the steam room. Here you can gently steam, wash yourself from taps, basins or black plastic buckets, or for an extra charge you can be rigorously scrubbed, massaged and expertly manipulated. In an interesting inversion of street etiquette, women often bathe with just the skimpiest pants or completely naked, and remove hair from the most intimate parts of their body, while men are very strict about wearing either a cotton wrap or swimming trunks, and wash their genitals privately facing the wall.

Several *hammams* are listed in the text, but by enquiring from your hotel you can find many others that are happy to accept foreign visitors. A minority of establishments, usually those directly attached to a mosque, do not like the presence of *Rumi*, as Christian tourists with only the slenderest relationship to Orthodox Byzantium are still called.

Health

No **immunizations** are officially required to enter Morocco. For peace of mind, though, you should be up to date on your typhoid, cholera, tetanus and polio protection, and you might talk to your doctor about the pros and cons of a hepatitis jab. No anti-malarial pills are necessary for the Imperial Cities, but they would be advisable if you ventured into the far south. **Tap water** is quite safe north of Marrakesh, though you may prefer to drink from the ubiquitous bottles of Sidi Ali and Sidi Harazem mineral water, which are considered by connoisseurs to be amongst the best mineral water in the world.

All-eventualities private **travel insurance** covering you for medical emergencies as well as theft need not be expensive and is the best protection against any serious health problems. If you have private health insurance you may already be covered—check the fine print. Moroccan **pharmacies** are usually knowledgeable, sympathetic and well stocked, and can often recommend a French-speaking doctor. They sell contraceptives, including the pill, but tampons, soap, shampoo and toilet paper are often easier to find in a general store. Even the most basic travel kit should include a good supply of painkillers and some proprietary medicine, such as Imodium, for rapid diarrhoea relief. Tom Owen-Edmunds, a very experienced travel photographer, carries a stock of seemingly innocuous things that can be put to emergency medical use. A tampon can become a dressing for a wound, condoms can be used for carrying water, and chewing gum a replacement for a missing tooth filling. Medical addresses for the big cities are given in the guide. The larger package-tour hotels often have a medical specialist. In an emergency, dial ✆ **15** for medical help, or ✆ **19** for the police.

Holidays and Festivals

The principal secular and religious holidays are observed by government offices, banks, post offices, public covered markets and some shops. Tourist restaurants and hotels continue in operation, though sometimes with delays entailed by a much diminished staff. On the days before a holiday there will be extra pressure on transport and hotel space. It is still too early to see if the new king, young Mohammed VI, will keep to his father's old calendar of celebrations since Hassan II's death on 23 July 1999.

Muslim holidays

These are based on a lunar calendar, which loses 11 days a year (or 12 in a leap year) against the Gregorian Calendar.

The great event of the Islamic year is the fasting month of **Ramadan** (which will begin in November in the years 2000, 2001 and 2002). To be in Morocco in one of the great cities during Ramadan is a fascinating experience, but it is not a good time to travel around the country. Ramadan, the ninth month of the Islamic lunar year, is the Muslim equivalent of Lent. The fast has remained a great institution in Islam and is cherished as an act that binds the whole nation, indeed the entire Muslim community, together in a month of asceticism. For all except the sick, travellers, children and pregnant women, Ramadan involves abstaining from food, sex, drink and cigarettes during the hours of daylight. It is an ancient custom, one that was in full force when the Prophet Mohammed was a child in Mecca, when this holy month was a time when a general truce reigned over Arabia and the demands of vengeance and tribal animosity were put aside. Non-Muslims are not involved, but you will find most cafés, bars and licensed grocers firmly closed. It is insensitive to smoke, eat or drink in public during Ramadan. It can be more rewarding to join Ramadan quietly as a volunteer, sharing the exuberance at dusk when the daily fast ends with a bowl of harira soup, and the café-restaurants fill up with customers and music. A spirit of relief breaks out across the nation and continues deep into the night. The 26th night of Ramadan, 'holy night' (when the first verse of the Koran was delivered to the Prophet Mohammed), is particularly magical, with young children paraded in glittering costumes in an endless promenade.

The feast of **Aid es Seghir** celebrates the end of the month of Ramadan, when the new moon is sighted. A few months later **Aid el Kebir** commemorates Abraham's sacrifice of a ram instead of his son, and is a great excuse for family reunions. The week before Aid el Kebir is colourful, as the streets are full of thousands of rams being led around on leashes like honoured members of the family. After the excitement of public prayers and the sacrifice on the morning of the Aid, the festival is mostly celebrated indoors. Shops, souks and some museums are closed for the week. Three weeks later is **Moharran** (or **Achoura**) the feast of the Muslim New Year, when almond cakes are baked, drums are beaten and gifts given to children and the poor. The fourth principal holiday is **Mouloud**, the Prophet's birthday, celebrated with presents for children and firecrackers on the street. In particular, there is a *moussem* (religious festival) at Zaouia-Moulay-Brahim in the High Atlas, south of Marrakesh; a candle procession at Salé; and the Aissawa *moussem* at Meknès.

moussems and festivals

Moussems and *ammougars* (the Berber version) were originally annual pilgrimages to the tomb of a saint; now the words are used for any festival, although most do still have religious roots. There are hundreds of local festivals throughout Morocco that celebrate a saint in either a day- or a week-long trading fair, with some feasting, dancing, religious music and *fantasia* display. In mood they are not dissimilar from an especially animated rural souk, and so for the vast majority of visitors may be of only passing interest. Even the major festival dates are impossible to predict accurately. Some depend on the harvest, the lunar cycle, the Muslim religious year, the national tourist office or the diary of the regional governor. You will have to ask the tourist office or a major local hotel for more accurate information, though even they are unlikely to know more than two months in advance.

The most rewarding festivals for a foreigner are the week-long Folk Music Festival staged in Marrakesh, usually in June; the week-long Festival of Sacred Music at Fez, usually at the end of May or beginning of June; a week-long jazz festival in Rabat in June; and the new week-long festival of *Gnaoua* music at Essaouira (accessible as a day trip from Marrakesh).

national holidays

1 January	New Year's Day
1 May	Labour Day
30 July	Feast of the Throne—celebrated with conspicuous amounts of bunting, processions, public feasts and music
14 August	Allegiance Day
21 August	King Mohammed VI's birthday
6 November	Day of the Green March
18 November	Independence Day

The Internet

If you are searching for flights, one of the best sites to try is *www.cheapflights.com*, which also has endless links to other Moroccan information from its destinations page: book recommendations, hotel possibilities, temperature guides and much, much more. The most extensive web guide to Morocco in English appears to be at *www.lexicorient.com /morocco*, which has entries on many of the places you are likely to visit and photographs to whet the appetite. *Www.maroc.net* is the country's most official website, dry as you would expect, with information on history, geography, culture and travel as well as links to government departments, etc. You may find their Maroc Search listings useful. For a very full listing of Moroccan links, turn to the directory prepared by Morocco's main university, *www.alakhawayn.ma/morocco*.

Kif

The Rif mountains grow some of the best common hemp (*Cannabis indica*) in the world. In the Ketama region its cultivation is legal (81,000 hectares/200,000 acres are currently planted) until another crop can be found that will grow as well on these denuded hills. The hemp (also known as marijuana) is planted in February and harvested in June. To collect their rich stores of pollen, plants are shaken inside a gauze-lined hut. The sticky mass is then kneaded into cakes. This resin is sold by farmers to the gangs who deal in the riskier but more profitable smuggling trade to Europe. The cut leaves and flowers are preferred by locals for their gentler aromatic smoke, which is inhaled from a thin pipe with a disposable pottery head. The flowers and seeds can also be made into *majoun*, an edible fudge.

In the north of the country discreet possession and use is, in practice, tolerated, and the police concentrate their activities on monitoring the big traders. The Moroccan law framed in 1954 is, however, quite explicit. Possession, purchase and transportation is illegal: the minimum penalty is three months' imprisonment and a 2,400dh fine; the maximum is five years and a 240,000dh fine, with the confiscation of any camouflage and transport involved.

Visitors who wish to smoke Moroccan kif can reduce the risk of receiving these penalties by buying small quantities for their own use, preferably not in Tangier or Tetouan, and by not travelling with any in their possession. As elsewhere, dealers also double as police informers. It would be foolish and quite misguided to attempt to smuggle kif. While possession of small quantities of kif in Spain is now legal, in Algeria you can be imprisoned for life for this offence.

About a dozen Britons and twenty Americans are arrested for drug-related offences each year in Morocco. Consuls are unsympathetic but professional, and try to visit within a week of imprisonment, every three months whilst on remand, and twice a year during imprisonment. The current penalties run on a rough quantity tariff: a girl hitching from Ketama to Chechaouèn with half a kilo strapped to her thigh was given a month in prison and fined; a New Zealand pilot caught loading a light aeroplane got five years and the full fine.

On a note of caution: all the alarmingly heavy tales of hassle that I have heard in the last twenty years involve kif. Never smoke somewhere or with someone who makes you the slightest bit uneasy. It is a recognized aspect of the drug that, as well as inducing laughter and an apparently increased perception, it can also cause mild paranoia.

Maps

Despite the great care taken over city maps in this guide, the medinas will often remain a maze to you for the first few visits. The free coloured tourist leaflets and the beautifully produced *Editions Gauthey* maps to Rabat-Salé, Casablanca, Marrakesh and Meknès are, however, a great help in getting to know the general street pattern.

There are a large number of national road maps to choose from. Bear in mind that any map that marks a border or even a difference in scale between Morocco and the western Sahara is liable to be confiscated. Kümmerly and Frey (1:100,000), Michelin sheet 169 (1:100,000), Hildebrand (1:900,000), and Reise und Verkehrsverlag (1:800,000) all publish full-colour maps, useful for advance planning. Road conditions do change and most maps contain one or two inaccuracies. The most accurate road maps are the large-scale (1:400,000) *Maroc, Carte Routière*, published by Editions Marcus, Paris, on sale throughout Morocco for 30dh a sheet, though they lack the clarity of full colour and are fragile. Moroccan official survey sheets of the High Atlas (1:50,000) are available in Imlil, the central base for High Atlas climbing.

In Britain the Moroccan Atlas survey sheets, some French-language walking guides and a wide variety of other regional maps can be obtained from Stanford's Map Centre, Long Acre, Covent Garden, London WC2E 9LP, © (020) 7836 1321. For specialist information for walking, *Guide Collomb: Atlas Mountains* (£11.95) is available from West Col Productions, Goring, Reading, Berks, RG8 9AA, © (01491) 681 284. The Royal

Geographical Society, Kensington Gore, London SW7 2AR, ✆ (020) 7589 5466, has an Expeditionary Advisory Service which runs weekend courses and can point you towards old reports and maps.

In the USA try either the Traveller's Bookstore, 22 West 52nd St, New York, NY 10011, ✆ (212) 664 0995, or The Complete Traveller Bookstore, 199 Madison Av, New York, NY 10016, ✆ (212) 688 9007. They also have a branch in San Francisco, 3207 Fillmore St, CA 92123.

Media

English-language newspapers are generally available in Marrakesh. French newspapers are more widely available, at about half the price.

principal newspapers

Al Alam (The Flag): venerable 53-year-old Istiqlal paper with a circulation of 80,000; French-language version is called *L'Opinion*.

Al Ichtiraki: socialist party paper with a circulation of 120,000; similar in tone to French newspaper *Libération*.

Al Ahdath (The Events): most independent-minded of all the Moroccan papers, with a circulation of 70,000 (and growing).

Le Matin du Sahara (French language) and **The Sahara** (Arabic): government papers with a circulation of 70,000. *Le Matin du Sahara* is worth buying, though its coverage, and certainly its opinion, seldom changes.

Al Jamaa: Islamist newspaper with a circulation of 5,000.

Amazir: weekly Berber newspaper written in Arabic with some use of Berber script.

However, Morocco remains a good place to shed your paper habit and pick up tuning into the World Service direct from London on 9.41 and 5.975mhz—31.88 and 50.21m.

There is little temptation, apart from being caught in a rainstorm, to visit a cinema in Morocco. If you do find yourself inside (tickets are around 10dh), you could become more fascinated by the audience than the film. The different cultural attitudes to humour, violence and romance always make fascinating study.

Money

The Moroccan currency is the **dirham**, which fluctuates between 12 and 15 to the pound and 7 and 10 to the US dollar. It is divided into 100 units, which are officially called *centimes* but are occasionally and confusingly referred to as *francs, pesetas* or *reales*. The denominations of notes are 200, 100, 50 and 10. There are silver-coloured coins worth 5, 2 and 1 dirham, and brass ones worth 50, 20, 10 and 5 centimes.

There are restrictions against exporting dirhams from the country, although you can usually buy Moroccan money in Málaga, Algeciras or Gibraltar. There are no black-market rates, though tourist bazaars and carpet shops may be persuaded to accept dollars and European currencies. Keep your **currency exchange slips** for when you leave the country, as you will only be allowed to change back up to half what you can prove to have changed in the first place.

You should bring enough cash to cover the first couple of days in Morocco. **Cash machines** (ATMs) are open 24 hours a day in all the big tourist resort cities; use your bank servicecard, credit card or cash card, matching the symbols (such as Visa or Cirrus) with those displayed on the machines. The maximum cash machine withdrawal is usually 2000dh. Standard international **travellers' cheques** in dollars or main European currencies are also easily exchanged in banks. Passports are required for most transactions. Major **credit cards** such as Visa and MasterCard are accepted in the smarter hotels and restaurants and a great many shops in the bazaars, though in the latter they might try to charge you the six per cent handling fee.

Moroccan **banks** display a wide range of tempting stickers on their windows but often don't match up to all their advertisements. There is usually one bank in every town that operates some form of foreign exchange desk, though you will usually save time by heading directly for either the Banque Marocaine du Commerce Exterieur (**BMCE**) or the Banque Credit du Maroc (**BCM**), which both take cards, travellers' cheques, Eurocheques and, of course, cash.

Opening Hours

Opening hours of **banks** vary depending on their location and the time of year. In the winter they should be open at least Mon–Fri 8.30–11.30 and 3–4; in the summer and during the month of Ramadan 8.30–2 is a likely minimum. Banking hours are usually longer in resorts and big cities. **Post offices** (once known as PTT but now relabelled La Poste) are open in winter Mon–Fri 8–3, and in summer 8–12 and 3–6. They sell stamps and can cash International Girocheques and receive *poste restante/*general delivery mail, although an established hotel usually makes a safer and more accessible address.

Museums are not well signposted, nor do they sell the postcards, catalogues and reproductions you would find elsewhere. They also decide their own opening hours: please treat the information given in this guide as an informed opinion, not an absolute authority. In general they are open daily 9–12 and 3–6, but will usually be closed on Tuesday and sometimes on Friday afternoons, as well as on all major national and religious holidays. Lunch breaks can sometimes spread over most of the afternoon. Custodians of national monuments cannot always be identified by an official cap, uniform or badge, but only by their possession of a book of entrance tickets: do not be haughty with unshaven, shabbily dressed, sleepy-looking individuals who are in the vicinity of a museum or monument if you wish to gain entrance. **Medersas** follow the same schedule, but will sometimes be closed for the whole of Friday.

Packing

A photocopy of the first four pages of your passport may come in handy if you mislay it for any reason. A corkscrew and a sharp knife are vital for picnics and peeling fruit. An alarm clock is useful for those early-morning bus departures. A suction bath plug will be needed in a surprising number of hotels, while a good lighter, a few candles and a torch are basic tools for exploring caves and simple hotels at night. On average, at least half of any holidaying group will be struck by a violent purge that might strike anytime anywhere. By packing a roll of soft toilet paper and a packet of Imodium and Nurofen you can earn undying gratitude.

To ease your passage around the country, buy a stock of presents (like those that you might fill a Christmas stocking with, and especially pens) for local children who have shown you around a village, put you on the right path or guarded your car. Anything with a football motif is usually eagerly received. My mother has travelled for years with a bag filled with goodies ranging from notebooks and small sets of coloured pens to more hazardous items such as whistles and water pistols that should only be given on departure.

Although shorts and swimwear are perfectly acceptable on the beach and in your hotel, you should not wear them anywhere else. Trousers and a short-sleeved shirt are acceptable for men; women wishing to appear respectable should pack a long skirt and a full shirt.

Photography

Why destroy the present for an unsatisfactory image of the past in the future?

Cameras are the symbol of the modern-day tourist driven by a mania to record, to move on, before you have the time to understand. Photographs give the illusion that one has the time to study these things later at greater depth. Even if you have the time for only the slightest sketch of a building or a landscape, it will imprint the image more vividly than a whole reel of film.

As a means of preserving images of wild flowers without picking them and of wild animals without killing them, however, cameras are entirely on the side of the angels. The two invaluable tips I have been given by a professional are to photograph at dusk and never put your subject in the centre of the frame.

Films can be bought and developed in most large towns. Excluding anything remotely military, you are free to photograph anything architectural. Do not photograph anybody, least of all a rural woman, without permission. Be prepared to tip for photographing animals or people at a tariff of around 10dh. Most museums forbid flash and operate a partial restrictive policy, like that which forbids photographs of the bronzes in the Rabat Archaeological Museum. This only seems to make sense as an opportunity for tips.

Police

The Moroccan police force is modelled on the French, and is divided into two—the Gendarmerie and the Sûreté. The Gendarmerie live under semi-military discipline, wear khaki serge and green berets and carry batons. They cover both cities and the countryside with a regular grid of barracks, and could be compared to a mixture of a county constabulary and a reserve regiment. The Sûreté are the grey-uniformed and armed police who patrol the roads and the cities, and to whom robberies from tourists will normally be reported to obtain a declaration for insurance purposes. They are more directly concerned with crime and law enforcement and are considered, as in France, more street-wise, sophisticated and corrupt: they are commonly referred to as 'Ali Baba and the forty...'

Grey customs officers may be seen, particularly on the northern coast, trying to control the flow of electrical goods smuggled in from Ceuta and Melilla, and kif being smuggled out. Prison officers wear blue. Firemen wear blue with red piping and might be seen trying to sell their calendars to unwary motorists, particularly on the road south of Tangier. The army, by comparison, look rather underdressed in their plain lovat-green uniform.

Sexual Attitudes

Abd as Slam, Malika's husband, is young and handsome. Like most young Moroccan men in Tangier, he dreams of finding a rich Christian woman who will take him to Europe or the States and make him a rich man.

The House of Si Abd Allah, Henry Munson

In the towns and among the Arabic-speaking mountaineers of northern Morocco, where pederasty is exceedingly prevalent, it is practically regarded with indifference...

Ritual and Belief in Morocco, Edward Westermarck

Moroccans traditionally have an uncomplicated attitude to sex—chauvinist to women and liberal to men—but a great respect for outward forms and standards of dress. Homosexuality is neither scandalous nor unusual and is socially treated not so much as a condition but as a mere matter of personal taste. The Koran cautions against celibacy: 'As to the monastic life they invented it themselves...many of them were perverse.' Against the confusion of Jewish or Christian sexual guilt, the Koran freely acknowledges sexual appetite: 'Your wives are your field, go in therefore to your field as you will but do first some act for your soul's good', and is only mildly disapproving of homosexuality—'come ye to men, instead of women lustfully? Ye are indeed a people given up to excess.'

AIDS awareness is very slight and public education and posters on the spread of the HIV virus have been low-key and unspecific. As yet, only the late King Hassan II managed to break through the general reluctance to air these matters publicly, and gave a few general talks on television. The bulk of the population continues to think of it as a disease that affects rich, white Europeans and Americans but that has no power over the Arab nation. Moroccans also tend to think of themselves as immeasurably more virile and potent than Western men. However chaste your intentions, why not pack some condoms beside the sun cream and romantic fiction?

women

In general, Moroccan men conceive of mature women in three guises: the mother whom they adore, the wife in whose modest conduct rests all the honour of her husband, and all other women, who are potential objects of their desire. This is particularly true of women who show themselves in the public domain of streets and cafés, let alone in bars and restaurants. Western women (especially in view of their power to bestow a foreign passport on the father of their children) are all near-automatically placed in the third category to a greater or lesser degree.

Morocco consequently tends to divide women travellers between those who couldn't cope and those who loved it. Dig a little deeper and you will often find that the former went alone or with another woman, and had never been to a Muslim country before. Of course there are single women who have holidayed happily in Morocco, but they tend to have a proven track record as independent travellers. If in doubt, err on the cautious side. There's no point in having a miserable trip, and no stigma attached to not feeling comfortable in a country where the men tend to see white women as possible lays and have little respect for them. If you do travel with a man, the most irritating thing will be the way in which any decision will be instantly referred to him by Moroccans. The easiest way to cope if you're alone is to play one of the stereotyped but recognizably 'less available' roles: the wife, the mother, the intellectual or the sportsperson. Unfortunately there are no easy ways to deal with a hand where you don't want it, but being soberly dressed will make you less of a target. Be open and straightforward, and don't be embarrassed to yell loudly at the man, in any language. He'll understand, and suffer the indignity of a public reproval. A sharp slap, satisfying as it might be, only seems to make things worse. In some of the larger towns it is not advisable for single females, or even female couples, to stay in the cheapest medina hotels.

On a more upbeat note, I once came across a group of six Australian girls who were travelling with six male high-school students that they had met up with in Tangier. The girls could take the Moroccan boys into the tourist zones where they would not otherwise have been welcome, while the girls were both protected, entertained and introduced to aspects of Moroccan domestic life that they would otherwise never have seen. I felt very envious.

For a sense of sorority go to the local women's *hammam*. Laughter and curious communication, if not outright friendship, will result. By way of reading matter, any of the studies of women and sexual politics by Fatima Mernissi make compelling if depressing reading (*see* **Further Reading** p.266). It is much, much more difficult for Moroccan women than one can possibly imagine. As Fatima Mernissi has observed, 'The conception of the woman as a lust-driven animal that must be kept under lock and key is one of the sickest and most disgusting aspects of Arab culture.' So is the sad record of male divorce and the neglect of their responsibilities as a father, though this has much more to do with poverty and lack of opportunity than any cultural determinant.

Shopping

Arab cities were designed with the **souk** or market at the centre of the community. Islam has none of the Christian anxiety about mixing trade and worship. The streets around a grand mosque are usually the busiest and the richest and are known as the **kissaria**. The outer walls of mosques are commonly obscured by workshops and stalls whose rent helps pay for the upkeep of the building. A new zaouia (religious college) or mosque was often the initial impetus that coalesced a trading community into existence. On Fridays you will notice a marked reduction in trade as the merchants shut up shop for noon prayers.

Moroccan crafts remain active and have recovered from the exodus of more than 250,000 Moroccan Jews, who were among the most skilled craftsmen in the country. The Jews were particularly prominent in jewellery, tailoring, weaving and non-ferrous metalwork. All large towns maintain a government-run craft centre called an **Ensemble Artisanal**, where traditional trades are taught and products exhibited for sale. Tourism greatly assists the craft economy, and it has been assessed that a fifth of any visitor's expenditure is on crafts.

A visit to a typical contemporary Moroccan home reveals a subtle difference in taste from the 'typically Moroccan' souvenirs of the souks. Rich embroidered cloth (covering cushions and day beds), nylon blankets and masses of deep-carved wood are dominant. The tiled floors are rarely covered by carpets. Ceramics tend not to be Islamic in decoration but plain glazed earthenware or a Chinese pattern for grand occasions. The radio, TV or tape recorder will be conspicuous and you notice the complete absence of any pictures (other than an obligatory photo of a Moroccan football team, the king and a calligraphic Koranic blessing). It is chiefly in the traditional embroidered kaftans worn by women, the low tables and all the impedimenta of a tea ceremony that the tourist bazaar taste and the domestic economy coincide.

blankets

The souks are all well stocked with loose-weave large brown and white blankets that make excellent bed covers. In the south you will come across brilliant patterns of tie-dyed cotton for the women's enveloping *haiks* and the enormous, many-coloured thick blankets of the Sahara region. Two of these can completely line a nomad tent and provide excellent protection against the bitter nights.

carpets

Only buy for your pleasure. Moroccan carpets are not an investment, but can be a continuous delight. To my mind the so-called **Royal** or Rabati carpets loosely based on a prayer rug have become charmless in colour and design, unless displayed en masse over some vast hall or courtyard. Of much greater interest are the products of the countryside. Ask to see the wild discordant weavings, often on a field of purple or madder red, known variously as **Chiadma, Oulad Bou Sba**, **Boujad** or **Rehamna**. Of equal mass but of much greater restraint in colour range and design are the **Marmoucha** rugs, especially those with a dark grid of lozenges on a white background. Whatever your pocket, however, you must visit the great carpet bazaars in Fez, Meknès, Rabat and Marrakesh. These are often housed in magnificent interiors, and the merchants will offer you tea while they display their still wonderfully tempting wares.

The **hanbel** or *arerbal* (the Moroccan version of the familiar Turkish killim) is woven, not knotted, though a rich pattern of embroidery can sometimes confuse this distinction. On the ground they have an even shorter life than carpets, but they are more flexible and can be used as hangings and throws, and can look especially lavish for picnics or as covers for day beds or dining-room tables. They should be much cheaper than carpets, with which they share many designs as well as the traditional nomadic production areas. All the more interesting ones are produced in the Middle or High Atlas, or at least to the traditional patterns that were developed in these tribal regions.

The Berber tribes of the Middle Atlas plateau dominate Morocco's weaving tradition. Travelling from Rabat southeast towards Midelt you will pass through or near the main weaving tribal zones: the **Zemmour** (around Khémisset), **Zaér** (around Rommani), **Zaïane** (around Khénifra, Moulay Bouâzza and Mrirt), **Beni-M'tir** (around El-Hajeb and Azrou) and **Beni-Mguild** (the old territory of which stretched between Azrou and Midelt). There is a basic similarity in texture and design throughout this large region. In their raw state at local markets, pieces are as likely to be found woven for a practical purpose and made up as saddlebags, belts, waistcoats, sacks, wall hangings, tent divisions or cushions, than as convenient lengths for your floor. A warm red, which used to be made from the madder root, provides the basic background against which the finely executed details are picked out in bright white cotton and black. Today, with the use of chemical dyes widespread, there are innumerable colour variations.

The designs, however, remain entirely geometric and generally rely on bands of plain colour alternating with richly worked bands of lozenges, diamond grids and elaborate crosses. A good weaver will brook no repetition in design and create a dazzling killim full of movement, colour and detail. A less inspired version can look static, lifeless and repetitive. The most elegant and hard-wearing killims, which rarely come up for sale, are often so heavy with sequins that the pattern is all but obscured. These are woven specifically for the weaver's wedding, and afterwards are displayed as a decorative hanging. On her death they are used as a cover for her corpse, the sequins glistening in the dusk as she is borne up to a hillside cemetery.

Another, smaller area of weaving is in the High Atlas mountains. These simple, dignified *hanbels* are known as **Glaoua**, after the Berber dynasty from Telouèt. They have a similar pattern of banded plain and decorated stripes, although usually have no colour and are woven from plain undyed black and white wool. In the area to the south of the High Atlas and Jbel Siroua (often referred to as Aït Ouaouzguite) these plain *hanbels* are worked over with an extra layer of knotted carpet work. In addition, a full range of colours can be used to accompany the dominant saffron hue to create a rich depth of pile, geometric design and colour. You will also find some more straightforward carpets with pale-green geometric designs worked onto a saffron field, and brightly coloured tent bands loosely based on the magnificent tradition of weaving ornate coloured borders into the local white woollen cloth.

In many of the carpet bazaars you will see the so-called '**message rugs**' with their bright colours and vivid row of pictograms such as camels, women and goats. These are popular trading items (of a size well suited for a child's bedroom) but are not in fact an indigenous Moroccan tradition, since they originated in southern Tunisia, in the region around the desert town of Gafsa.

ceramics

Pottery plates or large fruit bowls, particularly the traditional geometric designs of blue on white—glazed, plain or tinted green—translate well and seldom look out of place back home. The old ceramic centres of Morocco were Fez, Meknès and Tetouan, joined by Safi in the late 18th century. Today most of the pottery on sale in Morocco is made in either Safi or Fez. Good basic earthenware pots are also made in such typical Berber areas as the Ourika Valley, Et-Tleta-de-Oued-Laou, Amizmiz and Zaouia-Moulay-Brahim, as well as on the western edge of Marrakesh. Tamegroute in the southern Drâa produces a rough, green, glazed ware identical in look (if not in quality) to the medieval wares of North Africa.

clothing

The city souks are full of the distinctive clothing of the Maghreb: **gandouras** (collarless cotton smocks), **burnous** (woollen cloaks with hoods), **kaftans** (cotton 'nightshirts' for daytime with embroidered necks) and **jellabas** (full-length woollen tunics with hoods). Though they're vital for dressing up, you need conviction to wear them well in Morocco. Back home a *gandoura* can serve as an admirable nightgown, a *burnous* is excellent as an outdoor cloak, and a *jellaba* works well as a warm housecoat. Straw hats are useful in the summer, but no one should encourage any further manufacture by buying a hateful nylon **fez**. There are felt ones to be found, or lambswool 'Nehru' hats.

jewellery

It's still possible to find good pieces of traditional Moroccan jewellery, although you will have to hunt for it, and know your prices in advance. The opportunities for self-adornment are innumerable: silver crosses based on the traditional designs of the Tuareg and other Saharan tribes, green and yellow enamelled silver eggs from Tiznit, thick silver bracelets, a cascade of bangles, pairs of ornate triangular brooches linked by a chain, golden hand of fatima pendants, pierced coins, necklace medallions, small hanging boxes for miniature Korans or an Islamic prayer, or a thick rope of amber or cornelian beads interspaced with silver arrow heads. As well as all this there are the sumptuous necessities of a modern Moroccan marriage: golden tiaras, belts, bracelets, earrings and rings studded with emeralds and brilliants. Moroccan jewellers are an entirely courteous but comparatively restrained breed of salesmen. Even so, one sometimes returns with something that looks just too 'tribal' back home. Many an aunt and niece have become the surprised beneficiaries of Berber pieces that the buyer found impossible to wear.

leather

The distinctive Moroccan slippers, the pointed and trodden-heeled **babouches**, are immediately useful. They are for men and come in grey, white and yellow. You can also hunt for a softer chamois-leather version in a much larger field of colours. The heavily embroidered and gilded versions are supposedly for women, but tend to have little flexibility or much use except for a dinner party. Gilt-embroidered **belts** can be easily absorbed into Western dress. They look better and more amusingly ostentatious the shabbier the trousers they support. Check when buying, however, that the leather isn't cardboard, that it has been stitched, not just glued, and that the buckle is strong enough. Stamped and gilded red and ochre **portfolio wallets** come in a range of sizes. They are generally made of fine leather and make admirable cases for letters, documents, bills you have no wish to pay, or as a detachable binding for a book. The complete **desk sets** found in many leather shops (a blotter, envelope stand and desk-size portfolio) are also usually of a high quality. If you have time, ask for a favourite book to be Morocco-bound.

metal

There is a mass of decorated brass plates and silver-coloured implements in every bazaar. Candlesticks, mirrors, trays, incense burners, cake stands and ornate kettles attached to bowls (for the washing of hands before a meal) can be acquired before you even realized you had a need. The distinctive silver-coloured Moroccan teapot is the most attractive single item. The weak hinge of the lid and the failure of the insulating joints on the handle seem to be universal faults. Throughout Morocco, handkerchiefs are used for pouring and bent nails secure the lid.

minerals

For under £1/$1.50 you can pick up superb pieces of Sahara rose and amethyst from the High Atlas, south of Marrakesh. The three principal fossils are the spiral swirls of the goniates, the long cones of the orthoceres, and the compressed tapeworm-like forms of the trilobites. There are plenty of stalls selling these 400-million-year-old minerals on the roadsides of the High Atlas passes, and also in Marrakesh.

spices

Moroccan spices, principally cumin, *harissa* (hot pepper), paprika, ginger, saffron, cinnamon and bunches of fresh mint, coriander and parsley create the most colourful displays in the souk. The intriguing displays of the apothecary and cosmetic stalls are often found close by, selling blocks of silvery antimony, kohl (ground antimony for the eyes), henna (in leaf or powder), *ghassol* (a brown mud for washing), *snib* (for stopping shaving cuts), cochineal, porcupine quills, tooth-cleaning twigs, incense and dried Dadès roses.

wood

The skilled carvers and joiners of Essaouira, which is accessible as a day trip from Marrakesh (*see* p147), work upon odiferous thuja wood to create some of the most attractive and durable items that you can acquire in Morocco. Inlaid chessboards, backgammon sets, polished boxes and carved jars can be bought directly from the craftsmen. Watch out for the hinges, which are invariably shoddy, and hunt around for boxes that have snugly fitting lids. It is not a new trade, for the Romans were mad about thuja wood and spent fortunes on tables with knots and colouration that must have been in pleasing harmony with their liking for marble.

Sports

fishing

The streams and lakes of the Middle and High Atlas provide opportunities to catch a small local trout called *farios* and some imported rainbow. This could provide a few days' distraction, but is unlikely to make the basis of a holiday for a keen fisherman. The season starts on 31 March. Bring all your own fly-fishing equipment. Information is available from Roger Chaban's *La Pêche au Maroc*, Editions Alpha. Fishing permits can be obtained from Administration des Eaux et Forêts (Ministry of Water and Forests), 11 Rue Reveil, Rabat.

Coarse fishing is a more popular sport. The natural lakes around Moulay Youssef (east of Marrakesh) and Idriss (east of Fez), and El Kansera (west of Meknès) reservoirs are stocked with bass, perch and pike. Permits, official seasons, lists of approved reservoirs and lakes can be obtained from the Ministry of Water and Forests in Rabat. No permit is required to fish anywhere from Morocco's enormous coastline, where mackerel, bream, sea bass, red mullet or *loup de mer* (sea perch) can be caught from boat or line.

golf

Rabat has a 45-hole course at Dar es Salaam, 14km south of the city, set in an undulating area of cork woods (*closed Mon; green fee 120dh*). Mohammedia, near Rabat, has an 18-hole golf course beside the sea on wooded duneland. The Casablanca course has 9 holes, and is found in the middle of the race track. The Marrakesh Royal Golf Club, a picturesque if stately course with palms and flowering shrubs, was built in the 1920s by Pasha Thomi el Glaoui. Just a little farther out from town is the 200-acre Le Palmeraie Golf Palace, with clubhouse, hotel, thousands of palms and seven lakes, designed by Robert Trent Jones. The city's third course, the newest in Morocco, is the Amelkis, recently finished to the cost of $6 million.

For precise information on a Moroccan golfing holiday, contact the specialist tour operators listed on pp.8–9, or the Moroccan Royal Golf Federation, 2 Rue Moulay Slimane, Rabat.

hill walking and mountain climbing

The Ministry of Tourism has set up a Central Office of Information for the Mountains (CIM) and the Grande Traversée des Atlas Marocains (GTAM), a network of approved mountain guides, porters, village accommodation and hillside refuges. The full brochure of prices, addresses and itineraries can be acquired from CIM, Ministère du Tourisme, 1 Rue Oujda, Rabat, ✆ (07) 70 12 80/✆ (07) 76 09 15. Alternatively, you could look through the hiking expeditions run by the specialist British tour operators listed on pp.8–9.

riding

La Roseraie hotel at Ouirgane, south of Marrakesh, runs riding stables that offer anything from a simple half-day's ride to a week's expedition, complete with mule-borne tents. The hotel can be booked with a riding itinerary arranged through the travel agencies recommended on pp.7–10.

skiing

Oukaïmeden in the High Atlas, near Marrakesh, is one of the principal resorts. Snow can be found between November and March—see that section of the guide for details.

swimming and water sports

Among the principal beaches for summer water sports are Mohammedia and Essaouira, where donkey rides, water-skiing, sailboarding, pedaloes and paragliding can all be found. When swimming on the Atlantic coast, be aware constantly of the powerful undertow.

Study Resources

North Africa Travel, 3 Inglebert St, London EC1R 1XR, pools together book lists and travel tips as well as publishing an annual collection of travel essays and arranging a conference. The membership fee is £10 a year.

The **Society for Moroccan Studies**, c/o SOAS (School of Oriental and African Studies), Thornhaugh St, Russell Square, London WC1H 0XG, publishes a journal and arranges half a dozen lectures for an annual membership fee of £15.

The **Maghreb Bookshop**, 45 Burton St, London WC1H 9AL, ✆ (020) 7388 1840, run by Mohammed Ben Madani, not only stocks rare and out-of-print editions but is also the hospitable nerve-centre of the *Maghreb Review,* a scholarly quarterly review of North African affairs in French and English.

The **British-Moroccan Society**, 35 Westminster Bridge Rd, London SE1 7JB, ✆ (020) 7401 8146, is a more social affair dominated by ex-members of the Foreign Office. The society publishes an annual newsletter, arranges a drinks party at the House of Lords in the spring and a dinner party in a grand hotel in November, and sponsors an annual art exhibition.

Telephones

The central post office of any large town or city will normally have a separate **international telephone room** where an operator at the central desk sets up international calls, which are taken in a row of airless cabins. These telephone rooms often have longer opening hours than the post office itself and, though generally filled with a long queue, are much cheaper than phoning from a hotel. Estimate around 15dh a minute to Europe and 50dh a minute across the Atlantic. In addition, some post offices have recently been equipped with a line of international phone booths outside the building which are operated by coins or charge cards which can be bought at post office counters. These *téléboutiques* are well advertised and easy to operate. Buy cards (20 units for 40dh, 40 for 70dh and 100 for 160dh) at the desk, push into the machine and dial direct. In addition, most of these will send a fax abroad for around 50dh a go.

Deregulation of the telephone system has combined with satellite technology and the demands of Morocco's large expatriate population to encourage a real explosion of private telephone companies in cities and most of the towns.

For international calls first dial 00, then when you hear a tone, add the country code (44 for Britain, 353 for the Irish Republic, 1 for Canada and the USA, 61 for Australia, 64 for New Zealand) and then the local code and number, leaving out the initial 0 in area codes that have them. If you ask a friend to call you back, the country code for Morocco is 212.

The Moroccan telephone system has been completely overhauled in the last few years. All the former five-figure numbers have been promoted to six figures with the simple addition of another numeral. The country has been divided up into eight code-districts: (02) Casablanca, (03) Settat, (04) Marrakesh and Safi, (05) Meknès and Fez, (06) Oujda and

Sefrou, (07) Rabat, Salé and Kénitra, (08) Agadir and southern Morocco, and (09) Tangier and Tetouan. However, some out-of-the-way villages remain outside this system, and hotels and other places in these areas can still only be called through the operator.

It would not be fair to pretend that everything is quite so simple and straightforward as this basic outline might suggest. In practice, Moroccan telephone numbers are constantly being changed, there is no authoritative listing of numbers in any part of the country and, although we have double checked the numbers given in this guide, some of them will near-inevitably already be obsolete. When communicating with a hotel, try to use a fax wherever possible, as this will allow you to keep a receipt of the agreed booking.

Time

Morocco keeps Greenwich Mean Time throughout the year, so when Britain goes into summer time Morocco appears to be one hour behind.

Tipping

Be frequent but concise with your tips. Service charges and tax are added on to most restaurant and hotel bills, but a waiter will expect another 5dh a head. For helping you park a car and watching over it, 2dh an hour is standard throughout Morocco. 10dh is the going rate for photographs of camels, water-carriers and snake-charmers, depending on how keen you appear to be. Museum attendants also like the odd dirham or two or three extra, as do barmen, café waiters, hairdressers, hotel porters, bus luggage porters and petrol-pump attendants. Taxi drivers are not customarily tipped on top of the fare by locals, but since they have started using their meters I like to reward them for their honesty.

Toilets

There is no need to feel embarrassed about asking to use a lavatory for, unlike the staff in London pubs, no waiter or barman would dream of refusing a passer-by in need. Afterwards you could stop and order a drink, a simple coffee or Fanta, and leave an extra tip in grateful thanks.

Most classified hotels and large restaurants are equipped with Anglo-Saxon flush bowls, though water supplies and efficient drainage can be variable, particularly in summer. It is a wasteful system for a nation grappling with the recurring problems of drought, and has been established largely for the benefit of tourists.

Urban cafés and houses have a crouch hole and no paper, but a tap for washing your left hand and an old tin for sluicing. Outside the largest cities, public lavatories are unknown. Hedgerows, dung heaps, beaches and ruins are freely used by the locals.

Tourist Offices

The Moroccan National Tourist Board, the ONMT, and French-styled Syndicats d'Initiative are found in every city and even in most small towns in Morocco. They are useful as a source of official guides, glossy handouts, hotels, the dates of local festivals, the location of rural souks and the odd local map. They are seldom informative about local history, but very keen on the regular run of tourist sites, bazaars and large hotels.

The Moroccan Tourist Board is worth visiting to stock up on the full range of handouts. There is a useful booklet of all the classified hotels, a collection of package-tour prices, a sheet with the year's maximum hotel prices and half a dozen regional leaflets. There are several branches: 205 Regent St, London W1R 7DE, ✆ (020) 7437 0073/✆ 7437 0074; 2001 Rue Université, Suite 1460, Montreal H3A 2A6; 20 East 46th St, Suite 1201, New York, NY 10017, ✆ (212) 557 2520; 161 Rue St Honoré, Place du Théâtre Français, Paris 75001, ✆ 01 42 60 63 50; and 11 West St North, Sydney, NSW 2060, ✆ (02) 922 4999.

Where to Stay

One of the great joys of travelling in Morocco is the range and variety of hotels. You will intensify your enjoyment of the country if you switch freely between the most spartan and the most lavish accommodation. One night might be spent beside a bus station in preparation for a dawn departure, a second gazing at the stars in a place without running water or electricity, and a third wallowing in a luxurious oriental dream.

It is rare to find any Moroccan hotel, of whatever standard, without clean bedrooms. Bare stone floors will receive a daily wash and beds are made up with freshly laundered cotton sheets. The twin curses of the modern traveller—nylon bedding and a synthetic fitted carpet ornamented with cigarette burns—are rarely found in Morocco. Reliable supplies of bath water can be more problematical. Rationing has begun in some resorts, while even the grandest hotels can have their off-days, though moderately priced hotels and above can usually be relied upon. An American correspondent has suggested that most of his countrymen should begin their holiday in luxury hotels and gradually work their way down into something the British might find 'charming'.

Hotel Price Categories

The price categories used throughout the guide per night for a double room are:

luxury	over £100/$150
expensive	£50–£100/$75–$150
moderate	£20–£50/$30–$75
inexpensive	£10–£20/$15–$30
cheap	£10/$15 or under

In the body of the guide there is a complete price range of hotels to choose from in each of the three cities, plus in some of those places that are listed as possible excursions, particularly those towns that make lengthy day trips. Small hotels with character, gardens, fires in winter, a resident owner-manager and large double beds have been preferred.

The official Moroccan star classifications for hotels are not reproduced in this guide, as they are not necessarily a reliable indication of the relative expense or comfort level of a hotel, and can be seriously confusing, especially in the middle ranges. As in many countries they are based on a fairly arbitrary list of potential facilities (whether or not a hotel has a separate reception desk, a lift and so on) more than price. It can work out that a small two-star can be a good deal more comfortable and attractive than a four-star, or that a four-star can be cheaper than a three.

Instead, the classification used in the guide is simply based on prices, although this can still hide an enormous flexibility depending on room size, position, season and your bargaining ability. It is only possible to bargain down the published rates by fax (✉) or by telephone in advance, as once you have arrived in the lobby looking desperate the game is over.

History

Morocco was long known in the Muslim world as Maghreb el Aksa, the land of the farthest west. It was literally considered to be on the edge of the world, a place notorious for its powerful magicians and demon-like jinn. It is a country with an intense, almost insular, awareness of itself. In a sense it is an island, encircled by the seas of the Atlantic, the Mediterranean and the sand-sea of the Sahara. The land is further defended by four great mountain ranges (the Rif, Middle Atlas, High Atlas and Anti-Atlas) that run like vast ramparts across its breadth, breaking up the area's geographical unity and providing a secure mountainous refuge for the indigenous people, the Berbers, against both invaders and any central power. The Berber tribes of the mountains have remained in occupation of the land ever since the invention of agriculture.

Moroccan history is essentially the tale of a conservative society which has managed to triumph against all attempts at conquest. At the same time it has happily absorbed technical and spiritual innovations from the various foreign cultures that have tried to dominate the country. The first great change was from 1000 BC, when Phoenician traders brought settled agriculture and urban civilization to Morocco. The second came in the 8th century AD, when the cavalry armies of the Muslim Caliphate brought Islam, Arabic and the advanced culture of the Near East. Aristotle was being translated in the court of the rulers of Morocco when Oxford was still a muddy unlettered village. Arab military rule lasted only a few decades, but the spiritual and social message took deep root. All subsequent rulers of Morocco were legitimate only for as long as they championed Islam, either as reformers or as military protectors.

The third great revolution was in the 20th century, when the French, albeit for the selfish motives of a European power, implanted the scientific and medical advances of the Industrial Revolution in Morocco. Morocco's identity has been likened to the desert palm: rooted in Africa, watered by Islam and rustled by the winds of Europe.

Berber Roots (to c.150 BC)

Evidence of the camp fires and tool-making of the wandering bands of *Homo erectus*, who first crossed the Sahara to North Africa about a million years ago, have been discovered in the coastal sand dunes around Rabat and Casablanca. It was not until 10,000 BC that the melt waters of the last Ice Age separated North Africa from southern Europe, and the original inhabitants of both shores are of similar racial stock. The Neolithic Revolution, with the invention of both agriculture and stock breeding, reached the inhabitants of Morocco by about 3000 BC. It transformed the small bands of hunter-gatherers living in the area into communities of agriculturalists or nomads, and vastly increased the population. Stone circles in northern Morocco, such as that at M'Soura dating from around 1800 BC, prove that local tribes had strong contacts with the Megalithic culture of the Atlantic coast of Europe. There is also evidence of an ivory trade between the Tangier region and Spain.

At about this time we can begin to speak of the indigenous population of North Africa as Berber (from the Greek for 'barbarian'). They spoke a language of the Hamitic family related to ancient Egyptian. The men were devoted to war, polygamous, and allowed their women to do most of the agricultural labour. The horse, first bred in North Africa in this period, and the donkey were greatly prized, while in the savannah plains the chariot became a dominant element in war. A brief wet period allowed the Berber tribes to expand into the Sahara, an event recorded in cave paintings showing dreadlocked cattle-herders fleeing before conquering charioteers.

The Berbers enter the written history of the Mediterranean world via the trading settlements of the **Phoenicians**. By about 1100 BC these merchants from the coast of Syria had established a network of harbours along the North African shore which allowed them access to Cornish tin, Spanish silver and Saharan gold. The Phoenicians had a good eye for a harbour, and the shore of Morocco is dotted with their trading stations, such as Rusaadir (Melilla), Tingis (Tangier), Lixus (Larache), Sala Colonia (Rabat), Tit (Moulay-Abdallah) and Mogador (Essaouira). As well as their lucrative trade in metals and precious oils, the Phoenicians developed a more humdrum 'country trade' in corn, oil, fish, dyes, timber and ivory. These trading colonies were responsible for the diffusion of new skills to the tribes of the North African coast. The pottery wheel, an alphabet, improved weaving techniques, the art of masonry, new crops, arboriculture, iron and metal work were all Phoenician gifts to the Berbers of Morocco.

Roman Influence (*c.*150 BC–AD 429)

Effective dominion over the Phoenician colonies passed in the 5th century BC to Carthage, and with the defeat of Carthage in the 2nd century BC to Rome. The Romans exercised a loose protectorate over the extensive kingdom of Mauretania, which covered both Morocco and eastern Algeria. Mauretania remained an area of Phoenician culture (recalled by the Libyo-Berber script that can be seen carved on stones in the sub-Saharan region) and was ruled from the two capitals of Volubilis (in central Morocco) and Cherchel (in the centre of Algeria). Roman influence increased from 25 BC under Juba II, a Mauretanian prince who had been educated in the household of the Caesars in Rome.

The gradual absorption of Mauretania into the Empire was reversed by a widespread revolt in AD 42 which it took an army of four legions over three years to subdue. In AD 44 the Emperor Claudius officially annexed Mauretania, but the fierce resistance of the tribes left the Moroccan portion of the old kingdom much reduced in size. The frontier of Roman Morocco, known as the province of Mauretania Tingitania, extended just south of Sala Colonia (Rabat) and just east of Volubilis. There was no secure road east to Roman Algeria, whose western frontier reached Oujda and the river Moulouya.

The Romans' authority was continuously challenged by the Berber tribes, but within their frontiers they built upon the trade and settlement patterns of the Phoenician period to create a small but prosperous and civilized province. In addition to the magnificent ruins of the capital, Volubilis, their achievement is witnessed by lesser sites such as Lixus, Cotta, Banasa, Thamusida, Sala Colonia and Tamuda. As part of the reorganization of the Empire in the reign of Emperor Diocletian (285–305) the frontier was withdrawn to a defensive line between Tamuda (Tetouan) and Lixus (Larache). Volubilis was abandoned, but the two port cities of Tangier and Ceuta were protected. These remained under Roman rule until 429.

Vandals and Byzantines (429–704)

An army of the Germanic Vandals, led by Gesneric, invaded North Africa from Spain in 429, landing at Tangier. Although they were relatively few in number, their rule in North Africa lasted a century, until their defeat in 535 by the Byzantine general Belisarius. The Byzantines installed governors at Ceuta and Tangier, who remained dominant figures in local politics until the Arab invasion two centuries later.

The Arab Conquest (704–40)

The Arab conquest brought Islam to Morocco: a religion, a social code, a system of law and a new language that were to provide the central identity of all future Moroccan states. Islam's introduction was due not to peaceful missionaries but to Arab cavalry armies despatched by the caliphs, the political heirs of the Prophet. Within 25 years of Mohammed's death the first three caliphs had conquered an empire that stretched across Syria, Mesopotamia, Persia, Egypt and Libya. The Arab advance along the North African coast was delayed by a succession dispute, but in 682 **Uqba ben Nafi** made his famous raid. Partly a dazzling conquest, partly a missionary voyage of discovery, this is a cherished episode in Moroccan history, but the facts have long since been wrapped up in legend. The tale records that Uqba defeated a joint Berber and Byzantine army, was welcomed by Count Julian into Tangier, accepted the submission of Volubilis and went on to conquer the Haouz, the Drâa Valley and the Sous. Arriving at the Atlantic, he rode deep into the surf declaring, 'O God, I take you to witness that there is no ford here. If there was I would cross it.' This was all to no avail, for on his return east Uqba was ambushed and killed by an old adversary.

The Arab conquest of Morocco did not begin in earnest until 704, when **Musa ben Nasser** arrived at Kairouan in Tunisia to take up his appointment as commander of the western Arab army. Between 705 and 710 he advanced rapidly westwards, content to accept the nominal conversion of towns and tribes, which he enforced by establishing garrisons, notably at Tangier, Tlemcen and Sijilmassa. His aim was to secure Morocco in order to be able to proceed with the conquest of Spain. The prospect of an invasion of rich, plunderable Spanish provinces brought thousands of Berber warriors flocking to the Arab banners. In 711 an advance guard of 7,000 under the command of the governor of Tangier, **Tariq**, crossed the straits, first landing at what came to be known as Jbel Tariq, or Gibraltar. He was welcomed by many among the Christian and Jewish population of Spain as a deliverer from the harsh rule of the Germanic Visigoths. In one day's work at the Battle of the Barbate River, Tariq destroyed the Visigothic army. Muslim armies quickly occupied Spain, and the Arab advance into Western Europe was not checked until Charles Martel stood firm at Poitiers in 732.

In 740 a mutiny among the Berbers in the Arab garrison at Tangier lit a chain of rebellions that swept right through North Africa. Though the caliphate sent a succession of Arab armies, these were only able to reconquer Tunisia. Morocco, having absorbed the message of Islam, returned to its customary independence.

The Spread of Islam (740–1042)

For a while, northwestern Morocco found unity under **Moulay Idriss**, a kinsman of the Prophet who had fled civil war in Arabia. The tribes of central Morocco accepted him as a holy man and arbitrator. His son **Idriss II** established a unitary state based around a small army and the new settlement of Fez, which Moulay Idriss had founded in 799. Within a few decades it had grown into an influential city, filled with skilled craftsmen and noble Arab warriors who fled there from civil war in Spain and revolution in Tunisia. Fez became the cultural, political and economic centre of Morocco, from where Arabic language, religious knowledge and technical innovations spread into the rest of the country.

The political authority of Idriss II was lost when his kingdom was divided between nine sons on his death in 828. The various Idrissid princes soon fell under the influence of powerful neighbouring dynasties, such as the Shiite Fatimids of Tunisia and the Omayyads of Spain, who controlled many of the chief ports and towns of Morocco throughout the 10th and 11th centuries. This period also witnessed the gradual conversion of the Berber tribes of the interior by missionaries and warriors, many of whom claimed descent from the Idrissid princes. Idrissid ancestry is still a mark of prestige in Morocco, while the process of conversion is remembered in hundreds of different local folk tales that recall trials of power between Muslim holy men and diabolic magicians.

The Almoravids (1042–1147)

In the middle of the 11th century there was no Morocco, just a confused patchwork of half-converted Berber tribes, Arab trading cities, foreign garrisons and petty principalities. The Almoravids created Morocco. Their conquests welded the civilized northwest of the country to a vast Berber and Saharan hinterland and created a common identity. The Almoravid Empire marks a historical threshold, just as the Norman Conquest, which occurred in the same period, does for England.

The Almoravids were not a foreign power but a simple confederation of Berber tribes from the Western Sahara who had been united by **Ibn Yaasin**, a charismatic holy man from the Sous Valley. Determined to impose a pure Islamic state, he launched his crusade from the desert in 1042. A generation later, in 1070, the young Almoravid general **Youssef ben Tachfine** established Marrakesh as their advance northern base and principal city. By the 1080s he controlled central Morocco and Fez. In 1086 he landed in Spain at the invitation of the embattled Muslim states. He promptly defeated the Christians, but then proceeded to absorb the 26 principalities of Spain into his Empire. At its height the Almoravid Empire stretched from Spain to West Africa and from the Atlantic to eastern Algeria.

The empire sought to be the ideal Islamic state. The ruling class of princes and tribal emirs were deposed, and all taxes not sanctioned in the Koran were abolished. Islamic law according to the Malekite tradition was imposed upon society. Almoravid generals subdued even the remotest hill tribes, built stone castles on the summits of mountains to enforce their authority and encircled cities in protective walls. After the conquest of Spain, skilled craftsmen were brought over to build and decorate mosques, fountains and public bath-houses. Talented Andalucían secretaries, employed in the court, brought increased literacy and the Maghrebi script to the country. The Almoravid sultans also made a practice of consulting the doctors of Islamic law before making any major decision, even in matters of war. This council, the *ulema*, remained a central feature of the Moroccan state. The sultans sought recognition from the caliphs of Baghdad for their title, *Amir al Muslimin* (Commander of the Muslims), which aptly expresses their championship of orthodox Islam.

There was a dark side to Almoravid rule. The great flowering of Andalucían mysticism, poetry and intellectual enquiry seen in the previous two centuries was suppressed. Their insistence on collecting only Koranic taxes left them short of revenue, made up for by extortion. Their narrow puritanism led to the persecution of Jewish communities and the extermination of the last Christians in Morocco.

Ali ben Youssef succeeded in 1107. He completed the conquest of Muslim Spain and his generals advanced the frontier by adding Lisbon and the Balearics to the Empire. Ali reigned for 37 years and was responsible for the great building projects of the Almoravids: the grand mosque of Tlemcen (in Algeria), the Karaouiyne Mosque in Fez, and the Ben Youssef Mosque and Koubba Ba'Adiyn in Marrakesh. His sons, though, lost control to a rival Berber dynasty, the Almohads, who stormed Marrakesh in 1147 and killed Ishaq, the last Almoravid sultan.

The Almohads (1147–1248)

Medieval Morocco reached its zenith of confidence and achievement under the Almohad Empire, whose rule extended over Spain, Morocco, Algeria and western Libya. The Almohads had much in common with the Almoravids. They too were a confederation of Berber tribes (though from the High Atlas not the Western Sahara) that had been united by the zeal of a charismatic holy man, **Ibn Tumert**, and led to final victory by his more pragmatically minded successor, **Abdel Moumen**, whose descendants inherited the Empire. An Almohad fleet dominated the waters of the western Mediterranean, and the monumental architecture of this period still dominates the cities of Morocco, such as the Hassan Tower and Bab Oudaïa in Rabat, and the Bab Agnaou and Koutoubia minaret in their major centre, Marrakesh. The regional capitals at Taza, Tlemcen, Tunis and Seville were also adorned, and great philosophers such as Averroes enjoyed the friendship of the sultan.

The Empire's first important reverse came in 1212, when the Spanish Christians inflicted a crushing defeat on it at Las Navas de Tolosa. It was a blow from which Muslim interests in Spain never fully recovered. Ferdinand III of Castile captured Córdoba in 1235 and Seville in 1248, leaving only the mountainous kingdom of Granada under its own independent Nasrid dynasty. Remorselessly, the Empire contracted. In Tunisia, an Almohad governor established the Hafsid dynasty, whilst western Algeria fell to a Berber tribe, the Ziyanids, who ruled from Tlemcen. In 1248 an Almohad sultan died whilst on campaign against the Ziyanids. His leaderless army was betrayed and then massacred on the eastern plains of Morocco by the Beni-Merin tribe. The Beni-Merin chieftain then promptly seized control of Fez (the chief city of the north) and founded the Merenid dynasty. However, it was not until 1276, when the last Almohad sultan was killed in the High Atlas, that the Merenids controlled the south of the country as well, and could feel secure on the throne of Morocco.

The Merenids (1248–1554)

The rule of the Merenid sultans is recalled by a series of dazzling architectural compositions. The ruins of the Chellah necropolis at Rabat, the sumptuous medersas that can be seen in Fez, Salé and Meknès, as well as numerous mosques, fountains and *fondouqs* scattered throughout the towns and cities of Morocco reveal the exquisite taste and wealth of this period. Merenid power and creativity was at its glorious peak during the reign of **Abou Hassan** (1331–51) and his son **Abou Inan** (1351–8). A series of ambitious campaigns seemed on the point of recovering the old territory of the Almohad Empire in North Africa, while the glittering new medersas (university colleges) helped train a generation of loyal officials to serve in Fez Jdid (New Fez), the separate and defensible royal city that they founded to the west of old Fez. Literary figures such as the great historian Ibn Khaldoun and Ibn Batuta (the Muslim Marco Polo) received the enlightened patronage of the court.

By the beginning of the 15th century it was a very different story. The Merenid State fell into the hands of a corrupt cabal of viziers, financiers and generals. Against a background of economic decline, the Portuguese and Spanish gradually seized control of most of the Moroccan ports, starting with the sack of Ceuta in 1419. By the mid-16th century the Portuguese cavalry controlled the Atlantic coast and had begun to penetrate deep into the interior. Marrakesh and Fez were defended only with the military assistance of the Ottoman Turks, who had already seized control of Tunisia and Algeria.

The Saadians and the Battle of the Three Kings (1554–1668)

From this point of apparent hopelessness Morocco unexpectedly recovered. The Saadians, an influential family from the Drâa oasis valley, led the fight against the Portuguese and made themselves rulers of southern Morocco in the process. By 1542 their success in expelling the Portuguese from Agadir, Safi and Azemmour had brought them the support necessary to dethrone the old dynasty which, surrounded by Turkish guards, hung on to power in Fez.

The true turning-point in Saadian power came in 1578, when they destroyed a Portuguese invasion led by the youthful King Sebastian at the battle of Ksar-el-Kebir. This is also known as the Battle of the Three Kings, since the reigning sultan, Sebastian and his treacherous Moroccan royal ally all died during the battle.

The throne passed to **Ahmed el Mansour,** 'the victorious' (1578–1603), who further increased his prestige and wealth by seizing control of the gold fields of West Africa. Ahmed el Mansour remodelled the state along the lines of Ottoman Turkey. External trade was encouraged and with the revenue from customs duties he was able to fund a professional army, recruited from Andalucían exiles, Christian renegades and Turks, that was untarnished by tribal loyalties. He gave audiences from behind a screen, introduced the scarlet parasol that is still a distinguishing mark of a Moroccan sultan's sovereignty, and built the palace of El Badia in Marrakesh to be the magnificent ceremonial heart of his court. Provincial leaders were enticed away from local politics to the glittering life of the capital. His rule was that of an enlightened despot: in the words of the chroniclers, 'he sweetened his absolute power with much clemency'. In Marrakesh the magnificent ruins of El Badia, the serene elegance of the Ben Youssef Medersa and the glittering opulence of the Saadian Tombs survive to give a suggestion of this near-fabulous period of history.

In 1603 a vicious war of succession between the Saadian princes shattered the prosperity of the state. For much of the 17th century the Saadian sultans were mere shadows locked in their Marrakesh palaces while real authority was exercised by a jumble of petty powers that included the pirate republic of Rabat-Salé and four rival dynasties of sheikhs who controlled the Berber tribes in the western Rif, Middle Atlas, High Atlas and Anti-Atlas.

The First Alaouite Sultans: Moulay Rachid and Moulay Ismaïl (1668–1727)

The Alaouite prince **Moulay Rachid**, from an Arab holy family long resident in the oasis of Tafilalt, succeeded in seizing the throne in 1668. His family still holds it to this day.

During the 54-year reign of his younger brother, **Moulay Ismaïl** (1672–1727), the Portuguese were expelled from their fortresses on the Atlantic coast, the English were driven out of Tangier, and the Turks pushed back on the eastern frontier to the line of the present border with Algeria. Morocco is filled with evidence of the constructive nature of Moulay Ismaïl's reign. He founded towns, built bridges, ports and forts, and secured the safety of roads. He encouraged trade and reformed religious life, purging unorthodox cults but restoring shrines and mosques.

Moulay Ismaïl deliberately neglected the existing capitals of Fez and Marrakesh with their rebellious citizens and built up Meknès to be the new administrative and ceremonial centre of the nation. Meknès was also the headquarters of the sultan's black slave army of 150,000 men, which functioned as both a corps of engineers and the brutal instrument of his authoritarian regime. There were a number of bloody campaigns against the mountain tribes and frequent instances of despotic tyranny. The sultan's proudest boast was that he had made Morocco safe enough for a woman or a Jew laden down with jewellery to travel across the breadth of the country without being troubled.

Decline and Isolationism (1727–1822)

A vicious period of civil war followed Moulay Ismaïl's death as the slave regiments championed a swift-changing variety of his heirs. None of his descendants could hope to equal his power. They ruled as much by consensus and arbitration as by decree. The authority of the government was restricted to the fertile coast, river valleys and towns—the Bled el Makhzen, the 'land of government'. The dry plains and mountains were known as the Bled-es-Siba, the 'land of dissidence', where the tribes respected only the spiritual authority of the sultan and had no time for his tax-gatherers and ministers.

Sidi Mohammed (1757–90) was one of the most astute sultans of the period, beloved by the towns for his firm but fair rule and by the nation at large for his expulsion of the Portuguese from El-Jadida. He maximized government revenue by concentrating the export trade at Essaouira, which he built up into the elegant town it is today. He also played a clever game with the European nations and kept their influence at a minimum by a quick-footed policy of encouraging competition between them. His son, **Moulay Sliman** (1792–1822), changed to the ultimately disastrous policy of isolationism, attempting to seal Muslim Morocco from any contact with Europe. His foreign policy was dominated by suspicion of all the Christian powers and a particular loathing for the French Revolution. Despite being offered Ceuta and Melilla he refused to recognize the upstart Bonaparte as king of Spain. All exports were banned, a 50 per cent duty imposed on imports, and European consuls were confined to Tangier in an attempt to keep outside influence firmly at bay.

The Growth of European Influence (1822–1904)

Moulay Sliman ignored the claims of his inadequate sons and nominated his nephew, **Abder Rahman** (1822–59), to succeed him on the throne. It was during his reign that Morocco felt the full force of the growing power of France. The sultan had provided some support for the Algerian tribes during the French invasion of Algeria, but this policy was shattered in 1843 when a Moroccan army was destroyed at the Battle of Isly (outside Oujda) and the ports of Tangier and Essaouira were bombarded. The tribes' reaction to these humiliating national defeats was to rise in widespread revolt against the sultan.

Suddenly aware of his nation's military vulnerability, the sultan played on the strong and traditional Anglo–French rivalry. He made approaches to the British, who were interested in opening up Morocco to their traders and obsessed by keeping the Straits of Gibraltar open for their shipping. As a corollary of British diplomatic support against the French, the 1856 Treaty of Tangier removed all the sultan's restrictions on trade except his monopoly on tobacco and arms. It instituted a flat 10 per cent customs rate and introduced consular courts and privileges which soon deprived the sultan of any control over his nation's trade. Spain as well as France soon became envious of British influence. In 1859, as the sultan lay dying, a Spanish army advanced from Ceuta to defeat a tribal army and occupy the city of Tetouan. The tribes rose again in revolt against their defeated government, and British protection was revealed to be a false and illusory hope.

Abder Rahman's son Sidi Mohammed (**Mohammed IV**, 1859–73) was faced with a problematic inheritance. The Spanish demanded a crippling indemnity of 100 million pesetas before they would leave Tetouan; a pretender to the throne appeared in the Rif; and the Rehamna tribe pillaged Marrakesh. The Spanish left Tetouan in 1862, paid off by a British loan which required the surrender of customs revenue and its administration by the British and Spanish. Internal dissidence was subdued by 1864.

The unhappy start to the reign was followed by a remorseless growth in European influence. By 1900 there were over 10,000 European residents in the country. Foreign consuls in the ports of Tangier and Casablanca organized lighthouses, port works, sanitary services and a national postal service, increasingly supplanting the sultan's sovereignty. The consular privileges of the treaty of 1856 put European merchants and their many Moroccan agents beyond the law of the sultan. As a graphic illustration of this trend, between 1844 and 1873 the national currency lost 90 per cent of its value. Trade was conducted in the French five franc coin.

Sultan **Moulay Hassan** (1873–94) attempted the almost impossible task of modernizing Morocco while keeping the nation's independence. On his accession in 1873, he began a programme of reform. Whilst instituting this, however, he still had to maintain central authority through the traditional system of annual military campaigns. The students he dispatched to Europe to learn the latest medical and engineering skills returned unable to cope with the political realities of their homeland.

The sultan attempted to stabilize the currency by minting the Koranically approved *riyal* in Paris, but it was of such quality that it was hoarded or smuggled abroad. At the Conference of Madrid in 1880 he attempted to limit the ruinous extent of consular privileges, and a limit was set of two agents per country in each port; but no European power except Britain respected these terms. Military reforms proved just as difficult. When the European powers blocked his schemes, he wisely balanced their influence: there was a French military mission, a British chief of staff ('Caid' Maclean), the German Krupp firm was given contracts for coastal defence, and the Italians built and ran a munitions factory at Fez. Moulay Hassan exhausted himself in the service of his country, reasserting order and personally dispensing justice in regions that had not seen an official of the sultan for a hundred years. He died while on campaign in 1894.

His two sons presided over the last stormy decade of Moroccan independence. Useless Western products were enthusiastically acquired, their purchase financed through ruinous foreign loans. **Abdul Aziz** (1894–1908), surrounded by a court composed of European adventurers, unscrupulous salesmen and doctors, became alienated from his traditional advisers and political realities. Meanwhile, the tribal chiefs and *caids* (magistrates) appointed by Moulay Hassan, notably in the High Atlas mountains, expanded their power in the vacuum created by the disordered central government.

The Imposition of French Rule (1904–36)

It is doubtful whether any ruler could have successfully resisted the anarchy created by the advance of French power in Morocco at this time. In exchange for a free hand in Morocco the French had begun to negotiate a series of bargains with the other colonial powers: Spain was offered territory in northern and southern Morocco, Italy a free hand over Libya, while the French agreed to recognize Britain's rule over Cyprus, Egypt and the Sudan, with the additional promise that Tangier would remain a demilitarized zone.

French control was tightened in 1904 when Abdul Aziz accepted a loan of 50 million francs from a consortium of French banks. In 1906 the Conference of Algeciras ratified the various secret negotiations that had been taking place between the Europeans over the future of Morocco. The French army had slowly been occupying oases on the eastern frontier since 1900, but in 1907 the lynching of a few Europeans in Marrakesh and Casablanca gave them the excuse for direct intervention. Oujda was occupied in the east, and 3000 French troops were promptly landed at Casablanca. The 'Moroccan Crises' of 1905 and 1911, when Imperial Germany sought to gain influence in Morocco, only spurred the French into more aggressive action, to deny access to the country to their greatest rival.

Sultan **Moulay Hafid** (1908–12), faced with simultaneous French and Spanish invasions and internal rebellions, accepted the inevitable and signed the Treaty of Fez (1912), which established colonial rule over Morocco. The nation was carved up into Spanish and French spheres of influence: the French took everything of value, leaving only bare bones for their rivals. The Spanish protectorate consisted of Ifni (an enclave in the Anti-Atlas), a stretch of desert south of the Drâa Valley, and the mountainous Rif coast of northern Morocco.

The French takeover of Morocco was not entirely unopposed. Two weeks after the Treaty of Fez was signed, revolution broke out in Fez, eighty Europeans were lynched and the walls were manned. In the south, El Hiba, 'the Blue Sultan', raised the black banners of revolt and marched up from the Sahara with a tribal force of 12,000. French artillery and machine guns, though, did for them both, and by September Marrakesh had been occupied.

The colonial regime soon became critically short of manpower, as the storm clouds of the First World War became apparent. Deals were struck with the Glaoui brothers, a pair of ex-government ministers from the Berber High Atlas, who were armed and encouraged to build up a private army to secure the south. Taroudannt was taken in May 1913 without the use of a single French soldier, and the first French resident general, Marshal Lyautey, was able to hold central Morocco with a skeleton military presence. However, the Rif, Middle Atlas and the areas south of the High Atlas remained beyond his control until reinforcements in 1921 allowed the conquest to proceed. It was not completed until 1936.

It was in the rugged eastern Rif, in the Spanish zone, that the colonial powers encountered the most serious military resistance. The rebel leader **Abdel Krim** defeated a Spanish army in July 1921. It took several years and a full-scale combined Franco-Spanish campaign under the command of Marshal Pétain to subdue him.

Tangier was left as a demilitarized zone. A constitution in 1923 provided the international city of Tangier with a ruling council of consuls, a small house of representatives and the *mendoub*, the representative of the sultan. In practice, French and Spanish officials dominated the administration, the Italians gave the best parties, and the British created some beautiful gardens.

The Achievements of the French Protectorate (1912–56)

Peace, with the end of tribal pillage and administrative extortion, led to a rapid growth in population and trade. In 1921 Morocco had a population of three million. After only thirty years of French rule this had risen to eight million.

Apart from military conquest and administration the Protectorate's chief concern was to develop Morocco's agricultural and mineral wealth. French banks financed major public works, and the government attracted capitalist investment into mining and agriculture by a tempting package of low taxes, cheap labour and land.

By 1953, irrigation, expropriation and purchase had created one million hectares of cultivable land under French ownership concentrated in the fertile coastal zones. In 1951 there were 325,000 Europeans in the country, including a rich controlling minority of 5000 and a sub-class of 80,000 'poor whites'. An impressive infrastructure of roads, railways, ports, administrative centres and dams was developed to provide water and power for the settlers and facilitate the economic exploitation of the country. Hospitals, schools and hotels were also built for the use of settlers and a tiny minority of the traditional Moroccan ruling class of *caids*, merchants and sheikhs. Even by Independence in 1956 less than 15 per cent of the Moroccan population had received any sort of education.

The Second World War

Morocco was involved in the events of the Second World War as a Protectorate of France. After the conquest of France by Nazi Germany in 1940, her overseas possessions passed under the control of Marshal Pétain's Vichy regime. Pétain strove to maintain a degree of neutrality, but a series of British and Free-French attacks soon pushed Vichy into a tacit alliance with Germany. After the entry of the USA into the war many of Pétain's generals in North Africa began to enter into covert discussions with the Allies, and in November 1942 a British-American force stumbled ashore in the Casablanca landings that 'liberated' Morocco.

It was a near farce: the soldiers were all horribly seasick and the whole thing had been arranged in advance by secret negotiations. Morocco was promptly placed under the Free-French administration of De Gaulle, and in January 1943 Roosevelt and Churchill met in the country for the Casablanca Conference. In a meeting with Sultan **Mohammed V** the American President gave private encouragement that the post-war era would bring a return of sovereignty to Morocco.

By the end of the war there were 300,000 Moroccans under arms. They formed a very substantial portion of the French forces that fought alongside the Allies in Italy and then in France itself after the collapse of the Pétain regime in 1942. It was the Moroccan 4th Mountain Division that in May 1944 broke the Gustav Line. The Moroccan 2nd Division captured Monte Pantano in 1943 and, transferred to France, also won great respect for crossing the Rhine under heavy fire on 31 March 1945.

The Struggle for Independence (1947–56)

Though there was no immediate political evidence for it, the Second World War saw a transformation in the relationship between France and Morocco. France had been humiliated, whilst Moroccan forces had contributed to the liberation of Europe. The European colonial powers had been replaced by the anti-colonial world leadership of America and Russia. India and Egypt, which both rapidly achieved independence at the end of the war, pointed the way for Morocco.

Mohammed V had been chosen by the French in 1927 to succeed his father for his apparent docility. He proved to have an unexpectedly strong character and enjoyed the moral high ground against a series of unimaginative generals who served as Residents. The sultan resisted all of Vichy France's anti-semitic measures and refused to receive a single German officer, and while 200,000 French Jews died in Nazi concentration camps he protected all 300,000 of his Jewish subjects. By 1953 the sultan was so clearly identified with the popular demand for independence that the French authorities deposed him and exiled him to Madagascar. By the summer of 1955 the campaign of civil disobedience for the sultan's return had escalated into widespread violence and the French were threatened by an incipient armed rebellion. The situation in Algeria, where the FLN revolt had erupted in 1954, helped concentrate their minds. The French decided to quit Morocco (and Tunisia) with good grace in order to concentrate on holding on to Algeria. The Spanish and the 'international protectors' of Tangier were forced to follow suit. In November 1955 Mohammed V returned to a tumultous popular reception, and by March 1956 the French had formally recognized Moroccan independence.

King Mohammed V (1956–61)

Upon independence the sultan restyled himself as King Mohammed V to emphasize his position as a modern constitutional monarch removed from the practices of the pre-1912 regime. In the euphoric first years of independence a national government established schools, universities and newspapers, and elected regional assemblies. The Sufi brotherhoods—many of which had become involved in pro-French politics—were reformed; orthodoxy and public morality were reaffirmed; and massive public work schemes were launched. In the early burst of nationalist enthusiasm labour battalions absorbed unemployment and created some lasting monuments, such as the Route de l'Unité road across the Rif, which joined the road systems of the hitherto separate French and Spanish Protectorates.

For all this wave of modernization Mohammed V was quietly determined that the monarchy should always remain the controlling force in national politics. The **Istaqlal**, the sole national party, which had played a central role in the struggle for independence, was seen to pose a potential threat. It dominated the first cabinet, although Mohammed V insisted on retaining control over the army and the Ministry of the Interior. By 1959 the left wing of the Istaqlal under Ben Barka had broken away to form the UNFP (Union Nationale des Forces Populaires) and ranged themselves in a socialist alliance with the UMT labour union; the centrist rump of Istaqlal then established their own union, the UGTM. The rural Berber hinterland, meanwhile, remained suspicious of the urban Istaqlal, and with discreet support from the king a new and conservative party, the Mouvement Populaire, was formed.

Crown Prince Hassan was given the task of creating a royal army. Units of the Liberation Army were absorbed within this new force, which, by recruiting experienced veterans of French service, soon rose to 30,000 men. In 1958 and 1959 rebellions in the Rif, the Saharan oases and the Middle Atlas tested the army's discipline and efficiency. The more radical and militant members of the Liberation Army were meanwhile directed south to the unofficial siege of the Spanish enclave of Ifni and the struggle to gain control over the western Sahara.

The Early Years of King Hassan II, the 'Great Survivor' (1961–75)

In February 1961, at the height of his powers, King Mohammed V died during a routine operation on his nose. He was succeeded by his 32-year-old son, Hassan II, who foreign observers did not expect to last more than a few years. In fact he would rule Morocco for 38 years with an iron fist. Much of this success was due to his political adaptability. He freely confessed that at least 40 per cent of his decisions had been wrong, but he never once relaxed his control over the realities of power: the army, the police and the local governors.

The new king excluded the socalist UNFP from government by forming a cabinet from the Mouvement Populaire and Istaqlal in June 1961. In December 1962 a referendum was held to give popular approval to Morocco's **first democratic constitution**. The UNFP called for a boycott, but this failed due to lack of support from the labour unions. The new king, having won the referendum, no longer felt the need for Istaqlal support, and sacked its members from his cabinet.

The first parliamentary elections were held in March 1963. The Ministries of Agriculture and the Interior assisted the electoral victory of the FDIC, a royal coalition headed by the Mouvement Populaire. Istaqlal was strongest in the older cities and successful farming areas such as Tadla, Doukkala and the Rharb; UNFP in the new cities of the coast—Rabat, Casablanca and Agadir—and throughout the Sous Valley; the Mouvement Populaire's greatest support came from Marrakesh and the Berber hinterland as well as Oujda, Taza and Nador.

The socialist UNFP increasingly identified itself with the Arab republics of Egypt and Algeria, which its supporters publicly cited as role models for Morocco. The local elections of July 1963, and the conspicuous but fixed FDIC victory of an 85 per cent vote, encouraged the UNFP to think in terms of revolutionary change. The king responded by arresting over 130 UNFP militants on treason charges later in the month. Ben Barka, the leader of the UNFP, fled to Paris and widened the political breach by calling on the Moroccan army not to resist Algeria in the border war fought in the Sahara during the winter of 1963.

The first parliament was a failure. In two years of existence, it passed only three minor bills. A three-year plan drawn up in 1964 was aborted as the planners had failed to consult the Finance Ministry. A short-lived liberal party was formed around disgruntled technocrats appalled by the jobbery and factional intrigue that dominated the parliament. The student and worker riots of Casablanca in March 1965 encouraged the king to dissolve parliament in June and rule directly, though he retained most of the parliamentary cabinet. Ben Barka was assassinated in Paris that August, in a plot that was traced back to the Moroccan Ministry of the Interior. The king, in an adroit political move, then borrowed a popular UNFP issue and initiated the nationalization of foreign businesses and farms.

By August 1970 a new constitution was prepared and approved in a national referendum that gave the king increased influence over parliament. Istaqlal and the UNFP boycotted the elections, with the result that the parliament was made up of loyalist placemen. As a result of this narrowing of the field of power there were two coups d'état. A group of senior army officers had grown disgusted at the scale of corruption in government and the extent of patronage and client networks. In the Coup of Skhirate in July 1971 they attempted to purge the king of his existing advisers, who were to be replaced by a puritanical reforming military council. In 1972 there was another failed coup when the king's aeroplane was ambushed by Air Force jets but was saved by a quick-talking pilot. Investigations traced the plot back to General Oufkir, the widely feared Minister of the Interior. The following year, in March 1973, bands of armed men crossed the border from Algeria in the hope of sparking off a popular rising. It never got off the ground, but the public trial was used to accuse some of the left-wing opposition of treasonable rebellion.

The Later Years of King Hassan II, the 'Unifier' (1975–99)

If the first 14 years of King Hassan's reign earned him the nickname of the 'Great Survivor', his later period of rule allows him to be considered the 'Unifier'. In 1975 the king orchestrated a march of 350,000 civilians south to reintegrate the Spanish colony of Rio de Oro (western Sahara) into greater Morocco. This 'Green March' buried the political problems of the past in a surge of nationalism. It was a brilliantly timed political gamble which caught the Spanish government paralysed by the lingering death of General Franco. The resulting war against a group of the Saharan tribes, united under the **Polisario** movement for independence in the western Sahara, prolonged the mood of national unity. Libya and Algeria supported the Polisario, but this 'revolutionary' alliance led to firm backing for Morocco from both Saudi Arabia and the United States.

After a shaky start the war was won militarily. A methodical system of well-patrolled sand walls, begun in 1981 and completed in 1987, excluded the Polisario fighters from all but the frontier fringes of the province. This policy of practical action was matched by a 'hearts and minds' programme that sought to win over the Saharan population with new housing and development schemes. The enhanced pay, equipment and prestige afforded to the army kept it loyal to the king. Meanwhile, the Polisario, locked up in their refugee camps around the Algerian town of Tindouf, gradually lost the support of their hosts. In 1989 a UN-sponsored ceasefire was agreed and King Hassan met with Polisario leaders for talks in Marrakesh. His hand was further strengthened in 1992 when the foreign minister of the Polisario defected to Morocco, and the Algerian government seemed to renounce the idea of an independent western Sahara. Ever since the ceasefire there has been talk of a UN-monitored referendum, but the question of who is eligible to vote will be decisive.

The enormous cost of the war, an estimated $1 billion a year, added to Morocco's already grave economic problems. Strikes in 1979 led to the arrest of activists, but wages were increased to keep abreast of the annual 10 per cent inflation rate. The political temper was heated by these strikes, and later that year teachers and students demonstrated against the presence of the deposed Shah of Iran, who had sought refuge with the king.

By June 1981 the situation had been aggravated by a succession of bad harvests that increased basic food prices just when the International Monetary Fund (IMF) insisted that the state subsidy on food must be reduced. A day-long demonstration against the IMF cuts degenerated into looting and rioting. The police restored order after many casualties, and some of the organizers of the original demonstration were prosecuted. Local elections were held in June 1983, but the scale of the royalist victory suggested heavy-handed electoral influence. Parliamentary elections were subsequently cancelled and the king assumed emergency powers in October, though again he skilfully checked criticism by assembling a cabinet from a broad spectrum of political parties. In January 1984 the events of 1981 were repeated as the IMF insisted on further heavy cuts in subsidies in exchange for vital loans. Riots broke out throughout Morocco. The king withdrew the cuts in question, but at the same time heavy police action against rioters and political dissidents put 2,000 men behind bars.

The state of emergency lasted only six months, and by the summer of 1984 a new parliament had been elected which produced a moderate government committed to economic reform. There was much work to be done. The internal tax situation was in an anarchic state, with all the big earners such as tourism, agriculture and property speculation enjoying an official tax holiday. The state phosphate industry that bestrides the domestic economy ran at a paper 'loss', while a flourishing black market, covering much the same ground, turned over an estimated $5 billion a year.

The IMF provided the new reforming administration of Morocco with a series of loans to restructure its industry and gradually create something approaching a free market. Though there is still much to be done a bold start has been made in creating an open stock exchange, statutory accounting for businesses, VAT, independent management, cuts in the top-heavy civil service, and some accountability in the state phosphate monopoly. A policy of privatization, initiated in 1989, has already disposed of some of the enormous state sector, although, as in many such schemes elsewhere, it is the small profitable concerns that are easy to sell off while the monolithic loss-makers remain. These reforms have attracted an increasing amount of foreign investment and there are now over 1000 foreign companies in operation, mostly concentrated around the tourist, part-assembly and textile trades, which look to the EU as their natural market.

Though the man in the street is much more concerned with Morocco's relations with the rest of the Arab world, it is the European Union that is the country's vital trading partner. The rejection of the 'Muslim applications' of both Morocco and Turkey to join the EU during the 1990s has allowed a more pragmatic spirit to be introduced into later negotiations for a free-trade agreement between Morocco and the Union. Of the EU countries, relations with the old colonial powers of France and Spain remain dominant. Over 40 per cent of Morocco's imports come from France and Spain, and also the bulk of her invisible earnings through tourism and guest workers. Both countries have proved generous suppliers of government loans, technical assistance and arms. Despite the nationalization of foreign-owned land and businesses in the 1970s, both France and Spain have a substantial stake in the Moroccan economy, for French and Spanish banks hold influential shareholdings in Morocco's own chain of commercial banks. The Spanish territories of Ceuta and Melilla are not yet a major issue of confrontation, although it is easy to imagine they could become a tempting nationalist diversion in any future period of popular unrest.

The connection with France remains very strong. Thousands of young Moroccans finish their education in a French university, and there are still thousands of skilled French technicians, teachers and governmental experts employed by the government of Morocco. French and Moroccan troops have even performed joint operations, such as the 'policing' of Zaire in 1979. US support and aid throughout the Polisario war has drawn Morocco quite firmly into the Western camp. Bases have been put at the disposal of American rapid deployment forces and Voice of America relay stations have been established.

In June 1988 several decades of mutual hostility between Morocco and Algeria were ended with the restoration of full diplomatic ties. This was followed in the spring of 1989 by the Maghrebi Union Treaty between all the countries of northwestern Africa—Libya, Tunisia, Algeria, Morocco and Mauritania. This surprising turn of events had as much to do with the economic difficulties of Algeria and Libya, and mutual anxiety at the growth of an isolationist Europe, as the common culture of the Maghreb. This block of nations is known as UMA (Union de Maghreb Arabe), which has pleasing associations with the Arabic word *umma*, which refers to the wider community of Islam. The alliance did not have any dramatic consequences, but for a time allowed an easing of border controls that permitted Morocco and Tunisia to sell food to new importers such as Libya and Algeria. However, the collapse of Algeria since 1992 into ferocious violence between the established FLN regime and army and the Islamic fundamentalists of the FIS has led the Moroccan government once again to seal the Algerian border, undoubtedly motivated to a considerable extent by concern to head off any contagion of fundamentalism within its own territory.

There was no display of Maghreb unity during the Gulf War of 1991. King Hassan rode the conflict with consummate skill. His early pledge to send Moroccan troops to join the Alliance forces put him in good standing with all those powers—the USA, Saudi Arabia, the Gulf States and Western Europe—on whom Morocco is dependent for loans and investment. Faced with massive popular demonstrations in favour of Saddam Hussein he was forced to back down from his original strong pro-Alliance stance, but in the aftermath of the war Morocco did not suffer the sudden withdrawal of aid that affected so many Arab states.

The 1993 elections to parliament produced few surprises and confirmed the king's control of the political life of the country through the offices of his feared Minister of the Interior, Si Basri, the successor to Oufkir. In 1994, seemingly at the height of his powers, he hosted a Middle East Economic Summit at Casablanca attended by both the Israeli prime minister, Yitzhak Rabin, and Yasser Arafat, president of the PLO. The next year he knew he was dying, whilst his regime was hit by criticism of Morocco's human rights record and a withering World Bank report which attacked corruption and administrative lethargy.

Nothing in his life would quite match the shrewdness with which he prepared for his death. Political prisoners were released and a new constitution drafted to create a bicameral parliament, the 325 members of the lower house to be elected, the upper house—a 270-seat Chamber of Advisers—to be filled by old office-holders and an indirectly elected assortment of the great and the good. The 1997 elections seemed to be (for once) free of the manipulations of the government. A centre-left coalition won a majority and in 1998 the old king appointed his first socialist prime minister, the 75-year-old **Aberrahmane Youssoufi**. A quiet spirit of optimism prepared the country for Hassan II's death on Friday 23 July 1999, when the nation was swept by a spontaneous explosion of grief.

King Mohammed VI (1999–)

Hassan's 36-year-old eldest son ascended the throne as Mohammed VI, and quickly distanced himself from his father's henchmen. In a series of public tours to such forgotten and depressed corners of the regime as the eastern plains and the Rif mountains he revealed a compassionate interest in the plight of the poor and unprotected. On 9 November he sacked the deeply unpopular Minister of the Interior, Si Basri, but awarded him the Medallion of the Throne (the kingdom's highest honour) in acknowledgment of 30 years of loyal service to the late king. At the same time restrictions on the press were lifted and old exiles welcomed back (such as Abraham Serfaty and the family of Mehdi Ben Barka), while the young king's friends began to be placed in key positions of power. For the moment, relations betweeen the palace and the socialist prime minister are excellent. There is much to be done.

No one can be certain of the future. From the past you learn that Islam, anarchy, regional loyalties and nationalism are consistent if contradictory features of Moroccan history. But it seems clear that only a strong man can rule a nation of such triumphant individualists.

The Moroccan Economy

Farming is the most important element in the economy. Despite its rapidly growing population, Morocco remains almost self-sufficient after a good harvest, when the land yields about 4 million tons of wheat and 3 million tons of barley. Rainfall is still an absolute barometer of the national mood. In 1998 good rainfall allowed a 6.5 per cent growth in GDP, while in the following arid year it fell to just 0.2 per cent. Half the population works on the land, producing cereals and root crops from 8 million hectares as well as grazing animals over a vastly more extensive area. Excluding beasts of burden such as mules, donkeys, horses and camels, the nation's livestock numbers 18 million sheep, 6 million goats and 3.5 million cattle. Exportable agricultural goods such as sugar, citrus fruits, early vegetables and potatoes are principally produced by a few large well-irrigated estates established by the French in the Haouz Plain around Marrakesh and the Rharb. These are in the hands of a wealthy minority, while the masses survive on 20dh a day. It is estimated that 80 per cent of villages have either no schools, paved roads, running water or electricity.

Industry is concentrated on the Atlantic coast around Casablanca, Rabat and Kénitra. The urban work force is estimated at 5 million, of whom 1 million are unemployed—this in a country without any welfare support. Industry employs about 15 per cent of the population and is principally involved with the processing of the country's enormous phosphate deposits and its agricultural products (such as olive oil, flour, milk, fish, fruit and vegetables). A second tier of industry includes cement works, tyre and textile factories. **Traditional crafts**, such as hand weaving, leather work, metal work, pottery and carpet-making are still broadly distributed among traditional towns and cities. **Mining** and

construction employ another 15 per cent of the population, with lower numbers of workers absorbed by running the tourist industry, utilities and government services.

Customs duties, as throughout most of Morocco's history, provide the bulk of state revenue. Foreign exchange comes from three major sources: US$1bn in receipts from between 1 and 2 million migrant workers, $610m from tourism, and $480m from phosphates. These figures help fill the $2500 million gap in the balance of trade. The export of fruit and vegetables to Europe is a lesser earner and this market has been severely threatened since the entry of the similar Mediterranean agricultural economies of Spain, Portugal and Greece into the EU in the 1980s. **Fishing**, though still a small earner of foreign cash, has been an area of continuous growth for several years. Morocco now lands over 500,000 tonnes a year, largely composed of the world's largest sardine catch.

An unlikely but valuable national resource is the king's friendship with the royal families of Saudi Arabia and the Gulf States. Generous loans, help in rescheduling debts, a daily 'allowance' of 50,000 barrels of oil, and outright gifts have propped up the Moroccan economy on numerous occasions. In 1985, for instance, $250m suddenly appeared in the ledgers of the foreign currency reserves when all other sources were known to be exhausted. Over-ambitious central planning, government waste, inefficient tax collection, a bungled attempt to quadruple the world phosphate price and the desert war have pushed the load of **foreign debt** perilously high. Twenty-five per cent of all government expenditure goes to service the interest of this debt, whilst 50 per cent is pledged to official salaries. The room for political manoeuvre is not large.

Problems

The major issue in Moroccan politics would appear to be to democratize the country and yet maintain the stability, peace and unity afforded by the autocracy of the monarchy. Too many of the country's intellectuals and entrepreneurs remain outside the system of local and national government, while too many of the influential merchants and industrialists remain outside the system of law and tax-gathering. Without frightening them out of the country, revenue must yet be raised from this small but immensely prosperous class. This could then be spent on much needed social and educational aid for the 60 per cent of the nation who are illiterate and live below the poverty line. It is too early even to dream about land reform.

The economy has seen a steady annual growth of 2.8 per cent a year, but this achievement is constantly undermined by the equally **fast-growing population**. From 8 million in 1952 it has now grown to more than 27 million. Over half the population of Morocco is under 20, and the majority of this age group is unemployed, especially those with university degrees. There has yet to be any evidence that the population growth rate is slowing down. Family planning is still restricted to the small professional urban class. In any case, popular myth considers it a Western-funded plot to restrict the size of the Arab nation. Population growth is accompanied by a shift from the conservative society of the countryside to the radical identity of the shantytowns, which house more than 20 per cent of the urban population. The old solution—of migrant work in Europe—is no longer an option. Whichever way you look at things, this augurs future political stress.

Despite the dramatic and terrifying events in neighbouring Algeria, **Muslim fundamentalism** does not seem to have emerged as a difficulty in Morocco, although (typically) the Rif may yet prove to be an exception. The old role of the sultan as the Commander of the Faithful has been carefully retained. Morocco has never witnessed a split between the *ulema*, the Islamic hierarchy, and a determinedly secular government, as so many other Arab states have. The daily TV weather report provides an example of the natural religious conservatism of Morocco and the opportunities for consensus. The predictions of the weather were at first considered impious by the *ulema*, but once the announcer started to add enough *insha' Allah*'s (if God wills it) there was no further complaint. However, the young king will have to show that his regime can deliver economic and social growth or risk the alienation of the rising generation. It is noticeable that the foremost Islamist politician, Abdessalome Yassine, remains unaffected by the new liberal wind.

Moroccan Themes

As Muslims and Christians approach books from different ends, so do they architecture. This is less of a philosophical division and more to do with a difference in climate. Islamic architecture aims to enclose space, to create a sheltered garden from a wilderness. Architectural decoration, of pavilions, fountains, raised paths and pools, is reserved for the interior of this enclosure. European traditions are the complete reverse: gardens emanate from outside the house, decoration is reserved for the exterior of a structure, and the interior has more to do with a collection of rooms isolated from the environment than any feeling of a defined space.

In architectural detail both Christendom and Islam share the same classical influences, though Islam has more fully identified itself with the domes and arches of Christian Byzantium. Muslim architects in North Africa rejected horizontal beams early on and began experimenting with horseshoe arches. This was developed into a pervading, almost obsessive regional theme. The tracery of the interlocking arch is ubiquitous: rising from walls to support domes, or in serried ranks to support the roof of every major mosque, and defining the lowest tier of every interior courtyard. The squinches, the awkward corners left by a dome, are filled by muqurnas, which can appear like disordered dripping stalactites, though in their origin they are highly ordered tiers of arches. The surface of the arch itself is next adorned, with circular half lobes, tracery and muqurnas. By the 19th century the style had become debased; to see it with its early confidence and elegance you must visit the monuments of the Almoravids, Almohads and Merenids.

North African architects also moved away from using columns as a central structure and developed rectangular piers to support their arches. Columns that freely borrowed their capitals from classical, Egyptian and Persian styles were increasingly used as mere decoration. Often combined in pairs, they flank a window frame or define the edge of a horseshoe arch, or appear so ornate and thin as to be almost free-standing beside the load-bearing pier of an arch. In short, the column becomes vestigial.

The construction of the port town of Essaouira (which is accessible as a day trip from Marrakesh) in the late 18th century by a Christian architect in the service of the Moroccan Sultan provides a first taste of the Neo-Moorish style of architecture. This became widespread only in the late 1920s, when the French colonial administration began to construct a whole new infrastructure of post offices, railway stations, judicial and administrative offices. The Neo-Moorish style took elements of Morocco's medieval heritage and used them, totally divorced from their structural relevance, as mere decorative details and façades for otherwise entirely Western buildings. It was an inversion of the whole historical development of Islamic architecture, yet seems to work well. So far the style remains largely restricted to public buildings and hotels, though some newer housing developments are beginning to incorporate its repertoire.

Kasbahs

A Moroccan kasbah (or Qasaba) can be a fortified manor house, the citadel of a city, an isolated government garrison or a tribal fort. A key to its definition is not so much its scale as its purpose, for a kasbah should be the domain of a ruler, be he sultan, governor or just a tribal chieftain. Most of the ancient cities of Morocco retain a large portion of their outer walls, but the kasbah (the government citadel containing palace, barracks, prison, arsenal and treasury) has too often decayed beyond recognition. Rabat provides an honourable and accessible exception. The walls of Essaouira are in even better condition, for they were built on the best European principles in the 18th century. Such fortifications are not always described as a kasbah, for there is a parallel military terminology which uses names such as *mahalla* (a fortified marching camp); *rabat* (or *r'bat*), meaning both a castle and a fortified base for the holy war; *hisn*, 'stronghold'; and *bordj* (or *burj*), a 'tower'.

The rise in power of the High Atlas *caids*, and particularly the Glaoui tribe, has left the southern region of Morocco studded with decaying kasbahs from which they administered their feudal domain. A Glaoui kasbah can still be seen at Telouèt, which can be visited from Marrakesh. At their best these kasbahs fuse the dazzling variety of traditional Berber battlemented exteriors with finely proportioned interiors that drew on Andalucían palaces for their inspiration. The Berber hill tribes were more capable of defending themselves than oasis- or valley-dwellers. They could afford to live in smaller family units, but stored their corn in communal stone-built hilltop fortresses which are known as an *agadir* (plural *igoudar*), *igherm* or *tighremt*, depending on which Berber dialect region they are in.

Marabouts and Koubbas

Throughout the cities, towns, villages and countryside of Morocco you will observe the koubbas, the domed tombs of marabouts—Muslim holy men. They are a striking feature of the Moroccan landscape and can range from a simple whitewashed, earth-walled hut to an opulent chamber covered by a green-tiled pyramid roof. The marabout's tomb may be obscure, half-ruined and forgotten, or stand at the centre of a great city surrounded by a maze of outer courtyards around which stand dependent mosques, markets, *hammams*, schools and charitable institutions. As well as the size of the shrine, the nature of the holy man can vary. The venerated Lalla or Sidi could be a reforming sultan, a fearless warrior of the *jihad*, a Sufi master, the near-legendary ancestor of a tribe, the founder of a city, a pious protector of the poor, a learned arbitrator, or an Islamic identity for an old pagan deity of the mountain, river, forest or field. The one thing they have in common is *baraka*, which means both an enhanced spiritual standing and the power to benefit a pilgrim with a blessing.

The koubba is often the centre of spiritual life for the women of the area, as well as functioning as an asylum and a charitable centre. In the countryside it may also be the site of a weekly market or an annual *moussem*. These *moussems* may officially be held in honour of the saint but also function as exuberant secular festivals, popular social events, trade fairs and marriage markets.

Medersas

The earliest residential religious college in the Islamic world, or medersa, was built in Persia in the 9th century. Medersas were not built in Morocco until the 13th century, under the patronage of the Merenid sultans. Until then teaching took place in the courts of a mosque or in the houses of learned men. The earliest surviving Moroccan medersa, the Seffarine in Fez (1280), clearly shows the origin of this religious college in the town house of a lecturer. Later medersas drew more heavily on Andalucían decoration and the architectural developments of Cairo, though the basic plan of an open-air court surrounded by an upper storey of student lodgings and leading to a prayer-hall remains consistent. Marrakesh, Salé and Meknès each have a medersa that is open to the public, and Fez has three.

Mosques

Unlike Turkey and Egypt, Morocco does not allow those of other faiths to enter a mosque, nor in many cases Muslim cemeteries or the tombs of holy men. There are exceptions, most important of which are the Tin-Mal Mosque in the High Atlas south of Marrakesh, the new Grand Mosque of Hassan II at Casablanca, and the tomb of Sultan Moulay Ismaïl in Meknès. There is no doctrinal basis for this exclusion, which seems to date from the period of the French Protectorate. The colonial authorities wished to avoid confrontation, and also believed that it would be useful for Moroccans, everywhere faced by the reality of European power, to have somewhere which was beyond the influence of foreigners. There was also an older tradition (born from a thousand years of warfare) of excluding Christians from even entering within the walls of a city; the sanctuary of Moulay Idriss, near Fez, remained inviolate until the 20th century. However, allowing non-Muslims to meet an intelligent and sympathetic believer who can dispel centuries of European obscurantism is something that is worth extending even further.

Although most mosques in Morocco are closed to non-Muslims, you are of course free to admire the exterior details such as gates and minarets. 'Mosque' literally means the place of prostration. At its simplest it can be an open-air space with a small niche, the mihrab, that indicates the direction of prayer towards Mecca. These mosques are known as *msalla* and can be seen outside the walls of Marrakesh and Fez, where they are used during festivals. The next stage in the development of the mosque can still be seen in use in poorer rural areas: a wall is built to enclose the prayer area and the mihrab extrudes, to appear like a white sugar-loaf. It is only a small further development to roof over the prayer-hall, leaving an open-air court, the *sahn*, exposed at the opposite end to the prayer niche. The sahn or an adjoining building could be equipped with basins or a fountain for the ritual washing enjoined in the Koran.

Byzantine influence from Syria was strong in the construction of the cathedrals of Islam, the first grand mosques. The tendency to embellish the central aisle of the mosque with arches, pillars and domes strongly echoes the nave of a church. That characteristic Islamic feature, the minaret, was initially developed from the short towers that used to define a Byzantine churchyard. The first Muslim architects also borrowed from previous religious practice and elaborated the mihrab into a cave-like half-dome, upon which the two declarations of faith were carved, whilst the exterior of the niche was covered by an arch and flanked by two columns.

The walls and floors of Moroccan mosques are kept free of architectural decoration. The white pillars and arches may carry some simple carving, but there is seldom any colour beyond the hip-height reed matting pinned along the walls, and the carpets on the floor.

Decoration is reserved for elaborate chandeliers and the pulpit-like minbar. The original minbar, used by the Prophet for his lectures at Medina, had six steps. He used a lower step in order to leave the throne symbolically empty. More steps were added by his successors to allow them to sit further from the throne, and so make clear their lesser spiritual authority.

The only substantial traditional mosque that a non-Muslim may enter in Morocco is also one of the oldest. The half-ruined Tin-Mal Mosque in the High Atlas was built by the Almohads in the 12th century. It is contemporary with the great achievements of Moroccan architecture: the Koutoubia Mosque of Marrakesh and the Hassan Tower of Rabat. The minarets of the Koutoubia and Hassan led to the creation of a characteristic style. Moroccan mosques all echo these two tall, square towers, which should be capped with a lantern that is exactly a fifth the size of the tower.

Palaces

The Roman ruins of Volubilis, near Fez, contain a number of palatial houses that are similar in design to the lesser palaces of later Muslim rulers. Moroccan palaces have an inconspicuous exterior and a covered hall that leads to a central open-air court. Around the walls of this court are arranged four public reception rooms or pavilions. The women's quarters are secluded from this male preserve and were known as 'the forbidden', the *harem* court. This arrangement of courts could be endlessly repeated or expanded in scale. The entire complex was known as the *dar* and a suite of rooms around a court a *bayt*. The *méchouar* was a space outside the immediate palace confines but within the outer walls where a ruler could review military parades or receive selected portions of the populace.

The oldest accessible palace in Morocco is the ruined 16th-century El Badia in Marrakesh. Of the palaces built in the 17th century by Sultan Moulay Ismaïl, the Oudaïa in Rabat is well preserved and open to the public. Meknès, for all its past glory, gives little insight into palace architecture. Of the royal palaces built in the 19th century, only the Dar Batha in Fez is accessible. There are, however, a number of lesser viziers' palaces that have survived from this period and are open to the public: the Palais Jamaï Hotel in Fez, the Dar Jamaï Museum in Meknès, the Bahia and the Dar Si Saïd in Marrakesh.

Flowers, Trees and Gardens

The Prophet said: 'If the end of the world happens while one of you is holding a palm tree that you are about to plant, do not get up before having planted it, if possible.' Such an appreciation of the value of plants, so gently put, informs the Moroccan attitude towards the care and cultivation of their own plots, and the land is filled with the exuberance and beauty of plants which flourish under the clear skies of the Maghreb.

The progression from a Mediterranean to a desert ecology occurs in a diagonal belt across the country. Water supply rather than latitude is the key to plant identification. To the east the desert virtually reaches the Mediterranean, whilst in the south, around Marrakesh, irrigation allows groves of olive, orange and cypress trees to flourish. Plant growth ceases from June to August and begins properly with the rains in October. Some species flower throughout the winter but most perennials peak in March and April.

The real beauty of Moroccan flowers and trees lies not within the courtyards of the harems, but all around you, and all year round, even on city streets. Flowering trees along the boulevards, almost all imported from South America, decorate the streets from January onwards. The early yellow pom-poms of mimosas give way in April to the delicate blossoms of the coral tree (*Erythrina caffra*) and the pink calodendrum. May sees the jacaranda trees reveal their flowers of indescribable blue, and in June the delicate tracery of Jerusalem thorn (*Parkinsonia*) is lit up by an eruption of yellow flowers. The handsome evergreen leaves of figs and magnolias provide shade during the summer months. In December the extraordinary *Montanoa bipinnitifida* blazes with huge white daisies. Over the walls of the swanky out-of-town villas tumble hedges of bougainvillea, jasmine, passion flower, podranea, solanum, honeysuckle and roses, with the powerful fragrance of *Cestrum parqui*, charmingly known as *galant de nuit* in French, filling the June night air. And everywhere, of course, are palm trees, stretching up to the sky, providing a vertical counterpoint to the horizontalism of much of the urban architecture.

The clear blue flowers of larkspur, used in the ceremonial garlands of Egyptian mummies and undimmed 3000 years later when the tombs were opened, still overcome the dust of Moroccan roads and roundabouts in early summer. The sickly fragrance of *Datura* (angels' trumpets) is everywhere in villages and towns. It has been used as a (dangerous) hallucinogen since ancient times. The Greek doctor Theophrastus prescribed: 'If 3/20 of an ounce is given, the patient becomes sportive and thinks himself a fine fellow...four times the dose, he is killed.'

In the souks the musty smell of boxes and bowls turned from thuja wood from the Atlas fills every woodworker's shop. An ancient tree, esteemed by classical writers from Homer to St John, thuja is still much sought-after. Its convoluted grain patterns of knots, spirals and veins are identified as tiger-, panther- and peacock-eyes by the cognoscenti, who prefer wood the colour of wine mixed with honey. Cicero paid one million *sesterces* for a thuja table, and Pliny mentioned the tree, 'which has given rise to the mania for fine tables, an extravagance with which women reproach the men when they complain of their vast outlay upon pearls.'

Roses figure heavily in Moroccan agriculture and horticulture. Rose bushes surround the pisé walls of Marrakesh, and the mass production of roses for export is big business, providing the florists of Paris with fine long-stemmed, sweet smelling blooms. The ancient damask rose *trigintipetala* is grown on a massive scale in Dadès, and is known as *beldi* in Arabic and *rose de Mgouna* in French. Cultivated for the distillation of rose-water and used as a handwash by Muslims, it is grown in hedgerow-like strips.

Traditional enclosed Moorish gardens aim to create a harmony of audible flowing water and restful shade thrown from elegant trees, typically laurel, cypress and olive. Roses, violets, jasmine, hollyhocks and blossoming fruit trees were traditionally planted chiefly for their scent. Modern gardens borrow some of these themes but are often dominated by 19th-century imports such as Australian mimosa, Brazilian bougainvillea and the 'boulevard palm' from the Canary Isles. A tour of traditional gardens in Morocco would include the Chellah and the Kasbah in Rabat, the Dar Batha and Palais Jamaï Hotel in Fez, the Dar Jamaï Museum in Meknès, and conclude with the Mamounia Hotel, the Ménara Gardens and the vast Aguedal Gardens in Marrakesh. The latter, more agriculture than horticulture, are still a living exponent of the tradition. The rhythm of the walks radiating from the massive central basins through acre upon acre of olive and orange grove lends a calm, reflective solitude all the more striking in its proximity to the bustling streets of the city.

Of the botanical gardens, Yves St-Laurent's celebrated haven, the Majorelle Garden in Marrakesh, is a collection of spiky plants rather than a garden, and any tranquillity is shattered from 9am onwards by hordes of tourists. The Jardins Exotiques at Bouknadel outside Rabat are much more extensive and overgrown, and less visited.

Islam

Allah is a noun which can be translated as 'the divinity' or 'the only and true God'. Islam literally means 'submission' or obedience to the divinity. Koran means 'the recitation'—the announcement of the word of God to Mohammed via the archangel Gabriel. This at its simplest is the Muslim religion: recognition of and obedience to the single divinity whose will is clearly stated in the Koran.

The Prophet Mohammed is not considered divine but a mere human mouthpiece for divine will. There is no veneration for a single historical act in the life of Mohammed, in contrast to Christianity, in which the moral teaching of Christ can be obscured by his miraculous birth, crucifixion and resurrection. Nor does Islam encourage any hopeless if heroic attempt to imitate the perfect life of a Christ figure. Instead it establishes a moral code that it is possible for the entire community to follow, and which assures salvation for those who honestly attempt to obey and damnation for those who ignore it or fail. It is acknowledged that man is deeply flawed, but great trust and hope is placed in the all-compassionate and merciful God.

Islam is not considered a new religion but a reformation of the ancient monotheistic worship of Abraham. The teachings of Mohammed presented an opportunity for the squabbling Christian and Jewish sects to unite on the common basics of belief. Moses, St John the Baptist and Christ are honoured in the Koran as prophets, but although Christ's birth is seen as miraculous he is not considered to be the son of God. Such a subdivision of divine power is regarded as impossible in monotheistic Islam, although a kind carpet-seller sympathetically suggested to me that if Christians could believe that Christ was filled with the breath of God rather than being his son there would be little disagreement between the two faiths. Towards the end of his life Mohammed realized the impossibility of converting all Christians and Jews. The direction of prayer was changed from Jerusalem to Mecca, and while he still instructed his followers to respect the 'peoples of the book' his views hardened. From the tolerant words of his early teaching, 'Will you dispute with us about God? When he is our Lord and your Lord! We have our words and you have your words but we are sincerely his', the Prophet progresses to, 'O believers! Take not the Jews or Christians as friends.'

The Prophet Mohammed

Born in Mecca in 570, the young Mohammed was left an orphan and brought up by a succession of relatives from the influential Koreisch clan. As a young man he served as agent for Chadjilla, a wealthy widow 15 years his senior, whom he later married. Mecca was the centre of pagan Arab spiritual life, and Mohammed and his wife joined the circle of Hanyfs, puritanical seekers after enlightenment. The Hanyf venerated the religion of Abraham and were familiar with Jewish, Christian and Persian doctrines. These influences are repeatedly acknowledged in the Koran: 'Nothing has been said to thee which has not been said of old by apostles before' and 'Every people has had its own apostle'. Mohammed received his first revelation in 610, 15 years after his marriage, when he was 40 years old. The archangel Gabriel appeared to him in a cave outside Mecca that he used frequently for prayer and meditation. He was at first doubtful about the revelations but, encouraged by his wife, risked ridicule and shared the word of God. His ardent monotheism and criticism of the pagan worship centred on Mecca won some followers but even more enemies. Eventually the protection of his clan proved inadequate and, to avoid assassination, he fled to the city of Medina on 15 June 622, which is taken as the start of the Hegira, the Muslim era.

Mohammed was welcomed to the oasis of Yathrib (thereafter known as Medina el Nabi, or 'city of the Prophet') and invited to become its arbitrator, the learned figure who decided disputes within the community. There he established a theocratic state, and ironed out practical moral and legal codes for his community as well as the practice of prayer. From Medina he waged a defensive war on the Meccans and gradually subdued the surrounding Jewish and pagan tribes. By 630, two years before his death, his authority extended over all Arabia, and he proved magnanimous in victory. His enemies were pardoned and loaded with gifts, while the Prophet returned to his simple house built from palm trunks and canes.

The divisions within the Muslim world originated over the succession to the Prophet's leadership. Shiites believe in the claims of Ali (his cousin) to have succeeded Mohammed, while the Sunni accept the legitimacy of the first three caliphs. Sects such as the Ismailis, Druze and Kharijites all have their own beliefs on what the rightful succession should have been.

The Koran

'The recitation' was first dictated to the illiterate Mohammed by the archangel Gabriel in his cave above Mecca. More verses were revealed to the Prophet in succeeding years, and were memorized and then written down by his followers. The Caliph Othman established the first written version 18 years after the death of Mohammed, in 650. Its 114 unequal chapters, the suras, containing 6,211 verses, were assembled carefully but in order of length, which has given the Koran a chronologically haphazard order. The suras have names, but these, 'The Cow', 'The Bee', 'The Ant', have no significance other than as a memory aid. There are four main themes: the worship of Allah, the Day of Judgement with the division between heaven and hell, stories of earlier prophets, and proclamations and social laws. A collection of the Prophet's sayings and traditions remembered by his companions was also assembled, but despite great efforts there is no definitive edition of this Hadith. In Morocco the *caids* follow the Malekite tradition, one of the four schools of orthodox Islamic law.

The Five Pillars of Islam

The Prophet codified the religious life of his community into the five pillars of Islam: daily prayer, the pilgrimage to Mecca, the fast of Ramadan, the giving of alms, and acceptance that there is no other divinity but God. There were originally only three daily prayers, but some time after the Prophet's death this was increased to five. The first is known as *Moghreb* and is said four minutes after sunset; *Eshe* is said when it is dark; *Soobh Fegr* at dawn; *Dooh* at noon, just after the sun has passed its zenith; and *Asr* midway between noon and sunset. At each mosque a muezzin announces prayers by calling, 'God is great. I testify that there is no God but God. I testify that Mohammed is his prophet. Come to prayer, come to security. God is great.' For *Soobh Fegr*, the dawn prayer, an extra inducement, 'Prayer is better than sleep', is added.

Alone or in a mosque the believer ritually purifies himself by washing with water or sand (this ritual purification was standard practice in all religions of the Near East, including early Christianity). Then, turning to Mecca, the believer stands with hands held up and open to proclaim that Allah is great. He then lowers his hands and recites the *fatiha* prayer still standing: 'Praise be to God, Lord of the worlds, the compassionate, the merciful, king of the day of judgement, thee do we worship and your aid do we seek. Guide us on the straight path, the path of those on whom you have bestowed your grace, not the path of those who incur thy anger nor of those who have gone astray.' The believer bows with hands on knees and completes a full prostration. Kneeling up again, he recites the *chahada*, a prayer for the Prophet. The three positions of prayer have a symbolic meaning: standing distinguishes the rational man from an animal, bowing represents the act of a servant to his master, and prostration abandonment to the will of God. On Fridays the noon prayer is recited only in the grand or licensed mosque. This is followed by a sermon, the *khutba*, given from the steps of the pulpit-like *minbar* (with the throne and higher steps left symbolically empty).

In some of the grand mosques there are specific doors for the use of women. These lead to areas screened off from the sight of men, often at the side or the back of the prayer-hall. This is, however, the exception. In most of Morocco the mosque is a completely male preserve, and women pray at home or in the prayer-halls that surround *koubbas*, the shrines of the saints (*see* 'Marabouts and Koubbas', p.65).

The pilgrimage to Mecca was an annual month-long event centuries before the Islamic era. Mohammed acknowledged the Kaaba shrine as the ancient altar built by the son of Abraham, and a specific Islamic calendar of events was imposed on a cleaned-up version of the old rituals in 630. For a poor man it could be the journey of a lifetime, and in the past it was restricted to the healthy and wealthy, who granted their marriage partners a temporary divorce in case they should never return from the hazards of the journey. On their return they were greeted with the proud title of *hajji*. The distance of Mecca from Morocco (750 days by caravan for the complete trip) increased the attraction of local shrines. Towns such as Moulay Idriss, near Fez, claimed that five pilgrimages there equalled the trip to Mecca.

The fast of Ramadan, during the daylight hours of the ninth month of the Muslim year, commemorates Mohammed's spiritual practices before the Koran was first revealed to him. The night of the 26th day of the fast, which commemorates the first recitation, is known as 'the night of power', and is filled with processions while the heavens are opened to hear the prayers of the faithful. It is a night apart, 'better than a thousand months...peace until the rising of the dawn'. Although the 26th is widely celebrated, it is not known for sure that this is the correct date, for it could be any of the last ten days of Ramadan. This leads to some regional variations and anxious scholarly debate. Ramadan was specifically based on existing Arabian custom and Christian and Jewish spiritual practices such as Lent.

The giving of alms is a continual duty for the Muslim. The *zahir*, or 'fortieth', tax originated out of this obligation and was the foundation of all direct taxation in the Islamic world.

Jewish Morocco

The late 1990s witnessed a minor renaisssance in Jewish Morocco, as Moroccan Jews who emigrated en masse to Israel have begun to return to visit the land of their forefathers. On a mountain road I was told by a Jewish pilgrim that there are two great holy places in the world where heaven and earth are in the closest and most occasionally violent proximity. First is the land of Palestine, but after that there is only Morocco. Tombs, cemeteries and synagogues have been restored on the back of this growing pilgrimage trade, which coincides with a new assertiveness by the Sephardic community within Israel.

Jews first came to Morocco in the ships of the Phoenicians, for they provided a skilled labour force experienced in the working of inland mines. Initially they were concentrated in southern Spain, but gradually became a ubiquitous presence in all the ports established by the Phoenician traders along the North African coast. A tradition records that this scattered community sent tribute to King Solomon to assist in the construction of the first temple. Archaeological evidence is scant, though Hebrew gravestones have been found in the excavations of the Romano-Punic capital of Volubilis, near Fez. The community was greatly strengthened by refugees fleeing the destruction of Judea in the reign of the Emperor Vespasian (69–79) and again in Hadrian's time (113–38), as well as following the failed Jewish revolt in Cyrenaica, in the east of present-day Libya.

The 'Dark Ages' following the fall of Rome are the unchronicled golden period of Jewish activity in Morocco, when missionaries converted whole Berber tribes and communities were established in every corner of the country. When Moulay Idriss first reached Morocco in the 8th century, the Jewish-dominated city of Sefrou, in alliance with the Meknassa tribe, was a key political force. As Islam triumphed, Jews were marginalized from political life, but established a key position in trade, metalwork, jewellery and similar crafts. In the 11th century, two rabbis, the philosopher-physician Maimonides and Yitzhak al Fasi, brought their intellectual culture to a golden flowering. During the Merenid period the first walled ghettoes (the *mellah*) evolved out of the traditional Jewish quarters of cities to facilitate the protection, self-government and efficient taxation of this wealthy community. In the cities Jews were ruled by their own *caids* and judged and taxed by their own officials, while in the countryside Jewish villages placed themselves under the protection of the local military power. A second great wave of Jewish settlement occurred after the fall of Granada in 1492, when the sophisticated urban Jews of Andalucía were expelled from Spain and settled in such cities as Fez, Tetouan, Azzemour and Rabat. In music, speech, dress, cuisine and architecture these refugees had much more in common with their fellow Moors (Muslim Andalucíans) than with the so-called Berber Jews, and this division remains today.

Jews were seen as a vital resource of the state and often held the most important financial posts in the administration, although when the Merenid Sultan Abdul Haqq tried to appoint a Jewish grand vizier he met widespread popular resistance. The ongoing distrust between Muslim Moroccans and the Christian Europeans, fomented by centuries of war and piracy, also meant that the Jews were in constant demand as middlemen by both antagonists. The Alaouite sultans in particular leant heavily on Jewish expertise. It was they who established the large and important Jewish community in Tangier, mostly recruited from the old community in nearby Tetouan, as well as those in Essaouira and Casablanca, most of whom were originally from Azzemour.

In the period of French dominance, European-based Jewish charities were quick to pour funds into Morocco for the education of the community. This effort was so successful that the native Moroccan Jews began to be co-opted into the settler community, though this never reached the level of assimilation (mixed with outbursts of anti-semitism from the French *pied noir*) seen in Algeria and Tunisia.

During the Second World War, King Mohammed V protected the 300,000 Moroccan Jews from the horrors that overtook their brethren in France and the rest of Europe. Nevertheless, although the Moroccan Jews had always enjoyed royal favour and formed one of the world's oldest-established Jewish communities, they remained apart from the majority community, and with the rise of nationalism under the Protectorate they were frequently regarded by other Moroccans as a privileged, semi-Europeanized group who had identified themselves too closely with the French and Spanish colonizers. The events of the Holocaust followed by the establishment of the State of Israel in 1948 galvanized attitudes and Jewish opinion. Emigration to Israel began immediately after the state's foundation, and the trickle of the late 1940s turned into a flood after the Suez Crisis of 1956 led to a wave of anti-Jewish feeling throughout the Arab world. By 1967 this mass migration was all but complete, although the thread has not been completely broken. Around 8,000 Jews remain in Morocco today, and Moroccan Jews, even after they have settled in Israel, are allowed to keep their Moroccan passports. The late King Hassan sought to use the bridge afforded by this community (especially when represented by such a figure as Moshe Dayan) in attempts to intervene in the turbulent waters of the Middle East.

Throughout this guide you will find information on accessible Jewish cemeteries and the location of the old *mellah* quarters. If you wish to try to make personal contact with the surviving communities, the following are useful contact numbers:

Fez: Madame Danielle Mamane c/o Marocaines, 12 Boulevard Chéfchaouni (next to the Grand Hotel), ✆ (05) 62 23 94, ✉ (05) 94 22 51;

Marrakesh: Henri Cadoch, ✆ (04) 44 87 54;

Rabat: Community Centre, 9 Rue Ismail, ✆ (07) 72 45 04.

Moorish Decorative Arts

Morocco has an active tradition of decorative art which was first developed in Moorish Spain. This rich heritage combines geometric, floral and calligraphic themes in a distinctive style that also remains true to the mainstream traditions of Islam. Throughout the country you will find dazzling examples of decorative art carved into stone, cedar and plaster; painted on tiles, furniture, ceilings and ceramics; or assembled in tile mosaics.

Islamic art draws attention away from the real world to one of pure form. Titus Burkhardt defined Islamic art as the way to ennoble matter by means of geometric and floral patterns which, united by calligraphic forms, embody the word of God as revealed in the Koran. Of these forms of decoration only the calligraphic can be considered an Islamic invention, though the way all are combined is distinctively Islamic. Decorative themes from architecture provide many of the motifs for the lesser arts of ceramics, cabinet-making, embroidery and carpet-making.

Geometric decoration presents a direct analogy to spiritual truths, for both direct attention away from the confusing patterns of the world to find hidden cores of meaning. From the muddled three dimensions of the physical world geometry creates a clearly defined two-dimensional order. But beyond the ordered geometric patterns a single hidden point rules the kaleidoscopic images of the surface. Thus all relates to the one, just as on the Day of Judgement all that has been created will return to the single entity of the Creator. Time, space, angles, planes, lines will collapse in on themselves and the physical universe will return to the One. There is no God but the one God.

Islam also inherited earlier Semitic religious traditions that saw sacred art as having an essentially geometric and mathematical nature. Many familiar Islamic geometric patterns were borrowed from Egypt and Syria. Representational art was a dangerous distraction that could degenerate into graven images and paganism, but numbers and figures were seen as symbols that defined a perfect world, created by the single Creator. Islam also absorbed the Platonic and Pythagorean respect for the divine harmony of geometry and mathematics. Numbers and shapes in the Pythagorean and Cabbalistic tradition were connected to mystical properties: a pyramid with its six sides represented fire; a tetrahedron air; a cube earth; and an icosahedron water. The result was a detailed symbolic vocabulary which allowed hidden abstractions to be built into a pattern. The infinite repetition of geometrical patterns, the lattices, interlaces, overlays and borders, is also the perfect aesthetic accompaniment to the human ritual of Islam, the endless chanting of single phrases, the recurring ritual of daily prayer and the repetitious nature of the Koranic verses themselves.

According to the Koran every artist on the Day of Judgement will be challenged to breathe life into his work and on failing will be condemned. The floral art of Persia and Rome was not considered to fall under this interdict, and was eagerly borrowed by the first Muslim conquerors. Floral motifs—acanthus, peonies, tulips, roses, pine cones, vine leaves, pomegranates and palmettes—are also a constant reminder to the faithful of the rewards of paradise, for the Koran is full of references to the overhanging trees and fruits in heaven. The symmetry of flowers and seed pods also reveals the geometric hand of the Creator.

Many Muslims believe that Arabic is the divine language and that their language did not exist before the Prophet Mohammed received the first verses of the Koran. Archaeological evidence, though, shows that written Arabic developed from the Nabato–Aramaic script, which was itself a successor to Phoenician. The earliest Arabic inscription was found near Aleppo and has been dated to AD 512. There appear to have been four distinct Arabic scripts before the Islamic era. A reform by the Caliph Abdel Malik (685–705) established the two schools of calligraphy that exist today. These are kufic, an angular, solid, hieratic script, suitable for carving and ornamental texts, and cursive, a rounded flowing script (sometimes referred to as *Nashki*), suitable for everyday use.

This reform did not check the continual development of scripts, which continued evolving until the spread of printing. Among the more characteristic is the graceful Persian *Taliq;* the variant cursive of *Rihani*; *Tughra*, the cryptic Tartar lettering; the thick, stout *Riqa* script of the Turks; *Sayaquit*, the secret script of the Seljuk clerks; and the opulent *Diwani* of the Ottoman court. *Ghober* script allowed for letters to be carried by pigeon post and could be read only with a magnifying glass, whilst the different tones of *Manachir* could indicate reprimand or satisfaction before even the first letter had been read.

Up to the 12th century, Morocco remained dominated by the old cursive script of Kairouan, in Tunisia. This was replaced by the distinctive Maghrebi script which had been developed in Andalucía, and preserved an ancient synthesis of kufic and cursive. Abdelkebir Khatabi and Mohammed Sigilmassa in *The Splendours of Islamic Calligraphy* (*see* **Further Reading**, p.269) describe it as 'Virile and generous with angular outlines, both horizontal and vertical well emphasized and accompanied by large cursives open at the top.' Maghrebi script was written in black with ink prepared from scorched wool taken from a sheep's stomach. The official standard pen was composed of 24 donkey hairs, though dried reed was a common substitute. A red copper pen was used for marriage documents, a silver or stork-beak pen for a special friend, and a pomegranate sliver was used for an enemy.

Cursive and Maghrebi can be found in architectural decoration, though a plain kufic or floral kufic are much more common. Beyond their own attraction, horizontal bands of script are often used to bind together different sections of materials and decoration, as the Koran binds the community of Islam.

Music

The cry of the muezzin, summoning the faithful to prayer, is the most distinctive, universal and haunting sound in Morocco. In a large city such as Fez or Marrakesh the principal mosque has the honour of initiating the call, which is then picked up and echoed by dozens of lesser mosques. It is most impressive in the comparative quiet and diffused light of the early morning and evening, when it mocks the daytime bustle of the secular world.

Travelling through Morocco you will automatically be exposed to the music of the country as you sit scrunched up in a *grand taxi* or bus. Few cafés would feel complete without the sound of a radio, cassette player or television, while at markets, festivals and urban squares such as the Jemaa el Fna in Marrakesh there is always live music. No market, however small, is complete without at least one cassette stall selling a colourful assortment of their own 45-minute recordings. These barrows carry a broad selection, ranging from Egyptian singers such as the great Ulm Khaltoum, West Indian reggae and some major Western bands, to the home-grown stars of *chaabi*, Moroccan popular music.

The centre for today's Moroccan music industry is Casablanca, where the main contemporary pop influence—Algerian Rai music—is most common. Moroccan Rai stars, such as Cheb Khader and Chaba Zahounia, and their Algerian counterparts create the most prominent sounds on today's urban soundtrack. In most cases they replace traditional instruments with electric and digitalized equivalents, but in their inspiration still draw heavily on a rich seam of Arab and indigenous musical traditions. You will win instant street kudos by asking for a tape by any of the big Moroccan names such as El Hussein Slaoui, Lafkih Laomri, Nass el Ghiwane, Abselam Cherkaoui, Lhaj Amar Ouahraouch, Lem Chaleb, Jil Jalala or Muluk el Hwa.

Berber Music

The music of the Berber people is of ancient origin and inextricably linked with movement and dance. It is an astonishing example of the tenacity of an oral heritage which preserves a combination of dance, poetry and drama that could almost come from pre-Homeric Greece. There are musical differences between the three main dialect regions of Berber speech: the Tariffit of northern Morocco, the Tamazight of the Middle Atlas and the Tashelhit, or Chleuh, of the south. There is also a division between the music of the villagers and that produced by travelling musicians.

In village music (variously known as *ahaidous*, *ahidus* or *ahouach*) flutes, drums, rhythmic hand-clapping and large choruses predominate. The choruses, composed of long lines or circles of men and women, dance around the musicians as they perform. Soloists, known as *inshaden*, sometimes supported by two accompanists or by the sound of their own violin, improvise lyrics within the basic framework of these distinctive choral chants. As well as there being a difference in dialect, the music of southern Morocco is quite distinct as it is based on the pentatonic scale (like that of West Africa), while the other two regions use seven notes. Until the 20th century, traditional village music remained largely unknown to a wider audience, as it was considered improper to perform outside the tribal region or to seek any financial gain. Fortunately, folk festivals and recordings have changed this.

Traditionally, travelling musicians, usually groups of four, were led by a singer-poet, supported by a violin, tambourine and flute. He sang of heroic qualities, such as martial bravery and impossible love, into which he skilfully wove gossip and topical references to local politics, as well as flattering or chiding his hosts for their hospitality. These troupes bore a striking resemblance to the bards of Celtic Europe and the medieval troubadours of France. At the start of the 20th century they began to add female vocalists to the line-up, whose job was to echo the poetic refrain and to dance. These groups were increasingly based in the new urban centres of the coast, and replaced the older tribal tradition. Today's professional performers (male *shioukh*, female *shikat*) form a near-hereditary guild, and enjoy the kind of celebrity and notoriety that touring actors in the West experienced a hundred years ago. The groups are known as *ameziaren*, though in southern Morocco they can be referred to as *rwais*.

Two groups of particular eminence are the Jajouka and Daqqa. The Jajouka are known for their 1969 recordings with the Rolling Stones. They are a unique caste of musicians from the Jebala foothills in the western Rif. They perform on *ghaita, lira, guenbri* and drums to create a pagan ritual music that invokes the gods of fecundity and energies in a way similar to the ancient rites of Pan. The Daqqa of Marrakesh perform a ritual dance for the religious festival of Achura, accompanied by percussionists playing the tar drums and *n'far* trumpeters.

Further listening: *Brian Jones Presents the Pan Pipers of Jajouka* (Rolling Stone, London); *Berberes du Maroc*—from the far south (Le Chant du Monde, Paris); *Anthologie des Rwâyes* (4 CD Sous Berber collection, La Maison des Cultures du Monde); *Najat Aatabou: Goul el Hak el Mout Kayna* (Blue Silver); *Najat Aatabou: The Voice of the Atlas* (GlobeStyle); *Master Musicians of Jajouka: Apocalypse Across the Sky* (Axiom); *Bachir Attar: The Next Dream* (CMP); *Medium Atlas Range: Sacred and Profane Music* (Ocora); *Marrakesh Festival* (Playasound); *Maroc: Chants et Danses* (Chants du Monde); *Mohamed Rouicha: Ellil Ellil* (Sonodisc); *Mohamed Rouicha: Ch'hal Bkit Ala Alli Habit* (Sonodisc); *Festival de Marrakesh, Folklore National du Maroc* in 2 vols; *Rais Lhaj Aomar Ouahrouch: Musique Tachelait* (Ocora). Lyrichord, 141 Perry Street, New York, NY 10014, publishes a good selection, including Rwais from the High Atlas and a collection of Sufi music.

Al-Ala: the Classical Music of Andalus

The classical music of all the Maghreb countries is firmly based on the heritage of Moorish Spain. It is a lyrical and instrumental repertoire that has been elaborated over the last 200 years from verses written during the 700-year Muslim occupation of Spain, but which in turn had their origins in ancient Baghdad. The original reconstruction of these venerable verses was made in Morocco towards the end of the 18th century by Al-Hayek, under the enthusiastic patronage of two sultans, Mohammed ben Abdellah and Moulay Sliman. He completed his work in 1799, and the resulting manuscript provided the basis for the three collections of the modern repertoire, each based on a particular oral history and dynastic memory.

Of the original repertoire of 24 symphonies, or *nuba*, only eleven have even partly survived, though even this fragment takes some 90 hours to be sung right through. Each *nuba* is based on a specific mode that reflected one of the hours of the day, and is divided into five main rhythmic phases: the prelude (*mizan*), broad (*muwassa*), increased (*mahzuz*), quick (*inshad*) and fast (*insiraf*). Each *nuba* simultaneously passes through five tempo changes: *al bacit, al qaim wa nsif, btayhi, darj* and *quddam*. The sung poetry in the *nuba* is based on a corpus of classical Andalucían verse and later additions in similar tone and style.

Al-Ala is associated with the urban middle class, particularly from those cities that benefited from Andalucían refugees. In Morocco it is performed by extensive orchestras that use the lute, two-string viol, tambourine, vertically played European violin, and clay and skin drums. As well as the three big orchestras in Casablanca, Rabat and Fez, there are others from Tetouan, Tangier and Oujda. The latter follows the traditions of Algeria and performs the *gharnati*, believed to be the specific heritage of Granada. Going even farther east, other variations include *malouf,* played in Constantine, Tunisia and Libya, while a distant cousin called *moshahat Andalucía* can be found in Egypt, Syria and the Lebanon. A further offshoot of Andalus is preserved by the Sephardic Jews of Morocco, who added liturgical singing to the common tradition in the form of psalmodies and responsorial anthems.

These days Al-Ala is in healthy condition. There are conservatories in all the major cities; the complete *nuba* are available on a number of recordings; academics are currently notating all the varieties; and the Moroccan Royal Academy has commissioned a definitive edition of Al-Hayek's original manuscript.

Further listening: The complete *nuba* repertoire has been recorded and is being issued in several CDs (over several years) by La Maison des Cultures du Monde, Paris. For other recordings of Andalucían music see also *Fez Orchestra: Classical Music of the Andalucían Magreb* (Ocora); *Ustad Massano Tazi: Classical Andalucían Music from Fez* (Ocora); *Orchestre de Meknès: Musique Andalouse Marocaine* (Sonodisc); *Orchestre de Fez: Irabbi Lward* (Sonodisc); and for a crossover between the music of Muslim Andalus and the flamenco of Spanish Andalucía, *El Lebrijano and Orquesta Andalusi de Tanger, Encuentros* (GlobeStyle).

Gnaoua

The word 'Gnaoua' refers to both a spiritual brotherhood (originally based around communities of black slaves), a musical troupe and a style of music closely related to that produced in West African countries such as Mali and Senegal. It is strikingly distinctive, whether you concentrate on the music (usually produced by drums, castanets and a distinctive long-necked flute), the characteristically African beat or the cowrie shell caps of the whirling Gnaoua dancers. It is a confirmed favourite with tourists, whether in their hotels or the Jemaa el Fna square in Marrakesh. It has always had a public aspect, for the Gnaoua were employed to exorcize evil spirits and built up a variety of acts that include *l'fraja*, the show, designed to entertain crowds.

Gnaoua is at its most impressive at a *lila*, an all-night ritual held on religious feast days where the great Islamic saints and prophets as well as the spirit world are invoked, while dancers take turns to swirl to the point of exhaustion and possession. In such trances they will bang their heads on the stone flagging, eat glass and cut themselves with knives, all without apparently inflicting damage. The instruments used are iron castanets, a big t'bal drum and a large bass-gimbri lute with a camel-neck skin stretched over a walnut body.

Further listening (Gnaoua and Sufi): *Mustafa Baqbou* (World Circuit); *Hadra of the Gnawa of Essaouira* (Ocora); *Gnawa Music of Marrakesh: Night Spirit Masters* (Axiom).

Arabic Song: Guedra, B'Sat and Melhun

In the Saharan provinces south of the Anti-Atlas Mountains, the Hassani Arabic dialect became dominant in the 13th century. The most famous musical song-dance of this region is *guedra*, the erotic, swaying dance of the Saharan women, performed on their knees. It shares many of the West African influences of Gnaoua spirit music. There is also the more light-hearted tradition of *b'sat*. This developed as an annual festival of popular theatre, one in which music and lyrics were inextricably mixed into the farcical shows of the actor-storytellers. These shows are very popular in festivals such as Aid el Kebir, and can often be seen at the Jemaa el Fna in Marrakesh. As well as for their musical background, they are being examined with renewed interest as a source of indigenous drama for local television and theatre.

Melhun represents a much more polished and literate tradition, as indicated by alternative names for the style which translate as 'the gift' or 'the inspiration'. It is believed to have derived from the pure Arabic poetry of Andalucía, which was first converted into a popular strophic verse some time in the 12th century, before being transformed into a rhythmic formula at the time of Merenid rule. Each song would begin with an instrumental prelude that was then followed by short, sung verses marked by choral and instrumental refrains; a gradual, accelerated rhythm marked the end. The songs' subject matter was the many themes made familiar in the Sufi-inspired medieval poetry of Andalucía—images and ideas such as the beloved, wine, gardens, sunset and night—and could be taken at a popular level or understood as metaphors for a spiritual quest. There was also a tradition of satire (known as *lahjou, ashaht* or *addaq*) which could be combined with prophecy (*jofriat*) to bring a strong political content to the songs.

Sufi Music

All Morocco's rich musical heritage was used by the Sufi brotherhoods in the composition of ritual chants and dances. These have a spiritual goal which is directed at the performers, not the audience, and may extend over many hours before reaching their sudden conclusion. It is a form of music that is inaccessible to the non-initiate, let alone a non-Muslim, but remains a vital force and influence in the lives of many of Morocco's leading musicians. The Derkaoua, Hamadasha and Aïssoua are three of the most influential brotherhoods, though their influence has necessarily taken a second place to that of the Gnaoua. Instruments generally used are a simple oboe and cymbals as well as a variety of clay and skin drums.

Musical Instruments

Percussion instruments: *bendir*—round wooden frame drum sometimes with snare; *deff*—square wooden frame drum; *t'bal*—large wooden round drum played with sticks and hung round the neck; *daadouh, guedra, harazi, darbouka, goual, taarija, tbila*—clay and skin drums in descending order of size; *karkabus/qarqaba*—iron castanets; *naqus, nuiqsat and handqa*—all two-inch iron castanets; *tar*—tambourine.

Stringed instruments: *ud*—lute, usually the six-course Egyptian-style, round-backed version; *kamanja*—the Western violin, but played vertically on the knee; *rbab*—the two-string viol, with a bow that is a short iron arc holding strands of horsehair; *guenbri/gimbri*—the most popular lute, a sound box made of the shell of a turtle, covered with goat skin with one or three strings along its neck (the body of a treble *guenbri* is customarily pear-shaped, the bass rectangular, and that with a round-backed body with six or three strings is known as a *lotar* or a *soussi guenbri* and used to be limited to southern Morocco); *hajouj* or *sentir*—large bass *guenbri* with a rectangular walnut body covered with camel-neck skin and goat-gut strings; *swisdi*—small two-string lute; *kanum*—Arabic zither or psaltery with 26 triple courses.

Wind instruments: *awwadat*—metal pipe, played like a straight flute; *lira/gasba*—flutes; *nai/nira*—Arab bamboo flute; *rita/ghaita*—super oboe-like flute with double-reeded mouthpiece, used by snake charmers; *n'far*—one-note processional trumpet, of copper.

Sufi Brotherhoods

Alongside the formal practice of Islam there has always been a parallel tradition of Sufi mysticism. A Sufi attempts to go beyond mere obedience to Islamic law and reach for experience of God in this life. Ali, cousin and son-in-law of the Prophet and the militant hero of early Islam, is considered to be the originator of this mystical approach to Islam and the first Sufi. Traditions record that Ali received the secrets of the mystical life, which were considered too dangerous to be written down and revealed to the unprepared mass of mankind. The secrets are reserved for initiates who must first make themselves capable and prove themselves worthy of receiving this body of inherited oral instruction.

The mystical discipline has been passed down through the generations in a human chain of masters, each of whom trained his disciples to succeed him. Sufi brotherhoods arose as aspirants gathered around a celebrated mystic who evolved into the master, or sheikh, of the community. Branches obedient to the teaching of a popular master might be formed throughout the Muslim world; as new brotherhoods formed they were all proud to be links in this one chain of spiritual succession.

The first Moroccan Sufi master was Sidi Harazem of Fez, whose name now features on a popular brand of mineral water. He was succeeded in the tradition by two great scholars of the 12th century. Abu Medyan of Tlemcen, who died in 1198, and Abdessalam ben Mchich, who died in 1228, are central to the brotherhoods of northwest Africa (the latter is also known as the master of Jbel Alam, and is the patron saint of the Jebala region of Morocco). These influential masters combined the teaching of Sidi Harazem with that of the great Eastern masters, Al Jilani of Baghdad and Al Ghazzali. The life of a Sufi was not always easy or safe: the 12th-century Almoravid Sultan Ali ben Youssef burnt all Al Ghazzali's books and sentenced to death any Muslim found reading them.

Despite the fervent opposition of the 'fundamentalist' Almoravid and Almohad dynasties, the brotherhoods survived underground. Their spiritual heir was Abou el Hassan Ali ech Chadhili, who died in 1258 and from whose teachings arose 15 separate Sufi brotherhoods, many of which survive today. Al Jazuli in Fez, who taught and wrote *The Manifest Proofs of Piety*, was a continuation of this tradition. After his death in 1465 there was another explosion of brotherhoods, who all considered themselves his heirs.

The Sufi brotherhoods, whatever the exact pattern of their spiritual regime, all owe total obedience to a sheikh, their master. Most brotherhoods practise asceticism, and include charitable works and teaching among their activities. Initiates use spiritual tools in their search for *wajd*, ecstatic experience of the divine, including *hizb*—recitation, *dikr*—prolonged recitation, *sama*—music, *raqs* and *hadra*—dancing, and *tamzig*—the tearing of clothes. For an outsider the most common Sufi trait is indifference to the concerns of the world. This trend was developed by the Aïssoua and Hamadasha brotherhoods into self-mutilation to show indifference to pain, while the more off-beat practised the prolonged contemplation of a beautiful young man, an ephebe, who was believed to embody the divine.

Wildlife

Even the most distant and desolate wilderness landscape is likely to be a seasonal grazing ground for a village or nomadic herd. By day you are more likely to find herds of goat, sheep and camel than wild beasts, but it is possible, even without entering the guarded sporting and forestry reserves of the Administration des Eaux et Forêts, to spot wild boar, Barbary apes, a range of mountain cats, the ubiquitous red fox and the smaller desert fox with its bat-like ears. Most of these can be seen only at dawn, dusk or briefly caught in a car's headlights by night.

If you sleep anywhere near water you will be serenaded by a chorus of frogs and toads. In the daytime their identity can usually be patched together from squashed bodies on the roadside. They may include the Berber toad, green toad, green frog, western marsh frog and Mauritanian toad. Without even moving from a café chair it is possible to spot and photograph a variety of insect-hunting lizards. The Moorish gecko, Spanish wall lizard and chameleon all seem particularly tolerant of the presence of humans. The species of the mountains and deserts are harder to spot, although patches of sand will often be dotted with the winding tracks of the spiny-tailed sand lizard, the Algerian sand lizard and the Berber skink, or 'sandfish'.

The mouflon or wild mountain sheep, from which all the world's varieties of sheep derive, is indigenous to North Africa. Early Moroccan rock carvings of a sun set between the twin horns of a sheep, and Egyptian records, hint that the cult of Amon, the horned-god of the sun and the herds, originated in the Maghreb. The people of this area may also have first perfected the practice of nomadic herding. Dominant tribes sometimes maintained sacred herds that acted as their standard or totem. The horse was a late arrival to Morocco (from *c.*1600 BC), while the Arabian camel was not successfully bred in the Moroccan Sahara until about AD 600. Nomads and herdsmen still recognize the sacred animals of a herd, such as the *Saiba*—the chief mother, the *Bahira*—the eleventh calf, and the *Hami*—the senior stallion. In a widespread custom that extends throughout Africa and Arabia, a sacrificial calf is designated from birth and left free to graze over any field or boundary. Dedicated to a saint or spirit, it is sacrificed at their shrine and then consumed at the communal feast.

Birdlife

Birds are easily the most impressive of Morocco's wildlife. There is a large number of resident species, as well as dazzling and vastly varied concentrations of migrant flocks, which generally come to Africa for the mild winter from October to March and fly across the Mediterranean for the European summer.

The swift, swallow and crag martin are respected as birds inspired by Allah to protect the harvest and remove noxious insects and reptiles. They can be seen in showy evening flights above the rooftops of cities such as Fez and Marrakesh. The stork is Morocco's other great holy bird, and there are numerous legends to explain their constant attitude of prayer and symbolic prostration whenever they rest. Hospitals were established in Fez and Marrakesh to care for injured birds, where they could recover or die peacefully in protected enclosures.

The striped hoopoe is conspicuous during its migration, but is trapped by Moroccans, for its heart and feathers are powerful charms against evil spirits. The barn owl, a permanent resident, is recognized to be the clairvoyant ally of the Devil. The owl cries out the name of a fore-doomed individual who can only escape by cursing the owl with its own hidden name. Even a normal owl cry has the power to kill a child unless there is someone to spit and curse as they fly overhead. The Tangier raven is also viewed with suspicion, and always lays its eggs on 21 April. Killing a raven soothes the evil eye, whilst a raven's liver, tongue, brain and heart are made into useful antidotes.

Take a moment to look more closely at the Moroccan versions of familiar birds. Sparrows turn out to be mainly of the Spanish race (with rich chestnut heads and a pronounced black bib) and occasionally rock sparrows (with smartly striped heads). Chaffinches are most exotic with slate-blue heads, olive-green backs and salmon-pink underparts. The starling is not *vulgaris* but *unicolor*, which is to say spotless. Magpies sport a neat tear-shaped mark behind the eye in brilliant turquoise blue.

Crested larks are common along roadsides; buntings (corn, cirl, rock and house) are easily seen on top of walls and telephone wires; pigeons turn out to be turtle doves or rock doves with bright white rumps; glorious blue rollers and smart ginger, black and white hoopoes are widespread summer visitors; summer evenings are filled with the screeching and aerial displays of swifts and pallid swifts; herds of cattle are invariably accompanied by a few white cattle egrets; and common bulbuls sing delightfully from every bush in gardens and parks.

Certain bird species now so rare as to be threatened with extinction, but still appearing in Morocco are the bald ibis, the slender-billed curlew, and bustards (Houbara, Arabian and great).

Marrakesh

Marrakesh the Red is the heart that beats an African identity into the complex soul of Morocco. The city walls, overlooked by the Koutoubia minaret, are framed by the towering blue wall of the High Atlas mountains. From outside, the city promises much, but at first it may seem to contain nothing more than a vast transitory souk. The Jemaa el Fna, the celebrated square at the centre of the medina, is full of visiting farmers, as well as snake-charmers, story-tellers and fortune-readers. Marrakesh is strikingly African compared with the Atlantic character of Casablanca, and the intensely Arab attitude of Fez; yet it is not some desert border town but a city with a long and proud record as an imperial capital. The name Marrakesh, corrupted by European travellers, has provided us with the word Morocco. The derivation of the word Marrakesh is more problematical. It means to 'cross and hide', a reference to its first role as a fortress beyond the mountains.

The Phoenicians, Romans, Arabs and Idrissids ruled over a mere portion of Morocco, a patchwork of hills and the northern Atlantic coast. The Empire of Morocco was first created not by any of these distinguished, alien powers, but by a Berber tribe from the depths of the western Sahara. They were the first to forge a Moroccan identity by linking a vast continental hinterland to the civilized lands of the northwest. Marrakesh was the Berber capital, a city where they embraced Islam and an urban culture on their own terms. Here they brought together, like heraldic symbols of the future state, palm trees from the desert and craftsmen from Andalucía.

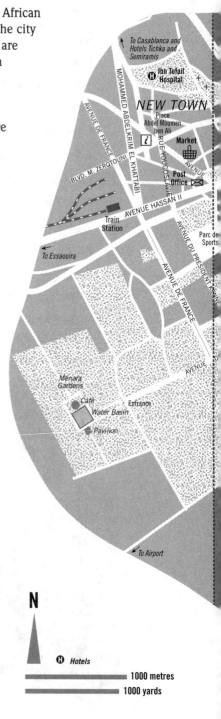

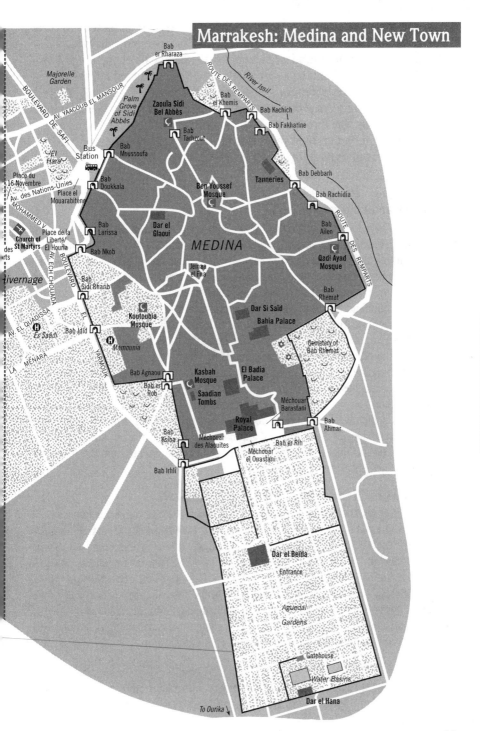

Majorelle Garden

BOULEVARD DE SAFI

AV. YAACOUB EL MANSOUR

Bab er Rharaza

ROUTE DES REMPARTS

River Issil

Palm Grove of Sidi Abbès

Zaouïa Sidi Bel Abbès

Bab el Khemis

Bab Kechich

Bab Fakharine

Bab Tarhzout

Bus Station

El Hara

Bab Moussoufa

Bab Doukkala

Ben Youssef Mosque

Tanneries

Bab Debbarh

Bab Rachidia

Place du 16 Novembre

Av. des Nations-Unies

Place el Mouarabitene

MOHAMMED V

Church of St Martyrs

des rts

Place de la Liberté/ El Houria

Bab Larissa

Dar el Glaoui

MEDINA

Bab Ailen

Qadi Ayad Mosque

Bab Nkob

hivernage

AV. ECH CHOUADA

BOULEVARD

EL

AV. EL QUADISSA

Bab Sidi Rharib

Jemaa el Fna

Bab Rhemat

Es Saâdi

Koutoubia Mosque

Dar Si Saïd

Bahia Palace

ROUTE DES REMPARTS

LA MÉNARA

YARMOUK

Bab Jdid

Mamounia

Cemetery of Bab Rhemat

Bab Agnaou

El Badia Palace

Bab er Rob

Kasbah Mosque

Saadian Tombs

Méchouar Barastani

Bab Ahmar

Bab Ksiba

Royal Palace

Méchouar des Alaouites

Bab er Rih

Bab Irhli

Méchouar el Ouastani

Dar el Beïda

Entrance

Aguedal Gardens

Gatehouse

Water Basins

To Ourika

Dar el Hana

The city's guaranteed dry heat, the heady atmosphere of its souk, its celebrated monuments and the nearby High Atlas mountain valleys have a universal appeal. It is a fascinating city, the central objective of most visitors to Morocco, but be aware that you will not be alone: Marrakesh is, alongside Agadir, Morocco's chief tourist destination. It is also undeniably demanding. As always in Morocco, take things slowly and do not try to rush your way through its precious store of monuments. Marrakesh has stood for a thousand years, has now endured generations of starstruck travellers, and its thick-lidded eyes will not be stirred by much.

History
Foundation and Empire (1062–1147)

Archaeologists have found that the site of Marrakesh has been almost continually occupied since Neolithic times, but the modern city has its origins in an Almoravid garrison town of the 11th century. In 1062, Abu Bekr, an early commander of the Almoravids, threw up a wall of thorn bushes to protect his camp and built a fortress amid his tented army, the Ksar el Hajar, 'the tower of stone'. Nine years later he appointed his young cousin, Youssef ben Tachfine, to command this new post. The meteoric conquest of Morocco and Spain by Youssef ben Tachfine from this base marks the true foundation of both the city and the Almoravid Empire. Marrakesh's position on the border of three agricultural regions meant that it soon eclipsed the older towns of Aghmat and Nfis to become the main market for the farmers of the Tensift valley, the nomadic pastoralists of the plains and the Masmuda Atlas tribes. It still has that feel to this day. It was Youssef ben Tachfine's son and successor, Ali ben Youssef, who built the great circuit of walls, two large mosques, palaces and fountains, which were all superbly decorated by Andalucían carvers. The Almoravids brought the technology of desert survival and used it to improve the city's seasonal water supply. Long *khettera* (pipes) were built to carry water underground from the High Atlas mountains to the houses and gardens of Marrakesh.

The Capital City of the Almohad Empire (1147–1269)

After decades of warfare between the Almoravid Sultans and the Almohads, whose headquarters were tucked up in the High Atlas mountains, the walled city of Marrakesh finally fell in 1147. The Almohads deliberately demolished any evidence of the previous dynasty and remade the city in their own image. It did, however, remain the capital city of a great empire, and the monumental buildings of this period—the Koutoubia Mosque, the El Mansour Mosque, the Bab Agnaou—still dominate the city. Almohad princes ruled on in Marrakesh decades after the rest of their empire had fallen into the hands of rival dynasties. Like the Almoravids before them, they were fated to die defending the walls of the city, which were finally breached by the Merenids in 1269.

A Decaying City (1269–1524)

Under the Merenid sultans (1248–1465) Morocco was ruled from Fez, and Marrakesh stagnated into a provincial town. By the early years of the 16th century even this comparative prosperity had ended. Portuguese cavalry raided up to the walls of the city, Ottoman Turks were poised to advance from the east, and the authority of the central government, threatened by dozens of rival dynasties, had shrunk to the area around Fez. In 1524 the dilapidated city welcomed the rule of Mohammed ech Cheikh, forceful founder of the Saadian dynasty, whose power was based on the tribes of the south. Using Marrakesh as his base, Mohammed ech Cheikh succeeded in subduing the rest of the country. He was murdered in a High Atlas valley by an Ottoman assassination squad. The governor of Marrakesh promptly ordered the murder of six of his sons, to clear the succession for Abdullah el Ghalib.

The Golden Capital of the Saadians (1524–1668)

The reigns of Abdullah el Ghalib and his half-brother Ahmed el Mansour, 'the victorious' (also known as *El Dehbi*, 'the golden'), witnessed a magnificent revival in the prosperity of Marrakesh. Abdullah founded the *mellah,* rebuilt the kasbah and the Ben Youssef Mosque and Medersa, and built a hospital and the new Mouassine Mosque. Ahmed built the incomparable El Badia Palace and the Saadian Tombs, and sprinkled the city with fountains, *fondouqs*, libraries and *hammams.* The prosperity of Marrakesh in these centuries was partly based on a thriving trade in sugar, saltpetre, cotton and silk. The city became the collection and transit point for the produce of the Sahara and sub-Sahara—slaves, gold, ivory, gum arabic and ostrich feathers—which was then exported through the Atlantic ports.

Alaouite Marrakesh, the Twin Capital (1668–1912)

The vicious civil wars of the late 17th and early 18th centuries, in which Marrakesh was repeatedly besieged and plundered, were a disaster from which it never entirely recovered. Sultan Moulay Ismaïl (1672–1727) restored the religious shrines of the city but decided to rule from a new capital in Meknès. Later Alaouite sultans attempted to check the city's continued decline by alternating government between Fez and Marrakesh, and many of the city's finest buildings date from the 18th and 19th centuries. The comparative order and prosperity of Moulay Hassan's reign (1873–94) is revealed in the large number of opulent merchants' houses and the palaces of the Bahia and Dar Si Saïd, built by viziers during the minority of his son, Abdul Aziz.

But the city remained pitifully backward. At the turn of the 20th century there were no wind or steam mills in the city, and trade depended on pack animals being safely escorted past the Rehamna tribe to Essaouira.

The 20th Century and Beyond

Growing European influence was bitterly resented, culminating in the lynching of a French resident, a Dr Mauchamp, after he attached an aerial to his roof in 1907. Personal resentment against Dr Mauchamp was intense, from both native healers and city traders who were infuriated that with his aerial the doctor could discover prices in Essaouira days before they could. The city mob for their part were convinced the aerial was a sorcerer's device, for it was well known on the streets, and with some truth, that Mauchamp had great knowledge of the occult. This lynching proved to be one of several incidents that provided the excuse for the French landings in Casablanca in the same year. Five years later the French army occupied the city, having destroyed the tribal army of El Hiba, the Blue Sultan, at Sidi-Bou-Othmane.

Marrakesh became an important centre of French influence in the south, though the city's old predominance was deliberately shattered with the location of the new commercial centre at Casablanca. In Marrakesh the French built a new town, 'Guéliz', to the west of the old city, its ordered avenues and quiet leafy suburbs overlooked by their enormous army barracks. Within a generation they had adorned the region with roads, hotels, pylons, railways, schools, irrigation works and hospitals. Apart from the roads, these technical advances were for the benefit of colonial farmers and the caidal allies of the French. Their chief ally was Si Thami el Glaoui, the fabulously wealthy Pasha of Marrakesh, who ruled a medina in which an estimated 20,000 registered prostitutes lived.

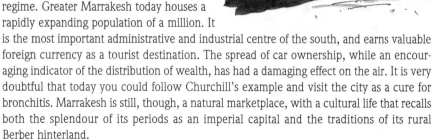

Independence in 1956 brought a swift and bloody end to the pasha's corrupt regime. Greater Marrakesh today houses a rapidly expanding population of a million. It is the most important administrative and industrial centre of the south, and earns valuable foreign currency as a tourist destination. The spread of car ownership, while an encouraging indicator of the distribution of wealth, has had a damaging effect on the air. It is very doubtful that today you could follow Churchill's example and visit the city as a cure for bronchitis. Marrakesh is still, though, a natural marketplace, with a cultural life that recalls both the splendour of its periods as an imperial capital and the traditions of its rural Berber hinterland.

Orientation

Marrakesh is an easy city in which to orientate yourself. The straight central street of the New Town, Av Mohammed V, runs with the Koutoubia minaret, which is just west of the Jemaa el Fna, as its focus. The areas around Av Mohammed V and the Jemaa el Fna support most of the offices, hotels, cafés and banks.

The minaret of the Koutoubia Mosque and the Jemaa el Fna are the dominant images in the medina of Marrakesh. Even if you avoid all other conventional tourist sites, and explore only the most reclusive quarters of the medina, these two will remain at the centre of your experience of Marrakesh.

by air

The Marrakesh–Ménara international airport, ✆ 44 78 62, is 5km southwest of town. There is, theoretically, a **bus** to the city every half-hour, no.11, but it is not always in evidence. There are *grand* and *petit **taxi*** ranks at the airport—drivers can be quite extravagant in their demands, though 50dh is usually considered an acceptable tourist rate (*see below* 'by taxi'). As well as international flights there is a regular schedule of internal RAM services to Casablanca (for Rabat) and two a week to Fez. Further information and prices are available from the RAM office, 197 Av Mohammed V, ✆ 43 62 05. Return tickets should be reconfirmed here a day or two before departure.

by rail

The station, off Av Hassan II, ✆ 44 79 47, is a five-minute walk west from Place du 16 Novembre. Four trains a day travel north to Casablanca (4hrs), where you can connect with trains to Rabat and Fez (via Meknès), and there is a new direct service to Fez at 9am.

Arriving in Marrakesh, you are likely to be met by touts as you leave the station. Take a *petit taxi* (licensed for up to three people) and get rid of your luggage at a hotel. Thankfully, a sea change in manners has occurred since the taxis have started using their meters. If the meter is not working, allow 10–15dh for the drive to your hotel. Alternatively, catch a no.3 or a no.8 local bus from the station to the Jemaa el Fna.

by bus

CTM and other bus companies all depart from the modern depot just outside the Bab Doukkala on Place el Mouarabitène. It is usually worth buying tickets a day in advance. Take your time to sort out the various alternatives on sale from the kiosk windows, and you can mull over the final details of your travel plans in the station's garden-café. As ever, travel by CTM whenever possible.

There are currently around eight buses a day to Rabat (5–6hrs), almost hourly departures for Casablanca (4hrs) and three a day to Fez (11hrs).

Local buses depart from Rue Moulay Ismaïl, beside the triangular garden at the southern end of the Jemaa el Fna. **No.1** goes right along Av Mohammed V to below the Guéliz hill; **no.2** passes the Bab Doukkala bus station; **nos.3 and 14** head along Av Mohammed V and Av Hassan II to the train station; **no.4** goes along Av Mohammed V and then on to the El-Jadida road; **no.5** goes on to the Béni-Mellal road (useful for Souk el Khemis); **no.6** passes the Quartier Industriel (and the youth hostel); **no.7** goes to Av Hassan II and farther northwest; **no.8** runs along Av Mohammed V and Av Hassan II; **no.10** goes to Bab Doukkala and the Safi road; and the elusive **no.11** runs to the airport via the Ménara Gardens.

by taxi

Petits taxis are found along the length of Av Mohammed V, by the covered market in the New Town, by the bus station, train station and by the Jemaa el Fna. Bargaining a decent price used to be an exhausting part of Marrakesh life, but the use of meters is now widespread. Take advantage of these little cabs whenever possible. Find **grands taxis** in the Jemaa el Fna, outside the post office in the New Town, by the bus station and by the Bab er Rob; a place to the Ourika Valley should cost 20dh. As a group you might want to hire a taxi for a day to Ourika or up the Tizi-n-Test, for which you will have to pay around 300dh.

by car

You will not need a car in the city until it is time to leave. The smaller **car hire** companies offer cheaper deals, but this is often reflected in the condition of their cars and their legal contracts. One misadventure that ended up with a protracted two-day negotiation at a police station has given me a bias towards the more reputable mainstream operators: Avis, 137 Av Mohammed V, ✆ 43 37 27; Europcar-InterRent, 63 Blvd Zerqtouni, ✆ 43 12 28; Hertz, at the airport, ✆ 43 16 35, or 154 Av Mohammed V, ✆ 43 46 80; and especially the English-speaking team at Always, Complex Kawkab, Centre Guéliz, ✆ 44 67 97, 🖂 43 09 38, who will deliver the car to your hotel.

You can **park** anywhere off the Av Mohammed V in the New Town—providing the pavement is not decorated with a red-and-white no-parking stripe—in any big hotel, or at the Jemaa el Fna in front of the Hôtel de Foucauld. There is also a car park in an old covered bus depot immediately beside the CTM Hotel. Another useful place is the car park behind the Koutoubia Mosque, approached off Av Mohammed V.

Bicycles can be rented from the Hôtel de Foucauld, on Av El Mouahidine in the southern corner of the Jemaa el Fna, ✆ 44 54 99; and **mopeds** from the Peugeot garage, 225 Av Mohammed V, as well as from two places out on the Casablanca road: Marrakesh Motos, 31 Blvd El-Khattabi, ✆ 44 83 59, and Adoul Abdallah, 14 Blvd El-Khattabi, ✆ 43 22 38.

by carriage

For a horse-drawn carriage that seats five, 60dh an hour is a price to aspire to, but it may be easier to settle one overall price for a tour of the ramparts and gardens. In the last few years the carriages have been equipped with a municipally approved list of maximum prices, which is an aid but not a conclusive element in the bargaining process. I usually end up paying 120dh for a rampart tour and, with just one or two suggestions, leave the route up to the driver.

On one trip, when my birthday coincided with the feast of Achoura, this rather hackneyed tourist excursion proved to be one of the most enchanting journeys of my life. We set off before dusk with both of the kerosene side lamps lit, and drove for hours, passing mosques with their silent queues of seated paupers waiting for the traditional festival charity, and through unknown back streets thronged with young children beating their festival drums, demanding presents and dancing around bonfires that scattered wild shadows on the glowing red walls. When it came to paying, the driver had lowered his price (perhaps because the back wheel came off twice), but we then doubled it as our two-year-old daughter, who had sat mesmerized with delight on the driving bench, had clearly fallen in love with both the ancient driver and his horse.

Marrakesh ☎ (04–)   *Tourist Information*

The **tourist office**, Place Abdel Moumen ben Ali on Av Mohammed V, ☎ 44 88 89, and the *syndicat d'initiative*, 176 Av Mohammed V, ☎ 43 47 97 (*both open Mon–Fri 8.30–12 and 3–6*), give away familiar free leaflets with maps and lists of hotels, and arrange the hire of guides, but do not provide much else.

The main **post office** is halfway along Av Mohammed V at the major junction of Place du 16 Novembre (*open Mon–Sat 8–2*). There is a **telephone** section tucked into the right-hand side of the building, with a separate entrance for the after-hours service that continues until 9pm. There is a good sub-post office housed in the prominent neo-Moorish public building on the southern side of the Jemaa el Fna (*open Mon–Fri 8–2*), which also has a telephone section as well as a line of card-operated booths on its western wall. In addition there has been a recent explosion in private telephone kiosks linked up to satellite systems.

Banks: The BMCE, as ever, is first choice for banking services. Their main branch is in the New Town at 144 Av Mohammed V, ☎ 43 19 48 (*open for currency exchange Mon–Fri 8am–8pm*). In the old town there is a selection of banks, just south of the Jemaa el Fna on Rue de Bab Agnaou, which include a *bureau de change* booth run by Banque Populaire, and branches of Crédit du Maroc and SGMB, while there is a BMCI branch on nearby Rue Moulay Ismaïl.

Eglise des Sts Martyrs, Rue Imam Ali, ☎ 43 05 85, offers Mass on Sundays at 10.30am and 7pm (July/August 9.30am and 7.30pm) and on weekdays at 6.30pm.

emergencies

For the **police**, at the Rue Ibn Hanbal station, dial ☎ 19; for the **fire brigade**, dial ☎ 16. Dial ☎ 15 for an **ambulance**, or use the private ambulance service that operates from 10 Rue Fatima Zohra, ☎ 44 37 24. There are two large **hospitals**; Hôpital Ibn Tofail, on Rue Abdel Ouahab Derraq, ☎ 44 80 11, and Hôpital Avenzoar, on Rue Sidi Mimoun, ☎ 42 27 93.

There is an **all-night pharmacy**, the Pharmacie de Nuit, on Rue Khalid Ben Oualid, ☎ 43 04 15, and an enormous selection open during normal shopping hours. The Bab Ftouh Pharmacie on Jemaa el Fna, ☎ 42 26 78, or the Pharmacie Centrale, 166 Av Mohammed V, ☎ 43 01 51, are among the most usefully placed.

Among the English-speaking **physicians** in the city there is the well-established Dr Perez, 169 Av Mohammed V, ☎ 43 10 30, and Dr Hamid Mansouri, on Rue Sebou, ☎ 43 07 54. English-speaking **dentists** include Dr Gaillères, 112 Av Mohammed V, and Dr Hamid Laraqui, 203 Av Mohammed V, ☎ 43 32 16.

The Koutoubia Mosque

The minaret of the Koutoubia Mosque appears at its most elegant from a great distance. Approaching Marrakesh from the High Atlas, the tower rises magnificently above the barely perceptible city, and you can begin to understand the veneration in which it is held locally. The interior of the mosque (and minaret) are, of course, closed to non-Muslims. The dusty wasteland that once surrounded it has been converted into a tidy garden, while the surrounding ruins—of the earlier mosque and elements from the Almoravid palace—have been exposed, stabilized and enclosed within a piazza. An elegant new paved street now allows the visitor to walk right up to the mosque and pass below the towering minaret.

This wasteland was once the centre of the city. The Almoravid Sultan Ali ben Youssef rebuilt his father's mosque and added a new palace to the south, on the site of the present Koutoubia, but both buildings were razed to the ground when the Almohads captured Marrakesh in 1147. Abdel Moumen, the Almohad sultan, immediately started on the construction of a new mosque, but the work was pushed forward too quickly. It was found wanting (among other faults it was incorrectly aligned to Mecca) and was dismantled soon after its completion. The excavations have clearly revealed this first mosque immediately to the north of the present one. Undeterred by this failure, Abdel Moumen ordered a fresh start. This, the Koutoubia, followed the same plan, though it was slightly wider and with an interior dominated by a forest of horseshoe arches resting on solid square pillars decorated by pairs of pilasters. Five domes rise along the high, wide central aisle to focus attention on the mihrab prayer niche. At the opposite end, the open-air *sahn* courtyard, the place for ritual ablutions, also served as the customary place for lectures on the Koran and Islamic law before the construction of medersas in the 13th century.

Owing to the vagaries of the site, the minaret was positioned in the northeastern corner of the mosque. It was only completed in the reign of Abdel Moumen's grandson Sultan Yaacoub el Mansour, one of the world's greatest architectural patrons, who was also responsible for the Giralda Tower in Seville and the Hassan Tower in Rabat. From its 12m by 12m base the minaret rises to almost 70m. It was built from an internal ramp that climbs between its double walls. This connects six rooms that increase in delicate ornamentation as they ascend. Each side of the minaret has a different decorative scheme, and the boldly carved lancet windows are a study in Almohad design. The decoration culminates in the rich interlinked arches of the top storey, above which is a last surviving band of faïence decoration. The rough stonework of the tower decreases in size as it rises. This work would originally have been obscured by plaster and decoration, as the restored minaret of the Almohad Kasbah Mosque shows. Fortunately no similar restoration work is planned on the Koutoubia.

Above the faïence band a decorative battlement frames the domed minaret, which was built in a strict one-to-five proportion to the tower, the golden rule for all Maghrebi minarets. On the summit a wooden gallows flies a blue or green prayer flag on Friday, beside three golden balls surmounted by a tear. These are thought to be the gift of Yaacoub

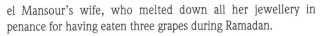

el Mansour's wife, who melted down all her jewellery in penance for having eaten three grapes during Ramadan.

The new mosque was once enclosed by streets where hundreds of copyists, scribes, binders and booksellers kept stalls. It is from this surrounding souk of books, the *kutubiyyin*, that it takes its name. For its inauguration in 1158 Abdel Moumen had a spectacular trophy to display, for he had just acquired from conquered Córdoba one of the four original copies of the third Caliph Othman's official compilation of the Koran. From these all later texts descend.

The imposing walled building just to the southeast of the Koutoubia is the French consulate. South of this stands the **Place Youssef ben Tachfin**, overlooked by a modest tomb. This is the traditional tomb of the great warrior and founder of Marrakesh. His grave was despoiled by the Almohads but reconsecrated by the Merenids in the 14th century. The tomb is left open to the sky, the only dome that the spirit of this desert warrior will accept.

The Jemaa el Fna

Three hundred metres east of the Koutoubia Mosque lies the great central square of the medina, the Jemaa el Fna, popularly translated as 'the place of the dead', a suitably chilling phrase which adds a whiff of exoticism and savage justice to an otherwise undeniably lively place. A less entertaining but probably correct translation is 'the mosque that came to nothing'—a sly reference to the Saadian Sultan Ahmed el Mansour's abortive attempt to build a mosque here.

The square has always been at the centre of medina life, and started as the formal *méchouar* in front of the Almoravid kasbah. When the Almohads moved the kasbah to the south of the city, official processions were increasingly staged there, but in essence the Jemaa el Fna has always been as it is now, a popular forum for entertainment, celebration, riots, gossip and business.

At dawn it is an empty wedge of tarmac, surrounded by parked cars, shuttered cafés and bazaars, an area of no architectural interest. As the morning progresses a perimeter is formed by lines of barrows selling nuts and freshly squeezed orange juice, and the edges of the square erupt in a sea of shops. The centre is filled by a random and changing assortment of snake-charmers, storytellers, acrobats, dentists, water-sellers, scribes, monkeys, clowns and dancing boys, who during the day direct most of their skills to camera-carrying tourists.

But at dusk the Jemaa el Fna comes into its own, and returns to its true audience of visiting Berber farmers from the plains, desert and mountains. Lines of kitchens set up their groaning tables, braziers and benches beneath hissing gas lamps. Here you can dine on an assortment of salads, vats of brewing goat's-head soup, fresh grilled or fried vegetables, chicken, fish and mutton. You can move from table to table trying different platefuls and

break off to wander among the musicians and the story-
tellers. Sharp young street kids hiss 'Hashish!', veiled
women offer trinkets, or sit beckoning by their stock
of woven baskets and woolly hats. Blind beggars
cry 'Allah!' as they extend a bowl or fix you
with one accusing, rheumy eye. Innocent-
looking children with beguiling almond
eyes solicit, or try rather clumsily to
pick your pockets. From worn tarot
cards, the waddle of sacred doves,
ink dots, cast bones or your palm,
incidents from a possible future
will be divined by hunched
figures perched on low stools,
surrounded by the instru-
ments of their trade. As
the evening progresses
the crowds thin, the
kitchens close, and small
knots of musicians are
left, surrounded by a
crouching audience furtively
smoking pipes.

This is the right time to seek
out powerful music influenced
by the many spiritual brotherhoods—the Aïssoua, Derkaoua,
Hamadasha and Gnaoua—freed
from the irrelevancies of a purely
tourist audience. The repetitive
and rhythmical music produced
on their drums, flutes, crude
violins and *guenbris* (long, few-
stringed guitars) is far
removed from light entertainment. Shuffling dancers are
animated by a spirit that plays
upon piety and continence at
one moment and then sends
lewd, erotic displays in the
next breath.

The Jemaa el Fna is a rich but undeniably exhausting carnival. It seems

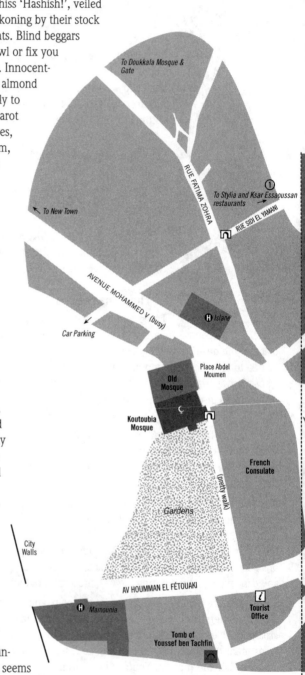

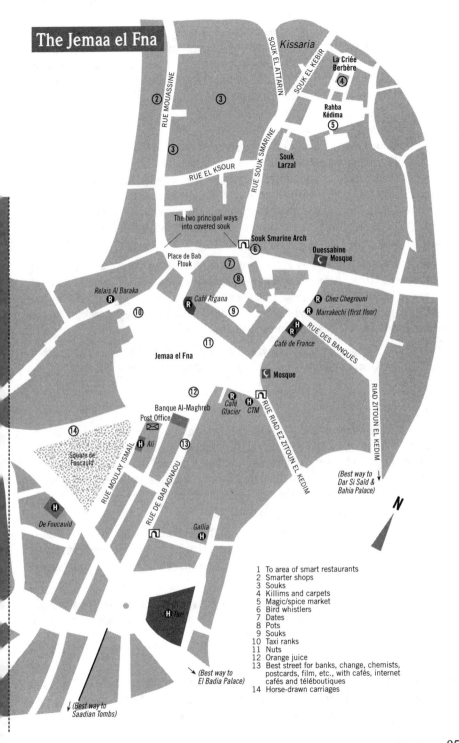

The Jemaa el Fna

Kissaria

SOUK EL ATTARIN

SOUK EL KEBIR

RUE MOUASSINE

SOUK SMARINE

La Criée
Berbère
④

Rahba
Kédima
⑤

② ③

③

③

RUE EL KSOUR

Souk
Larzal

The two principal ways
into covered souk

Souk Smarine Arch
⑥

Place de Bab
Ftouk

⑦

⑧

Ouessabine
Mosque

Relais Al Baraka
R

⑩

R Café Argana

⑨

R Chez Chegrouni

R Marrakechi (first floor)

RUE DES BANQUES
R H

Café de France

⑪

Jemaa el Fna

Mosque

⑫

Banque Al-Maghreb
Post Office

R Café
Glacier
H CTM

RUE RIAD EZ ZITOUN EL KEDIM

RIAD ZITOUN EL KEDIM

⑭

H Ali

⑬

Square de
Foucauld

RUE MOULAY ISMAIL

RUE DE BAB AGNAOU

(Best way to
Dar Si Saïd &
Bahia Palace)

H
De Foucauld

Gallia
H

N

H Taxi

(Best way to
El Badia Palace)

(Best way to
Saadian Tombs)

1 To area of smart restaurants
2 Smarter shops
3 Souks
4 Killims and carpets
5 Magic/spice market
6 Bird whistlers
7 Dates
8 Pots
9 Souks
10 Taxi ranks
11 Nuts
12 Orange juice
13 Best street for banks, change, chemists,
postcards, film, etc., with cafés, internet
cafés and téléboutiques
14 Horse-drawn carriages

95

somehow to encapsulate much of the fascination of Morocco: the difference, the colour and the energy of its alien culture, compounded by a rarely diminished sensation of being a stranger on the edge of any understanding. If you haven't managed to find a nearby hotel bedroom, there are a number of cafés that surround the square where you can rest and watch in comparative serenity, and stock up on loose change.

The Medina Souks

Beyond the northern edge of the Jemaa el Fna stretches the great souk of Marrakesh. It is a triumphant, labyrinthine marketplace, a glittering display of all the traditional arts and regional crafts of Morocco, grouped together by trade in separate but interlinked streets and courtyards. Compared with the woodcarvers' areas in Essaouira or the souks of Fez it has relatively few workshops, though there are turners, carpenters, weavers, dyers and tailors to be found. Only in the Souk Haddadine (the blacksmiths' quarter) do the makers outnumber the dealers.

The souk is not best appreciated at the tail-end of a bemusing and exhausting tour. It should be dipped into: chosen areas gently explored and discovered at different hours of the day. The traditional trading period is in the morning, but the hours before dusk are the busiest for traffic, both human and motorized, when the souk becomes so packed that the crowds of people seem to sway and move in unison.

For your first visit employ a guide to show you the main streets and features. Then, armed with a little knowledge of the street pattern, you can afford to explore—the earlier in the morning the better.

Rue Souk Smarine

Along the northern edge of the Jemaa el Fna a range of bazaars and the Ouessabine Mosque hide the main, arched entrance to the principal street, the Rue Souk Smarine. Here, before entering the souk proper, you can find a pottery and a spice market. The whole area is often obscured by shifting displays of clothing laid out on canvas. These pavement vendors are constantly on the look-out for police; they operate against an echoing soundtrack of bird whistles and hustling calls.

Rue Souk Smarine is, however, easy enough to identify. It is broad, well paved and shaded from the sun by a high trellis cover. Commercially, it is dominated by the cloth merchants, whose shelves groan under the weight of hundreds of bolts of bright silks and embroidered cloth for kaftans.

Interspersed amongst the cloth merchants are tailors, who have been joined by a number of upmarket bazaars with halls stacked full of carpets half-hidden behind gleaming gates of brass, and who accept all manner of credit cards.

Rahba Kédima (Magic Market)

About 150m along Rue Souk Smarine two right turns lead into a distinctive open space, the triangular-shaped piazza known as Rahba Kédima, which used to be the old corn market. Until the 19th century it was forbidden to export grain, as it was considered immoral to

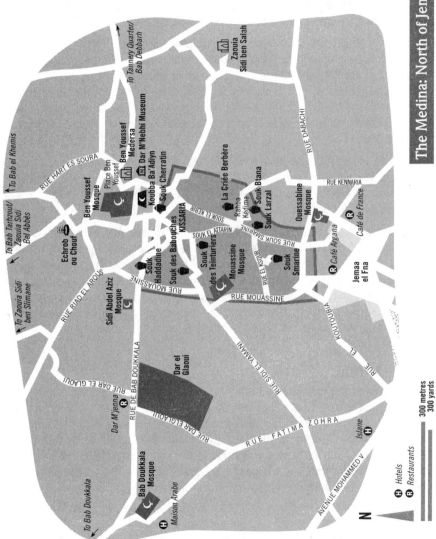

The Medina: North of Jemaa el Fna

To Tannery Quarter/
Bab Debbarh

Zaouia
Sidi ben Salah

RUE DABACHI

Ben Youssef
Medersa

Dar M'Nebhi Museum

RUE HART ES SOURA

Place Ben
Youssef

Koubba Ba'Adiyn

Souk Cherratin

La Criée Berbère

RUE KENNARIA

To Bab el Khemis

Ben Youssef
Mosque

Souk Btana

Souk Larzal

To Bab Taghzout/
Zaouia Sidi
Bel Abbès

KISSARIA

SOUK EL KEBIR

Rahba
Kédima

Ouessabine
Mosque

Café de France

Echrob
ou Chouf

SOUK EL ATTARIN

RUE SOUK SMARINE

To Zaouia Sidi
ben Slimane

RUE RIAD EL AROUS

Souk
Haddadine

Souk des Babouches

Souk
des Teinturiers

Mouassine
Mosque

Souk
Smarine

Café Argana

R Café de France

Jemaa
el Fna

Sidi Abdel Aziz
Mosque

RUE MOUASSINE

RUE ELKSOUR

R Café Argana

RUE MOUASSINE

Dar el
Glaoui

KOUTOUBIA

Dar M'jenna

R

RUE DE BAB DOUKKALA

RUE DAR EL GLAOUI

RUE SIDI EL YAMANI

RUE EL

RUE DAR EL GLAOUI

RUE FATIMA ZOHRA

Bab Doukkala
Mosque

To Bab Doukkala

Maison Arabe

Islane

H

AVENUE MOHAMMED V

N

H Hotels
R Restaurants

300 metres
300 yards

97

profit by feeding Christians to the discomfort of poor Muslims. The place has a few vegetable stalls at its far end, but is dominated by spice and magic stalls.

The latter are hung with strange curtains of dried eagles, mountain foxes, hedgehogs, snakes, porcupines, lizards and unnamed grim relics in pots. These ingredients are used in the concoction of love potions, stimulants and aphrodisiacs—a female magic which helps to balance the many male-dominated features of Moroccan life.

The trinity of Maghrebi cosmetics are very prominently displayed: silvery blocks of antimony which are ground into kohl—a powder which both outlines the eyelids and stimulates an attractive watery sheen that protects eyes from soot and dust; henna in all its variety—green leaves, powder or ready-made pastes for dyeing hair and the intricate decorative tattooing of hands, face and feet; and pottery saucers of cochineal, which is used as a rouge. Also look out for sacks of dried Dadès roses, a deliciously fragrant and cheap pot pourri.

In the centre, veiled ladies sell knitted woollen hats and reed woven shopping baskets and raffia trays. The northern face of the piazza is usually hung with killims and carpets—a bright blaze of madder red and saffron yellow which almost obscures the two entrances to La Criée Berbère, the dark textile marketplace.

Before entering this haven of carpet dealers you might discover two other small places to the south of the Rahba Kédima. **Souk Btana** used to be dedicated to the auction of sheep and goat skins, cured and uncured, but has now been tidied up. These pungent goods have been replaced by dozens of stall holders. **Souk Larzal**, a small rectangular square with a small covered arcade in its centre, has kept more of its medieval atmosphere. Wool is still auctioned off to spinners and dyers, but in the evening the square is transformed into a secondhand clothes market with some fine embroidered kaftans and gilt work amongst the dross.

La Criée Berbère

Off the northern side of the Rahba Kédima two entranceways lead into the narrow Criée Berbère, a tight, enclosed space lined with displays of killims, killim cushions, killim waistcoats, carpets and woollen burnouses. Most trading here is done from the shops, but auctions of goods are often held in the morning and evening. Moroccan auctions are distinctive affairs: the auctioneer walks around with odd composite bundles of stock, shouting the current price in the hope of attracting a larger one. Buyers and sellers sit to one side eyeing each other. Nothing seems to get sold very quickly.

This auction square was used before 1912 for the sale of slaves, at dusk on Wednesdays, Thursdays and Fridays. These auctions were only for the disposal of stock at the lower end of the domestic market, as influential clients would expect private and advance viewing. Galla women were considered the most attractive, but girls of the Hausa country fetched the best prices as they were considered more cheerful and neater. In the 1840s about 4,000 slaves were sold in Morocco each year, but by 1870 there was such a glut that prices dropped below $3. Even before then the common rate was two slaves for a camel, 10 for a horse, and 40 for a civet cat.

A left turn from here leads you past an artful selection of bazaars to the main street, or you can retrace your steps to Rue Souk Smarine.

The Kissaria: Souk el Kebir and Souk el Attarin

Just past the Rahba Kédima turning, Rue Souk Smarine splits into the **Souk el Kebir** (on the right) and the **Souk el Attarin** (to the left).

The Souk el Kebir passes a jewellers' alley on the right, before the alleys of the Kissaria open up on your left. The Kissaria is traditionally the heart of a souk, and in Marrakesh specializes in clothes, with stalls selling modern Western clothes, traditional cotton *gandoras*, woven blankets and arrays of Western-influenced open-necked kaftans for women.

Farther along Souk el Kebir are the aromatic stalls and small courtyards of the carpenters and wood-turners who make wooden screens and book holders. On the right-hand side, after an arch labelled Souk des Sacochiers, a skilled craftsman makes elaborate embroidered saddles and all the trappings of an Arab cavalier. Almost opposite, at 127 Souk Chkaria, craftsmen will Morocco-bind a favourite book for you, although covers for video cassettes are more in demand. If you bear left at the far end of the souk, you will find yourself in **Souk Cherratin**, a collection of alleys with a few leather, wood and metal craft stalls.

The Souk el Attarin takes you on much the same journey as the Souk el Kebir, though the alleys of the Kissaria will appear on the right. There are, however, three of Marrakesh's most celebrated sites to be discovered just on or off this alley.

The first, and easiest to find, is the **Souk des Babouches**, the section of Souk el Attarin devoted to the sale of slippers. This quarter, with its dazzling display of bank after bank of gilt-embroidered slippers, arrayed in every colour alongside those in fake animal skin, suede, polished leather, burnished leather or velvet, is like swimming in a jewellery box.

Continue farther along to the narrow turning into the **Souk Haddadine** (blacksmiths' quarter). During working hours the cacophony of hammer blows is enough to guide you there with your eyes closed. It is a triumphantly messy zone, full of rusting sections of iron plates and cut rods. The ice-blue glow of acetylene torches illuminates the tiny workshops packed full of industrious smiths dressed in grime and denim. They can make anything here, but at the moment the souk is producing vast quantities of lanterns, fire tongs, weather vanes, tables and yet more lanterns to be exported to Europe.

The third great site in this area is the **Souk des Teinturiers** (dyers' quarter)—reached by either of two alleys to the left of Souk el Attarin. On a good day the whole alley can be hung with vast swatches of wool drying in the sun. The combination of bright primary colours is irresistibly photogenic. As a passing tourist you might snap away free of charge, although film crews will be charged for the pleasure. There are some good shops in this section: old junk shops as well as a young man making genuine felt hats and fezzes. If you continue, passing under an arch, you will emerge out by the Mouassine fountain on your left—a triple-bayed recess with one or two working water taps. The great bulk of the **Mouassine Mosque** is hidden behind houses.

A left turn past the Mouassine Mosque takes you down the wider and uncomplicated Rue Mouassine, lined with some of the better-stocked tourist bazaars, which brings you out into the Place de Bab Ftouk and the Jemaa el Fna.

Ben Youssef Medersa, Koubba Ba'Adiyn and Dar M'Nebhi

There are three monuments open to non-Muslims in the medina: the Saadian Ben Youssef Medersa, the Almoravid Koubba Ba'Adiyn and the private museum housed in the 19th-century Dar M'Nebhi palace. The medersa and the koubba are two of the finest buildings in Marrakesh, some would say in all Morocco, and no visit, however short, should exclude these architectural treasures. They are relatively easy to find as they are both associated with the Ben Youssef Mosque, just to the north of the covered souk.

From the Jemaa el Fna head up the main souk artery, the Rue Souk Smarine/Souk el Kebir for 450m, turn left at the far Y-junction and then right under an arch and left again along a broader street to reach an open square, the Place Ben Youssef. This is usually occupied by at least one football game, while the mosque walls are draped with long, spinning strands of tailors' silk. The entrance to the koubba is behind the wall on your left, the museum is on the right, and the medersa down the alley to the right of the mosque.

The Ben Youssef Mosque

Above the square rises the green-tiled roof and minaret of the Ben Youssef Mosque. A mosque was first built here by the Almoravid Sultan Ali ben Youssef, in the 12th century, as the central mosque of the medina. It was then twice as large as the present building. The Saadian Sultan Abdullah el Ghalib attempted to make Ben Youssef the most popular and esteemed mosque in Marrakesh. By this time it was in ruins, so he had to rebuild it entirely, along with the neighbouring medersa, and to cap his work he presented it with a large library.

The mosque, however, did not survive the well-intentioned improvements of his successors. What you now see dates entirely from the early 19th century, when an ancient and beautifully carved Almoravid fountain was also destroyed.

The Ben Youssef Medersa

Open Tues–Sun 8–12 and 2.30–6; closed Mon and Fri am; adm.

The medersa was founded by the philanthropic Merenid Sultan Abou Hassan in the 14th century as part of an educational programme that established Koranic colleges in Fez, Taza, Salé, Meknès and Marrakesh. In 1564 it was restored by order of Saadian Sultan Abdullah el Ghalib, who created the largest medersa in Morocco, a feat which was completed in under a year. It was part of his ambition to make the Ben Youssef Mosque an intellectual centre to rival Fez. Dedicatory inscriptions to the sultan can be seen on the lintel of the entrance gate and along the prayer-hall.

You may have to knock at the inconspicuous door to the right of the covered arch to enter. A long twisting passage then leads to the entrance hall, a secretive Marrakeshi feature not found in any Merenid medersa (they have proud portals and direct entrances). From the hall, stairs lead up to over a hundred plain wooden rooms where students lived, each sharing small courtyard skylights. This is another distinctive feature, for earlier medersas used windows overlooking the central courtyard to provide a central decorative theme.

The open **courtyard**, a great interior space of peace and silence, centres on a marble basin and is flanked by two galleries of solid pillars. Directly opposite is the entrance to the prayer-hall. The richness of decorative detail never disturbs the graceful simplicity of the plan: an initial height of *zellij* mosaic is broken by two bands of tile and plaster carved with Koranic inscriptions, which lead up into the ornate plaster and cedar carving. The court-yard has a distinctive grandeur touched with an element of severity not found in more intimate Merenid medersas.

The **prayer-hall** is divided into three aisles by four marble columns, and a further four enhance the arched mihrab, which carries the two traditional inscriptions of the Muslim declaration of faith. Go upstairs to see the students' rooms arranged around internal light-wells, their sparse dignity enlivened by the elaborate details of the carved wood balconies and turned window frames. The students (known as *tolba*, or reciters) were allowed to lodge here for six years whilst they memorized the Koran and studied the commentaries and laws. In the summer they wandered through the country, begging, listening to marabouts, and reciting their verses throughout the night at rural festivals.

The Koubba Ba'Adiyn (Kobbat el Mourabitine, Kobba el Baroudiyine)

When this building was rediscovered in its sunken position in 1948, French art historian Gaston Deverdun exclaimed that 'the art of Islam has never exceeded the splendour of this extraordinary dome'. The koubba is all that remains to hint at the glory of 12th-century Almoravid Marrakesh. It is a small pavilion covering a shallow ritual washing pool in the outer courtyard of the mosque, and is still surrounded by brick cisterns and latrines that once enclosed it. The koubba introduces many of the shapes that become so familiar in later Islamic architecture.

The plan itself is simple enough: a rectangular two-storey domed structure pierced by arches. At ground level a pair of scalloped arches face each other; there are twin horseshoe arches on the longer sides. These silhouettes are repeated in the rows of three and five inset window arches on the upper storey, where scallop and horseshoe have been joined by an impaled turban motif. A decorative battlement frames the dome, which is decorated with a band of interlocking arches and surmounted by a series of diminishing seven-pointed stars.

Standing inside you look up into a dome of astonishingly bold, confident, solid yet supremely elegant and disciplined carving. The remains of a Kufic frieze announcing its creator, Ali ben Youssef, can just be made out. Above this rests an octagonal arched dome, its interlaced scallop arches infilled with rich foliate carving upon which hang shell-shaped palmettes. The corner squinches are framed by *muqurnas*, elegant spanning arches that in later centuries degenerated to appear like dripping stalactites. The *muqurnas* ring a seven-pointed star that frames an eight-podded dome, which in turn echoes the triumphant, deep carving of the central cupola.

Both the exterior and interior carvings play with the strong African sun to create pools of dark shadow and contrasting patches of light. The light shows up well the confident architectural origins of the Spanish Moorish style. The gradual debasement of this style into a mere veneer of decoration can be seen progressively at the medersa, the Saadian Tombs, the Dar M'Nebhi, and finally in the modern hotels of Marrakesh.

The Dar M'Nebhi (Musée Privé de Marrakesh)

Open daily except holidays 9–12.30 and 3–6.30; adm; © (04) 39 09 11.

This opulent turn-of-the-20th-century palace has been converted into a museum owned by a charitable foundation, supported by an American-style Association of (rich) Friends. To one side of the entrance courtyard there is a well-stocked bookshop full of posters, art books and cards, and there is also talk of opening a café. The museum's exhibits are mainly items on loan from state museums or rarely seen pieces drawn from Moroccan private collections.

The Fortunes of the Menebhi

The M'Nebhi (Menebha) family no longer possess either of the great palaces in Fez and Marrakesh that bear their name. They are descended from a clan of the Arab nomad tribes that held a privileged military position and were settled by the Alaouite sultans on the good grazing ground between Marrakesh and Essaouira. The family rose to a great position at the turn of the 20th century, when one of the most promising young cavalry officers in Sultan Moulay Hassan's army, El Mehdi bel Arbi El Menebhi, rose to become Minister for War to the boy sultan Abdul Aziz. As was customary, this Menebhi made a great fortune from his position and elevated his less talented nephews and sons to various official positions. After Moulay Hafid replaced his brother on the throne, Menebhi arranged for his transfer to Tangier, where he served as the *mendoub*, the sultan's representative. His charm, erudition, bubbly wit and hospitality endeared him to the foreign community and especially to the British, who showered him with honours, including a knighthood. He attended the coronations of three kings at Westminster Abbey. Even as an old man, seated on a comely mule, he was delighted to escort his guests out to picnics and pig-sticking parties in the woods around Tangier. On one such expedition, when things were on the point of getting ugly, the old minister plucked a lance from a neighbour and deftly transfixed a maddened boar so that nine inches of spear protruded on the farther side. The startled onlookers were left wondering what he had been like in his prime.

The heart of the museum is the enormous internal courtyard, in which three marble fountains play beneath the subdued light that filters through the modern steel-and-stretched-canvas roof. Exhibits on show in the rooms alongside include two vast plates, one imported from Andalucía, the other from the Saharan oasis of Tafilalt; a circumcision kaftan; an 18th-century painted dowry coffer from the Rif; a sumptuous red velvet- and gold-embroidered Jewish wedding dress; and Lucine Vola's collection of textiles. The latter includes two fine Glaoua *hanbels*, but is richest in Beni Yacoub and Aït Ouaouzguite work. These two tribal regions on the southern slopes of the High Atlas have specialized in producing restrained bands of brightly coloured embroidery on cream or white woollen *haiks*, though the work currently on sale in the south has long since fallen from these high standards.

In a secondary courtyard there is a small collection of modern Moroccan art, of much greater interest than the orientalist imagery culled from French and British magazines that is also on show. There is a fine example of Hassan el Glaoui's work, with his view of a royal procession centred on the mounted figure of the sultan with his crimson parasol. An artist of much greater influence is Farid Belkahia, who has looked to Saharan-derived imagery and traditional designs painted on leatherwork and drums for his parchment-like canvases.

Another key figure, Fatima Hassani, is also represented here. Her poster-bright colours (taken from traditional embroidery), henna-like decorative details, and her concentration on depicting—and glorifying—female-dominated spaces have touched upon a rich new artistic vein. Other pictures include Jacques Azema's disturbingly iconic view of three boys in a *hammam*, Ben Haim's powerful portrait of a lady in red and yellow, and Mohammed Ben Allal's picture of a basket-weaver at dusk.

The palace's toilets are also a wonderful feature, and on your way out (passing some press photographs of the great and the good at the royal opening) look out for two large pale-green tiles with a central rivetment hole. These 11th-century tiles were once fixed to wooden batons at the summit of the Koutoubia minaret, and so are among the oldest known examples of Morocco's long tradition of *zellij* tiling. Their celadon-like colouring and simplicity of form provide a tantalizing insight into a lost world of colour. It is all too easy to see the Almoravids and Almohads in an austere stone-like monotone, in the same way that we mistakenly visualize the Normans and Romans.

A Walk Past the Lesser Monuments in the Northern Medina

North of the medersa stretches the great bulk of the medina, without souks, bazaars, guides or many tourists. Modern houses have for the most part replaced the pisé buildings, but the streets retain their labyrinthine design and you can wander freely through this living maze, catching glimpses of old *fondouqs*, mosques, *hammams* and bakeries. The route outlined here takes you past the notable sights of the area, and will give you a feel for this less-explored section of the medina. Unless you are a Muslim, however, you can only look at the monuments in this area of the medina from the outside. It is a long walk: if you are short on time or energy, leave it for another visit.

Turn right from the Ben Youssef Medersa, and then left down a covered passage. As you re-emerge into daylight you face a crossroads where Rue Baroudienne joins Rue Amesfah. Both these streets are lined with a number of elegant 16th- and 17th-century *fondouqs*, which are still very much in use as craftsmen's and tradesmen's courtyards. They are well worth a discreet look inside.

Turn right up Rue Assouel, passing several more *fondouqs*, the most elegant of which is beside the monumental decorated fountain on the left, the **Echrob ou Chouf**, which translates as 'drink and admire'. A left turn by the fountain, up Rue Diar Saboun, takes you into Rue de Bab Tarhzout, which is often half-filled by a souk of secondhand clothes.

In medieval times the **Bab Tarhzout** marked the northern edge of the city, but in the 18th century Sultan Sidi Mohammed extended the walls to include the zaouia suburb of Sidi Bel Abbès, one of the seven saints of Marrakesh, within the city.

Zaouia of Sidi Bel Abbès

The direct approach to the shrine is through an arch lined with an expensive and elaborate arcade of jewellers. The zaouia, mosque and tombs are forbidden to non-Muslims, but by going to the left or the right of the main entrance you can get impressive views into the extensive complex and of the great pyramidal shrine.

The zaouia rose beside the grave of the Sidi in the cemetery of Sidi Marwan, which at that time was just to the north of the city walls. The existing buildings are the work of the 18th-century Alaouite Sultan Sidi Mohammed, who, apart from extending the city walls and rebuilding the entire shrine complex, added a further gift of a medersa courtyard with two flights of horseshoe arches.

Es-Sebti, the Seven Saints of Marrakesh

Combinations of seven saints or seven sleepers reach back beyond Islam and Christianity to an older universal myth. In Morocco, Ceuta, Jbel Hadid, Fez and Marrakesh all share in this common tradition. In the 18th century, Sultan Moulay Ismaïl removed various unorthodox Berber aspects of the annual celebration of Marrakesh's *es-Sebti*, and at the same time rebuilt the sanctuaries of the historical, orthodox saints. A new week-long *moussem* was established, which began at the shrine of Sidi Lyad, moved on to Sidi Youssef ben Ali, Sidi Abd el Aziz, Sidi el-Ghawzani, Sidi es Suhayi and Sidi ben Slimane al Jazuli before culminating at the major shrine of the city, that of Sidi Bel Abbès.

Sidi Bel Abbès (1130–1205) was born in Ceuta but moved south to establish a hermitage outside Marrakesh. His learning, moral sermons, miracles and ascetic lifestyle gained him a widespread popular following. The Almohad Sultan Yaacoub el Mansour invited him into the city and presented him with buildings and funds to carry on his good works. Centred on his shrine, these continue today: city merchants support the zaouia in running a number of schools and hostels, and in feeding the blind each evening. A number of potent legends still circulate in the city—that Christians venerate Sidi Bel Abbès as St Augustine, for instance, and that he haunts the minaret of the Koutoubia Mosque each night until he is certain that all the blind have been fed.

The Zaouia of Sidi ben Slimane al Jazuli

Turning back through Bab Tarhzout, a right turn takes you past the covered Souk el Mjadlia and out below the zaouia of Sidi ben Slimane al Jazuli, another of the seven patron saints of Marrakesh. Its distinctive green pyramid roof and neighbouring mosque can be seen from alleys to the north and south of the zaouia, but the street beside it is closed to non-Muslims.

Sidi ben Slimane al Jazuli was one of the great Sufi mystics of Morocco, and his followers went on to found important religious institutions throughout the country. Al Jazuli's book, *The Manifest Proofs of Piety*, remains a seminal mystical text. As well as being famed as a spiritual teacher, he was a leading figure in the struggle against Portugal and his embalmed body would became a powerful totem in the *jihad*. Buried at Afugal in Haha province for a few decades, his body was brought to Marrakesh by the Saadians in 1523. Six Saadian princes were murdered shortly afterwards in a palace coup. They were buried together beneath a single koubba beside Al Jazuli's shrine, giving a further bizarre resonance to the legend of the seven.

Walk down to a dusty crossroads square below the zaouia. Ahead and to your right you will see the minaret of the Sidi Bou Ameur Mosque. Turn left below the minaret to walk down Rue Dar el Glaoui.

The Dar el Glaoui

At the junction between Rue Dar el Glaoui and Rue de Bab Doukkala is the massive bulk of the Dar el Glaoui, the palace of Si Thami el Glaoui, Pasha of Marrakesh, which was built in the early years of the 20th century. Impressive in scale if not in detail, it is now in use as a Trade Union headquarters. In recent years visitors have been allowed in to admire the garden and some of the principal rooms.

Dar el Glaoui was a place of legendary hospitality which from the 1920s to 50s entertained an international social élite including Roosevelt, Churchill and Patton. Beautiful Berber girls or boys, opium or marijuana, Lafitte or Latour were offered to guests with the freedom and nonchalance with which other Moroccan houses offer mint tea. Compliant European females could rely on a parting gift of emeralds, and society figures fought for the chance to have been the pasha's friend for a night. However, behind the pampering of sophisticated guests lay French 'loans', illicit taxes, bribery, blackmail and protection rackets, and it was common knowledge that the thousands of Marrakesh prostitutes had the pasha as their ultimate pimp.

Only hours after the pasha's death in 1956 a crowd broke into the Dar el Glaoui. Such was their hatred for the pasha, who had allied himself very closely with the French colonists, that they preferred to destroy rather than loot the palace and even the cars were smashed and set on fire. The mob then had their vengeance on the traitorous henchmen and officials of the pasha, who were hunted through the streets of the medina. They were treated like the cars: beaten, stripped and then burnt alive on the rubbish dump outside the Bab Doukkala. It is said that King Mohammed V would not eat for seven days when he heard of this brutality, even though the men killed had been his bitterest enemies.

From the Dar el Glaoui you can walk due west along Rue de Bab Doukkala, which runs towards the gate of that name, to look at the **Bab Doukkala Mosque**, on your left. This was built in 1558 by Lalla Messaouda, daughter of a *caïd* of Ouarzazate, wife of a sultan and a redoubtable mother. While in exile in Istanbul she educated her two sons, later to be the great Saadian sultans Abdel Malik and Ahmed el Mansour. All that can be seen by non-Muslims is the slender elegant minaret to the northeast of the mosque and the elegant **Sidi el Hassan Fountain**, named after one of the founding professors of the medersa that used to be attached to the mosque.

Walk back to the Dar el Glaoui and go east for 300m until you reach the prominent crossroads with Rue Mouassine. Just up the street to the left is the **mosque and shrine of Sidi Abdel Aziz**, another Sufi follower of the teachings of Al Jazuli, who died in Marrakesh in 1508 and has entered the pantheon of the seven saints. While on this crossroads, look out for the gates to half a dozen *fondouqs*, some of which may be open. Try Nos.192 or 149 Rue Mouassine, which will reveal courtyards surrounded by galleries supported by high simple pillars and graceful cedar beams.

The Mouassine Mosque

South from the crossroads, 150m down Rue Mouassine, is the Mouassine Mosque, a monumental building established by the Saadian Sultan Abdullah el Ghalib in 1560, complete with baths, medersa and exterior fountain. The mosque has an equivocal local reputation. It is named after a prestigious local *shorfa* family but, during the building of the foundations, a 14th-century Jewish plague cemetery was unearthed. This is considered to have reduced the sanctity of the site, and rumours of a curse released in disturbing the grave of a cabbalistic rabbi began to circulate. The mosque is largely hidden from non-Muslims by the surrounding buildings, and there is little indication of the reported magnificence inside. The large triple-bayed **Mouassine Fountain**, with its ornate portico, is in a small square to the left of the mosque.

Imperial Marrakesh

The Marrakesh of the sultans has grown up since the 12th century in what is now the southern area of the medina. Here, the Almohads first established their kasbah, palaces, barracks and a royal mosque. Successor dynasties continued to develop the southern district into an Imperial City, but in a typically Moroccan way paid scant regard to the achievements of their predecessors. The Royal Palace—not open to the public—therefore stands on ground that has seen a dazzling succession of pavilions, courts and gardens.

The glories of imperial Marrakesh include the massive and very impressive ruins of the 16th-century Saadian El Badia Palace, which contrast perfectly in their state of decay with the Saadian Tombs, which have survived completely intact from the same period. Apart from exploring two 19th-century viziers' palaces, the Bahia and the Dar Si Saïd, you can also lose yourself in the dark alleys of Marrakesh's ancient Jewish quarter, the *mellah*.

The best way to approach this quarter is on foot, walking south from the Jemaa el Fna. Start by heading down the café-lined and pedestrianized Rue de Bab Agnaou to a roundabout dominated by the Tazi Hotel. To your right is the Place Youssef ben Tachfine. Cross straight over, passing a fort and keeping the medieval kasbah wall to your left shoulder. 500 metres south you stop before two imposing gates. The intermittent wall on your left is not an old city wall but marks out the inner city, the kasbah quarter of sultans, the Imperial City.

Bab Agnaou and Bab er Rob

The official entrance into the city lay through the Bab er Rob; the Bab Agnaou guarded the entrance into the kasbah quarter, the city within the city. *Agnaou* is a Berber word that translates as 'the mute ram without horns'. A less prosaic but more logical translation names it 'the Guinea gate'—the southern gate leading to black Africa, the homeland of the sultans' guards. It was built on Sultan Yaacoub el Mansour's orders in 1185, and has added prestige as one of the few stone structures in this city of pink pisé. It is carved from local 'blue' Guéliz stone, which is still being quarried to the north of Marrakesh. The semi-circular frieze has been delicately cut but is surprisingly assertive and strong.

The Kasbah Mosque

Passing through Bab Agnaou you approach the Kasbah Mosque, finished in 1190 by Sultan Yaacoub el Mansour. The long white exterior wall is capped with decorative battlements and for once left free of encrusted buildings to give an indication of its impressive extent.

The Merenids added a famous medersa to the Almohad mosque, but this was destroyed in a gunpowder explosion in 1569. The Saadian Sultan Abdullah el Ghalib restored the damaged mosque, which has been touched up every 200 years since, by Sidi Mohammed in the 18th century and more recently by Hassan II. These pious restorations have kept it from looking its age. The minaret, however, retains its original decorations: the simple *revêtement* of celadon green tiles, the first stirrings of Morocco's love affair with *zellij* (geometrical mosaics of cut tile). For a Muslim the principal approach is through the great domed northern gate which looks across the extensive open *sahn* court to the domed mihrab flanked by four Omayyad columns of jasper. Beside the mihrab a door leads to the enclosed garden courtyard of the 16th-century royal necropolis—the Saadian Tombs.

The Saadian Tombs

Open daily 8–12 and 2–6; adm; visits often in the company of a guide, tips accepted.

The tombs are one of the most visited sites in Morocco, so in order to recapture some sense of serenity and isolation try to go either early in the morning or in late afternoon. A tight, thin passage to the south of the mosque was cut through the protective Saadian walls in 1917 for the use of non-Muslims. (Before this the only entrance was through a postern gate beside the mihrab.) Coming through it, you enter an ancient rectangular enclosed garden, planted with trees, cascading shrubs and rosemary hedges. This is the cemetery of the *shorfa*, the descendants of the Prophet, which had been in use for centuries before any Saadians arrived in Marrakesh. The identity of most of the open-air mosaic graves is lost, but the Merenid Sultan Abou Hassan was buried here before his corpse was moved on into the greater state of Rabat's Chellah in 1351. The first Saadian sultan, Mohammed ech Cheikh, was buried here in 1557, in a tomb covered by a simple koubba. The existing koubbas were all built by Mohammed ech Cheikh's third ruling son, Ahmed el Mansour, in two stages. First he built a pavilion around his father's simple tomb, where he also buried his mother, Lalla Messaouda, in 1591. Later he built the hall of twelve columns to be his own mausoleum, and attached to it a prayer-hall. The extraordinary interiors of both koubbas can be examined from their thresholds.

The **prayer-hall** is the first hall on your left as you enter; it extends south of Ahmed el Mansour's tomb. Four clean pillars support elegant high horseshoe arches which, with the skylight, divide the roof space into eight rectangles. The decorated mihrab niche can be seen to your left. Although it has the most pleasing dark, simple sepulchral quality of them all, this was never intended as a tomb. It contains, however, a plethora of them, mostly the resting places of Alaouite princes from the 18th century. There is a sad little nest just to the left of the mihrab where half a dozen plague victims, the children of Sultan Sidi Mohammed, were buried between 1756 and 1777. The large tomb to the right, surrounded by a wooden balustrade, is one of the many resting places of the Black Sultan, the Merenid Abou Hassan.

The **Hall of Twelve Columns** is the central mausoleum of Ahmed el Mansour. The three central tombs are surrounded by a colonnade of twelve decorated marble pillars, and the intensely carved upper plasterwork appears like gilded lace. The dome is even more fantastically rich, and prolonged inspection induces an almost physical sense of nausea. Decoration has overwhelmed form to produce a heady mystery, a pointillist scattering of reflected gilded light and depth that verges on a spiritual unworldliness. It is with relief that you concentrate on the layer of white script interwoven with black flowers, the lower area of *zellij* mosaic and the clean sober tombs at ground level. The central tomb is of course that of Ahmed el Mansour, who died in 1603. To his right is his son and successor Zaidan, who died in 1628, and to his left that of his grandson Mohammed ech Cheikh II, who died in 1655. There are 33 other tombs of Saadian princelings, although only 15 are identifiable by their inscriptions. Immediately behind the tomb of Ahmed el Mansour is an inscription commemorating his father.

Through this magnificence a small darkened room can be glimpsed to the right: the **Hall of Three Niches**. An inscription in the middle niche commemorates Ahmed el Mansour's elder half-brother, the great building sultan of Marrakesh, Abdullah el Ghalib. The large tomb at the back is associated with Abou Hassan, who died an exile in the High Atlas in 1351.

Crossing over unidentified *shorfa* tombs, you pass the old entrance that led out of the Kasbah Mosque on your left. This used to be covered by another dome, but now the three sheiks' tombs are left open to the elements.

The **Second Koubba** is overlooked by two ornate loggias and a prayer-hall which was Ahmed el Mansour's first creation. The loggias' slim white marble pillars bear a lintel of carved cedar that supports the green-tiled roof. The prayer-hall, where a number of Saadian and a few 18th-century Alaouite princes are buried, is refreshingly clear of decoration other than the tranquil patterns of *zellij* mosaic. The burial chamber is decorated with

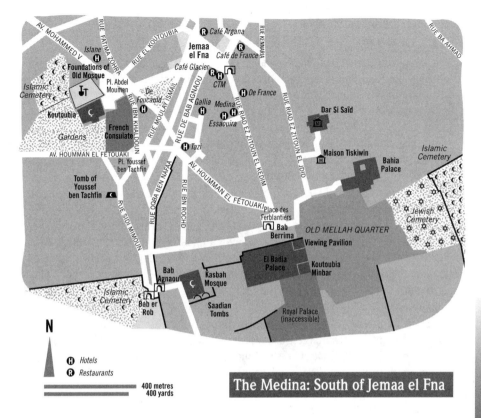

The Medina: South of Jemaa el Fna

stalactites and contains four tombs. Ahmed el Mansour's mother, Lalla Messaouda, is buried in a niche next to the wall on the right, beneath a commemorative inscription. The tomb to her left is that of the Sultan Abdullah el Ghalib, to his left that of Sultan Mohammed ech Cheikh, who died in 1557. The final tomb is that of the mad Alaouite Sultan Moulay el Yazid, who reigned for three years before his death in 1792.

Walking from the Saadian Tombs to El Badia Palace

To find El Badia Palace from the Saadian Tombs, return to Bab Agnaou, turn right and retrace your route back up Rue Oqba ben Nafaa for about 150m and then turn right again on to Av Houmman el Fétouaki. After about 600m you will arrive in the dusty square known as the **Souk du Mellah**, where oranges, fruits and olives are often sold. From the Souk du Mellah pass through one of two gates to the right into the Place des Ferblantiers, a large rectangular *fondouq* where metalworkers can be seen at work. Among other unusual processes, strips of unused Safi canning metal are cut to make intricate brass lanterns. Passing through the southern gate, the Bab Berrima, you enter a double-walled space familiar to anyone who has tramped the Imperial City of Meknès. The outer wall divides the imperial kasbah district from the civil medina; the massive wall further south, decorated by storks' nests, encloses El Badia Palace.

El Badia, the Incomparable

Open daily except holidays 8.30–11.45 and 2.30–5.45; adm.

The palace was started in 1578, five months after the Battle of the Three Kings put enormous wealth from Portuguese ransoms and captured booty into the hands of Ahmed el Mansour, 'the victorious', who was further boosted by efficient management of the Sous sugar trade and the capture of Timbuktu in 1598, so that el Mansour also became known by the honorific *el Dehbi*, 'the golden'. He employed the finest craftsmen in the world, and Montaigne, on his travels in Italy, saw sculptors carving marble pillars of extreme height and delicacy for the palace. It was he who recorded that the Moroccan sultan exchanged sugar, pound for pound, for these marbles.

Entering the palace, now in ruins, through a series of crumbling walls, you find yourself in a massive empty rectangular courtyard, crossed by a rigid grid of paths which lead to a central pool—90m long with an island—and flank four sunken gardens. The paths were actually raised to allow room for a great vaulted underground water system. The four sunken gardens would have been planted with sweet-smelling flowers: roses, violets, jasmine, acacia and hollyhocks, and with orange trees and tall cypresses, palms and olives for shade. A Moorish garden drew its chief glory from the arrangements of trees and running water, and flowers were almost entirely prized for their scent.

In the centre of each of the four massive walls pavilions were built, flanked by smaller pools and fountains. The largest of these was known as **Koubba el Hamsiniya**, the pavilion of fifty pillars. Opposite it stood the crystal pavilion, to the north was the green hall and to the south 'the Hayzouran', named after the sultan's favourite wife.

In his book *Black Sultan*, Wilfrid Blunt describes:

> *walls and ceilings encrusted with gold from Timbuktu...gaily decorated boats to entertain the King and his guests in the cooler hours of the evening... Its vast halls were filled with fountains, and in looking-glass ceilings far overhead the fish appeared to swim, reflected from the cool waters of marble basins. There was a domed hall where golden stars set on a blue ground gave the appearance of the heavens themselves. Long fish ponds between the alleys ended in grottoes and arbours.*

In the northeastern corner a staircase gives access to a viewing platform (which used to be closed and occupied by a military guard whenever the Royal Palace was in occupation). The prospect of the palace is superb, as are the views south to the Jbilet hills across the medina. In the northwestern corner of the palace courtyard a staircase leads down into the so-called apartments of the ambassadors. Excavations have exposed the courtyards of a terrace of three 'houses', each of which was centred on a little fountain courtyard.

In the southeastern corner of the courtyard, a gate leads to a smaller series of yards and cellars. In the shadow of the present Royal Palace, this is an intriguing area where you can see the slave pens, old potteries, baking ovens and the remains of the *hammam*. These ruins only constitute the ceremonial court of the palace: el Mansour's private apartments for himself, four wives, dozens of concubines, children and ministers extended to the south and west.

El Badia, an almost impious borrowing of one of the 99 names of God, was finished in 1603 only a few months before the death of its creator. Descriptions of the celebratory feasts and inaugural gifts are of almost unsurpassable splendour. During a lull in one of the festivals, the ageing sultan asked his fool for a compliment on the palace, to which was returned the famous reply that 'it would make a fine ruin'. Indeed, before the century was out, in 1696, Moulay Ismaïl had spent twelve years stripping the palace bare in order to embellish Meknès.

The Koutoubia Minbar

Open museum hours; adm.

A room in the southeastern corner of the courtyard has been set aside to display the minbar of the Koutoubia. This pulpit is one of the world's great treasures to have survived from the early Middle Ages. Commissioned by the third Almoravid sultan, Ali Ibn Yusuf Ibn Tashfine, in 1137 from the craftsmen of Córdoba, it took eight years to make the one thousand panels which were then assembled in Marrakesh. It stood to the right of the mihrab in a special hidden recess from out of which it rolled, almost miraculously, so that the imam, staff in hand, could ascend halfway up and deliver the noon-day Friday sermon. Revered even by the Almohads (who destroyed everything connected with the previous dynasty), it remained in use until 1962. A beautiful book and multilingual storyboards explain every detail.

The Mellah

From the Bab Berrima, Rue Berrima runs east of the El Badia outer walls past intriguing dark entrances into the heart of the *mellah*. You eventually emerge, after 600m, in a *méchouar* outside the present Royal Palace, where the walls and guards are distinctly off-putting.

In 1558, some hundred years after it occurred in most of Morocco's other cities, the Jews of Marrakesh were moved into a *mellah* on the orders of the Saadian Sultan Abdullah el Ghalib. The sultan created a secure quarter for them beside the royal palace, protected by walls and entered through only two gates. They were a talented community of traders, metalsmiths, bankers and linguists, a useful and valuable asset for the sultans, who have seldom shared the anti-Jewish feelings of their subjects. The community was governed by an *ulema,* a council of rabbis, ruled by a separate *caid*, and maintained its own cemetery, gardens, souks and fountains.

For some time the Jews prospered as middlemen between Moroccan Muslims and Christian merchants, but were recurrently accused by the populace of spying whenever there was a war. This antagonism grew with the strength of Portugal in the 15th and 16th centuries. Whereas learned rabbis had once been invited to lecture in mosques, it became accepted practice that if a Jew strayed into a mosque he was given the choice of immediate conversion or being burnt alive. Jews had to remove their hats and shoes when walking past a mosque, and in a royal city were forbidden to wear any shoes at all outside their own quarter.

But within the *mellah* walls the community grew into one of the most populous and over-crowded in Morocco. Before 1936 there were 16,000 Jews living here, but with the foundation of Israel in 1948 and the Suez Crisis in 1956 the community disintegrated, either moving to more tolerant Casablanca or emigrating.

Only a handful of Jews are left here, but the distinctive tall, cramped houses lining low but regular narrow streets remain. Within the quarter, mostly to the north, the traditional Jewish specialist trades of jewellery, textiles and tailoring remain. At the centre of the quarter is the small **Place Souweka**, with its fountain. If you are interested in visiting the **old synagogues** which have now been converted into houses and shops, you should find a young guide here or ask advice from the Jewish–American hostel in the *mellah*. Fessaine Synagogue (or Asim), built in 1840, remains in use as a small 20ft by 20ft house of prayer. On the eastern edge of the *mellah* is an extensive Jewish cemetery separated from the larger Muslim one by the city's outer wall. Until a few years ago it was a wilderness of shrubs and mating dogs, but now it is kept secure and the tombs are frequently whitewashed.

The Bahia Palace

Officially open daily 8.30–12 and 2.30–6, but often closed for receptions and conferences; adm.

From the Place des Ferblantiers, which stands just before El Badia Palace, follow the road north and then east to the long garden entrance of the palace ahead. If you manage to get into the palace, you will find it a perfect contrast to the vast sunbaked simplicity of El Badia. The Bahia, 'the brilliant', contains a series of paved courtyards, dark interior reception halls and Andalucían gardens, built by two generations of 19th-century grand viziers.

Si Mousa was vizier to Sultan Sidi Mohammed ben Abderahmane (1859–73), and his son, Ba Ahmed, served Sultan Moulay Hassan and became the powerful regent of the child-sultan Abdul Aziz. Their choice of architecture was highly traditional and, as father and son gradually amassed over eight hectares of the city, they created a maze of passages, connecting doors, courtyards, gardens and pavilions. However, fortunes created by a sultan's officials always return to their master eventually. Ba Ahmed was exceptional in having been able to enjoy his father's inheritance and his own wealth until the hour of his death, for a provincial *caid* or pasha in Morocco could expect to be squeezed of his ill-gotten gains any time after just a decade in office. Not until Ba Ahmed lay dying did the sultan's guards quietly replace the viziers at the doors of the Bahia Palace. Before the corpse had grown cold, they had stripped the palace of all portable possessions, and a few days later nothing remained but the great empty building as it is seen today.

The oriental complexity of plan, the locked side doors, beckoning passages and the ghosts of French and Moroccan courtiers (it was lived in by the resident-generals after 1912 and is still used on occasions by the Royal Family) give it an undeniable charm. The guided tour will take you through a dazzling series of reception halls with their great panelled Moorish ceilings of carved, painted and gilded wood. It is, though, the low empty range of the extensive concubines' courtyard, the garden courtyard and the courtyard of the four official wives that provide some of the most powerful, enduring and melancholic images of this palace. It is impossible not to feel sympathy for the imprisoned women who once inhabited this gilded cage, even though they themselves no doubt felt protected, pampered and privileged.

The Dar Si Saïd (Musée des Marocains)

Open Sat–Mon and Wed–Thur 9–11.45 and 2.30–5.45, Fri 9–11.30 and 3–5.45; closed Tues; adm.

Walking up Rue Riad ez Zitoun el Jdid towards the Jemaa el Fna, turn right opposite the neighbourhood mosque to find this secluded museum. Si Saïd was the idiot brother of Ba Ahmed, though they shared the same slave mother and powerful vizier father. He held a number of court posts as extra sinecures for his brother, whose palace communicated with the Dar Si Saïd by an underground tunnel. The Dar Si Saïd is more modest and attractive in plan than the Bahia, and greater attention has been paid to the detailed decorative work. Worthy of attention in its own right as a town palace, it also houses an important collection of the decorative arts of southern Morocco.

The entrance passage of the **Museum of Moroccan Arts and Crafts**, lined with doors rescued from the decaying kasbahs of southern Morocco, leads to a magnificent marble fountain bowl carved for Abdelmalik ben Abi, grand vizier to the Omayyad Caliph of Córdoba, Hisham II. It was carried away from Spain by the Almoravid Sultan Ali ben Youssef to embellish the Marrakesh mosque that bears his name. The figurative carving (on the sides a central imperial eagle is seemingly supported by two mountain goats, with a pair of apes on the outspread wings) would not have survived the fundamentalist cleansing of the Almohad period, and it was fortunate to have lain buried in ruins until discovered by excavations in 1926. You also pass a curious old fairground machine on your way to the delightful courtyard, with green and white pavement, fountain and central pavilion almost lost among bird-filled trees.

In the long room to the left is an uplifting display of the many Berber jewellery traditions of southern Morocco: the gorgeous fibules and green and yellow enamel eggs of Tiznit, the red stones set in dark silver from the Western High Atlas, the elaborate filigree from Jbel Siroua, the black-on-silver repoussé designs from the Tafilalt Oasis, and thick bracelets from Jbel Bani. On the other side of the courtyard there is male jewellery, as worked into ornamental daggers, powder horns and long-barrelled flintlocks. The two smaller rooms are dedicated to ceramics: one housing the traditional yellow, green and blue decorated wares produced in the great centres (Safi, Marrakesh and Fez), and also the traditional green slipware of Tamegroute, while the other is filled with different examples of the local red wares produced in the countryside and the mountains.

The **collection of carpets** includes many of the best examples you will find in southern Morocco, several of which are on view in the magnificent upstairs apartment. Stylistically they are divided between Berber and Arab. Those produced by the Arab tribes of the plain are sometimes collectively known as Tensift, or individually identified as Rehamna, Oulad Bou Sbaa, Chiadma, Ahmar or Boujad. Typically they are very long and narrow (to fit the dimensions of a tent, or the interior of a kasbah), and dominated by fields of madder red and purple with an almost abstract use of geometric designs floating in and out of scale with each other. By way of a contrast those carpets and *hanbels* (similar to killims) produced by Berber tribes such as the Glaoui of the High Atlas and the Aït-Ouaouizarht of the Jbel Siroua region are set against a predominately black and white background with details worked in gold, yellow, red and blue. They are both more ordered and more colourful, though once again they use an entirely geometric repertoire of patterns. The figurative shapes—those brightly coloured strip pictograms so beloved of the bazaars—are not indigenous to Morocco, even though their influence was already apparent in the 19th century. They come instead from southern Tunisia, and in particular the Gafsa region.

The collection concludes with some ornate and sometimes beautiful pieces of local **carved cedar**—heavy dark doors, the delightful doors within painted Moorish gates, turned window frames and screens, among them some 16th-century Saadian work recovered from El Badia.

Maison Tiskiwin (Bert Flint Museum)

Open 8.30–1; adm; if you turn up on Saturday at noon you might be lucky enough to get a personal tour from the proprietor, otherwise you will be left to the tender mercies of his bored housekeeper.

The entrance to this private museum, on 8 Rue de la Bahia, is reasonably easy to miss—overshadowed by the group of three neighbouring bazaars. It houses another collection of Moroccan decorative art, put together by the Dutch anthropologist Bert Flint during three decades of field work in Morocco. The house, ranged around a traditional Moorish courtyard, is itself reason enough for a visit, and the exhibits offer an overview of the traditional material culture of Morocco. Unless you are already familiar with the material, or Moroccan museums, you might find the labelling rather sketchy. The highlight of the collection is the Zemmour room, with its dense collection of Middle Atlas weaving on floor and walls forming a bit of textile heaven for the nomad-dreaming but urban-bound visitor. The vivid patterns on the leatherwork he has collected from around the various Sahara regions are enough to fuel a sketchbook with dozens of derivative designs. The exit from the museum rooms goes through the kitchen courtyard with its orange tree, and you are meant to pass quickly through the private rooms, which are, however, equally intriguing. You might have to pinch yourself to prevent the feeling of having strayed into a design-magazine article as you take in the faultless blending of traditional High Atlas weaving and bold modern carpets.

A Tour of the Ramparts

The pisé walls of Marrakesh respond with a dazzling range of colours to different degrees of light. They glow with changing hues of pink, ochre, gold and brown against the startling backdrop of High Atlas peaks and clear blue sky. Stretches of the walls wind through a wilderness of dusty graves; elsewhere they are overhung by rustling palms or interrupted by frantic streams of traffic. Elsewhere again they are found decorated with drying skins, sheltering a souk or a passing flock, or enclosing the processional court of the palace of a king. The walls are a shifting pattern of colour and life, at once both monotonously extensive and the city's richest aesthetic treat.

Alarmed by the growing Almohad threat from Tin-Mal, the Almoravid Sultan Ali ben Youssef decided to protect Marrakesh with walls in 1126. He asked his generals for tactical advice and consulted his astrologers for an auspicious date to start work on them. Within a year a 10km circuit of 9m-high walls, defended by 200 towers and pierced by 20 gates, had been built. This has been constantly repaired and occasionally expanded but still substantially follows the 12th-century plan.

A 16km walk around the city walls of Marrakesh would be arduous at any time of the year. Ideally you should travel by horse-drawn cab. The trip can be broken at Bab el Khemis for the souk, and Bab Debbarh, for a look at the tanneries, but the rest of the gates are likely to be of only passing interest. A circuit of the walls would ideally end with a leisurely afternoon picnic in the Ménara or Aguedal Gardens.

Leave from the Jemaa el Fna, where horse-drawn cabs, taxis and bicycles are easy to find, and take the Av Mohammed V, passing the town hall on your right and the orange-tree-shaded park of Moulay Hassan opposite. Crossing through the line of the city walls at the Bab Nkob breach, follow the walls round to the right, passing the double crenellated towers of the Bab Larissa in the corner to approach the Bab Doukkala.

Bab Doukkala

The massive but unequal towers of this Almoravid gate are now isolated to the left of the modern entrance to the medina. If the doors are open, go in to examine its dark, twisting defensive passages. The gates guarded the road to Doukkala, the fertile coastal region between El-Jadida and Safi inhabited by Arabic-speaking Berber tribes who were considered to be among the more loyal and dependable subjects of the sultan. Just within the gate, to the right, are the impressive modern green-tiled law courts.

The area outside the gates, despite being used by a busy and modern bus station and passing fairs, retains a melancholy air. To the south of the bus station is the cemetery and **koubba of Sidi Bennour**, which belonged to the El Hara, the old leper colony.

Pass two small gates, Bab Boutouil and Bab Moussoufa, to reach the **palm grove of Sidi Bel Abbès**. Inside the walls here is the zaouia of Sidi Bel Abbès; despite the fact that he was the venerated patron saint of Marrakesh, his zaouia was in a suburb outside the city until the walls were extended in the 18th century.

Souk and Bab el Khemis

The northern end of the medina has spilled beyond the walls around the Souk el Khemis, the Thursday market. Fruit and vegetables are sold throughout the week here, though livestock trading is still concentrated on Thursdays.

From the souk enclosure a road passes between the cemetery of Sidi Ahmed Ez Zaouia and a lunar landscape of baked mud and refuse to approach the old Almoravid Fez gate which when rebuilt became known as Bab el Khemis. Just before the gate, on the left is the **koubba of Sidi el Barbouchi**, the saint of the slippers, and straight through the gate within the walls is the **zaouia of the Derkaoua Sufi brotherhood**. The road to the left leads to a series of yards where scrap, broken machinery and bruised food are traded by the most impoverished on the grounds of the old Christian cemetery. It is a powerful, disturbing place, threatening only through its misery. It was at the centre of an insurrection in January 1904. A revolutionary mob led by the cobblers' guild marched under black flags to the cemetery and there exhumed the graves of Christian missionaries. The skulls were impaled to serve as standards that led the mob in its assault on the money-lenders in the *mellah*, the merchants in the souk and the kasbah of the pasha.

Return outside the city walls, then follow the road south beside a magnificent stretch of wall and an extensive cemetery through which snakes the dry bank of the river Issil. The cemetery is often flecked with the bright colours of drying skins as you approach Bab Debbarh, the tanners' gate.

Bab Debbarh

The entrance to the tanners' quarter is beneath the ancient Almoravid towers of Bab Debbarh, through a twisting three-chambered passage. By one of the gate-towers there is a door to the precarious roof, which, if open, provides the best view over the tanneries. If the gate is closed there will be no difficulty in finding a young guide to give a quick tour of the tannery vats. They are at their busiest and least pungent in the morning.

Continue south, past Bab Rachidia, to reach **Bab Ailen**, a strong portal named after a Berber tribe that inhabited land to the east. In 1130 an Almohad army descended from the High Atlas to besiege the city. They concentrated their assault on this gate, but were driven off by Almoravid cavalry who sallied out from the neighbouring gates. Just within the gate is the minaret and extensive shrine of the **Qadi Ayad Mosque**. This was built by Sultan Moulay Rachid in the 17th century to hold the tomb of Moulay Ali ech Cherif, the holy ancestor of the Alaouite dynasty. Two later sultans, Moulay Sliman (1792–1822) and Mohammed IV (1859–73), chose to be buried here beside him.

The Southern Ramparts

The angle in the southeastern corner of the walls is filled by the enormous **cemetery of Bab Rhemat**. To the east stretches a modern suburb, and a green-tiled koubba peeks over the houses to your right. This shrine covers the grave of a 12th-century saint, Sidi Youssef ben Ali, who is remembered for his great piety—he continued to praise and thank God even for the gift of leprosy that killed him. The twin towers of the **Bab Rhemat/Aghmat** were betrayed by a Christian regiment in the service of the Almoravid sultans, who opened the gate to the Almohads in 1147. If you pass under the gate here and continue a kilometre into the medina along Rue Ba Ahmad you can see the exterior of the **zaouia of Sidi ben Salah**, its carved minaret inset with green tiles rising above a jumble of roofs, arches, passages and gates. This complex was built in the 14th century by the Merenid Sultan Abou Said Othman.

Continuing outside the city walls, pass beside the cemetery wall to reach the **Bab Ahmar**, which was rebuilt by Sultan Sidi Mohammed in the 18th century. The gate was reserved for the use of the sultan on the feast of Mouloud. The area inside the gates used to house the barracks of the Bouakher regiment of black soldiers, who had a religious cult based around a jujube tree that grew from the gate. To the south, 3km of walls enclose the Aguedal, the private gardens of the sultan.

Pass through the Bab Ahmar to enter a number of processional squares or *méchouars* to the south of the royal palace. From **Méchouar Barastani** pass through 'the gate of the winds', the Bab er Rih, to go into the smaller **Méchouar el Ouastani**. In the south-western corner a double wall allows private communication between the palace and the Aguedal. The Bab El Arhdar, just before this on the left, may be left open for the use of the public. Beyond is the great **Méchouar des Alaouites**. The **pavilion of Essaouira** in the middle of the southern wall and an artillery magazine in the corner were both built by Sidi Mohammed in the 18th century. The pavilion was used for diplomatic receptions, parades and for reviewing *Fantasia* displays. Pass out through the city walls at **Bab Irhli** and turn left.

The **koubba of Sidi Amara** is just south of here, on the right, and 800m farther on is the **Sqallet el Mrabit**. This elegant ramped fortress was built by Sidi Mohammed in the 18th century to house a mobile squadron from the 600-strong regiment of cavalry he kept permanently posted to defend against the Rehamna tribe. Beyond it you can see the white mihrab of the **msalla**, an open-air mosque used during religious festivals.

Just north of Bab Irhli, the **Bab Ksiba** leads to the Derb Chtouka district, once the site of an Almohad fortress. In the 19th century this was still a government kasbah, occupied by the Mokhazines who guarded the sultan's prison.

From Bab er Rob to Bab Sidi Rharib

After extending the city to the south in the 12th century, the Almohads were left with a potentially vulnerable angle in the southwestern wall, which they protected by building the **Bab er Rob**. *Grands taxis* collect up passengers and local buses stop here. There is a souk for cheap pottery and fruit extending around the gate, which is named after raisin juice, perhaps a memory of an old dried-fruit market or a morbid reference to the executed heads that in former times were displayed from the battlements. Just inside the Bab er Rob is the most elegant gate in Marrakesh, the **Bab Agnaou**. This carved stone arch once led from the medina to the Imperial City.

To the west of the Bab er Rob the walls are hidden by the **cemetery of Sidi es Soheili**, another of the seven saints of Marrakesh, whose koubba is beside the cemetery gate, Bab ech Charia. After a detour around the outside of the cemetery you will eventually reach the long wall that contains the garden of the Mamounia Hotel, the entrance of which is just inside the next gate, the Bab Jdid. North of this gate is the **Bab Makhzen**, which used to form a direct entrance to the 12th-century Almoravid kasbah and today is still reserved for the use of the king. This is no inconvenience, as the **Bab Sidi Rharib**, just 200m north, will lead you just as directly back to Av Mohammed V, with the main streets of the New Town to the left and the Jemaa el Fna and the medina to the right.

The Gardens of Marrakesh

The gardens of Marrakesh are often packed with locals and visitors alike, but do not let this discourage you: there is no better way of sheltering from the afternoon heat than by picnicking in the Aguedal or the Ménara gardens. The main market on Av Mohammed V in the New Town sells everything you need: wicker baskets, wine, cheese, fresh bread, pâté and a bewildering selection of olives, nuts and fresh fruit.

The Aguedal Gardens

Open periodically especially weekends, but often closed if the Royal Palace is occupied.

Pass down the dirt track through the orchards to the 200m-square main tank, the Sahraj el Hana, or 'pool of health', next to the pavilion of **Dar el Hana**. You can still enjoy its tranquil rooftop view south to the Atlas peaks, or join the knots of Moroccan families picnicking under the shade of the surrounding trees. On the far side the ruins of a gunpowder factory are being turned into a waterfront palace. From the roof of the Dar el Hana you might have witnessed the death in 1873 of the Sultan Mohammed IV, who drowned while boating with his son on the tank. A forlorn, almost wistful, acceptance of fate is beautifully expressed in the official epitaph: 'He departed this life, in a water tank, in the expectation of something better to come.'

He was not the only sultan to die in the Aguedal Gardens. On 9 April 1672, after the feast of Aid el Kebir, Sultan Moulay Rachid took out a spirited horse to gallop away his ennui through the orange groves of the Aguedal. In the morning, the court poets sang, 'The tree's branch did not break the skull of our imam out of cruelty; nor from ingratitude, unmindful of the duties of friendship. It was out of jealousy of his slender figure, for envy is to be found even among trees.'

These gardens were established in the 12th century by the Almohad Sultan Abdel Moumen. Two enormous tanks were built and filled by pipes that tapped the Ourika stream. By the 18th century, however, the walls had decayed, the water had been diverted and tribesmen grazed the orchards. The present garden is the creation of Sultan Abder Rahman (1822–59), who reclaimed the water rights and rebuilt the walls, although his successors still had to keep a constant guard against tribesmen, especially the nomadic Rehamna, who enjoyed nothing more than raiding the sultan's garden.

In the 19th century a succession of pavilions was built in the gardens, most notably the **Dar el Beïda** provided for the harem of Moulay Hassan. However, the garden's primary purpose was always to be an efficient and very profitable private agricultural estate. Two visitors from Kew who saw it in 1840 estimated that its 40 acres gave the sultan produce worth at least £20,000 each year.

The Ménara Gardens

Orchards open daily; free. Royal Pavilion entrance by admission ticket.

The Ménara Gardens are 2km west of Bab Jdid. It is an agricultural estate of irrigated olive orchards and gardens that have been planted around a massive water tank. Like the one in the Aguedal Gardens, the tank was built by the Almohads in the 12th century, but what you now see was established in the 19th century by the Alaouites. Mohammed IV replaced the outer walls, refurbished the tank and built the green-tiled pavilion in 1869 to replace a ruined Saadian one. There is a a wonderful, tranquil view over the great expanse of water from its open, balconied first floor, where the royal party would picnic whilst musicians played out of sight on the ground floor. Walk around the tank to catch the celebrated view of the pavilion set against the High Atlas mountains and reflected in the waters. Stop for a sandwich at the café or just to buy bread to feed the enormous carp, which will churn up a small frenzy of turbulent water with their gaping wide mouths as they descend on leftovers.

The Majorelle Garden

Open summer daily 8–12 and 3–7; winter daily 8–12 and 2–5; adm.

The Majorelle is a privately owned botanical garden off a side street in the New Town, north-west of the medina opposite the wholesale market on Av Yaacoub el Mansour. It was created by two generations of French artists, Jacques and Louis Majorelle, and is now owned by the couturier Yves Saint-Laurent (who was born in Algeria). It is an immaculately manicured walled garden full of pavilions, paths and rills painted a bright Mediterranean blue. The admirably lush botanical collection is especially strong in cacti. The Majorelles' old studio has been turned into a small museum (*separate adm; closed Mon*), which displays the present owner's idiosyncratic collection of Maghrebi decorative art: carpets, ceramics, textiles, woodwork and jewellery, as well as a gallery filled with some of the Majorelles' original canvases.

The Mamounia Garden

This lush formal garden with its central pavilion was established in the 18th century by Pasha Mamoun, governor of Fez, and was later bequeathed to the sultan. It then served as the crown prince's residence, and was occasionally lent to visiting diplomats, until the era of French rule when it was turned into a luxury hotel (*see* p.120). The hotel's charm was drastically reduced by its 1986 renovation, and somewhere in its marble halls there should be installed a constant video of the old interior as preserved in Hitchcock's 1956 film *The Man Who Knew Too Much*. The 300m sweeping wall of bougainvillea and the quiet, undisturbed half-dozen regular plots of olive and palm trees are supposedly reserved for residents. Ignore this restriction, though it is as well to dress up a bit and buy a cup of coffee on the terrace.

The Palm Grove (La Palmeraie)

Follow the Fez road east for a kilometre past the Bab el Khemis, then take a signposted left turn for an 8km drive through the palm grove to the north of the city. The Almoravids are credited with planting this grove, but palms in Marrakesh are useful only for wood, shade and desert imagery, for they are too far north ever to bear fruit. Olives or oranges would be a more useful crop, and the palm grove has a deserved aura of neglect. The pisé walls, fragments of irrigation systems and barren palms might be entertaining if it weren't being turned into a smart suburb of villas, time-share holiday homes and hotels.

The New Town, the French-built city of neat avenues and apartment blocks to the west of the old walled city, is known as Guéliz. The name derives from a local corruption of '*église*', for the **Catholic Church of St Martyrs** was the most remarkable building throughout the 1920s and 30s. Arguably this is still true today, with its cool, spacious interior lit by a clerestory of yellow and red glass to flood the basilica with warm light. It is dedicated to the five early Franciscans who travelled from Italy to Muslim Seville and then on to their martyrdom in 1219. Fortunately the priest and the imam of the mosque (both on Rue Imam Ali) now maintain an excellent relationship. The **Hivernage**, a garden suburb of hotels and villas, stands immediately west of Bab Jdid and Bab Makhzen. The mature gardens of the inter-linked Hotel es Saadi and the Casino make for a pleasant, tranquil stroll, particularly when combined with a drink beside the hotel pool or the piano bar.

There are also some recent buildings in the New Town that toy with the New Carthage style, a fusion of traditional Moorish and Saharan styles spiked with the odd detail from Egypt and Tunisia, that might be of interest. In particular, look for the recent work of the Tunisian-born French architect Charles Bocarra, responsible for the design of the much talked-about Tichka Hôtel (*see* 'luxury' under 'Where to Stay') and the opulent Les Deux Tours villa in the Palm Grove (*see* 'The Gardens of Marrakesh' earlier), as well as the great mass of the Marrakesh Opera, which now dominates the junction of Av de France and Av Hassan II, near the railway station.

Marrakesh ✆ (04–)   **Where to Stay**

Wherever you wish to stay in Marrakesh, book early, or at the very least start your quest for a room early in the day. The essence of the city for a visitor is firmly around the Jemaa el Fna, the bustling square that stands in the centre of the medina. All the cheaper hotels are found here, and many of these, such as the **Gallia**, can hardly be bettered. If you want to go slightly upmarket and have the addition of bars and restaurants, there are three good places still within the walls of the old town: the **Islane**, the faded **De Foucauld** and the **Tazi**. In summer you may find that a hotel with a pool and a garden for sunbathing is more important than a view (and the surrounding noise and diesel fumes) of the Jemaa el Fna. In that case there are four hotels, the **Imilchil**, **Yasmine**, **Lalla Hasna** and **Ibis Moussafir**, in the New Town that are small enough to have both some character and a pool. In the world of luxury hotels, the choice is between the well-decorated but out-of-town **Tichka**, the calm unpretentious atmosphere of the **Es Saâdi**, or the world-renowned glamour of the **Mamounia**.

luxury

The **Mamounia**, on the edge of the medina along Av Bab Jedid, ✆ 44 89 81, ✉ 44 46 60, is an old palace (*see* 'The Gardens of Marrakesh' earlier) which was converted into a fabulously elegant hotel in the colonial period. It was Winston Churchill's favourite haunt, and his suite is preserved with his books, bed and photographs of him painting in the garden. It remains a supremely elegant and distinguished hotel. It cannot be intimate, with 200 bedrooms, but the choice of bars, terraces and restaurants scatters the guests around in their own chosen corners. Topless blondes dominate the poolside, and you are forced into a tie in the dining room, but the garden, its position in the city and its cooking remain superb. Off-the-street prices start at around $230 for a double room, though it is possible to pay much less by booking through an agency, or much more by taking your own suite or villa in the garden. It offers a whole alternative world, with its four bars, four restaurants, eight boutiques, a good bookshop and casino.

The **Es Saâdi Hôtel**, on Av El Quadissa, ✆ 44 88 11, ✉ 44 76 44, occupies the heart of the Hivernage quarter of the New Town. It has half as many rooms as the Mamounia, and is about half the price. The courteous service makes the Es Saâdi exceptional, and wins devoted customers back year after year.

The **Tichka Hôtel**, ✆ 44 87 10, has a structure by Charles Bocarra and an interior designed by the American Marrakeshi socialite Bill Willis; these have given it an undeniable cachet. It is popular with the media, and you may well see a passing film crew, a fashion shoot or two, and a handful of 'ideas-brokers' working their mobile phones poolside. Meals are served at the well-dressed tables beside the pool. There are fires in the sitting room off the lovely entrance hallway in the winter, a *hammam* in the basement and a Moroccan restaurant. It is situated in Semlalia, the uninteresting far northern edge of the New Town. To find it take the road for Casablanca, and watch out for a clutch of hotel signposts on the right.

Just as we are going to press, the **Hotel Amanjena**, ✆ 40 33 53, ✉ 40 34 77, *www.amanjena.com*, has opened 7km outside Marrakesh, designed in the style of a traditional Moroccan palace, with 40 luxurious one-, two- and three-bedroom pavilions. The staff are discreet and multilingual, and the only drawback seems to be the presence of an 18-hole golf course that backs on to the hotel. Needless to say, don't even think about staying there if you're on a budget.

luxury (in the medina)

There have always been a number of elegant old courtyard houses in the medina which have taken in guests. Their address is kept a secret, exchanged like a favour between friends. Fortunately the identity of two such new hotels can be given without breaking any confidences. Guests are met at the airport or train station, so there is no need to reveal their exact location.

La Maison Arabe, just west of the Bab Doukkala mosque, is an oasis of calm, a delightfully intimate old town house with just a dozen rooms. Apart from breakfast, guests eat out or simply take tea or drinks in the courtyard. Guests may use the pools of two luxury hotels, and dine locally at the nearby Pavilion restaurant. Ring Nabila Dakir, the elegant multilingual manageress, ✆ 39 12 33, ✉ 44 37 15.

Riad Enja is the most elegant hotel in Morocco, perhaps the world, the vast mansion of the Jelloun family, restored to its days of 18th-century glory by a Swiss designer and a Swedish architect. The rooms are operatic in scale and furnishing, enriched with Marrakeshi silk throws, Quantamaine textiles and a daily scattering of rose petals. Gilt glasses and plates transform meals into feasts, presided over by the charismatic hostess. Tucked away to the east of the souk, it isn't easily accessible by foot, let alone by car, and it's not suitable if you want a TV or mini-bar—but it's perfect for the well-heeled shopper. Reservations should be made with Ursula Haldimann, ✆ 44 09 26, ✉ 44 27 00.

expensive

Just west of the Koutoubia Mosque off Av Houmman el Fétouaki, and almost opposite the Mamounia, is the well-positioned but inconspicuous **Chems Hôtel**, ✆ 44 48 13, a functional motel-like place with its own car park, pool, bar and small garden. The similar **Les Almoravides**, on Av Mohammed V at Arset Djenan Lakhdar, ✆ 44 51 42, is also within the walled old town, north of the Ensemble Artisanal. The large **Hotel Marrakesh**, ✆ 43 43 51, ✉ 43 49 80, has a central position on Av Mohammed V (on the northern corner of Place de la Liberté), and its smart row of boutiques breathes a bit of town life into the place.

The much praised **Semiramis**, ✆ 43 13 77, ✉ 44 71 27, is out in the Semlalia quarter on the far edge of the New Town, beside the Tichka Hôtel. Its standards of calm efficiency have made it a favourite stop-over for airline crews.

Imperial Borj, ✆ 44 73 22, ✉ 44 62 06, is well placed in the Hivernage quarter. No marks for architecture, but this massive chunk of marble-veneered concrete is run with aplomb. There is a popular buffet in the dining room beside the pool, while some of the rooms face out to the Koutoubia Mosque.

Mansour Eddahbi, ✆ 44 80 43, ✉ 44 90 82, stands on the wide and elegant Av de France. The Mansour, with 450 bedrooms, is the largest and grandest of the hotels in this category and offers the most extensive facilities.

moderate

In the New Town, just west of the ramparts and south of Av Mohammed V, is the comfortable **Le Grand Imilchil**, ✆ 44 76 53, ✉ 44 61 65 (front door on Av Ech Chouada), with a pool, bar, restaurant, a small garden and 90 bedrooms, all with their own bathrooms. Nearby, but dropping a notch in price, there is the **Yasmine**, ✆ 44 61 42, which is also just outside the walls at the meeting of Rue Boualaka and Av des Remparts, and also has a pool. It is usually a quiet place and has a bar and restaurant. The **Ibis Moussafir**, ✆ 43 59 29/✆ 43 59 35, ✉ 43 59 36, just alongside the railway station on Av Hassan II, has a bar, restaurant, small pool and modern bedrooms at an affordable price. Although it is on the western edge of the New Town, there is never a shortage of taxis, which gather in the station forecourt. The privately owned **Lalla Hasna**, 247 Av Mohammed V, ✆ 44 99 72, ✉ 44 99 94, right in the centre of the New Town (named after the proprietor's daughter), has a café, two restaurants, a small but welcome pool and briskly clean bedrooms.

La Maison Alexandre-Bonnel, 4 Rue Derb Sania, off Rue Sidi el Yamani (west of the souks), © 42 98 33, or mobile © (01) 46 15 08, in the heart of the medina, is a small traditional house that has been fully modernized and has a roof terrace. Bed and breakfast is offered in their home by the Herculean-sized Christophe and his English-speaking wife. It is ideal for self-contained couples or a family taking over all three rooms.

inexpensive (and dead central)

The **Hôtel Gallia**, 30 Rue de la Recette, © 44 59 13, ✐ 44 48 53, on a turning off Rue de Bab Agnaou due south from the Jemaa el Fna, is a discreet, calm, functional but very friendly hotel with resident turtles and 20 rooms arranged around two internal courtyards. Book at least two weeks in advance. **Hotel Sherezade**, 3 Derb-Djaina Riad Zitoun-el-Kedim, ©/✐ 42 93 05, on a turning to the left of Rue Riad ez Zitoun el Kedim, is a 16-room hotel, around a courtyard, with a fine view from the rooftop terrace. Some rooms have showers. The **Hôtel de Foucauld**, on Av El Mouahidine, © 44 54 99, ✐ 44 13 44, overlooks the triangular wooded park just west of the Jemaa el Fna. It has a pleasantly faded neo-Moorish interior, hip baths, a licensed restaurant, and an English-speaking manageress, Maria, who also rents out bicycles. It might be considered a bit worn to Californians, but by English reckoning it is well above B&B standards. The **Islane**, 279 Av Mohammed V, © 44 00 83, ✐ 44 00 85, stands within the medina walls, just outside the hassle area of the Jemaa el Fna, almost directly opposite the Koutoubia Mosque. It has a licensed restaurant on its rooftop (no bar service without food), a popular local café on the street, and 23 well-appointed bedrooms. Noisy but dead central. The **Grand Hôtel Tazi**, © 44 24 52/© 44 21 52, in the southern end of the medina on the corner of Rue de Bab Agnaou and Av Houmman el Fétouaki, has 60 comfortable rooms, a restaurant, a pool and an invaluable roof-terrace bar. Though clean, it's not in the first flush of youth. The less characterful **Hôtel Minaret**, 10 Rue Dispensaire, is just behind.

cheap

All of the six hotels listed below are characterful, safe and well-established places that overlook, or are within a stone's throw of, the Jemaa el Fna. The **Hôtel Ali**, on Rue Moulay Ismaïl, © 44 979, ✐ 43 36 09, on the street that runs beside the triangular garden square west of the Jemaa el Fna, is a popular backpackers' choice and has a busy central courtyard café-restaurant. The rooms are scrupulously clean, although they can be a bit stuffy, and the international trekking clientele can be a bit earnest. The **CTM**, © 44 23 25, in a superb position next to a café on the southern side of the Jemaa el Fna, has a balconied roof terrace which overlooks the square, and a cool internal upstairs courtyard around which are the large comfortable bedrooms. Breakfast is served on the terrace, the maids Brika and Fatima take in washing, and there is a secure lock-up garage in the old bus station next door. The **Oukmaiden**, © 44 10 38, has a fine position overlooking the northern side of Jemaa el Fna. Like the CTM, it is one of the first budget hotels to get filled up.

Along or just off the Rue Riad ez Zitoun el Kedim (facing the CTM on the southern side of Jemaa el Fna, this narrow arched alley is to your left) there are three good places to check out: at no.197 there is the popular and friendly **Hôtel de France**, ✆ 44 30 76; and about 30m farther down the street a right turn leads you to two of the best cheap places in town: the family-run, hospitable and much praised **Hotel Medina**, 1 Derb Sidi Bouloukat, ✆ 44 29 27, and its almost-as-popular neighbour, the **Essaouira**, at no.3, ✆ 44 38 05.

camping

The **Camping Municipal**, ✆ 43 17 07, is on Av de France in the New Town. It is an unappealing site part-shaded by eucalyptus, with a café-restaurant and desultory pool patrolled by the more desperate hustlers. It's much better to try a cheap hotel.

Marrakesh ✆ *(04–)*   **Eating Out**

In this city you can dine lavishly in magnificent surroundings, and eat cheap fresh local food in one of the world's great public spaces, but you can also just as easily be served a succession of dull, overpriced meals. It is a city that has been living off tourism for generations, and has developed a large range and variety of restaurants. All will be well if you go for extremes: eating either very cheaply or the very best you can afford.

expensive (banquet restaurants in the medina)

It is essential to book in advance for dinner in any of these three sublime restaurants, which combine some of the best traditional cooking in Morocco with a visual feast of furnishings, textiles and pictures in traditional town houses of an almost dream-like seclusion. For what they offer they are extremely good value (allow $50 a head for an almost embarrassingly opulent evening), but be aware that menus, if offered at all, are only for information or for selecting from the number of courses (anything between three and eight) that the house has prepared for all its guests that night. If you have the capacity for it, or have starved yourself beforehand, try them all.

Dar Yacout (La Maison de Saphir), 79 Sidi Ahmed Souissi, ✆ 31 01 04, is a well-established restaurant, founded by the American Charlie Munroe, but now presided over by Mohammed Skhiri, the honorary Moroccan-British consul. It is hidden away down a dark street off the Rue el Gza (250m north of the Bab Doukkala, within the old walls): for your first visit you should take a taxi, which will be met at the end of the street by a lantern-bearing watchman. Hold your breath as the magical interiors get revealed, enriched by the hand of Billy Willis, the uncrowned king of expatriate Marrakesh society. At the end of the evening, coffee is served on a terrace that provides a serene view over the surrounding streets.

At **Dar M'jenna** (also spelt Marjana, or known as La Maison), 15 Derb Sidi Ali Tair, ✆ 44 57 73, the master of the house, Chaaouqui, presides over aperitifs in the courtyard before you get so much as a whiff of the lavish feast of a meal that is served in the high, narrow old dining room, with a continuous supply of wine all included in the price. **Ksar Essaoussan**, 3 Derb Chorfa El Messaoudyenne, © 44 06 32, is off the Rue des Ksours alley, which is found by going through an archway off the Rue Fatima Zohra (from the Islane hotel-café, turn left along Av Mohammed V, then first left on to Rue Fatima Zohra for 250m, with the arch appearing on your right at a road junction, after which the way is signposted). While not the least lavish, it is the quietest and smallest of the three, established as a way of working retirement by Parisian chef Jean-Laurent Graulhet. Before dinner visitors are usually welcome to make a tour of the house, which retains many of its original 17th-century details. *Closed Sun.* An honourable choice if the others are booked up is a near neighbour of the Ksar Essaoussan, the **Stylia**, 34 Rue Ksour, © 44 35 87, which remains stylish and very good.

expensive (lunch in the medina)

If at lunchtime you are looking for good traditional Moroccan cooking in an elegantly appointed restaurant with a drinks licence, there are three good addresses that spring to mind. They are also open in the evening.

The **Relais Al Baraka**, © 44 23 41, is tucked in the northwestern corner of the Jemaa el Fna, beside the offices of the Commissariat de Police. You can dine from three extensive menus, in the tranquil fountain court or in the two dining-room pavilions that flank it. **Le Restaurant Marrakeshi**, 52 Rue Banques, © 44 33 77, has a good kitchen and an extensive menu, and is large and easy to find on the northeastern corner of the Jemaa el Fna. It also has the essential midday asset of a roof terrace overlooking the street life in the square. If you are in the southern half of the medina, the **Douriya** Moroccan restaurant, 14 Derb Jedid Hay Essalame, © 40 30 30, is perfectly placed just north of Place des Ferblantiers off Av Houmman el Fétouaki. Ask for a table in one of the three private rooms off the upper terrace to avoid the noise of the ground floor.

expensive (dinner)

If you are hoping to mingle with the *haute monde de Marrakesh* in the evening, start with cocktails at the Mamounia and then head for either of the following four restaurants. Book a table in order to avoid disappointment. The **Villa Rossa**, 64 Av Hassan II, © 43 08 32, on the northern side of the avenue between Rue de Yougoslavie and Rue Mohammed Beqal, is a well-established meeting ground with an Italian fish-based menu, plus an associated boutique and jazz bar. *Closed lunchtime.* The equally highly regarded **La Trattoria**, 179 Rue Mohammed Beqal, © 43 26 41, in the New Town, is also an Italian restaurant, decorated by Bill Willis and under the direction of Giancarlo. *Closed Mon.* The third, **Le Pavilion**, 47 Derb Zaouia, © 39 12 40, @ 44 37 15, in the medina, is in a traditional court-yard house in a little dead-end by the Bab Doukkala mosque, easily accessible by taxi. Although the setting is archetypally Moroccan, the menu is determinedly French, in deference to locals escaping from couscous and *tagine*. *Closed lunchtime and Tues.* **La Rotonda**, 19 Derb Lamnabha, © 44 00 98, is perhaps the most stylish and certainly the most expensive of the four, situated beyond the

Saadian Tombs, off Rue de la Kasbah. The first floor of this old courtier's palace is occupied by a Moroccan restaurant, the second by an Italian restaurant with a bar—and a magnificent view— on the roof terrace. *Closed lunchtime.*

moderate (in the medina)

The **Pizzeria Venetia**, 279 Av Mohammed V, ✆ 44 00 81, is the roof-top restaurant of the Islane Hotel. It looks directly out at the Koutoubia Mosque and has a number of classic Moroccan dishes on its menu as well as pizzas and the familiar Italian standards. The restaurant at the **Hôtel de Foucauld**, on Av El Mouahidine, ✆ 44 54 99, offers a filling five-course set meal at reasonable prices, as well as a mixed Moroccan-French and Italian menu (and has a drinks licence). The cooking is sound if uninspired, but you get to eat and drink in a high-ceilinged Moorish dining room with a fine old whirring fan, and the almost-as-elderly waiters have great gravitas. The **Grand Hôtel Tazi**, on Rue de Bab Agnaou, ✆ 44 24 52, is slightly further down the culinary pecking order, but the terraced bar tends to stay open longer. It is the sort of place where you order a *salade niçoise* to keep your wine company.

moderate (in the New Town)

Restaurant El Fassia, 232 Av Mohammed V, ✆ 43 40 60, stands aside from the norm for restaurants anywhere in Morocco. It is an exceptional place, run by a staff of women who have achieved the rare balance of a committed approach to Moroccan cooking without degenerating into an orientalist feast. Here you can order single dishes, not whole meals, from a well-thought-out menu in a modern Islamic-style interior.

Safran et Cannelle, 40 Av Hassan II, ✆ 43 59 69, ✆ 43 42 74, just farther along from Villa Rossa, is a new addition—a small Moroccan restaurant on the ground floor of a New Town apartment block. **Le Jardin**, on Rue Oum Rabia, one block west of Place de la Liberté, ✆ 43 38 39, is a small and convivial restaurant locally celebrated for its crêpes and grilled meats, eaten on wooden plates. Despite its name it has no garden, but meals are served in summer on a sun-dappled terrace.

Restaurant Le Jacaranda, 32 Blvd Mohammed Zerqtouni, ✆ 44 72 15, at the northern end of the New Town opposite the strategic tables of the Brasserie des Negociants on the busy Place Abdel Moumen ben Ali, has a fire in winter, air-conditioning in summer and a French menu that takes full advantage of the fish and shellfish available from the coast. *Closed Tues and Wed lunch.* The **Café de la Paix**, 68 Rue de Yougoslavie, ✆ 43 31 18, is an attractive café, with a mixed French and Moroccan menu and tables placed outside in a shady garden, filled with the noise of a tinkling fountain. The cooking is not inspired, but it's a perfect place for a cold beer and a light, reasonably priced lunch of cheese omelette followed by a *tagine* and finished off with ice cream.

The **Bagatelle**, 101 Rue de Yougoslavie, ✆ 43 02 74, nearby, is a surviving relic from the colonial period, a calm and distinguished place with admirably poised waiters and an almost exclusively local clientele. It is an excellent venue for a long, slow lunch, starting with a bottle of chilled rosé and finishing with the house's renowned chocolate mousse. *Closed Wed and Sept.* **L'Entrecôte**, 55 Blvd Zerqtouni, © 44 94 28, is another Franco-Maroc corner of Marrakesh. This briskly efficient steak house, run by Isabelle and Gilles, also has Italian and fish dishes on the menu. *Closed Sun.* Dropping a notch in price and style, **Le Petit Poucet**, 56 Av Mohammed V, © 43 11 88, on the corner of Rue Mohammed el Bequal, is another survivor from the colonial era.

cheap (in the medina)

You will find in the evening that food can hardly taste more exotic than if you eat from the barrow grill-restaurants in the centre of the **Jemaa el Fna**. Wander around first, sniffing out the most extensive and succulent of the restaurants before you succumb to the brilliant multilingual sales chatter and plonk yourself down on a bench. The portions are reasonably small, so you can easily justify trying a broad selection of daily offerings. It may be as well to check prices in advance, though most of the kiosks charge between 20 and 30dh for a meal if you appear to be reasonably in control of your mind.

If you are looking for a slightly more relaxing and longer meal you can use one of the terraced café-restaurants that overlook the northeastern corner of the Jemaa el Fna. The **Café de France** and especially the **Restaurant Argana** are popular places—you may have to wait a bit for a table—that only charge about twice as much as the stalls on the square. Otherwise, try any of the cafés along Rue Bani Marine or Rue de Bab Agnaou (the streets leading south from the Jemaa el Fna), particularly the **Café-Restaurant Oriental**, 33 Rue de Bab Agnaou, or the **Restaurant Etoile de Marrakesh**, which serves dinner until midnight.

At lunchtime, when there are fewer, if any, grill-stalls, you can still eat in the northeastern corner of the Jemaa el Fna. **Chez Chegrouni**, at Nos.4–6, has a terrace that overlooks the *place* where you can eat a nourishing meal of soup, salad, brochettes and sweetened yoghurts. The service is friendly and honest, if a little erratic.

If you find yourself in the southern medina around lunchtime, the rooftop **Café-Restaurant El Badi** (signposted on the street just west of Place des Ferblantiers) is also enthusiastically recommended. Filling three-course Moroccan meals are served almost on the same level as the storks' nests on the neighbouring walls of El Badia.

cheap (in the New Town)

The **Agdal** café-restaurant, 86 Av Mohammed V, stays open from breakfast to dinner, and can fulfil any need for a cheap meal in the New Town. It has a scattering of tables on the pavement.

cafés (in the medina)

Overlooking the Jemaa el Fna, the traditional choice to make is between the battered chairs on the terrace of the **Café de France** or those of the **Café Glacier**, beside the CTM, as your theatre from which to read, play cards, sip drinks, watch life on the square and eavesdrop on other foreigners. A popular alternative is the **Argana Café**, whose sun-shaded first-floor terrace dominates the northwestern corner of the *place* (directly across the square from the post office).

cafés (in the New Town)

In Place Abdul Moumen ben Ali, at the meeting point of Av Mohammed V and Blvd Mohammed Zerqtouni, the cane chairs of the **Café Renaissance** and **Brasserie des Negociants** look across the traffic at each other. The former has a lift up to a rooftop terrace, where non-Muslims can be served drinks and enjoy a view of the sunset. Their new neighbour, the **Café Siroua**, 20 Blvd Mohammed Zerqtouni, ✆ 44 62 26, completes this trinity of places for the *hommes d'affaires*, which includes most of the local estate agents. Another meeting place is the **Boule de Neige**, 30 Rue Yougoslavie, beside the **Pâtisserie Hilton**, which is popular with an elegant coterie of local women. Other local haunts include the **Firdaous Café**, on Av Mohammed V, and the **Café-Pâtisserie Zohor** on Rue de la Liberté, near the covered market. For cakes, **Al Jawda** pâtisserie, 11 Rue de la Liberté, ✆ 43 52 19, is the best in town.

bars

Apart from the restaurants detailed above, the only places for an affordable drink in the medina are the Tazi or De Foucauld hotels. If you are looking for some cocktails to be washed down to the tinkling of a piano, head for **Le Churchill** in the Mamounia Hotel, **Omar Khayoun** in the Pullman Mansour Eddahbi Hotel, **Le Star's House** on Place de la Liberté, or the bar in the Es Saâdi Hôtel. In the New Town there are a large number of bars outside the big hotels, but they are a male preserve and can be unsettling for Western men, let alone women. They chiefly serve half-litre bottles of beer in quick succession. The Prophet Mohammed said that wine is both a great sin and a great advantage to man, but that the sin is greater than the advantage. Hangovers also seem particularly intense in the African sun. The **Haouz** is on Av Hassan II, the **Iceberg** on Av el Mouahadine, **L'Escale** on Rue Mauritania, the **Marché** at 44 Rue de la Liberté, the **Poste** on Rue el Imam Malik, the **Taverne** on Blvd Mohammed Zerqtouni and **Tony Bar** on Rue Abou Bekr Esseddiq.

Marrakesh ✆ (04–)

Shopping and Services
Moroccan crafts

The Marrakesh souk has as extensive a range of Moroccan crafts as anywhere in the country. However, the bazaar merchants are also used to extracting some pretty fabulous sums from rich and careless visitors who have come straight off the aeroplane into this Aladdin's Cave. You may find that you will have to spend even more time and energy than normal bargaining things down to a decent price. Before going into the souk, check out the quality in the Dar Si Saïd and Merehbi museums and at the **Ensemble Artisanal**, on Av Mohammed V inside the medina walls. If all you want to do is quickly gather together a hamper full of gifts, it's easiest to head straight for the covered market on Av Mohammed V in the New Town, which has good displays of reasonably priced fossils, minerals and pieces of Safi pottery in among the trays of dates and fresh fruit.

For antiques, fine craftwork, pictures and old books, together with one or two fine pieces of embroidery and jewellery, have a look at **L'Orientaliste**, 15 Rue de la Liberté, ✆ 43 40 74, in the New Town, run by Madame Amzallag. Her husband Claude Amzallag also runs one of Marrakesh's best leather-goods shops, **Place Vendome**, 141 Av Mohammed V, ✆ 43 52 63 (established 1948). They will make goods to order to your specific requirements. Also in the New Town, you can find an interesting range of traditional and more modern decorative pieces at Isabelle Castagnet's interior-design shop, **Maison d'Été**, 17 Rue de Yougoslavie, ✆ 43 60 61.

In the medina, Mustapha Blaoui at **Trésor des Nomades**, 128 Rue Mouassine, ✆ 44 59 06, has an engaging stock of old doors, battered tables and lamps ancient and modern among a clutter of other decorative pieces.

On the edge of the city on the Safi road there is a factory (Quartier Industriel, Sidi Ghranem, Route de Safi, Guéliz, ✆ 49 25 29) run by two Spanish brothers, **Roberto and Gerardo Ruiz**, who produce striking ironwork tables, chairs, shelves and beds. They also stock ceramics, will add a *zellij* mosaic top to the table of your choice, and can arrange shipment. For a greater discovery there is no replacement to visiting the Souk Haddadine yourself in order to pick out the lanterns of your choice. The best selection is held by **Abdelhakim Abou el Aibada**, 3–5 Rue Semmouine (on the edge of Souk Haddadine), ✆ 44 12 82, mobile ✆ (01) 20 83 03, ✆ 42 72 37, who can also help with air freighting. For the carpets produced by the Arab tribes of the plains have a look at the stock held in **Bazaar Chichoua** (chez Mustafa), 5 Souk des Ksours, ✆ 44 07 13. The other great source is of course the dealers that cluster around the Rahba Kédima.

clothes

One of the great disadvantages of clothes shopping in Marrakesh is that the exquisite embroidery and tailoring is all too often imposed over ugly synthetic cloth. However, the Baroudi brothers understand European needs (and prices); visit their elegant boutique, **Beldi**, 9–11 Souikat Lakeour (first bit of Rue Mouassine from the Jemaa El Fna direction), ✆ 44 10 76.

books and newspapers

There is an English-language bookshop in town, the **American Bookstore**, 3 Impasse du Moulin, off Blvd Mohammed Zerqtouni, but for most purposes the elaborate but not overpriced **kiosk** in front of the Mamounia Hotel has the best selection of books, guides and newspapers. Other bookshops can be found in the lobby of the Tichka Hôtel and the newsagent in the gardens of the Es Saâdi Hôtel. For glossy art books go to the shop in the private Menebhi Museum in the medina. To feed your daily newspaper habit go to the two stands pitched by the covered market on Av Mohammed V, or the even more comprehensive selection by the main post office on the corner of Av Hassan II and Av Mohammed V.

food

In order to assemble a picnic, or stock up on wine, go to the covered market in the heart of the New Town on Av Mohammed V. There are several good grocery shops, which stock local wine and stay open after the market has closed, on the other side of the avenue.

photographs and film

There are three shops selling and processing film in the medina at the Jemaa el Fna end of Rue de Bab Agnaou.

laundry

Most hotels will be happy to do your laundry but, if not, make use of **Blanchisserie du Sud**, 10 Rue de Bab Agnaou, ✆ 44 33 31, in the medina, or the **Oasis**, 44 Rue Tarik Ibn Zaid, ✆ 43 45 78, in the New Town near the covered market.

Marrakesh ✆ *(04–)*   **Sports**

go-karting

There is a go-kart track at the Kart Hotel, about 12km out of the city, ✆ 44 81 63, which has 800m and 1360m tracks (*open daily 9am–midnight*).

golf

Marrakesh has three superb courses: the 1920s **Royal Golf Club**, 6km out on the road to Ouazazite, ✆ 44 43 41/✆ 44 44 03; the 200 acre **La Palmeraie Golf Palace**, ✆ 30 10 10; and the **Amelkis**, the newest and most expensive in Morocco (*see* **Practical A–Z**, p.38).

hammams

There are *hammams* throughout the medina. There are a couple on Rue Riad ez Zitoun el Kedim (southeast of Jemaa el Fna) that are used to accepting Europeans, but the most magnificent interior is undoubtedly at **Hammam Dar el Bacha** on Rue Fatima Zohra (northwest of Square de Foucauld), with both male and female sections. In the New Town the **Hammam Salama** on Blvd de Safi (behind the petrol station near the Majorelle Garden) has been recommended, though the *hammam* in the basement of the **Tichka Hôtel**, ✆ 44 87 10, wins an even more loyal following as it employs one of the city's most skilful masseurs.

hill walking and mountain climbing

Marrakesh is superbly located as an initial base for a walking holiday. Hill walkers can easily drive out in the morning to explore the lower valleys of the High Atlas passes or the Central High Atlas.

riding

The **Royal Club Equestre** is 4km out of town on the Asni road, ✆ 44 85 29. There are two riding schools just outside the city: **Club de l'Atlas**, ✆ 43 13 01, near the Ménara Gardens, and **Club Equipitage**, ✆ 44 85 29. There is also a polo club, ✆ 43 53 83, with a pitch about 4km out of town along the Béni-Mellal road. The Résidence La Roseraie at **Ouirgane** (a third of the way along the Tizi-n-Test pass into the High Atlas, *see* p.136) has a superb stable of Arab thoroughbreds which can be taken out for anything from a half-day to a week's camping in the hills.

skiing

This is possible but not predictable at Jbel Oukaïmeden in the High Atlas (*see* pp.142–3) any time from November to March.

swimming

You could save up your swimming energy for battling the Atlantic surf at the beach of Essaouira, just a few hours away to the west. There is a popular **municipal pool** in the Moulay Abdessalam Garden, entered from Rue Abou el Abbes Sebti opposite the Ensemble Artisanal on Av Mohammed V. There is a small admission charge for this pool, and it's full of exuberant hordes of adolescent Marrakeshi boys—which could be either a personal heaven or purgatory. For more tourists and tranquillity you can also buy a day ticket and use the small pool at the **Grand Hôtel Tazi** in the medina.

tennis

Aside from the three dozen or so courts and professional instructors found in the grounds of almost all the four- and five-star hotels, there is the **Royal Tennis Club**, ✆ 43 19 02, at Jnane El Harti, off Rue Oued el Makhazine.

Cultural Centres

The **French Cultural Centre** (*open Tues–Sun 8.30–12 and 2.30–6*) is on Rue de la Targa. It runs a garden-café and a library, and arranges a full schedule of films, lectures and exhibitions.

The **American Language Centre**, 3 Impasse du Moulin, off Blvd Mohammed Zerqtouni (*open Mon and Sat 9–12 and 2.30–6.30; Tues–Fri 2.30–6 only*), has a small library, a bookshop and noticeboard and puts on a weekly film.

Marrakesh ✆ (04–)   **Nightlife**

There are two fairly recent additions to Marrakesh's nightlife that, beneath a transatlantic shimmer, have blurred the established division between the introverted world of the tourist complexes and the promenade cafés beloved by locals. The **Complexe Jet d'Eau** is on Place de la Liberté, and contains a restaurant, snack bar and Le Star disco. The **Palais des Congrès** on Av de France is an even more shocking piece of mall glamour for the burgeoning world of the charge account. It contains seven restaurants, five café-bars, two nightclubs and one luxury hotel for the *homme d'affaires*.

The two best-equipped discos in Marrakesh are the **Paradise** in the Pullman Mansour Eddahbi Hotel, on Av de France, ✆ 44 82 22 (*open 10pm–7am; adm*

80dh), and the **Cotton Club**, at the Hôtel Tropicana, Lotissement Semlalia, ✆ 43 39 13 (*open 9pm–5am; adm 60dh*). Other clubs include **Byblos** at PLM N'Fis on Av de France, ✆ 44 87 72, the **Charleston Disco** at Place Abdel Moumen ben Ali, ✆ 43 11 36, below the Grand Café Atlas, and **Le Diamant Noir** in Le Marrakesh Hôtel on Place de la Liberté. An alternative would be to hire your own **folklore troupe** for a moonlit picnic or dinner party. Try El Haj Allal, 96 Rue Mouassine; Eddibyn Mohammed, 160 Rue Mouassine; or Haj Mohammed Baba, 36 Derb Dabachi.

casinos

Dress up a bit but don't overdo it: men wearing a dinner jacket will probably be mistaken for a croupier or a waiter. The busiest is the **Mamounia Casino**, ✆ 44 89 81, in the celebrated hotel on Av Bab Jdid. It has its own small restaurant, ✆ 44 45 70, 🕮 44 41 32, which you can book any time between 9pm and 2am. The other, older casino in Marrakesh is run by the **Es Saâdi Hôtel** and stands in the heart of the Hivernage district on Av Quadissa, ✆ 44 88 11/✆ 44 70 10.

fantasias

Fantasia evenings are staged several times a week most of the year, and are bookable through the larger hotels or the organizers. The three principal pitches include **El Bordj**, ✆ 44 63 76, **Zagora**, ✆ 44 52 37, and the renowned **Chez Ali**, ✆ 44 81 87, run with great style by an Italian-Moroccan family. Though they are arranged almost entirely for the benefit of tourists, they are undeniably well managed and impressive circus events that are seen at their best in the added romance of the night. Torch-lit entrances lead to caidal tents where traditional food is cooked before your eyes while skilled musicians and dancers entertain, leading to the finale of horse-borne acrobatics, the spectacular *fantasia* charge of Arab horsemen, fireworks and swirling processions of musicians, all set amid illuminated towers and stirring martial music.

Festivals

The annual **National Folklore Festival** is held in El Badia Palace for two weeks at some point during each summer. For all its orchestration it is perhaps the most rewarding festival in Morocco for a visitor to attend. It presents a fascinating opportunity to hear the distinctive varieties of Berber tribal music, and the chants and dances of the Sufi fraternities. Groups perform here who would not dream of any professional career. The festival takes place every evening from 9pm to midnight, and admission is just 50dh. At the same time the small pavilions to the north and southwest of the palace are opened, and you can see exhibitions as well as the permanent collection of excavated ceramics and an old minbar from the Koutoubia. There is, unfortunately, no way of predicting the festival's dates, which can be any time between May and September.

The main **Fantasia Festival** is held outside the city walls at the end of July; the *moussem* of **Sidi Abdel Kader ben Yassin** is in September; and the **contemporary arts fair** is held in November.

South of Marrakesh the *moussem* of Setti Fatma at the head of the Ourika Valley is held in August, the *moussem* of Sidi Boutamane in September, and the zaouia of Moulay Brahim holds its *moussem* after Mouloud.

Day Trips from Marrakesh

The highest and most dramatic range of mountains in North Africa, the High Atlas, rises immediately south of Marrakesh. This jagged horizon of ethereal blue peaks is a lodestone that draws visitors out from the city. The two great sights of the region, the **kasbah of Telouèt** and the **mosque of Tin-Mal**, however, make lengthy day trips from Marrakesh. The High Atlas can be crossed by only three mountain passes, of which only one, the Tizi-n-Babaou that links Marrakesh to Agadir, is open all year round. The Tizi-n-Test, that connects Marrakesh to Taroudannt, and the Tizi-n-Tichka to Ouarzazate are cut off by falls of snow and rocks for several weeks every year. As well as these crossings, three other tarmac roads intrude into the mountainous region, allowing easy access to the Ourika Valley, Jbel Oukaïmeden and the village of Amizmiz. For a day trip into the mountains, the **Ourika Valley**, with its selection of restaurants, is the obvious choice. The Ourika river sparkles and gurgles over rounded boulders and through the dappled shade of poplars, and even in the midsummer heat of Morocco the valley can appear like some image from an English pastoral poem. And yet, amid this tranquillity it can reveal a darker nature. One night a few Augusts ago it was suddenly transformed into a raging torrent for a few murderous hours, when a thunderstorm up among the distant peaks of the High Atlas announced the unleashing of a violent rainstorm that took the whole region by surprise. Roads, houses, bridges were swept aside in the confused hours of the night, and when by morning the water had receded it left a residue of drowned animals and humans—rarely from the indigenous Berber communities, who had kept to the hillside dry-stone houses of their ancestors—mixed among uprooted trees and river-flung boulders. This is a land that has always demanded great hardiness from its inhabitants.

Long before Marrakesh was founded, the Berber tribes of the High Atlas region practised a seasonal migration. In the winter they brought their flocks down to the plains, planted crops during the brief spring, and then through the summer slowly worked their way back up to the cooler Alpine grazing of the highland peaks. The foundation of a strong central authority at Marrakesh in the 11th century disturbed this pattern. The Almoravids, with their desert technology, improved the irrigation of the plain and established efficient gardens and a sedentary population on the most fertile tracts. Arab tribes who came to the region in the service of the sultans were rewarded with tracts of Berber tribal land below the foothills of the Atlas. By the 19th century most of the Berber tribes had been expelled from the plains by the fierce cavalry of these nomadic Arab tribes. The Berbers either stayed to work as sharecroppers on the plain for an alien landlord, or moved up into the mountains in order to remain free sedentary farmers. There they remain today.

Another possible day trip from Marrakesh is the enchanting Atlantic town of **Essaouira**, a 4hr journey by bus. Here you can swim, wander through the town's souks, and eat at one of the many excellent fish restaurants.

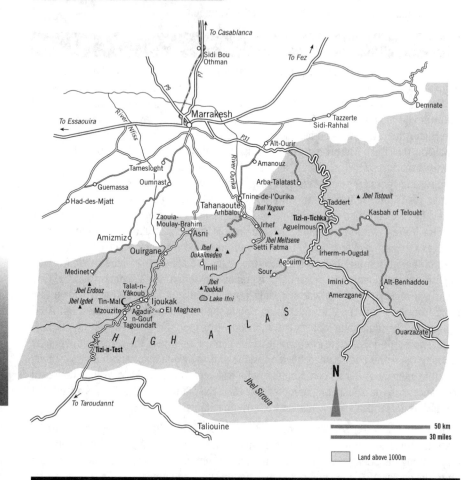

To Casablanca
Sidi Bou Othman
To Fez
Demnate
To Essaouira
River Nfiss
Marrakesh
Tazzerte Sidi-Rahhal
Aït-Ourir
Tamesloght
Amanouz
Arba-Talatast
Guemassa
Oumnast
Tnine-de-l'Ourika
Jbel Tistouit
Had-des-Mjatt
Tahanaoute
Jbel Yagour
Taddert
Kasbah of Telouèt
Zaouia-Moulay-Brahim
Arhbalou
Tizi-n-Tichka
Amizmiz
Asni
Irhef
Aguelmous
Jbel Meltsene
Ouirgane
Jbel Oukaïmeden
Setti Fatma
Irherm-n-Ougdal
Medinet
Imlil
Agouim
Imini
Aït-Benhaddou
Jbel Erdouz
Talat-n-Yâkoub
Jbel Toubkal
Amerzgane
Jbel Igdet
Tin-Mal
Ijoukak
Lake Ifni
Mzouzite
Agadir n-Gouf
El Maghzen
Sour
Tagoundaft
H I G H   A T L A S
Ouarzazate
Tizi-n-Test
Jbel Siroua
To Taroudannt
Taliouine

N

50 km
30 miles
Land above 1000m

The Tizi-n-Test

The Tizi-n-Test pass crosses the High Atlas to link Marrakesh and Taroudannt through 200km of mountain road. It can be closed by snow or made more dangerous by ice any time between December and March, and each year some portion is destroyed by falling rocks or a swollen mountain stream.

Nevertheless, it is definitely worth venturing up here: you will have the opportunity to climb the highest mountain in North Africa, to visit one of only two mosques in Morocco (along with the Hassan II in Casablanca) open to non-Muslims, and to admire a succession of ruined kasbahs. Or you might simply come for the clear air and to walk in the high valleys.

There are eight **buses** daily from Marrakesh to Asni (90mins), which leave from Bab Doukkala bus station and call at the Bab er Rob stop on their way south. If you are heading farther up the valley you should take the dawn departure (either 5 or 6am) for Taroudannt.

A place in a *grand taxi* will get you to Asni or Zaouia-Moulay-Brahim in three-quarters of an hour for 12dh. Or you could bargain with a *grand taxi* and hire him for between 200 and 300dh for a whole day trip.

Tahanaoute

Thirty-one km from Marrakesh on the Taroudannt road, the S501, you pass the strikingly picturesque village of Tahanaoute on the far side of the riverbed. A cascade of pisé houses surrounds a great rock which shelters the **shrine of Sidi Mohammed El Kebir**, whose festival is celebrated at Mouloud. It was the subject of Winston Churchill's last painting in 1958. Tahanaoute proper is a kilometre further, an ancient marketplace on the border of the mountains and plains where a **souk** is held each Tuesday.

Zaouia-Moulay-Brahim

Beyond Tahanaoute the road twists up above the meandering course of the river as it flows past the five knuckles of black rock that protrude into Moulay Brahim Gorge. A cluster of **cafés** line the roadside and the riverbed just before the turning uphill to the village of Zaouia-Moulay-Brahim; they look out over a wooded hill on the other side of the river. This hillside zaouia is one of the most important centres of spiritual life in the region. A fortnight after Mouloud a great festival is held here. A camel is sacrificed at the gates of the town, and its head and skin are taken down to honour two nearby springs that are used for ritual washing by men and women. The 3hr trek to the koubba on the summit is an integral part of the pilgrimage. Gaily caparisoned horses stand patiently on the banks of the riverbed beside mounting stools for the use of pilgrims in need of a photographic souvenir of themselves in the pose of a cavalier.

Even outside the festival, Moulay-Brahim remains a popular day-trip destination for Marrakeshi families. The town is formed from a small maze of streets that extend in a confusion of levels, courts and paved passages around the central shrine. This has a distinctive green pyramid roof; a wooden bar has been placed below the minaret as a barrier to non-Muslims. The rest of the village, with its cafés, pilgrim trinket stalls, two surviving potteries and hill views, is open and the population is pleasantly welcoming.

Asni

This pleasant roadside village, 15km farther south, is the local administrative centre and the destination for most *grands taxis* from the Bab er Rob in Marrakesh. Apart from the opportunities for walking from the hotel here (Imlil, Zaouia-Moulay-Brahim and Ouirgane are all within easy reach), it could be worth a visit for the busy **souk** held here on Saturdays. From Asni a partly tarmacked road leads up to the hamlet of **Imlil**, which is the centre for hill walking in the **Toubkal National Park**. The park is named after the highest mountain in all North Africa and embraces some of the most striking and awesome highland scenery in Morocco. If you want to walk in the park, you must make proper preparations and set aside several days. Maps and guides can be found in Imlil.

Ouirgane

Continuing on the main Tizi-n-Test road, the hamlet of Ouirgane lies 16km south of Asni. It mainly consists of two celebrated hotels, whose gardens face each other across a stream which drains the western face of Jbel Toubkal to merge with the river Nfiss just below the village. Four km south of Ouirgane there is the intriguing mass of drystone walls that forms the hilltop agadir at **Tagadirt-n-Bour**, to the right of the road. Possible strolls from the village include the two-hour walk up to villages such as Tikhfist, or to a mountain waterfall in the company of local guides.

Eating Out

expensive

The **Résidence La Roseraie**, ℅ (04) 43 20 94, is made up of some two dozen apartments scattered around an extensive riverside garden (a fusion of raw Morocco and bourgeois France) which also contains two swimming pools and a stunning mass of rose beds, all confined within a horizon of wooded mountains. There is a restaurant and bar, where a portrait of Caid Goudafa by E. Varley hangs.

The original riverside riding stables were swept away in a horrific midsummer flood in 1996, but have been replaced by a new block safely uphill where the immaculately groomed thoroughbreds and the stable donkey can be admired. A health centre has also been established above the mineral stream, although the pseudo-medical nature of spa life compares unfavourably with the joys of walking or riding in the magnificent hinterland. The hotel is one of the best places from which to ride in Morocco, and can organize anything from an hour's tuition within the grounds of the estate to a week-long expedition into the mountains.

inexpensive

Le Sanglier Qui Fume, ℅ (02) 12 12 08, is one of Morocco's surviving colonial institutions, described by Paul Bowles in 1959: 'Lunch outside in the sun at Le Sanglier Qui Fume. Our table midway between a chained eagle and a chained monkey, both of which watched us distrustfully while we ate...Madame is Hungarian and lives in the hope that people coming through Ouirgane will speak her language or at least know Budapest...obviously disappointed in us.'

The dining room is dominated by large dogs and a collection of kasbah oil paintings by Holbing, an ex-German professor in Marrakesh. In recent years the hotel hit a troubled patch with the departure of Madame Thevenin-Frey and a legal dispute amongst the various heirs to the property. Even if the rooms may have deteriorated a little, the French cooking remains as good as ever.

Si Taieb, a Caid of the High Atlas

Si Taieb succeeded his father as *caid* of the Goundafa tribe in 1883 at the age of twenty. His father, after a lifetime of rebellion, had sued for peace with the government and sent a legendary gift to the palace at Marrakesh: a hundred male slaves, each leading a horse and a camel; followed the next day by a hundred slave girls each leading a cow and a calf. Once in power, the young *caid* launched a campaign of aggressive expansion. He had at his disposal a tribal force of 5,000 men and his own slave guard of 500. By 1900 he had trebled the size of his domain, a fact which increasingly drove the rival High Atlas *caids*, the Glaoui and M'Touggi, into an alliance against him. In the words of the latter, 'He is a hill man who has discovered the plains. It will not be easy to get him out.' R.B. Cunninghame Graham has left a description of Si Taieb holding court in 1901: 'Forty years of age, thick set and dark complexioned...not noble in appearance but still looking as one accustomed to command; hands strong and muscular, voice rather harsh but low, and trained in the best school of Arab manners, so as to be hardly audible... His clothes white and of the finest wool...his secretaries never stopped opening and writing letters, now and then handing one to the *caid*...slave boys, in clothes perhaps worth eighteen pence, served coffee.'

In 1906 the rival *caids* seized their chance, for Si Taieb had been called to Fez. Their combined forces descended to plunder the Nfiss valley and burn the kasbah of Talat-n-Yâkoub. Si Taieb returned to find his homeland in desolation, and for six years never left the valley. Lyautey, the French Resident-General, was the only man who could entice the warrior *caid* from his mountain realm. In 1912 the lowland kasbahs of Amizmiz and Aguergour were returned to Si Taieb, and at a stroke he was restored to his pre-1906 position. He was also given arms and money for the conquest of the Sous Valley. After the capture of Taroudannt in 1913 he was honoured by being created *naib*, representative of the sultan in the south. In 1917 he was appointed pasha of Tiznit, and for seven years he remained in command of this frontier of the desert war. In 1924 he retired to his mountain kasbahs, where he died four years later, aged 65.

After his death his feudal authority was dismantled and replaced by the even rule of French officials, while his lands were divided between his son, Lhassen, and two nephews. A pleasant white house of spacious courtyards can be seen attached to the end of the kasbah of Talat-n-Yâkoub. This is the house of the *caid's* grandson, an electrical engineer from Casablanca.

Tin-Mal

Another few kilometres south, the Almohad **mosque of Tin-Mal** emerges high up on the opposite bank of the river, a fortress of the faith with its high walls and strong towers. It is usually empty of tourists, yet must be considered one of the most memorable sites of

Morocco, the sole survivor of the 12th-century city of Tin-Mal and one of only two mosques in Morocco that a non-Muslim may enter. Its striking position, deep in the High Atlas mountains, is equalled only by its extraordinary history.

The mosque has been restored, and a small museum built to house various architectural fragments. The track from the road has also been repaired, and you no longer have to clamber across a broken bridge. Small boys lie in wait for visitors and will enthusiastically lead you to the custodian, Mohammed Filali, who may be in the company of his young son or one of his three hazel-eyed daughters. You might add a tip onto the price of your admission ticket. The mosque may be closed to tourists on Fridays, when the village of Tin-Mal uses it.

The Mosque

You enter through a small but sturdy door in the corner of the main tower which used to be reserved for the imam, the leader of the prayers, and the *khatib*, the pronouncer of the Friday sermon. The mosque is now roofless but this increases rather than diminishes the splendour of its interior. Deep shadows cast by the surviving brick columns and horseshoe arches contrast with an expanse of sunbaked wall which reflects the mountain sunlight to give the whole of the interior an enchanted roseate glow.

The central tower has been placed immediately above the mihrab, the arched niche which indicates the direction of Mecca. The dome above the mihrab and the arches that link with the domes underneath the two corner towers were richly decorated to draw the worshipper's attention naturally in this direction. The central aisle would also have boasted more elaborate details. All the other aisles would have been supported by horseshoe arches, embellished by bas-relief columns of which a few survive. At the opposite end to the mihrab is the *sahn*, the open-air court for worshippers to wash themselves, which has its own entrance arch and would have once contained an elaborate marble fountain. Either side of the *sahn* are two prayer-halls which, screened and provided with their own entrances, could be used by women. The old gates piled up against the outside walls are from the Koutoubia Mosque at Marrakesh, rejected secondhand gifts from the sister mosque built by the Almohads.

In its prime the whole mosque would have been spotlessly white. Excavations unearthed not so much as a fragment of a green-glazed roof tile or a single piece of *zellij* mosaic, otherwise ubiquitous elements in any Moroccan shrine. Almohad Tin-Mal remained true to its puritanical origins, and was composed of just bricks, wood and white plaster. The three brick towers are an unusual feature in that they are built above the actual prayer-hall of the mosque. Most minarets are quite free-standing and rarely aligned with the mihrab. The corner minaret towers were crowned by lanterns, but the central one did not reach much higher than it does today. You can climb up its staircase and look south down the Nfiss Valley to the Goundafa kasbah of Agadir-n-Gouf, which crowns the central hill. As testament to the restraint of the restoration programme, a pair of owls have already started nesting in one of the domes.

Ibn Tumert and Tin-Mal

Ibn Tumert was a religious reformer who desired to enforce his puritanical doctrine over the Muslim community. A Chleuh Berber, he was born in one of the small villages on the northern slopes of the Anti-Atlas mountains and travelled east towards Mecca to study in the intellectual centres of the Islamic world. He was a well-known and controversial figure before his return to Morocco, and by 1124 he had selected Tin-Mal to be the citadel of his theocratic state.

It became a place of total obedience where he trained the mountain tribes for war against all who would not accept his authority. Dancing, music and singing were banned, art placed under his severe direction and codes of dress established which denied any ornamentation. Ibn Tumert lectured the Berber tribes in their own dialect, but taught them the Arabic Koran in a characteristically authoritarian manner. Long lines of warriors would each be given a word of the Koran as their name and by obediently calling out their new names in turn could learn whole *suras* of the Koran. As a capstone to his authority, Ibn Tumert gradually led his community to recognize that he was the *Mahdi*, the prophesied successor of Mohammed.

After two years at Tin-Mal he led a series of expeditions that enforced his authority in the valleys of the High Atlas, and consolidated these victories in 1128 by a bloody forty-day purge of the tribes. In 1129 three Almoravid armies attempted a joint assault on Tin-Mal. Though these were beaten off, Ibn Tumert's own siege of Marrakesh that same year ended in a costly defeat. The death of Ibn Tumert in 1130 was kept a secret from his followers for three years while his chosen successor, Abdel Moumen, consolidated his authority. In 1148 he captured Marrakesh, which became the administrative capital of the empire while Tin-Mal degenerated into the Almohad cult centre, secure treasury and favoured burial ground.

In 1154 Abdel Moumen subtly shifted the Almohads from a movement of religious reform to a dynasty invested in his own family. The great mosque of Tin-Mal was finished as a triumphant cult centre in the same year that Ibn Tumert's own children, grandchildren and cousins were quietly disposed of.

Tin-Mal Village

There is a ruined kasbah at the centre of the village, as well as a mosque, a Koranic school and an old water tank which produces a regular crop of edible frogs. Past the village (a kilometre north on the main road) the old city walls of Tin-Mal lead up from the riverbank to the heights above. Tin-Mal was both the first and the last bastion of the Almohads. It was finally stormed in 1276 by the Merenids, who, though they respected the great mosque, left no house standing, no tomb undefiled, and no citizen of Tin-Mal alive. However, the historian Ibn Khaldoun, who visited Tin-Mal a generation later, found

Koranic reciters had returned to the mosque. When they entered the valley in 1924 French administrators found the area around the mosque covered in old shrines of which there is now no trace.

On one side of the village square stands an olive press which was built from one family's savings accumulated in 16 years' emigrant labour in France. The owner is usually happy to show you the mill and explain the process, finishing off by selling you a litre or two of his Tin-Mal olive oil.

The Ourika Valley and Oukaïmeden

The Ourika is a narrow valley that cuts deep into the High Atlas. As you intrude south down the valley, the mountains rise ever more precipitously and the area of cultivation diminishes further. At the head of the valley, constricted terraced gardens, their walls constructed from round river boulders, their bright crops shaded by slender almond trees, appear like some vision of the Promised Land. The gardens are productive throughout most of the year, since the Ourika stream which drains the northeastern face of Jbel Toubkal seldom runs dry.

In the summer, when Marrakesh can feel debilitatingly like a furnace, the Ourika Valley has a gentle trickle of cool, clear water, a breeze in the trees, trout in the river and oleanders that have just burst into flower. Small pottery workshops are found off the road and flour mills operate above the riverbed, fed by irrigation ditches that double as a source of power. For this constancy of supply the valley can pay an occasional but high price. Sudden fierce rainfall, especially in winter, carries a flood downstream which can rip out the sides of hills, bury houses in mud and boulders, and sweep all away in a great torrent of water.

In the past the people of the Ourika Valley were in a powerful position: they controlled the water supply to the city and gardens of Marrakesh, for old Moroccan law did not acknowledge the rights of any user downstream. In practice this meant that no ruler of Marrakesh could afford to have a hostile power in control of the valley, which has always been closely associated with the affairs of Marrakesh. This is still true today, and the lower reaches of the valley are lined with the villas of the richer Marrakeshis. It is a traditional place to relax, with a good selection of licensed restaurants beside the road.

Getting There

A fairly continuous stream of **buses** and *grands taxis* plies the road from the Bab er Rob in Marrakesh to Ourika. A place in a *grand taxi* should cost 20dh, though you might have difficulty in finding a taxi to Oukaïmeden in the summer months. Hiring a *grand taxi* for the day should cost 300dh.

Aghmat Rhmate

Twenty-eight kilometres from Marrakesh a signposted tarmac road leads off to the hamlet of Aghmat Rhmate. This was, until the arrival of the Almoravids in the 11th century, the principal town of the region. Now it boasts a café and the elegant tomb of El Mutamid, the poet prince of Seville (*adm free; tips accepted*). He was exiled here by the great Almoravid Sultan Youssef ben Tachfine, who accused him of conspiring with the Christians. The koubba, restored in the 1960s, is a copy of the Almoravid Koubba Ba'Adiyn in Marrakesh, with the dedication inscription replaced by one of El Mutamid's verses.

The Ourika Valley

At the entrance to the Ourika Valley, 33km from Marrakesh, you pass through the Monday souk of **Tnine-de-l'Ourika**, which has for that one day each week become a destination for coach tours. On the opposite side of the valley, across a bridge, is the settlement of **Dar-Caid-Ouriki**, the house of the *caid* of Ourika. The ruins of the kasbah and its garden are approached through the encroaching hamlet of farms. Dramatically placed below a geological fault, the ruins retain a certain aura. Abdallah, *caid* of the Ourika in the 19th century, was an early ally of the Glaoui, an alliance confirmed by his marriage to one of Madani's six daughters. This relationship did not, however, stop Madani's brother Si Thami el Glaoui from removing Abdallah and appointing his own brother, Mohammed el Arbi, to the influential caidship.

The village of **Irhef** is 5km farther up the valley. This used to be an entirely Jewish community, but only a few Jews remain and the Jewish charity school is now full of young Muslims.

Setti-Fatma, at 1500m, and nearly 20km farther, is the virtual edge of human habitation in the Ourika Valley. The last kilometre of road to Setti-Fatma takes the form of a washed bank of gravel, which is continually being swept away. Across the stream from the hamlet, a path crosses below a group of café-restaurants and continues up to a system of **seven waterfalls**. Getting up to the first fall with its plunge pool, sunbathing rocks and tiny café is a quarter of an hour's stroll partly under the shade of walnut trees (raided by Barbary apes), but it does include the odd rock scramble. The other, higher falls demand some experience of rock climbing, or at least a good head for heights.

Following a path above the eastern bank of the main river you reach the green-tiled **koubba** of Setti-Fatma (not accessible to non-Muslims), a popular burial ground as the tell-tale head- and foot-stones indicate. The window grilles of the shrine are covered in a web of cloth knots left by supplicants. This is the centre of a four-day *moussem* held in August which attracts Berber farmers and shepherds from all over the High Atlas.

Eating Out

Hotels get gradually seedier and accommodation cheaper as you proceed up the valley. All give Arhbalou as their address, but despite this they are easy to find, strung along the road.

First along the road, up a turning to the right, is the expensive **Ourika Hôtel**, ✆ (02) 12 09 99, which has a good view, a bar and good cooking but a slightly soulless air. The moderately priced **Auberge Marquis** is not far after the Oukaïmeden turning (at km 45). The bar is friendly and the tranquil licensed restaurant serves a reliably delicious *tagine*. It is run by Saida and Jean Pierre Blanc; reservations ✆/✉ (04) 48 45 31.

A few kilometres farther up the main valley (km 49) there is a knot of places. The **Kasbah Restaurant** on the right has been established in an old Glaoui pavilion. It can be overrun by tourists but retains a certain chaotic style. Almost directly opposite is the **Hôtel Amnougar**, ✆ (02) 11 08 37, which is a popular weekend base for Marrakeshis. It has a bar, pool, dining room and is moderately priced. Also on the left is the expensive **Le Lion de l'Ourika** restaurant, ✆ (04) 44 53 22, which has a palatial dining room, uniformed waiters and elaborate set meals.

One of the last in this group, tucked away up a drive to the right of the road (at km 52) and in its own garden, is the moderately priced **Auberge Ramuntchko**, ✆ (02) 31 91 02, with a bar, a fire-warmed dining room for winter, and an elegant terrace shaded with white umbrellas, filled with the sound of the river and basking in a magnificent view of the mountains. Its near neighbour **Dar Piano**, ✆ (02) 12 10 73, is an equal in cuisine.

The cheap places are all at Asgaour, where the tarmac road gives out. The best of these is the new **Tafoukt Hôtel**, though the village cafés such as the **Asgaour** are good for meals, as well as advice on walks and introductions to possible mountain guides. In Setti-Fatma itself the **Café les Cascades** and its neighbours prepare meals to order.

Oukaïmeden

Getting to Oukaïmeden, 'the meeting place of the four winds', provides at least half of the excitement of the place. Ten kilometres south of Tnine-de-l'Ourika, at the village of **Arhbalou**, a right turn takes you 30 twisting kilometres, up to the foot of Jbel Oukaïmeden. The road mostly climbs within sight of a mountain stream, the Asif Aït Leqaq, which has cut a series of steep canyons and waterfalls in the side of the mountain. Along the way you pass a string of stone and pisé Berber hamlets, perched way up but still surrounded by carefully tended terraced gardens, bramble hedges and orchards, even above suicidal cliffs. As you climb up to Oukaïmeden, at 2600m, you pass through a whole series of altitude belts that gradually dispose of olive trees, almonds, henna and walnut, leaving you in a barren area of windswept rock. Providing there is no cloud cover, there is a continual and magnificently changing view over the valleys of the High Atlas to the east and west or away to the north to Marrakesh.

The settlement of Oukaïmeden itself is no more than a fairly ugly assortment of skiing chalets and associated huts and services sheltered by a rising platform of barren rock. The face of the mountain is scarred by the pylons that support the half-dozen ski lifts. As you arrive you pass a small reservoir lake, well stocked with fish, and a barrier at which you must pay an admission charge (currently 10dh) to enter the resort. In winter this provides the best skiing in the country, and in summer it makes a good, well-supplied base for walking in the high valleys. What is more, around the town there is the most accessible collection of prehistoric rock carvings anywhere in Morocco. There is no view from Oukaïmeden, but a superb one from the Tizerag TV relay station, atop a peak at 2,740m, which is at the end of a road that winds up for another 2km beyond the resort.

The Rock Carvings

There is a map in the Club Alpin Français (CAF) hut in Oukaïmeden that shows the location of the carvings, but the club is often locked up. Ask to be guided by any of the locals to the half-dozen sites. The French, in their efficient way, built protective shelters around them, which have all now rusted down to a few inches. You can, if you don't like being guided, look for these telltale signs just to the right of the road above the reservoir as you enter the town; there are also some near the Angour hotel. Among the rocks you will find a collection of images that includes representations of shafted stone knives, Aztec-like ritual knives, some circular or stellar-solar shapes with rings, snake-lightning bolts, a male hunter beside a small deer, and an elephant with mouse-like ears and a penis but no tusks. They have all been dated to the 9th century BC.

Eating Out

There are a number of places open in Oukaïmeden which tend to be filled with unbearably hearty mountain types and the smell of their boots and socks. For choice use the **Hotel L'Angour**, for many years known as the Hôtel Juju, ✆ (04) 31 90 05, a great wood-lined mock-Alpine thing.

Sports

The **National Ski Centre** at Oukaïmeden is open from November to March. The best conditions are usually from February to March—and often coincide with an impassable road. The skiing is Scottish: icy in the morning, wet in the afternoon, with some potentially surprising patches of rock. There are half a dozen button lifts and a 1660m chair-lift. Day passes and ski hire are available from the local shop.

The Tizi-n-Tichka

The Tizi-n-Tichka pass crosses the High Atlas from Marrakesh to Ouarzazate and, like the Tizi-n-Test, can be blocked any time between December and March. It is an exciting and memorable journey, on a perfectly safe road that climbs twisting up through forests to the treeless summits of the pass. Just beyond the summit is the turning for the kasbah of Telouèt, the chief attraction of the journey.

Getting There

There are three buses daily crossing the pass from Marrakesh to Ouarzazate, but no buses or coaches make the trip along the dead-end side road to Telouèt. Telouèt Kasbah also has an odd local status and most taxi drivers would prefer not to go there, and try to dissuade you from going. The only option for the day trip to Telouèt is really hiring a **car** for the day.

To the Tizi-n-Tichka Summit

Aït-Ourir, 30km southeast of Marrakesh off to the left of the main road, is one of the string of market towns that nestles at the foot of the High Atlas. Good farm land stretches below, and the Tuesday souk is usually busy and empty of tourists. A well-built Glaoui residence can be seen to the south of the town, but it is inaccessible as it now houses an orphanage. You could eat at the reasonably priced **Le Coq Hardi**, ✆ (04) 48 00 56, a charming motel which has a garden and a licensed restaurant. It stands right beside the bridge over the river Zate, and can be filled at lunchtime with passing tour groups.

Beyond Aït-Ourir the road climbs quickly up into the foothills, after a few kilometres passing below the prominent **koubba of Sidi Lahoussine**. Just before the koubba a dirt track leads almost due south to the village of **Tidili-des-Mesfioua**. The Mesfioua, alone of the Berber tribes, succeeded in resisting the Arab tribes of the plains and held on to their area of the fertile plain of Haouz, centred on this village. They also preserved their traditions of tribal democracy and, up to the 20th century, suffered no autocratic *caid* to rule over them.

Twelve kilometres east of Aït-Ourir a tarmac road turns right up the Zate Valley, passing through a series of Mesfioua villages where the timeless, tireless pace of subsistence farming continues undisturbed by tourism. The road ends at **Arba-Talatast**, overlooked to the southwest by the twin peaks of **Jbel Yagour** (2723m) and **Jbel Meltsene** (3588m). The slopes of Yagour have some of the best-preserved prehistoric rock carvings in the area, while the summit of Meltsene is still rumoured to be used for the old Berber sacrifices celebrated on the equinox and solstices.

Back on the main road, the P31, you climb up through dramatic mountain scenery, the slopes covered in mixed woods of oak, pine and juniper. Perhaps the best view of these Mesfioua mountains is from the pass of **Tizi-n-Aït-Imguer**, at 1470m, where there is a particularly good view southeast to Jbel Tistouit, a summit looming up at 3224 m.

Taddert is a roadside village poised below the last 15km of twisting road that climbs to the Tizi-n-Tichka summit. Though unpromising at first sight, it makes a pleasant stop, with its line of cramped cafés, and the licensed but inexpensive Auberge Les Noyers can— despite its roadside position—be a good place to eat, with its terrace overlooking a mountain stream. A number of paths lead away from the sound of grinding truck gears to pisé farmhouses placed idyllically beside the terraced banks of mountain streams.

The **summit** of Tizi-n-Tichka, 'the gate to the pastures', is 2,260m high. From this central point in the High Atlas, a windblown, desolate expanse extends in all directions, though the immediate environment is ringed by the now customary mineral stalls. Four kilometres farther on there is a left turn for the kasbah of Telouèt.

The Kasbah of Telouèt

Telouèt is 21km east from the main road on a tarmac lane that leads past stunted pines and mineral-stained soil, which has given the ground a sanguinous hue in keeping with its reputation. Eventually you glimpse a minaret that rises from the low village of **El-Khémis Telouèt**, separated from the sprawling extent of the kasbah by the river Mellah. Above the kasbah, overlooking a prominent koubba in the centre of the cemetery, there is a simple hotel, the Auberge Telouèt, which provides meals.

Three generations of *caids* of the Glaoui tribe built extravagant structures out of wood and pisé to form this kasbah. Most of Telouèt is consequently an area of leached and shapeless mud banks. Broken spars and wattle frames protrude like the bones of some decaying leviathan. This area of ruin is screened from immediate view by the most recent, stone-built **White Kasbah**, with its layers of towers, buttresses, crenellations and curtain walls, built by Caid Brahim, Thami el Glaoui, between 1934 and 1955.

The Making of the Lords of the Atlas

The Glaoui first rose to fortune by aiding Sultan Moulay Hassan in completing a late crossing of the High Atlas in 1893. Moulay Hassan, the last of the great pre-colonial rulers of Morocco, rewarded them with a gift of munitions which was later followed by a position at his court. The Glaoui prospered in the service of the sultans: Madani el Glaoui served Sultan Abdul Aziz as minister of war, before advancing to become grand vizier (prime minister) to Sultan Moulay Hafid, while his brother Thami was appointed pasha of Marrakesh. The brothers used their new wealth and great position gradually to enlarge their influence over the Berber tribes of the High Atlas. The kasbah of Telouèt grew in stature with each new conquest of a village and submission of a tribe.

By 1907 the Glaoui had become key national figures, but their greatest hour came in 1912 when they became the sworn allies of the French. They undertook the expansion of French rule south of the High Atlas, and created an empire within an empire for themselves in the process. Thami succeeded his brother Madani in 1918 and inherited Telouèt on his cousin Hammou's death in 1934. Only the collapse of French power in 1956 toppled this aged but still avaricious warrior who, at his peak, had 600,000 souls under his care. Within a year of Independence the Glaoui chiefs were either dead, in prison, or in exile, their lands confiscated and their tribesmen disarmed. Each year their kasbah moves closer to its sentence of complete decay.

The road skirts the village to approach the kasbah from behind. Melted forms of old walls grow stronger where a few families squat with their chickens, dogs and children in the more weather-resistant corners. A gateway directs your approach through narrow walls that open into a large paved courtyard. Even the minaret of the kasbah mosque has been infected with the universal crumbling.

The amiable uniformed government custodian conducts tours of the main reception rooms of Caid Brahim's White Kasbah (tips accepted). The haphazard evolution of the palace becomes apparent in the eccentric route to these rooms, affording tantalizing glimpses of dark corridors, subterranean staircases and obscure sun-baked terraces. The dusty, long, echoing corridor to the reception rooms provides an astonishing contrast to the massive assertive confidence of these halls. The vulgarity of display mixes with detailed Moorish craftsmanship of the highest order to silence the visitor.

An ornate grille-window frames a significant view of the old kasbah of Telouèt on the edge of the village, with barely two of its walls left standing. The old kasbah is the size of a traditional fortress of a mountain *caid* and would have boasted little decoration beyond crenellated towers and motifs embossed into the pisé of the exterior walls. Inside, the rooms would most likely have been small, dark and infested. The halls of the White Kasbah of Telouèt are of another order and, though now empty of furniture, the absence of rich cloth, carpets, worked metal and wood seems merely to enhance the grandeur of the interior. The roofs above are still secure and you are allowed up to enjoy the excellent view. They were once decorated with great expanses of green glazed tiles, but these now lie in shattered heaps at the foot of the outer walls.

On the way out the custodian may point out a large windowless room, the **cinema**. Edward G. Robinson was Caid Brahim's brother-in-law. The screening of the latest fantasies from California seems bizarrely appropriate in this last outlandish product of feudal grandeur.

The rest of Telouèt is not officially accessible and is securely locked up. Every year the buildings become more dangerous, but the custodians can sometimes be encouraged to take visitors around. For the brave, the route to the kitchens, Hammou's Kasbah and the harem runs through another delightful maze of passages. The kitchens are vast, and recognizable chiefly by their blackened walls. The mixture of soot, melting pisé and exposed beams is impressive only in its size and the imminent danger of final collapse. Telouèt was entirely staffed by slaves except for one salaried French chef. Over a thousand slaves fled overnight when the news of the death of Si Thami el Glaoui reached the kasbah.

At the heart of Telouèt, physically and emotionally, was **Hammou's Kasbah**, a stark, square keep formed from massive walls, dark and featureless inside. Hammou was the cousin and brother-in-law of Madani and Thami, but remained violently opposed to the French, whom he would not permit to enter his feudal domain. He was the *caid* of Telouèt and ruler of the traditional mountain territory throughout the period of phenomenal growth in Glaoui power until his death in 1934. Stories of his occult powers blended with the grim truth of his violent, xenophobic and sadistic nature. *Sloghis*—hounds that could each kill a wild boar by themselves—trailed behind guests in the kasbah like some canine thought police, while the final bloody resolution of a tribal feud too often ended at the hands of Hammou in his labyrinthine cellars. These have long since collapsed to bury the evidence of this grim underworld.

The **harem courtyard** is beyond Hammou's Kasbah and is approached through a number of rooms. The central courtyard was equipped with large pools of water which have now cracked and drained. The cool rooms that open from this internal space, thanks to a trick of design, are not overlooked by any battlemented tower. Two ornamental fruit trees survive, and in spring still fill this breezeless space with the scent of cherry and apricot blossom. After the initial pleasure of discovery, the languid introspection and sterility of the harem creep back to repossess the spirit of the place.

Beyond these identifiable features you can wander freely among the curtain walls and acres of complete ruin. Banks of pisé now and then astonish you with their tremendous range in height, which hints at some past extravagant architectural form. Fragments of carved cedar, carved foliate arabesques and shattered tiles can be glimpsed buried deep in what appears at first to be nothing but bleached soil.

It may seem extraordinary that such a place as Telouèt should not be better preserved but, for a Moroccan, Telouèt is a monument to treason on a vast scale. The Glaoui were totally identified with the most extreme French colonial ambitions right up to 1956. Si Thami el Glaoui was deeply involved in the deposition of Mohammed V, and his officials had extorted and stolen for years. Allied with the French, they had hunted down those who worked for Independence and fought against the Liberation Army.

Essaouira

This is the most enchanting town on the Atlantic, and perhaps on all the coasts of Morocco. The old town and port, encircled by 18th-century battlements, overlook a scattering of barren, wave-worn islands. A great sandy bay sweeps out to the south, while wooded hills dominate the skyline to the east. The old parts of the town—the medina, the kasbah and the *mellah*—express the exoticism of Morocco: the dark alleys are broken with frequent arches, and the women of the town are mysteriously concealed under their enveloping *haiks*. At dusk the call to prayer echoes across the silhouetted skyline, unchallenged by the distracting sound of traffic.

History

Es-saouira, 'the little ramparts', has been known over the millennia as Amougdoul, Migdol, Mogdoul, Mogdoura and Mogador. The offshore isles are still collectively known as Mogador, a name that probably derives from the Phoenician *migdol*, a look-out tower. Phoenician sailors used these islands from at least the 7th century BC, while archaeological evidence suggests that the principal villa remained in occupation for a thousand years from 500 BC to AD 500.

In the 11th century the bay opposite the islands formed the chief port of southern Morocco. King Manuel of Portugal seized Essaouira early in his campaign to dominate the whole trade and coast of Morocco, and built a fort here in 1506. This fell to the Saadians even before Agadir, the main Portuguese base, was recovered in 1541, but the Saadian dynasty (who originated from the far south) preferred to use the port of Agadir.

The present shape and character of the town is entirely the achievement of Sultan Sidi Mohammed. Agadir had never been loyal to the Alaouite dynasty, and Essaouira was deliberately created to replace it. In 1760 the sultan used his captive French architect-engineer, Théodore Cournut, to design the walls and street plan of the medina, which helps account for their unaccustomed regularity. By the 19th century the port of Essaouira handled nearly half of Morocco's trade: importing Manchester cottons and exporting bales of ostrich feathers, almonds, gum arabic, ebony, ivory and dried camel skins. The commercial connection with Britain was strong, and tea was first imported to Morocco through this port, a drink which, with the addition of mint and French-imported sugar, took the nation by storm. The distinctive Moroccan teapot was first manufactured in Manchester by creating a fusion from the existing Andalucían and Yemeni patterns.

In the 20th century, an assorted group of artists, windsurfers and hippies have put up with the damp winds and fallen in love with the town, though only such cultural heroes as Orson Welles, Jimi Hendrix and Cat Stevens (who, as Yusuf Islam, still comes here frequently) are remembered much.

Getting There
by bus

All buses use the new bus station, plonked in some drab pot-holed streets about a 1½km walk from Bab Doukkala on the northern edge of the medina. Walking towards the conspicuous town walls from the bus station is relatively easy, though if there is a *petit taxi* around (anywhere in town should be under 10dh), take it. Walking to the bus station from Bab Doukkala, take the first right and second left, then continue along for 500m until you reach an assortment of cafés and the different booths of the bus companies, including CTM. There are at least six buses a day from Marrakesh (4hrs).

by taxi

Grands taxis operate from the bus station but will usually be happy to deposit arrivals on the open square between the port and the medina. A car from Marrakesh should cost about 300dh one way.

by car

Arriving by car, the main approach to the town, the coastal Blvd Mohammed V, leads directly to the car park (10dh a day) that stands between the port and the old town.

Tourist Information

The **tourist office** is in a shed in the square between the medina and the port. It is not often open, but has a beautiful wooden model of the northern ramparts. There are leaflets, but not another scrap of information.

There are four **banks** around or just outside Place Moulay el Hassan: the BMCE, Banque Populaire, BCM and Credit du Maroc.

The Port

The harbour is guarded by the L-shaped **Skala du Port**, the port bastion, where two castellated towers and great banks of cannon once commanded the northern and western approaches. Two land gates still control admission to the enclosed quays of the harbour. Do not be put off by the guards standing around by these gates: despite appearances you are perfectly free to join the rest of the town and take a leisurely stroll through the docks, in order to admire the massed nets, flag-fluttering floats and busy decks of the fishing boats. The sardine-fishing fleet, the third largest in Morocco, provides a great spectacle of activity in the early morning or after dusk. The southern edge of the quay is occupied by ship builders, working on a line of emerging wooden hulls that illustrate every stage of the fascinating process of construction.

The main entrance to the harbour is through the **Porte de la Marine**, which you may occasionally find shut. It is one of the town's most famous structures. Its 18th-century architect, Cournut, achieved an equable fusion of traditions—details from a classical gateway combine with the green-tiled pyramid roof of a koubba. It is, like most of the town, a forerunner of 20th-century neo-Moorish public architecture, achieved at a time when Morocco was assertively independent. The three crescents of the Moroccan navy—a device borrowed from the Ottoman Turks—stand proudly carved into the limestone by an inscription that records that the gate was erected by Sultan Sidi Mohammed in 1769, year 1184 of the Hegira.

Place Moulay el Hassan

The best place to get the flavour of Essaouira is Place Moulay el Hassan. The square is lined with elegant, tall white houses picked out in blue that help give it a tranquil and intimate atmosphere. The cafés seem to break down the strongest reserve: the travellers who have arrived for a day but stayed for a few weeks are quick to offer an exchange of books or some tedious but well-meaning advice. Do not ignore the beggars, like most of the other tourists, but befriend them immediately with a silver coin. They are a feature of the place, and there is nothing more rewarding than earning their salute in the morning rather than trying (ineffectually) to avoid their unremitting attention.

The Woodcarvers' Souk

In the casemates and pebble-paved courtyards below the north bastion of the **Skala de la Ville** battlements (lined with bronze cannon cast for Philip II and Philip III of Spain), some of the skilled joiners and carvers of Essaouira have their workshops. The rich, resinous smell of the wood is a great attraction and the craftsmen are usually happy to demonstrate their skills. Acacia and ebony are both dark woods that are contrasted very successfully with the pale wood of the lemon tree and the rich chestnut of thuja wood. Shells, mother of pearl, strips of silver and copper are also inserted to create astonishingly inlaid tables, chests and cabinets. Essaouira also has the best selection of trays, chessboards, dice cups, thuja boxes and backgammon sets. Similar work seen in other cities is likely to have come from Essaouira, and be more expensive. You should bargain in the bazaars, but the co-operatives in town and the casemate workshops have less time for negotiations and generally offer a reasonable first price. Any hinges and locks should be examined carefully—skill with wood is seldom matched with much love for metalwork.

The Museum

Open Wed–Mon 8.30–12 and 2.30–6; closed Tues; adm.

The ethnography museum of Sidi Mohammed Ben Abdallah is found on the southern side of Rue Laâlouj, the street which leads from the Skala de la Ville back to the centre of town. Originally constructed in the early 19th century as the town house of a pasha, it was transformed into the town hall during the French Protectorate, with the unfortunate addition of a monolithic central staircase that now completely dominates the central courtyard. The museum has been overhauled and extended, to become a delightful repository for the

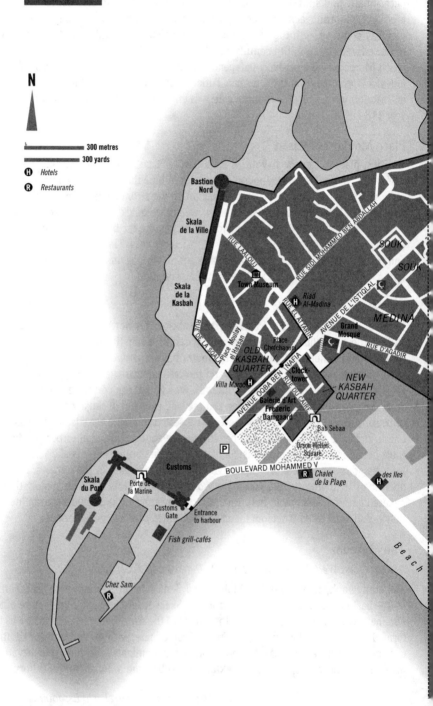

Essaouira

N

300 metres
300 yards

H Hotels
R Restaurants

Bastion Nord

Skala de la Ville

Skala de la Kasbah

RUE LAXIOU

RUE SIDI MOHAMMED BEN ABDALLAH

SOUK

SOUK

Town Museum

Riad Al-Madina

RUE EL ATTARIN

AVENUE DE L'ISTIQLAL

MEDINA

RUE DE LA SKALA

Place Moulay el Hassan

Place Chefchaoun

Grand Mosque

OLD KASBAH QUARTER

RUE D'AGADIR

Villa Maroc

AVENUE OOBA BEN NAFIA

Clock-tower

RUE DU CAIRE

NEW KASBAH QUARTER

Galerie d'Art Frederic Damgaard

Bab Sebaa

Orson Welles Square

P

Customs

BOULEVARD MOHAMMED V

Chalet de la Plage

des Iles

Skala du Port

Porte de la Marine

Customs Gate

Entrance to harbour

Fish grill-cafés

Beach

Chez Sam

traditional crafts, textiles, carpets, clothing, jewellery and weapons of the region, as well as of some early maps, engravings and sketches of the town.

The Medina Thoroughfare

From the main square outside the port, the high red archway with its green-tiled roof (sometimes used to house art exhibitions) leads to the old *méchouar*, now the tree-lined Av Oqba ben Nafia. This attractive broad avenue was originally an assembly place, where the garrison paraded and processions were marshalled. Avenue du Caire leads from the old *méchouar* to the strongly guarded Bab Sebaa. The triangular patch of open ground just to the south of the gate has been named **Orson Welles Square** and provided with a plaque to commemorate that fantastic polymath who was producer, director and principal actor of the film *Othello*, which was mainly shot here in 1949. Though his financial backers deserted him he won the affection of the town, who for a mere 2dh each a day provided him with all the craftsmen and extras he wanted, while everyone was fed on sardines.

The eastern side of Av Oqba ben Nafia is lined with hotels and a growing number of art galleries, led by **Galerie d'Art Frederic Damgaard**. The fortified western side of the avenue (once the city walls) is dominated by a distinctive clocktower beneath which is an archway leading into the small killim-lined and café-overlooked Place Chefchaouni. Pass under the second archway (occupied by Damgaard's framing workshop) to twist past more intriguingly furnished bazaars and inviting cafés before passing beneath the old kasbah and returning to Place Moulay el Hassan.

Alternatively, take the archway at the northern end of Av Oqba ben Nafia, which leads to the civil area of the old town and the central thoroughfare of **Avenue de l'Istiqlal**. To the right, on the eastern side, rises the minaret of the **grand mosque**, its spacious prayer-hall mostly tucked out of sight. The 200m-long avenue is largely devoted to kitchen and hardware stalls, piled high beneath the green-tiled overhang and framed by blue shutters.

The heart of the town's trading is reached at the central crossroads. The central souk area, known as **Souk Jdid**, lined with an arcade of short stone arches, is enclosed by twin gateways. Off to the west are courtyards housing fish, chicken and spice markets. To the east the *fondouqs* house old metalware and other secondhand goods, jellabas and killims, and the densely packed network of jewellers' booths. North of these souks, Avenue de l'Istiqlal, now lined with a blue-tiled arcade, becomes devoted to the vegetable and grocery trade.

The Beach

The beach to the south of the town, protected from the full force of the Atlantic surf and current, is one of the safer bays on this coast in which to swim. The area nearest the town is often occupied by football games and piles of seaweed, but as you walk farther out towards the **ruined fort** the sand gets cleaner and the beach emptier. This ruin is a remnant of Sultan Sidi Mohammed's defence system. Built on a rocky promontory, the fortress's compact walls have split but not disintegrated, despite being washed daily by the incoming tide.

Back from the beach, and screened slightly by the dunes, is the town's stumpy lighthouse, built beside the koubba of one of the town's patron saints, **Sidi M'gdoul**. There is a story about the origin of this saint which claims that he was a Scottish merchant called McDougall who saw the error of his hard-hearted ways and, having converted to Islam, settled down in a hermitage on the shore to help the poor of the town. The more historically minded will recall that Essaouira used to be known by its old Carthaginian title of Migdol, which gives the saint an even more venerable link to another widely scattered trading nation.

Essaouira ℂ (04–) | **Where to Stay**

expensive

The **Hôtel Villa Maroc**, 10 Rue Abdellah Ben Yacine, ℂ 47 31 47, ✆ 47 28 06, is one of the most delightful and most talked-about hotels in Morocco, discreetly tucked away on the edge of the medina—to find it go through the archway beside the clock on Av Oqba ben Nafia, turn left and walk down beside the wall for about 60m. It has the intriguingly confusing interior of a traditional house, but one which now proudly displays a scattering of exquisitely furnished sitting rooms lit by fires, and two dozen bedrooms arranged around a pair of interior courtyards. Breakfast can be taken on the roof terrace or in your room, while dinner (which should be booked in advance) is served at tables tucked around the courtyards. The interior, a fusion of bold Greek colours with a disciplined selection of Moroccan crafts, is a showpiece that has already appeared as background in dozens of fashion shoots. It is usually essential to book in advance, and to be safe you should reserve a room two months ahead, although in practice a last-minute cancellation may often leave a room or two free.

If you simply want a pool, reliable plumbing and a sense of spacious ease you will be better off in the **Hôtel des Iles**, ✆ 47 23 29. This well-established hotel stands in a prime position at the northern end of Blvd Mohammed V between the beach and the medina walls. It has 40 bungalows arranged around a garden and swimming-pool courtyard, with bar and restaurant nearby in the sturdy pre-war roadside block.

moderate

The old Hôtel du Pasha used to be *the* hotel in town, as its guest list of distinguished visitors proudly proclaims. After a long period of closure it has resurfaced as the **Hotel Riad Al Madina**, 9 Rue Attarine, ✆ 47 57 27, ▨ 47 57 27, with 27 bedrooms around a splendidly restored 18th-century courtyard. There is no licensed bar but the hotel has a fine view from the terrace and, though the decorator responsible for the renovation has at times tried much too hard to make an effect, especially in the bedrooms, the staff are cheerful and willing. The **Hôtel Tafouket**, ✆ 47 25 04, is on the southern end of town along Blvd Mohammed V, a fair distance from the medina but ideally placed for the sea and sand. Do not let the slightly unpromising exterior put you off: this 40-room hotel is run with a rare blend of efficiency and hospitality. It has its own bar, a good restaurant and faces the beach. A few blocks farther out from town is the **Villa Quieta**, 86 Blvd Mohammed V, ✆ 78 32 81, ▨ 78 34 21, a small luxuriously decorated house hotel which has been enthusiastically recommended by a beach-loving correspondent.

inexpensive

There are five good reasonably priced hotels to choose from. The **Sahara**, ✆ 47 22 92, and **Al Mechouar**, ✆ 47 20 18, are comfortable, slightly humdrum places but easy to find on Av Oqba ben Nafia. The latter is smaller, has its own bar and restaurant, and is generally preferable. For more medina atmosphere try the **Tafraout**, 7 Rue de Marrakesh, ✆ 47 29 02, or better still **Des Remparts**, 18 Rue Ibn Rochd, ✆ 47 25 08, the entrance of which is in the far lefthand corner (looking inland) of the Place Moulay el Hassan, where you will smell a bakery in the morning on the opposite side of the street. This is perhaps the dampest and least efficient of the five but is nevertheless a friendly place in which to stay, run by El Houcienne and his son Mustapha. Thirty rooms are arranged around a three-storey interior courtyard; the roof provides a spectacular view, perched above the ramparts, and a possible sunbathing spot if you can find a corner out of the wind. Deep in the heart of the medina is the **Residence El Mehdi**, 15 Rue Sidi Abdesmith, ✆ 47 59 43, a surprisingly modern place with televisions in every bedroom, a central courtyard with a parrot, a restaurant and the sort of cleanliness and domestic calm that you normally associate with a house, not a hotel.

cheap

The **Hôtel du Beau Rivage**, ✆ 47 29 25, above the Café de France in the Place Moulay el Hassan, is easily the best option in this bracket: clean and scrupulously honest, with some rooms overlooking the sea and others overlooking the *place*. If this is full, try the **Hôtel du Tourisme**, Rue Mohammed ben Messaoud, ✆ 47 20 75, perched on the medina walls, with clean simple rooms, cold water and cats. The **Pension Smara**, 26 Rue de la Skala, ✆ 47 23 34, is another good standby, though a somewhat bossy management offsets some of the charm of the view.

Essaouira ✆ (04–)

Eating Out
moderate

Chez Sam, ✆ 47 65 13, also known as the 'Restaurant du Port de Pêche', is at the far end of the port, a delightful clapper-built restaurant that at first appears to be a stranded boat-house. Its location, and a reputation for seriously fresh fish, are enough to guarantee a continuous flow of customers. Beware of the combination of low ceilings and walls clad with photos of movie stars who have dined here—it can catch you a surprising blow on the head. The service is famously erratic, so get a good view or plenty to drink so as not to get frustrated.

Chalet de la Plage, 1 Blvd Mohammed V, ✆ 47 21 58, stands on the seafront opposite the Hôtel des Iles, with a terrace directly washed by the tide. It serves alcohol and has a seafood menu and a range of cheaper local dishes. However, at lunchtime it can be rather busy.

You can also dine in the courtyard of **Dar Loubane**, 24 Rue de Rif, ✆ 47 62 96, a beautiful 18th-century palace just a few yards from the clocktower arch in the centre of the old town. It is furnished with modern orientalist pictures, Mogador memorabilia, some intriguing junk, a fountain and the patrons' beautiful dogs. It is licensed, and the competent menu embraces both French and Moroccan cooking.

cheap

There are four restaurants (none of which serves alcohol) that offer good cheap Moroccan food in and around Place Moulay el Hassan. The **Essalam**, ✆ 47 25 48, provides one of the cheapest and most perfunctory meals with its bargain rates for the set three courses. The café-restaurant **Bab Lachour** is only slightly more expensive, but calmer. You can eat outside on the café terrace, or upstairs in a first-floor dining room. On the eastern side of the *place* is another series of cafés that includes **Toufiks Restaurant** and **Café L'Horloge**. Toufiks serves a delicious vegetable *tagine* and freshly squeezed orange juice in its killim- and mat-strewn interior; L'Horloge occupies an old synagogue.

The **Riad**, 18 Rue Zayane, in the heart of the medina but well signposted, serves local dishes in imaginative menus amid a tranquil traditional atmosphere. A meal could start with harara, courgette and argan oil salad, then *tagine* with potato soufflé. The manager, Azriguine el Mostapha, is a charming, informative man. There are also the outdoor tables of the fish grill-stalls in the port to remember.

Fez

Fez, where all is Eden, or a wilderness.

Anon

Fez is the most complete Islamic medieval city in the world. Its history has for a thousand years also been the history of Morocco's political, commercial and intellectual life, even though it is now superseded by the modern cities of Rabat and Casablanca, and to some extent by its own New Town, built by the French after 1912.

The first independent Muslim kingdom of Morocco was established here on the plain of Saïss, upon the shell of the old Roman capital of Volubilis, by a great-grandson of the Prophet Mohammed, Moulay Idriss, at the end of the 8th century AD. The Idrissid state that was created by his son, Idriss II, stands at the core of Moroccan national identity. Idrissid Morocco declined as a political power after a mere century of rule, but it left behind a new city—Fez—where Islam, law, literacy, art, industry and skilled crafts had a safe refuge.

The citizens of Fez, the *Fassi*, became an urbane upper-middle class that were sufficient unto themselves. They paid lip-service to the current powers, but kept their true loyalty for the fallen Idrissid dynasty. In the heart of the city of Fez stands the ornate tomb of Idriss II, who, to be put in an Anglo-Saxon context, must be compared to some fallen Arthur descended from the family of Christ, and to whom many of the chief citizens can proudly trace their genealogical descent.

For all their pride and insularity the *Fassi* yet provided a vital pool of skills that were at the disposal of the Almoravids, the Almohads, and any dynasty that could unite the disparate regions of Morocco. Fez is most imperishably linked, though, with the Merenids, who through the 13th and 14th centuries presided over the most prosperous period of the city's history, as well as choosing it to be their

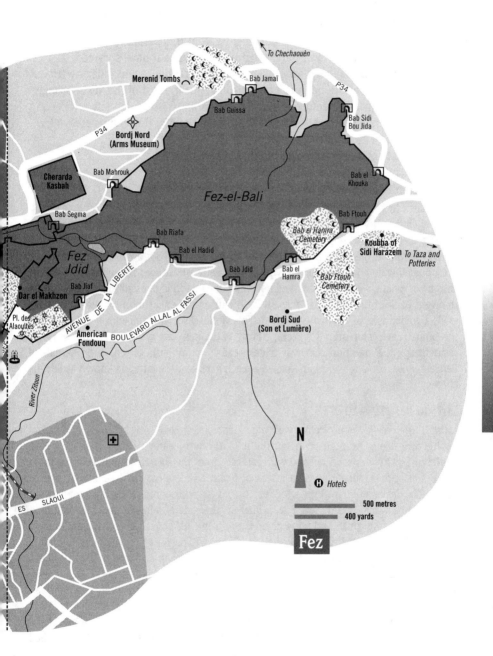

To Chechaouèn

Merenid Tombs

Bab Jamaï

P34

Bab Guissa

Bab Sidi
Bou Jida

Bordj Nord
(Arms Museum)

P34

Bab Mahrouk

Cherarda
Kasbah

Fez-el-Bali

Bab el
Khouka

Bab Segma

Bab Ftouh

Bab Riafa

Bab el Hanra
Cemetery

Koubba of
Sidi Harazem

To Taza and
Potteries

Fez
Jdid

Bab el Hadid

Bab Jdid

Bab el
Hamra

Bab Jiaf

Dar el Makhzen

Bab Ftouh
Cemetery

Pl. des
Alaouites

AVENUE DE LA LIBERTÉ

American
Fondouq

BOULEVARD ALLAL AL FASSI

Bordj Sud
(Son et Lumière)

River Zitoun

N

ES   SLAOUI

H Hotels

500 metres

400 yards

Fez

capital. There was no love lost between the sultans and the *Fassi*, however, despite the plethora of Merenid buildings in the city. The former dwelt in a separate walled enclosure, the palace city of Fez Jdid, where all the instruments of government were located.

Much has perished in the long decline from this period, and it is chiefly the old mosques, tombs and religious colleges that have survived, respected by each dynasty, every mutinous regiment and pillaging tribe. The medersas are open to non-Muslims, but the rest of the vast heritage of religious architecture remains inaccessible. Visitors are left to concentrate on the street pattern, the style of life, the sounds and odours, which remain triumphantly unchanged.

History
Foundation Legend

At his birth in 791 Idriss II inherited his father's kingdom, centred on the two existing cities of Christian Volubilis and Jewish Sefrou. He and his loyal regent Rashid decided to create a specifically Muslim city, and one day while travelling between the two cities they rested halfway, at the Ras el Ma spring. The boy Idriss followed it downstream to discover a wide, well-watered valley fringed with hills. Greatly encouraged by this gorgeous vista, and the prophetic welcome of an aged holy man, they decided to establish a settlement on the right bank of the river that year, in 799. During the excavation for the foundation walls a golden axe, a *fas*, was unearthed. This fateful discovery helped settle the form of the human sacrifice required if each gateway of the new city were to be protected by a resident spirit, a tradition that was widespread in many parts of the world. A pair of Persian exiles, or *Fars*, were buried alive at each gate, and the city was known as Fez, its citizens as Fassi.

Idrissid Fez (799–1075)

Idriss II ruled his kingdom from a walled city, containing his El Aliya palace and barracks for his 500-strong Arab guardon, on the left (northern) bank of the valley. This bare nucleus of a city was soon flooded with refugees from the turbulent politics of the more prosperous and Arabized Muslim states of Spain and Tunisia. In 818 a civil war in Andalucía drove 8000 refugees to Fez; they were presented with the empty right (southern) bank by Idriss II. Seven years later another tide of refugees fled a revolution in the holy city of Kairouan and were given land on the left bank. This settlement pattern remained for the next 250 years. Fez-el-Andalous and Fez-el-Karaouiyne were two quite separate cities that faced each other across the riverbed, each enclosed in its own walls. The Andalucíans were considered to have the prettiest women and the men were considered strong, brave, handsome and good farmers, but also just a little dull. The Kairouan men were considered more elegant, better educated but a bit over-partial to the luxuries of life. What they both shared was a strong Arab identity and an urban, literate, technical and intellectual culture far in advance of any mere Berber tribe. It was as if a fortified Manhattan were suddenly placed in the middle of the prairies.

Idriss II died in 828 and his tomb became the focus of the city's pride and identity, as it is today. His kingdom was divided amongst his squabbling sons, but the ruler of Fez was accepted as first among equals. During his grandson Yahya's reign the two grand mosques of Andalous and Karaouiyne were founded to give graphic evidence of the settlements' prosperity. In 917 Fez fell under the control of the Shiite Fatimid Empire, expanding west from its core territory of Tunisia. In 930 the Ommayad Caliphate of Córdoba took over, and ruled the city through a governor for over a century.

The Almoravid and Almohad Period (1075–1248)

In 1075 the Almoravid leader Youssef ben Tachfine captured Fez, just five years before he succeeded in uniting Morocco for the first time. The Fassi could not at first accept these unsophisticated Berbers from the Sahara, but they soon learned to benefit from their firm rule. Though Marrakesh was the political capital, Fez was better suited to act as the commercial hub of an empire that stretched from West Africa to the Pyrenees. The Almoravids dismantled the divisive twin walls and erected a single circuit to protect both districts. The endless bickering over river rights ended, for the Almoravids came from the desert and knew all about the efficient collection and distribution of water. Clean mountain springs were tapped and a network of pipes, sewers and mills prepared the ground for future expansion.

Water was also the tool by which the Almohads, based in Taza, at last seized control of Fez in 1146 after a long siege. Abdel Moumen built a dam upstream in order to collect a great head of water which he suddenly released; the resulting flood washed the walls around the valley clean away. The Almohads then marched in and demolished the remaining walls, declaring that 'only justice and the sword shall be our ramparts'. They also demolished any traces of Almoravid rule, on the flimsy basis that the architectural decoration of the previous dynasty had been impious. Later sultans ignored these early declarations and constructed a massive new perimeter wall. This still defines the extent of Fez-el-Bali, and some gateways and large sections, particularly to the north, are still in place.

Merenid Fez (1248–1465)

Abou Yahya, the chief of the Beni Merin tribe, captured Fez in 1248, the year that he had treacherously massacred the leaderless Almohad army. So important had the city now become that this date is taken to be the start of his reign. Though the period of Merenid rule was to prove the glittering zenith of the city's fortune, the Fassi never took to this dynasty, mere Berber chiefs of a nomad tribe from the eastern plains. They frequently rebelled against their new rulers, and in truth no dynasty has been able to win the city's affection away from the original Idrissid line. Abou Yusuf Yacqub reigned from 1259 to 1286 and firmly established Fez as the capital of Morocco. He did not, however, feel secure enough to dwell amongst his citizens. On 21 March 1276 he started work on Fez Jdid, 'New Fez', enclosing it in a double wall 750m away from the turbulent politics of Fez-el-Bali. It was known officially as *El Medinat el Baida*, 'the white city', and a portion of the river Fez served as a moat for its outer walls, which were crowned with crenellations and reinforced by square towers. The white city held the court and palace of the sultans,

the mint, baths, markets, three mosques—the Grand, the Red and the Flower—an aqueduct and separate quarters for the sultan's mercenary guard. Abou Yusuf Yacqub was the
first Moroccan ruler to build a medersa, a residential college for religious education. It was
an archetype which his successors developed and embellished into one of the great glories
of Fez.

In 1438 the barracks were enlarged and converted into the first separate Jewish quarter in
Morocco. Wealthy Jewish merchants had long been convenient targets in urban unrest, and
by placing them within the protection of the royal city the Merenids bound this community,
useful for its many skills and taxable wealth, to their service. One of the more disagreeable
services was the preservation of the heads of the executed in salt, before they were displayed on gates. The word for salt, *mellah*, soon became synonymous with a Jewish quarter.

The Decline of Fez after 1465

In 1465 the last Merenid sultan, Abdul Haqq, was dragged through the streets of Fez-el-Bali
before having his throat cut like a sacrificial goat. A council of Idrissid *sherifs* had planned
this bold insurrection, and they succeeded in ruling a republic for seven years. This political
experiment was finished by the Wattasids, the hereditary viziers of the Merenids, who
marched into Fez at the head of an army. Wattasid authority over the next century was
slowly reduced to Fez itself, as the Portuguese seized control of the coast and tribal dynasties fought over the rest. An earthquake shattered the town in 1522, and the Saadians, a
dynasty from southern Morocco, occupied Fez 19 years later. They made no secret of their
preference for Marrakesh, and their only constructive action was to build two artillery forts
with which to intimidate the city. In 1666 Fez welcomed the first Alaouite sultan, Moulay
Rachid, as a liberator, and he responded in kind by building another medersa here. This
rapprochement was quickly reversed: Sultan Moulay Ismaïl detested the city and did everything in his power to humble Fez and vaunt neighbouring Meknès. Most of the later
Alaouite sultans tended to alternate between Fez and Marrakesh, and it was not until the
reign of Sultan Moulay Hassan (1873–94) that decay was decisively checked. He built three
administrative palaces that physically and symbolically united Fez Jdid and Fez-el-Bali, and
most of the substantial Fassi merchant houses date from his reign.

The grip of the European powers strengthened after Moulay Hassan's death, and on 30
March 1912 Sultan Moulay Hafid was forced by the French to sign the Treaty of Fez, which
established the French Protectorate. The city reacted violently to the surrender of national
sovereignty, and on 17 April the European population was hounded through the medina
streets and lynched—over 80 mutilated bodies were stacked up before the palace gates.
The sultan's army joined the rebellion and manned the city walls, but the following day a
French force marched from Meknès and first shelled and then occupied the subdued city.

Sultan Moulay Hafid was removed to Rabat, where the government of Morocco has since
remained, and Casablanca became the still-unrivalled mercantile metropolis. Here in Fez,
the French built an ordered New Town of regular avenues well to the west of the old city
to house the European population in comfort and safety. Fez-el-Bali is now a unique
medieval survivor, fallen far from grace but remaining one of the most distinctive cities of
the world.

The city has a population of half a million and is divided into three parts. **Fez-el-Bali** (Old Fez) is the enigmatic and fiercely Muslim medina, a maze of hidden quarters, *fondouqs*, medersas and mosques, with narrow streets that remain inaccessible to cars. **Fez Jdid** (New Fez) is the 13th-century Imperial city to the west of the medina, still dominated by the royal palace and the *mellah*, the old Jewish ghetto. The French-built **New Town** is even farther to the west, a separate entity with wide avenues and new developments which would be without interest but for its cafés, hotels, restaurants, and convenience.

Fez ℂ (05–)   ***Getting There and Around***

by air

The Fez-Saïss airport, ℂ 62 48 00/ℂ 62 47 12, is 11km due south off the P24 road to Immouzer. Royal Air Maroc have an office at 54 Av Hassan II, ℂ 62 55 16, reservations ℂ 62 04 57, as well as a booth at the airport, ℂ 62 47 12/ℂ 65 21 61. Internal flights include a daily flight to Casablanca and a twice-weekly service to Marrakesh. The airport bus, no.16, leaves from Place Mohammed V, or pay 30dh for your own taxi, 5dh for a place in a *grand taxi.*

by rail

Travel by train whenever possible, trust no published schedule and buy your ticket and a seat reservation early and directly from the main station, which is located off the Av des Almohades on the northern edge of the New Town, ℂ 62 20 43. There are eight trains a day to Casablanca (8hrs) and two south to Marrakesh (8hrs) including a sleeper connection. A taxi ride, in a licensed cab with meter on, from the station to any centrally placed Fez hotel will be under 10dh.

by bus

Bus travel into and out of Fez can be slightly confusing as there are three bus stations. The busiest and most convenient is the new terminal just north of Fez-el-Bali's Bab Mahrouk. This has replaced the old mess of garages (still marked on some maps) around Place Baghdadi and Bab Bou Jeloud. It has its own café and is well served by *petits taxis*. The CTM have begun to use this terminal, as well as continuing with their own station in the heart of the New Town on Blvd Mohammed V, ℂ 62 20 43. If you should want to head east or north into the Rif there is also a local bus station by Bab Ftouh on the southeastern edge of Fez-el-Bali. The most frequent bus connections are west to Meknès (50mins), Rabat (4–6hrs) and Casablanca (8hrs), with at least twice-daily connections to Marrakesh.

Fez is one of the few Moroccan cities where local buses can be of real use to a visiting tourist. The route numbers are marked on the sides, not on the back or front as you might expect. Bus **no.1** runs between Place des Alaouites (the southwestern end of Fez Jdid) and Dar Batha (at the western end of Fez-el-Bali); **no.3** goes between Place des Alaouites and Place de la Résistance (in the northeastern corner of the New Town); **no.9** runs from Place de la Résistance to Dar Batha;

no.10 runs from Bab Guissa (the centrally placed northern gate to Fez-el-Bali) to Place des Alaouites; **no.16** runs from Place Mohammed V to the airport; **no.18** goes from the Place de la Résistance east via Bab Jdid to Bab Ftouh (the southeastern gate of Fez-el-Bali); and **no.19** runs from the train station to Place des Alaouites.

by taxi

Fez' red *petits taxis* use their meters and are therefore delightfully cheap and trouble-free. Taxi fares increase by 50 per cent after dusk or 9pm, whichever is earliest. In the New Town you should be able to find taxis on Avenue Hassan II (especially around the crossing with Blvd Mohammed V), at Place Mohammed V, the train station and in Rue des Normandes, off Blvd Mohammed V, which is a *grands taxis* park. In Fez Jdid try the Place des Alaouites, while in Fez-el-Bali they can usually be hailed outside all the principal transport gates: Place Baghdadi (between Bab Bou Jeloud and Bab Mahbrouk), the northern Bab Guissa, southern Bab er Rsif, southeastern Bab Ftouh and Dar Batha-Place Istiqlal (just south of the Bab Bou Jeloud).

Grands taxis can be found at Place Baghdadi (for a place to Meknès), Bab Jamai, Bab Guissa and Bab Ftouh in Fez-el-Bali. The rank on Rue des Normandes, just off Blvd Mohammed V in the New Town, is one of the most useful, and covers the destinations south of the city, if you should decide to venture that way.

by car

A car is a hindrance in Fez. If you drive into the city from the west or south you will invariably find yourself escorted by motorbike-borne 'guides'. There is absolutely no way to shake them off (apart from revealing a deep knowledge of the city in collo-quial Maghrebi), but treat them as a convenience, for they can lead you directly to your chosen hotel. It is as well also to be aware, though, that they are aiming for the greater prize of taking you round the medina and earning a commission from the bazaars and carpet shops. Once in Fez, get your hotel receptionist to recommend a secure parking place, then completely empty your car and forget about it.

A car could be useful, however, for day trips from the city. For **car hire** ask at reception in big hotels or go directly to such agencies as Avis, 23 Rue de la Liberte, ✆ 62 27 90, or 50 Blvd Chefchaouni, ✆ 62 67 46; or Europcar, 41 Av Hassan II, ✆ 62 65 45.

Garages: for Renault service, 26 Rue Soudan, ✆ 62 22 32; for Fiat, Auto Maroc, on Av Mohammed V, ✆ 62 34 35; or for problems with all makes of car try the Méchanique Générale, 22 Av Cameroun.

Fez ✆ (05–) **Tourist Information**

The two principal **tourist offices** are in the New Town: in the western corner of Place de la Résistance at the end of Av Hassan II, ✆ 62 34 60, and the Syndicat d'Initiative (SI), on the eastern side of Place Mohammed V on Av Mohammed es Slaoui, ✆ 62 47 69. However, most useful for the visitor is the SI booth (*open*

Mon–Sat 8am–7pm), beside Bab Bou Jeloud in Fez-el-Bali, where official guides, with their official gold medallion and working outfit of white cotton jellaba, red fez and dark glasses, can be hired.

Banks are mostly in the New Town. The BMCE on Place Mohammed V offers the most useful range of services, but there is also the BMCI, 10 Rue Assela, Banque Populaire and Crédit du Maroc on Av Mohammed V. In the heart of Fez-el-Bali there is a branch of Crédit du Maroc uphill from the Cherratin Medersa for currency exchanges. All large hotels will change money and travellers' cheques for guests.

The **post office** is in the New Town at the corner of Av Hassan II and Blvd Mohammed V (*open summer Mon–Fri 8–2; winter Mon–Fri 8.30–12 and 2.30–6; stamps sold Sat 8–11*). The telephone section (*open until 9pm*) has its own side entrance when the rest of the building has closed up. Other branches are found at Place de l'Atlas, and Place Batha in Fez Jdid.

Emergencies: The central police station is on Av Mohammed V, ✆ 19. There is an **all-night pharmacy** in the New Town on Blvd Moulay Youssef by the Place de la Résistance, ✆ 62 33 80. In the daytime there are dozens of chemists open in the New Town, and also one by the Bab Ftouh in Fez-el-Bali.

There is a **French consulate** on Av Abou Obeida Ibn Jarrah. The **Catholic Church** of St Francis, on Av Mohammed es Slaoui in the New Town, has Mass on Saturday at 6.30pm, and Sunday at 10.30am.

Fez Jdid

Though the most famous sites are in Fez-el-Bali, a walk through the simple street plan of Fez Jdid and a visit to the Dar Batha Museum make a good preparation for the heady and confusing alleys of the old town.

Place des Alaouites

From the Place de la Résistance in the New Town, Blvd Moulay Youssef leads directly to the Place des Alaouites, a kilometre away; or you can hop on the no.3 bus. This main entrance to the palace was created by King Hassan II between 1969 and 1971, as the ceremonial guard and great gates proclaim. On occasion this entire square is covered in a patchwork of carpets brought out by Fassis to honour some official guest. The gleaming brass doors were manufactured in the medina in 1971, and are kept clean by being rubbed with lemons.

The Royal Palace (Dar el Makhzen)

> *I believe this to be the finest single sight Morocco has to offer; one of the wonders of the world.*
>
> *The Traveller's Guide to Morocco*, Christopher Kininmonth

The royal palace occupies half of Fez Jdid and covers over 80 hectares. Within its walls is an inaccessible city that holds 700 years of pavilions, squares, gardens and palaces. It includes a mosque, the koubba of Sidi Mejaed, and a medersa built by the Merenid Sultan Abou Said Othman in 1320. Sidi Mohammed built the Dar Ayad el Kebira palace in the 18th century; Moulay Hassan the present royal apartments in 1880; and in 1980 another palace was added, the Dar el Bahia, for the Arab summit held the next year. There are rumours that the young king Mohammed VI intends to open it to the public.

The *Mellah*

The Grand Rue du Mellah runs from Place des Alaouites through the whole *mellah* district. The Jewish community had to walk barefoot within the three royal cities (Marrakesh, Fez and Meknès) and in front of a mosque, but by the 18th century the Fassi Jews had acquired the right to wear sea-rush socks outside the *mellah*. There are few Jews left, but a legacy of jewellers' shops, brocade, balconies, small windows with their tracery of iron grille work, and an air of business gives the quarter something of its old distinctive atmosphere. Tiny side streets lead off into a labyrinth of covered passages, underground workshops and timbered houses. A little way to the south is the Jewish cemetery, a great walled enclosure of whitewashed inscribed stones.

The Historic Synagogues of Fez

There are five historic synagogues in the *mellah*, most found off small alleys leading from Rue Merin. The largest, oldest and most important is the **Synagogue Rabbi Shlomo Ibn Danan**, on Rue Derb El Feran Teati, which has been restored as a historic monument. This can be visited free of charge during reasonable daylight hours, though you will need a guide to point out the deliberately inconspicuous door. The synagogue was built by Mimoun Bou Sidan, a merchant from Zaouiat Ait-Ishaq village in the Middle Atlas, during the reign of Moulay Ismaïl and named after a 19th-century scholar-rabbi. The synagogue later passed into the ownership of the well-connected Bensoussan family. It is a dark, powerfully atmospheric place, built hard against the *mellah* wall, with a subterranean *mikve* (ritual bath) and no space for women. Right next door is the **Synagogue Debada**, also on Rue Derb El Feran Teati, now a house and not normally accessible. **Synagogue Sabba**, Rue Derd El Wassa, is also a house, and the resident is unfortunately bored with visitors trying to see Morocco's most beautiful 18th-century synagogue. **Synagogue Dar El Ma**, 220 Rue Derb El Foukie, is tiny and tucked up two flights of stairs, but has elaborate wooden ceilings and cornices. It is also now a house, and its owners are friendly to interested visitors. **Synagogue El Fessaine**, Rue Derb el Fessaine, was the largest Jewish place of prayer built in the 17th century and is now in use as a sports hall.

Bab Smarine

As you approach the distinctive, crenellated, high gate of the Bab Smarine, restored in 1924, you pass through the glittering displays of the **jewellers' souk**. The Bab Smarine used to separate the *mellah* from the Muslim quarter, and before that marked the southern entrance of the city. Immediately beyond the arch is a covered food market which was established in an old granary built by the Merenid sultans. From the gate the Grand Rue de Fez-Jdid, lined with stalls and cafés, runs due north through the city to the

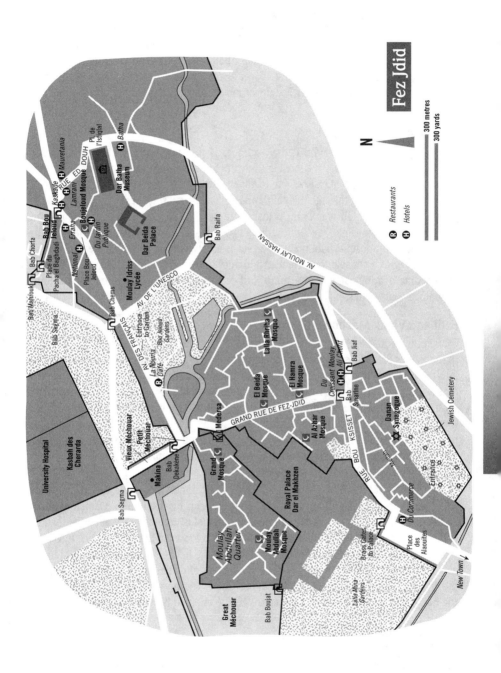

Fez Jdid

N

Restaurants
Hotels

300 metres
300 yards

PI. de
l'Istiqlal

RUE ED DOUH

Bab Batha

Dar Batha
Museum

Kasbade

RUE

Mauretania

Lamrani

Erraha

Bab Bou Jeloud Mosque

Bab Bou

National

Bab Chorfa

Place du
Pacha el Baghdadi Jeloud

Place Bou
Jeloud

Du Jardin
Publique

Dar Beida
Palace

Bab Raifa

Bab Mahtrouk

Bab Segma

Bab Chems

Moulay Idriss
Lycée

AV. DE L'UNESCO

Entrance
to Garden

AV. DES FRANÇAIS

La Noria
Café

Bou Jeloud
Gardens

AV. MOULAY HASSAN

University Hospital

Kasbah des
Cherarda

Vieux Méchouar

Petit
Méchouar

Bab Segma

Makina

Bab
Dekakène

Medersa

GRAND RUE DE FEZ-JDID

Grand
Mosque

El Beida
Mosque

El Hamra
Mosque

Lalla Rihita
Mosque

Du
Croissant Moulay

Al Cherif

Bab Jiaf

Bab
Smarine

Al Azhar
Mosque

RUE BOU KSISSET

Dianan

Synagogue

Jewish Cemetery

Royal Palace
Dar el Makhzen

Moulay
Abdullah Quarter

Moulay
Abdullah
Mosque

Enfrânes

Du Commerce

Brass Gates
to Palace

Place des
Alaouites

Great
Méchouar

Bab Boujat

Lalla-Mina
Gardens

New Town

165

outer walls. Along the way, on the right, is the **Hamra**, the red, and then the **Beida**, the white, **mosques**, built in the 13th century by the creator of Fez Jdid, Sultan Abou Yusuf Yacqub. The alleys to the left stop at the perimeter wall of the palace, beneath which is the pretty **mosque of Al Azhar**, built by Sultan Abou Inan in the 14th century, with a fine sculpted gate. The street opens out to form a small walled square known as the Petit Méchouar, under which the river Fez flows and in which is a gleaming back entrance to the royal palace.

Moulay Abdullah Quarter

A small arch to the left of the Petit Méchouar is the only entrance into the Moulay Abdullah district. This area is almost entirely enclosed by high walls and was chosen by the French as the *quartier réservé*, the red-light district, though there is little evidence of those days. Wandering through this calm residential area you soon pass the entrance of the **grand mosque**, which was built in just three years (1273–6) by Sultan Abou Yusuf Yacqub. Sultan Abou Inan was buried here in 1358 and a koubba was raised above his tomb beside the mosque. The main street leads after 200m to the **mosque of Moulay Abdullah**, with a conspicuous, slender minaret, built in the 18th century. The mosque has become a principal Alaouite tomb, full of the graves of princes and two sultans including Moulay Youssef (1912–27).

Petit and Vieux Méchouar

Back in the Petit Méchouar, at the northern end is the **Bab Dekakène**, sometimes known as the Bab es Siba. This massive, triple-arched Merenid gate served as the main entrance into the city and royal palace until 1971. Ferdinand, prince of Portugal, was imprisoned for six years in this gate after he had surrendered himself as hostage to allow his army to escape after a disastrous attempt to seize Tangier in 1437; his brothers refused to return Ceuta, near Tangier, to the sultan in exchange for his release. On Ferdinand's death his naked body, pierced through the heels like a butchered goat, was hung from the gate, where it swung for four days. His corpse was then gutted, stuffed with straw and put on show for a further 29 years.

On the far side of the arches there is the larger, walled Vieux Méchouar. On the left is the *Makina*, the old royal ordnance factory, built and run by the Italian 'Campionario Di Spolette' in the late 19th century. Although it now holds nothing more offensive than an export-orientated carpet factory, you will need permission from the tourist office to visit its huge vaulted halls. At the far end of the square on the left is the **Bab Segma**, a Merenid gate built in 1315. It was originally flanked by a pair of distinctive octagonal arches, like the gate to the Chellah in Rabat, although only one tower now survives. The smaller gate, the **Bab es Smen**, built in the 19th century, is the one that is used nowadays.

Bou Jeloud and the Gardens

The Avenue des Français leads due east from the Petit Méchouar 600m to the **Bab Bou Jeloud**, the main point of entry to Fez-el-Bali. For 500 years this area was a wasteland, caught between the cities of Fez Jdid and Fez-el-Bali, until it was developed in the 19th century by Moulay Hassan into the three palace gardens of Dar Batha, Bou Jeloud and Dar

Beida. The old Bou Jeloud Palace, symbolically, was entered from either Fez Jdid or Fez-el-Bali. Only one of these palaces, the Dar Batha, is open, and now houses the **Museum of the Arts and Traditions of Fez** (*see* below). Otherwise the area remains dominated by high walls that hide gardens, palaces and pavilions, while less attractive administrative buildings are left exposed.

There is an entrance just east of the Petit Méchouar to the **Jardins de Bou Jeloud**, a delightful park with palm-shaded formal walks, cut through with ornamental watercourses that feed the round but slightly disappointing pond. The most famous and restful corner of the garden (also accessible directly from the road) is **La Nouria** café, which overlooks a mill race and its namesake waterwheel. This wooden watermill is sadly stuck solid, but it recalls a time when all the backstreet workshops of Fez were powered by dozens of such gently moaning creatures. Just outside the back door of the café is the pitch of a photographer, who continues to make use of an old box apparatus complete with cape and tripod.

Halfway along Avenue des Français toward Fez-el-Bali is a crossroads. To the left is the keyhole arch of **Bab Chems**; to the right the Avenue de l'UNESCO divides the public Bou Jeloud gardens from the walled park, pavilions and palace of **Dar Beida**, now occupied by a school, the Lycée Moulay Idriss, and so not open to visitors.

Place du Pasha el Baghdadi

A left turn opposite the entrance to the Lycée Moulay Idriss takes you to the Place du Pasha el Baghdadi. Idle buses now no longer take over this dusty triangle of land, where nut, fruit and cake hawkers and *petits taxis* collect. At dusk small groups gather around the odd musician, or haggle over temporary displays of secondhand goods, particularly on the side of the square by the solid-looking **Bab Mahrouk**, the 'gate of the burned'. This was built in 1214 by an Almohad sultan, Mohammed en Nasir. It was first known as the Bab ech Cheria, the gate of justice, as this was the execution square. It received its new name after El Obeidi, a leader of the heretical Rif Rhomara tribe, and Ibn el Khatib, a harmless 14th-century intellectual, were burnt alive here. This was a savage punishment designed to deny any chance of resurrection.

To the right of the Bab Mahrouk is the **Bab Chorfa**, a strong gate protected by two elegant towers that guards the entrance into the **Kasbah en Nouar**, the kasbah of flowers, also known as the Filali Kasbah. Though now just another residential district with a busy, stall-lined central avenue, it was once the site of the central Almohad fortress, which was occupied by the pasha of Fez under the Merenids and then renamed the Filali Kasbah to honour Moulay Rachid, of the family of that name, in the 17th century. The original mosque is just to the right inside the gate. Its façade was restored in the 18th century by Sultan Moulay Sliman, at the same time that he repaired the battlements.

The Dar Batha Museum (Musée des Arts et Traditions)

Open Wed–Mon 9–12 and 3–6; closed Tues; adm.

Through Bab Bou Jeloud, turn right and then right again along the comparatively broad Rue Ed Douh for 100m to the café-fronted Place de l'Istiqlal, where another right turn takes you to the entrance of the Dar Batha Museum. Alternatively, take a taxi or the no.1 bus from Place des Alaouites straight to the Dar Batha, or catch the no.18 from Place de la Résistance.

The palace of Dar Batha was begun by Moulay Hassan and finished by his son Abdul Aziz (1894–1909). A range of green-tiled pyramid roofs emerges above the red walls to cover the apartments and galleries that now house the exhibits. An amply sized **Andalucían garden** extends within the walls, its grid of blue and white raised paths lined by lush trees and swathes of shrub and bamboo. It's a delightful place, the tranquillity of the enclosed garden appealing as much as the exhibits. In September and May concerts of Andalucían music are held here.

Inside, the cases of exhibits follow no particular scheme: astrolabes, Middle Atlas carpets, stamps, illustrated Korans, pens, Berber jewellery, embroidery, guns, rural pots and coins from either the Idrissids or Alaouites are interspersed with blue geometric ware from Fez. The corner rooms contain the larger pieces of carved cedar, plaster or stone that have been recovered from restorations and excavations of Fassi tombs, mosques and medersas, some of them dated to the Merenid and Saadian dynasties. As ever in Morocco, the achievements of urban Andalucían culture appear timeless, as objects from the 10th to the 20th centuries have a great deal in common. The true contrast is with products from the Berber tribes, even ones stationed close to Fez. Fez' past role as an oasis of technical skill and literate culture for the nation is well revealed by this charming jumble of exhibits.

Fez-el-Bali

The four major accessible sites of Fez-el-Bali—the Bou Inania Medersa, Attarine Medersa, Fondouq Nejjarine and the tanneries—can be seen in half a day. The lesser medersas, the exteriors of the ancient mosques, the hidden bakeries, *hammams*, *fondouqs*, workshops and alleys of the medina could take weeks to find—to understand the city fully you have to have been born a Fassi. To arrive at the medina with no intention of buying anything is to miss out on the central life of the city, but see all you wish before making the rounds of the bazaars. Then you can savour the ritual of commerce without impatience, delight in the gift of mint tea, the opulent decoration of the large bazaars, and the loquacious salesmanship.

Guides

Arriving at the medina, usually at the Bab Bou Jeloud, accept the need for a guide for at least your first half-day. He or she can show you intimate parts of the old city where an unescorted foreigner would not be welcome. Official guides can be found at the tourist office, outside all the major hotels, and from the Syndicat d'Initiative on Place Mohammed V in the New Town. These official guides are a professional body but their talk and itineraries can become uninspiring through repetition. Unofficial guides charge less and may try harder to please, although their routes are often given an erratic twist as they try to avoid the police, since they are illegal—but that remains their problem, not yours.

The Golden Age of Fez

At the beginning of the 14th century Fez-el-Bali had a population of 125,000. None of the houses was permitted to touch the city walls, which were lined with gardens and cemeteries and pierced by eight gates. Within the medina there were 785 mosques, 372 flour mills, 135 bakers' ovens, 93 public baths, 467 *fondouqs* and 80 fountains. Outside the walls, potteries, olive oil presses, sawmills, weavers' workshops, tanneries and smithies collected in three industrial zones around Bab Guissa, Bab Ftouh and along the riverbanks.

The medina was divided into 18 districts which each had a headman agreed upon by the chief residents. The caid, a magistrate learned in Koranic law, judged civil cases, with a deputy who specialized in marriage and divorce suits. There were 35 secretaries and accountants on the caid's staff helping to supervise the financing of pious foundations, hospitals and baths. The caid also acted as rector of the university and censor of intellectual life. The various medersas lodged 2,000 students in Fez while they pursued their studies in the Karaouiyne University. Lectures were given in the grand mosques after morning prayers; the university library was housed behind the mihrab of the Karaouiyne Mosque, and the courts of the various medersas or the houses of professors were used for smaller teaching groups.

There was a hospital for the sick without family, and a leprosarium outside the ramparts housed lepers in isolation. The muhtasib, the prefect of manners, kept surveillance over the baths, the honesty of exchanges, weights and measures, and organized a weekly inspection of prostitutes by physicians.

There were 150 guilds each under the protection of a patron saint, such as Sidi Mohammed Ibn Attab for the shoemakers and Sidi Mimum for the potters. Numerically, the corporation of weavers was dominant—500 workshops employed almost 20,000 workers— but the most powerful corporation was that of the semi-official water and drainage technicians. They and the water jurists alone understood the labyrinthine pipe system—the chief wonder of Fez. It filled fountains, public baths and mosque pools, drove 400 mills, and then 'the river doth disperse itself into manifold channels insinuating itself unto every street and member thereof to pass through countless conduits into sinks and gutters'.

Above the urban hierarchy, the sultan appointed a pasha as governor of the city. He occupied the Almohad fortress at the western end of the medina, held enormous power and directly ran the police, criminal trials and ordered executions.

The Karaouiyne Quarter

The square in front of the main city gate, the Bab Bou Jeloud, is a bustling throng of cafés, cheap hotels, taxis, buses, bemused tourists and confident young guides. Originally it was the site of another Almohad kasbah, itself built over the ruins of an Almoravid fort which had defended this exposed western edge of the city. Some of the kasbah foundations were found recently during building work on ground just to the west of the Bou Jeloud Mosque. The famous **Bou Jeloud triple arch** was built in 1913 by the French beside an earlier gate, just a year after they had occupied Fez. It served as a recognizable border between the native quarter of the medina and the administrative districts and resident-general's palace, which were established in the Dar Batha and Dar Beida in the first years of the Protectorate. The origin of the name of the gate is much discussed. It is thought to have started as Bab Abou El Jnoud, 'the soldier's gate', before being shortened and popularized to Bou Jeloud, 'the leather gate'. The gate frames the minarets of the Sidi Lezzaz Mosque and Bou Inania Medersa. The gold and blue tracery decoration represents Fez 'the blue'; the gold-green on the far side is for Islam.

Beyond the arch is an area lined by a few cheap hotels, food stalls and café restaurants, while straight ahead is the **Kissariat Serrajine**, a small courtyard lined with a glittering array of stalls selling embroidered leather, slippers and silverware. The medina's two major arteries appear here: Rue Talaa Kebira is down the narrow turning to the left, while Rue Talaa Seghira is to the right. They run roughly parallel to each other in a bow-shaped way, and are both lined with stalls, shops and bazaars. Periodically covered by arches and slats of bamboo, they later meet in the confused web of narrow streets known as the Kissaria.

The Bou Inania Medersa

Open daily 8–6, except Fri am, though you may be asked to leave during hours of prayer; adm.

Taking Rue Talaa Kebira, you approach the Bou Inania Medersa, 100m along on your right under a covered archway. The Bou Inania Medersa is the finest and largest in Fez. The **prayer-hall** is in active use, which saves the spirit of the place from disappearing under the flow of visitors. The entrance hall has a stalactite-domed roof; to the left is a room for the faithful to wash their feet. The main open-air court, paved in marble with a round, central pool, is surrounded by a carved cedar screen. There is a lecture hall at either side and a large prayer-hall at the end, across a marble-moated portion of the river Fez. The prayer-hall should not be entered by a non-Muslim, but it is fine to look at its mihrab, columned hall and minbar. The elegant **minaret** is clearly visible above the cedar-lintelled and green-tiled roof. The roofs are currently closed, owing to repairs, but when open they offer an exciting view over neighbouring roof tops and a barrage of minarets.

The Bou Inania Medersa is a direct importation of 14th-century Andalucían techniques to Morocco. All the materials—the *zellij* mosaic, the plaster, marble and cedar—carry a range of patterns, in excellent condition, that threaten to overwhelm the architecture. But the geometric swirls hide a single point: the detail of the floral patterns illustrates a divine symmetry, and even the array of stalactites breaks down into an ordered span of inter-locking arches. The cedar screen with its delicate weave of knots and stars seems to simplify into two dimensions, and invites a further reduction to the one-dimensional, single point. All can be seen as witness to the one God. The bands of Kufic calligraphy contain lines from the Koran.

Medersas were residential colleges for the learning of the Koran, and their endowments provided free board and lodging for students for six years, as well as the salaries of the

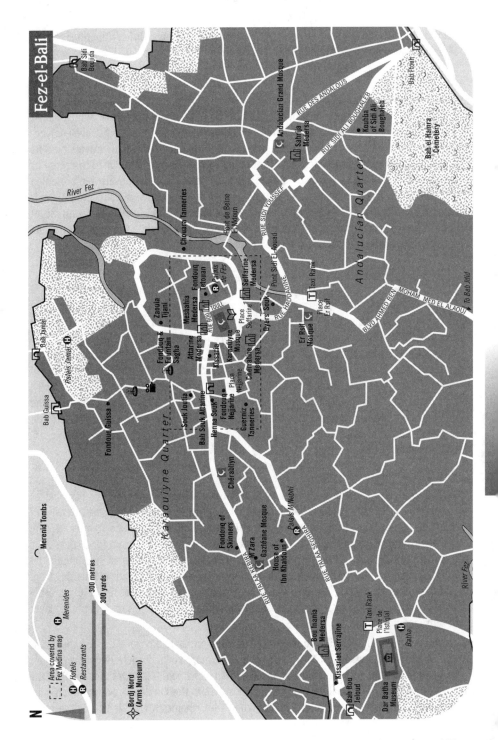

Fez-el-Bali

N

- **H** Hotels
- **R** Restaurants
- - - Area covered by Fez Medina map

Merenides **H**

0   300 metres
0   300 yards

Bordj Nord (Arms Museum)

Merenid Tombs

River Fez

Bab Jamaï
Bab Guissa
Palais Jamaï **H**
Fondouq Guissa

Bab Sidi Boujida

Andalucian Grand Mosque
Bab Froun

RUE DES ANDALOUS
Sahrija Medersa
RUE SID ALI BOUGHALEB
Koubba of Sidi Ali Boughaleb
Bab el-Hamra Cemetery

Chouara Tanneries

Pont de Beine El-Mdoun

RUE SIDI YOUSSEF

Andalucian Quarter

Zaouia Tijani
Mesbahia Medersa
Fondouq Tetouan
R Palais de Fez
Saffarine Medersa
Pont Sidi El-Aouad

Fondouq el-Fanfani Sagha
Attarine Medersa
RUE TOUIL
Kissaria
Karaouiyne Mosque
Place Saffarine
Tyers Souk
RUE HADDADINE
Taxi Rank **T**
Place Er Rsif

To Bab Jdid

Souk Joutia
Bab Souk Attarine
Place Nejjarine
Chérabliyn
Cheratine Medersa
Er Rsif Mosque
BLVD AHMED BEN MOHAM MED EL ALAOU

Henna Souk
Fondouq Nejjarine
Guerniz Tanneries
Place Vejjarine

Karaouiyne Quarter

Fondouq of Skinners
N'Zara
Baztéane Mosque
House of Ibn Khaldoun
R Palais M'Nebhi
RUE TALAA KEBIRA
RUE TALAA SEGHIRA

Chérabliyn

Bou Inania Medersa
Kissariat Serrajine
Place de l'Istiqlal **T**
H
River Fez
Batha

Bab Bou Jeloud
Dar Batha Museum

171

administrative staff and the professors. This had an obvious political function, for the Merenid sultans could counter regional loyalties and divisive spiritual brotherhoods by educating future governors, judges and tribal chiefs near their side and within a state-approved orthodoxy. A little of this political dimension has crept into the Bou Inania. It was built by Sultan Abou Inan between 1350 and 1357 on an area of wasteland set apart and so removed from the independent spirit of the Karaouiyne University, which feared his intentions. This powerful sovereign (who had deposed his own father) strove energetically to enhance his new foundation and supersede the traditional university. The medersa's sumptuous proportions and decoration were deliberately designed to eclipse its rival, and the sultan is remembered for his famously aestheticist response when presented with the costs: 'What is beautiful cannot be expensive at any price; what is enthralling is never too costly.' It is no surprise that several lines praising Abou Inan and his munificent generosity have crept into the decoration of the main court, while the dedication stone declares him caliph, the successor to the Prophet.

The Clock and Sahn

The scaffolding opposite the medersa gate on the left hides, high up on a carved lintel of cedar, a dilapidated row of thirteen windows with some brass bowls on the sills and the odd water spout. This is known as the water-clock, though no description has survived and no satisfactory explanation of its working has been devised. It is considered to have been the work of a magician rabbi, and was finished in 1357 in time for the medersa's inauguration. It may not have been a clock but a musical instrument of timed jets of tinkling water on brass, in celebration of the building, inside which is the medersa's *sahn,* or courtyard for washing. Male tourists used to be able to enter this working portion of the medersa complex and admire the court with its central marble basin, stone closets and impressive flow of water. It is now closed, hopefully in order to repair its rich but precarious plaster and cedar carving.

Rue Talaa Kebira

Farther down the street is the **zaouia of Sidi Ahmed Tijani**, one of the two Fassi lodges of this widespread Sufi brotherhood. The street continues downhill into the intensity of the medina—bazaars, bakeries, grill cafés, *zellij*-decorated fountains and *hammams.* The heavily loaded mules of the Guir Valley porters pause for no man: listen for '*Balak!*', the muleteers' look-out cry. The rich odours of olive oil, fresh mint, cedar shavings, leather, fat burnt on charcoal, kif, mule dung and human urine mix with the sounds of chanting from a Koranic nursery school, running water, hooves and the babble of business. Buy freshly squeezed orange juice, sweet cakes, fresh bread, or fried potato cakes to add another layer of sensual enjoyment.

As you begin to climb uphill you pass a row of blacksmiths, and beyond this, on the left, is an old **Merenid prison**, just like any other *fondouq* except for its noticeably heavier arches and colonnades where the prisoners would be chained. It is now the market for the butter and honey wholesalers. On the right, just before the **Gazléane Mosque**, an alley marked by a plaque leads to the house where Ibn Khaldoun (1332–1406), the great historian and sociologist, lived. Just beyond this turning is the **M'Zara of Moulay Idriss**, a monument that commemorates the place where the founder rested and envisaged the future city. On the left is the Derb bou Haj Mosque, and just beyond that the **skinners' fondouq** (*fondouq des peaussiers*), the yard where wet hides are scraped clean of fat and tissue. Some of the near-transparent, vellum-like finished products are then fitted here to ceramic drums and wooden tambourines. The oldest *hammam* in Fez is opposite the distinctive fountain on the right.

Cobblers' stalls increasingly dominate the street with their displays of slippers, and the second mosque on the right is the **Chérabliyn**, the slipper-makers'. This was founded by the Merenid Sultan Abou Hassan (1331–51), though only the minaret is original—which is all, apart from the gate, that a non-Muslim can see. Beyond the mosque there are a number of bazaars and then the **Souk Aïn Allou** area, where the fine leather-workers trade; their distinctive gold-stamped and decorated book-binding is still known as Morocco work, or *maroquinerie*.

Souk Attarine Gate

Beyond the Souk Aïn Allou look out for a modest gateway across the road marked by a rusty 'Souk Attarine' sign. The gate stands before a busy crossroad of paths and is a city landmark. It can be used as a starting point for short walks to the **Henna Souk**, to **Place Nejjarine** and to the **zaouia of Moulay Idriss II**, before heading farther along the main street to the **Attarine Medersa** and the great **Karaouiyne Mosque**.

The Henna Souk and Sidi Frej Maristan

Just before the Souk Attarine gate take the right turn and then, ten paces later, take the first left to bring you into the **Souk au Henné**, an intimate triangular *place* under the dappled shade of an old poplar tree. Here henna paste, hessian sacks of henna leaves, silvery blocks of antimony, rhassoul and dark, powdered kohl are weighed out and sold. More alarming is the display of the dried skins of lizards, snakes and small predators, with hutches of live hedgehogs and terrapins for magical pastes, aphrodisiacs and love potions. All the stallholders are happy to explain the use of their various products and can put you in touch with the local women who create the rich geometric patterns in henna with which hands and feet are decorated.

On the far side of the little *place* stands a normal-looking trading *fondouq* which occupies the site of the **Sidi Frej Maristan**, a mental asylum built in the reign of the Merenid Sultan Yacqub (1286–1307). A plaque on the wall proudly records this early example of enlightened medical care, and that Leo Africanus worked here as a doctor for a while. The Sidi Frej charitable foundation was also famous for running another hospital which nursed sick cranes and storks back to health, and respectfully buried these holy birds when they died.

Place Nejjarine and Fondouq Nejjarine Museum

Take the second right turn down a narrow alley before the Souk Attarine gate, and after 25 paces turn right again to walk down a vine-covered alley lined with workshops to approach

Place Nejjarine (the square of the carpenters). This is another of the medina's intimate places, which can be appreciated *en passant*, or at your ease in one of the small cafés. An elegant drinking fountain plays here into a basin of mosaic tiles, and cedar beams support a green-tiled canopy. On a weekday morning the carpenters can be found at work off any of the surrounding streets, adzing away at a twisted trunk, for instance, to carve a light, strong plough.

The 18th-century **Nejjarine Fondouq** dominates the *place*, with a great imposing ornamental gateway standing behind the fountain to frame one of the classic images of the city. The immaculate restoration of the *fondouq* has been paid for by Mohammed Lamrani, ex-prime minister and scion of an old Fassi family. Opened in 1998, at a cost of 18 million dirhams, it now houses the **museum of wood** (✆ *(05) 74 05 80*, ✉ *(05) 63 61 85; open Wed–Mon 9–12 and 3–6; closed Tues; adm*), a state-of-the-art collection of tools, wood types and historic exhibits all beautifully displayed, labelled, securely dated and odiferous. Look out for the low dowry chests, high marriage chairs, ornate window grilles, prayer beads, elegant musical instruments, fairground wheels and the *karraka*—school boards by which the Koran was learnt. Continue through the three storeys up to the roof terrace for the views, a 6dh mint tea at the café, and a chance to sit and collect your thoughts.

If you take the alley beside the *fondouq* you will be heading towards the smell of the **Guerniz tanneries**, which are just before the Sidi Moussa Mosque. These are the oldest of the three Fez tanneries; tradition has it they were established by Idriss II.

The Zaouia of Moulay Idriss II

Non-Muslims are not allowed into the sanctuary here, but you can get an excellent view of the interior from the edge of the women's gate.

Take the right turn just beyond (east of) the Souk Attarine gate, and after about 80 paces you will pass under a gate. Bear left, up through a street dedicated to the selling of nougat, for 19 paces before turning left (having ducked beneath the wooden bar that hangs across the alley), from where it is about 70 paces, along a street dedicated to selling votive candles and trinkets, to the best view into the zaouia of Moulay Idriss II.

Within the darkened sanctuary the tomb can be seen heavily draped in a rich embroidered velvet cloth, the *ksaoua*, and surrounded by baroque brass, flickering coloured candles, glittering lamps, offerings, European clocks and praying women. It is strikingly similar to a saint's shrine in Spain, Naples, Sicily or Greece, and round the corner of the sanctuary a hole lined by well-worn copper allows the devotees to touch the tomb. As well as being the patron saint of the city, Moulay Idriss II is especially appealed to by boys before circumcision and women before giving birth.

It is not known if the reforming Almoravids or Almohads suppressed the cult, but Idriss II's tomb was re-identified during Merenid rule, in 1307, after an uncorrupted body was unearthed here. The present zaouia was constructed in 1437, but it was the Wattasid dynasty (1472–1554) that developed it into a major cult centre. Throughout August the numerous guilds of the city still go in procession to the tomb and offer decorative gifts, animal sacrifices, religious chants and *nubas* of classical Andalucían music before starting

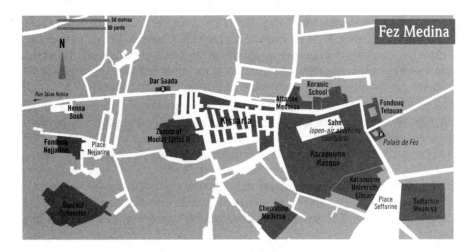

their festivals. In the 18th century Moulay Ismaïl restored the shrine, and until the 19th century it was hung with contracts by which the various towns and tribes tried to establish the exact terms upon which they accepted the rule of each new sultan. The right of sanctuary, *horm*, is still respected, and Sultan Abdul Aziz appalled the Fassi when he arrested the murderer of a European who had taken shelter beside the tomb.

The Kissaria

The Bab Souk Attarine is also the spice-sellers' gate that marks the entrance to the Kissaria, the dense network of traditionally expensive shops on an irregular criss-crossing grid of alleys and tiny shop-filled squares that cluster at the heart of the medina. This is a sublime area for shopping, a world away from the piles of tack in the enormous tourist bazaars. Here each proprietor sits in his own small booth with everything within reach. It fortunately remains an area dedicated to local needs—fine cloth, silk threads, jewellery, clothes, hats and blankets—and at night the whole Kissaria is locked.

On your first visit stay close to the main street. About 35 paces along the street (on your left) is the welcoming interior of the Dar Saada café-restaurant, while another 40 paces brings you past a quiet cul de sac (on your right) with a fine view of the minaret of the zaouia of Moulay Idriss.

The Attarine Medersa

Open daily 9–12 and 2–6, except Fri am; adm.

A hundred metres (225 paces) past the Bab Souk Attarine, on the left just as you enter a vaulted and confusingly busy crossroads, are the distinctive bronze doors of the Attarine Medersa. Built by Sultan Abou Said Uthman (1322–5) within a confined space, it does not have the grandeur of the slightly later Bou Inania, but is a finer, more delicate structure. It is at least as rich in its *zellij*, plaster and wood decoration, but with a lighter architectural touch emphasized by reflecting pairs of arches seemingly supported by thin stone pillars.

The plan is familiar: an entrance hall with stairs to the upper floors (with 60 rooms for students), and a central fountain court with a prayer-hall beyond. There are no lecture halls as the Attarine was designed as an addition to the Karaouiyne University, not a rival. You may enter the prayer-hall; the **mihrab** is to the right, flanked by pillars and lit by coloured glass windows. A bronze chandelier hangs from the cedar ceiling.

The **zaouia of Sidi Ahmed Tijani**, 200m north of the medersa, is the main lodge of this influential Sufi brotherhood founded by Sidi Mohammed Tijani in Algeria in the 18th century. Persecuted by the Turks, he fled to Fez. The brotherhood was a great ally of the Alaouite sultans, aiding them in religious reforms; when Moulay Hafid retired to Tangier in 1912 he wrote a scholarly work in praise of the order. Opposite the green-tiled minaret, go through an arch, then pass under another arch into a low and tight passage. Off to the left is the *fondouq* **of the weavers**, a dim, dilapidated but highly atmospheric old courtyard full of the noise of looms. The weavers are used to visitors. You can buy a silk-cotton *haik* or bed cover for 200dh.

The Karaouiyne Mosque

It is perhaps appropriate that this grand mosque at the heart of Fez and Moroccan culture should remain such an elusive building. Its outer walls are so encrusted with shops and houses that its shape is lost, while the four main gates offer intriguing but baffling vistas of a succession of pure white colonnades and simple rush matting with a woven red design. They occasionally frame a turbanned lecturer sitting cross-legged against a far wall.

First built in 859 by Fatima bint Mohammed ben Feheri, a prosperous refugee from Kairouan, the mosque was improved by a Fatimid governor in 933 and enlarged by Abd er Rahman III, governor of the Omayyad Caliph of Cordoba, in 956. Rebuilt by the Almoravid Sultan Ali ben Youssef from 1135 to 1143, it was finished a few years before the dynasty fell.

It is a rectangular space sufficiently large for 20,000 to say their prayers simultaneously. The roof is upheld by spacious round-topped arches supported on 16 arcades of 21 spans. An open-air court, the *sahn*, of four spans' width, is at the opposite end from the mihrab. Within this open court the Almohads placed a marble basin and the Saadian Sultan Abdullah el Ghalib added two flanking pavilions modelled on those of the Lion Court in the Alhambra at Granada. The chief glory of the mosque remains the **central aisle**, which leads up from the centre of the court to the mihrab. This is embellished with increasingly elaborate floral and Kufic script carved into the plaster as you advance, while the domes that span the arches are raised higher and higher as they approach the mihrab and are ribbed or vaulted with bold stalactite decoration. The carving is in mint condition as it was covered by the Almohads two years after it was finished and only revealed in the restorations of 1950. The mosque also houses one of the richest libraries of the Islamic world.

The best view of the mosque available to a non-Muslim is that from the roof of the **Palais de Fès** restaurant and carpet shop, 16 Rue Boutoil-Karaouiyne (*see* p.188), which has a wonderful, multi-level terraced café on its rooftop (and very elegant toilets). To find it follow the alley that skirts around the Karaouiyne Mosque. On your way, depending on which gates are open (10 of the 14 gates are opened on Fridays), you can see into the *sahn* and the main body of the mosque, but never as far as the central decorated aisle or the domes. On your left you will pass the locked door of the **Mesbahia Medersa**, closed for restoration at the time of writing. It was built in 1346 by Sultan Abou Hassan, and nick-named '*er rokham*', the marble, owing to his lavish use of the stone. The central white marble basin was brought over from a mosque in Algeciras.

Having turned the corner you pass on your left the ***fondouq* of the Tetouanis** (*Fondouq Tétaounine*), a fine 14th-century Merenid court used by Andalucían merchants from Tetouan. You are welcome to enter as there is a small carpet shop within. There is a less grand *fondouq* a few doors below and then the Palais de Fès, where you can sip mint tea, gulp mineral water and recover your strength as you enjoy the stunning view over the vast acreage of the mosque's green-tiled roof. The tall, distant minaret is that of the zaouia of Moulay Idriss II, while the lantern-less minaret on the grand mosque is the Trumpeter, from which Ramadan is announced; the nearest is the 10th-century white domed minaret that echoes the grand mosque of Kairouan, Tunisia. The mosque's internal court, the *sahn*, with flanking twin pavilions and dazzling blue and white floor, is also partly overlooked.

An Ancient Centre of Learning

The great library of the university, to which there is no entry, is stored behind the white walls between the Place Seffarine and the mihrab. Considering the physical state of the city, the library has survived well. It boasts a 9th-century manuscript Koran and an original manuscript of Averroës–Ibn Rachid amongst its 30,000 precious volumes.

The Karaouiyne University is one of the oldest in the world, dating from AD 850. Its origins lie in the teaching of the Koran in the mosque, just as Christian universities grew out of monastery and cathedral schools. Allied subjects such as grammar, theology and Koranic law were taught in informal lectures, with an accent on learning by heart rather than on debate or written papers. It is claimed that as a young French peasant boy the future Pope Sylvester II studied at Fez a century before Bologna, the first European university, was established. He certainly so aston-ished the European courts with his mathematical and astronomical knowledge that he was later accused of making a pact with the devil. In the 14th century 2,000 students, *tolba*, dwelt in the various medersas to be instructed by the *ulemas*, the doctors and professors. Ibn Rachid, Ibn Khaldoun, Leo Africanus and Ibn Batuta all participated in the intellectual milieu of Fez. In 1963 the university was 'national-ized', having been the single source of higher education until then.

Place Seffarine

Shaded by fig trees, this is by the southeastern corner of the mosque, the direction of the mihrab and prayer. It has a pleasant fountain and is full of metalworkers tapping away at an impressive range of pots and kettles, including some really gigantic ones for weddings.

This, like the Bab Souk Attarine, is a recognizable centre from which to explore this end of the medina—the Seffarine Medersa, Dyers' Souk and the Cherratine Medersa—or the tanneries, and the Medersa es Sahrija beside the grand mosque of the Andalucían quarter.

The Seffarine Medersa

A doorway on one side of the Place Seffarine leads into the Seffarine Medersa, which is still occupied by Islamic students, who will happily show a few affable visitors around (tips accepted); it is normally closed to groups and brusquer tourists. Established by Sultan Abou Yusuf Yacqub, the founder of Fez Jdid, in 1280, it was the first medersa in Morocco, and follows the design of a Fassi house, since professors used to lecture in their home when not using the mosque. Medersas had long been established in Egypt, Syria and Iraq, but with the additional gift of a library the sultan showed that he too was interested in education. The rooms and small pool arranged around the irregular courtyard have a simple domestic elegance, but the dilapidated central prayer-hall (offset from the irregular medersa courtyard) shows signs of the extravagance that would be unleashed in the Attarine Medersa 25 years later. It is good to see a medersa in use: the plain mattresses, heaps of books and notes and the normal squalor of student life add a vital missing in-gredient to empty tourist-thronged halls. The medersa roof has an intriguing outlook over the river mills, houses and bridges.

The Dyers' Souk

Continue on past the medersa door and drop down into the Dyers' Souk, the Souk Sabbighin or Souk des Teinturiers, which is on the riverbank to the right of the bridge. The swatches of bright-coloured wool draped over the street to dry are perennially photogenic. The vats of dye and the grave, grey-clothed vat masters are more disturbing. If you are with a guide, ask to be shown the riverside mill where seeds and minerals are crushed to extract the raw dyes. The millers wade through the thick, pungent waters of the stream, raking aside mounds of garbage in order to direct enough water into the workings of the mill—a vision of mingled squalor, rancid steaming waters and skilled medieval use of water power.

The Cherratine Medersa

Standing in front of the library at the top of Place Seffarine, turn left and walk along Rue Haddadine (lined with displays of teapots, kitchenware and jewellery) for about 90 paces and then turn right up Rue Cherratine. Walk for about 130 paces and, having passed the **Dar Sekka bazaar**, you will reach the twin bronze doors of the Cherratine Medersa, a dilapidated but delightfully unvisited corner of the city. It is an extensive complex built by the first Alaouite sultan, Moulay Rachid, in 1670 to celebrate his reunification of Morocco. From the bronze doors on the street an ornamental passageway leads directly into the calm, quiet order of the spacious interior courtyard with its central pool. One side opens directly into a high-vaulted mosque, the orientation of which allows the whole courtyard to be treated as a *sahn*. No windows break the severity of the walls: instead, the residential blocks, each looking into its own lightwell, have been cunningly placed off the three corners, approached through passages. The fourth corner houses the ablutions courtyard—

the only one in Morocco still in exuberant working order, with a fountain by the entrance and water-filled pool in the central courtyard, around which are ranged seven L-shaped closets. For its combination of privacy without prudery, and functionally inspired decoration mixed with a touch of grandeur, it is exemplary. It is no wonder that the Victorian closet-makers looked to the East for their inspiration.

Beyond the medersa there is a pretty triangular square, **Place Chemaïne**, where dried fruit is sold, and beyond that the Kissaria begins with several shops that specialize in lambswool hats and embroidered fezzes.

The Tanneries

The **Chouara** or Dabbaghin, the largest of Fez' three ancient tanneries, is on a terrace above the river Fez, a well-beaten 200m walk along Rue el Mechattine from the north-eastern corner of Place Seffarine. The powerful, distinctive smell is enough to guide you. Once there, boys will take you to terraces and courts where you can see the operations without being too much in the way. There is a rush of guilt as you attempt to stifle your initial nausea and notice that you are part of a stream of foreigners who arrive, look repulsed, take photographs, tip and leave. The honeycomb of vats, their assorted colours, processes and levels, have an endless fascination. The neighbouring roofs and hills are flecked with drying skins, a tone down in colour from the livid vats of saffron, poppy, indigo, mint and antimony. The scantily dressed tanners appear like so many human storks, their long elegant legs working through the pools, bobbing down to worry a skin and then striding off to wash at the fresh-water standing pipes.

The tanneries are worked by a mesh of specialist and cooperative guilds with their own hierarchies of apprentices, craftsmen and master craftsmen. A whole range of processes are undertaken here: fresh animal skins are treated and pounded in alternating liquid and solid vats of urine and pigeon shit; they are then scraped, wet dyed, scraped, and perhaps dry dyed, before being trimmed and sorted for auction.

Out of the Medina

From Place Seffarine a short walk downhill through the Dyers' Souk (avoiding the narrow bridge across the river into the Andalous side of the old city) and a right turn in the twisting street should drop you down into the sunbaked tarmac space overlooked by the green-tiled minaret of the **Er Rsif Mosque**. From here, local buses and *petits taxis* offer a quick means of leaving the medina. Alternatively, retrace your path, going uphill from the Bab Souk Attarine towards the Bab Bou Jeloud, or if you have the energy explore a different section of the old city by walking uphill to the Bab Guissa and Bab Jamaï.

From Bab Souk Attarine to Bab Guissa and Bab Jamaï

A turn north off the Souk Ain Allou, just after Bab Souk Attarine and 15m before the conspicuous Dar Saada restaurant, will take you into the **Souk Joutia**, the market for salt, eggs and fish. The Rue Hormis runs roughly north from this souk towards Bab Guissa. About 40m beyond the Joutia, and 20m to the right of the street, is an 18th-century *fondouq* and fountain, the central square of the **Es Sagha** district, which used to be a great haunt of jewellers. The elegant carved-plaster and cedar colonnades of the Fondouq Sagha are now one of the centres of the wool trade: raw spun wool is stored here, auctioned off and brought back from the dyers in bright-coloured batches to be sold to weavers and carpet-makers.

Back on Rue Hormis, bear left and climb uphill past a cinema, a local social centre that's surrounded by cheap grills and cafés. Off from here is another henna and spice market, the **Place Achabin**. The path snakes farther uphill, past a fountain on the left, to the area around Fondouq el Yhousi or Guissa. In the morning there's a distinctive aroma of cedar wood and singed hooves from the workshops of farriers, joiners and wood-turners. Ask to be shown the original **Fondouq el Yhoudi**, high up on the left, where Jewish merchants were based in the 13th century before the Merenids moved them to Fez Jdid. Replaced several times since then, the *fondouq* is now used for the sorting, grading and auctioning of tanned and dyed skins.

Below the **Bab Guissa** is a complex of three buildings, a 14th-century mortuary chamber and a 19th-century mosque and medersa, none of which are open to non-Muslims. To the right of Bab Guissa are the more elaborate Bab Jamaï and Bab Ferdaous, where you can find a no.10 bus to speed you back to the Place des Alaouites on the western edge of Fez Jdid, or a taxi to take you to the New Town or on a tour of the ramparts.

The Andalucían Quarter

This half of Fez-el-Bali is a quieter, residential area. It has the Sahrija Medersa, no bazaars, lots of local shops and, as a direct consequence of there being hardly any tourists, a much friendlier and more courteous population. It is likely to stay that way, for the quarter's great historical centre stands on the summit of a hill and has—even by Moroccan standards—a particularly elusive Grand Mosque (*Jemma el Kebir*, to a local). To get to it, or to the partial view from the side doors, there are two main approaches. From the Chouara tanneries, cross the conspicuous **Pont de Beïne el Mdoun**, the bridge of the two cities, into the Andalucían Quarter and then follow the Rue Seffah for about 500m as it climbs the hill. Alternatively, cross the river Fez at the smaller **Sidi el-Aouad** bridge (by Place Er Rsif), which is just off the Dyers' Souk below Place Seffarine. From here it is probably easiest to keep to the fairly level Rue Nekhaline for about 300m, until you turn right onto the Rue Seffah and trudge uphill.

The Andalucían Grand Mosque

One of the best views of the mosque is from a side gate that looks straight across the elegant *sahn* courtyard towards the white minaret, which is capped with a stumpy dome. It was first built by Meriem, the equally pious sister of Fatima, the founder of the Karaouiyne Mosque, but was largely rebuilt by the Almohad Sultan Mohammed en Nasir in the 13th century. The Merenids gave it a fountain and built two nearby medersas for students. They presented an entire library to the mosque in 1415, but this never developed into a separate university.

The Sahrija Medersa

This medersa 'of the pool' lies southwest of the Grand Mosque. It was built by Abou Hassan between 1321 and 1323, while he was still heir to the throne. When he became sultan he built another in the Karaouiyne Quarter, the Mesbahia Medersa, and commissioned others at Taza, Meknès and Salé. The Sahrija, which remains in partial use for the accommodation of Islamic students, is theoretically open to the public every day of the year (except Fridays) from 8am to 6pm, but in practice it is often locked up outside university terms. It is a dilapidated but enchanting jewel of the period, with a simple but harmonious plan.

A rectangular pool fed from a marble bowl surrounded by a worn grid of tiled drainage rills dominates the centre of the small courtyard, with splendid carved plaster, cedar walls and *zellij* mosaics touched with the true serenity of age. On the outer face of the prayer-hall you can still see the hinges of those typical Moorish hanging gates which would later become associated more with secular than with sacred buildings. The prayer-hall, with simple coffered ceiling and comparatively austere central mihrab, retains a venerable dignity. On two sides of the courtyard, behind wooden grilles, are the students' rooms, four of which have windows that overlook the pool. The medersa seems to have kept up with the proud traditions of its past by offering free accommodation to students drawn from a huge hinterland: Chad, Niger, Algeria, Mali… You are free, at your own risk, to explore the roof, but there is no view from there of either the Andalucían mosque or the other, inaccessible, Merenid medersa in this quarter, the **Medersa el Oued** (the river), which is sometimes known as es Sebbayin, the seven, as the seven approved styles for the chanting of the Koran were taught here.

Instead of retracing your steps, you could also continue south from the Grand Mosque/Sahrija Medersa out of the medina down Rue Sidi Ali Boughaleb. The **koubba** of this saint is on the right just at the beginning of the cemetery. The saint is not actually buried here, but the shrine remains an important popular cult centre. The ill and the mad surround the koubba on Tuesday nights, and wait for the saint to appear in their dreams and suggest a cure. The **cemetery of Bab Hamra** on the right should not be entered by non-Muslims and has a local reputation as the resort of black magicians. At **Bab Ftouh** you can find a taxi to get round the ramparts, or take a no.18 bus back into the New Town.

A Tour of the Ramparts

Before leaving Fez try to witness dusk from the hills. Flame-coloured light plays on the ochre walls and flickers finally over the high minarets. The sky is full of pigeons and swallows enjoying the evening flight; smoke from thousands of kitchens floats upwards from the medina. Then you are hit by the call to prayer.

A 15km circuit round the outer walls by taxi gives an excellent overview of the city. The surrounding hills, particularly at Bordj Sud and by the Merenid tombs, all provide magnificent views over Fez-el-Bali.

Fez Jdid

Starting from the Place de la Résistance in the New Town, take the southern exit, for Taza, which descends into the river Zitoun valley. The outer walls of Fez Jdid rise to your left, enclosing the *mellah* and the Jewish necropolis, which is entered through the Bab Jiaf. Schools and hospitals cluster around the Bab Jebala/Bab Riafa, which leads to the area that Moulay Hassan developed in the 19th century to unite Fez-el-Bali and Fez Jdid. An electrical sub-station on your right marks the site of an old aqueduct; opposite is the Bab el Hadid.

Below the walls a great artesian fountain ensures that there is a patch of bright-green grass around the splash pool. Near here are the discreet walls of the American Fondouq, a charitable hospital for animals. As the road swings closer to the walls you pass Bab Jdid, which provides direct bus and taxi access into the heart of the medina.

Bordj Sud

Crossing over the river Boufekrane here, the approach track to Bordj Sud can be seen to your right. This fort was built by Portuguese prisoners of the Saadian Sultan Ahmed el Mansour (1578–1609) as part of a system that was designed as much to intimidate the Fassis as to defend them. The fort is partly in ruins now, but it would have had a good field of fire over the Andalucían and Karaouiyne districts that rise either side of the now invisible river Fez.

Bab Ftouh Cemetery

Pass below the vast cemetery of Bab Ftouh, studded with the whitewashed koubbas of holy men—non-Muslims are not usually welcome on this hill. All the great professors of the Karaouiyne University are buried here, and on the summit there is an open-air mosque, a *msalla*, used for the great feasts of Aid el Kebir and Aid es Seghir. Around the *msalla* are the koubbas of the Sebatou Rijal, the anonymous seven saints who, according to local tradition, brought Islam to Morocco.

At the lower eastern corner of the cemetery is a koubba to **Sidi Harazem**, who came to Morocco from Arabia and, before retiring to a life of poverty and silence, taught at the Karaouiyne Mosque. He was so skilful a debater that he silenced the most agnostic and sophistic of jinn, and has become the patron of Koranic studies and students in general. The ancient festival of Sidi Harazem takes place in spring. An equivalent of the European Lord of Misrule is elected, and they process up to the Andalucían Grand Mosque to officiate as the student sultan for Friday prayers. Now a humorous affair, in the past it was a great occasion for political unrest. The final resting place of the Sidi's bones is a contentious issue: they are not claimed to lie here but in Marrakesh, or in the nearby spa of Sidi-Harazem. Below the cemetery is the Bab Ftouh, to the left of which behind the walls stretches the cemetery of Bab Hamra.

Beyond Bab Ftouh to the Potteries

The **Potters' Quarter**, with its distinctive chimneys belching black smoke from kilns still fuelled by orchard prunings and dried olive pressings, has been moved away from the medina and is now found 1km east of Bab Ftouh just off the main Taza road. Turn left by the blue-tiled tower of the Boissons Talounite café, and a left turn at the next dirt cross-roads leads directly to the **Poterie Fakh-Khari**, ✆ (05) 64 93 22, well geared to receiving visitors, with a café and two showroom shops. In the compound you can watch apprentices kneading the raw clay, skilled potters working it on wheels, the stacking and unstacking of furnaces, and schools of fluent painters decorating plates, bowls and hotel ashtrays, while in other rooms teams of young boys cut glazed tiles to be the raw ingredient for the *zellij* mosaics made by the master craftsmen. There is no admission charge, prices are not bad and there can be an encouraging murmur of business from designers and exporters commissioning special pieces.

Otherwise, continue east of Bab Ftouh to pass the eastern gate, Bab el Khouka. An extensive suburb has here sprawled out beyond the old city to obscure most of the eastern walls. The next gate, **Bab Sidi Bou Jida**, is named after the koubba of that saint, which is on your right. He can be compared to St Jude, the patron saint of lost causes, and is greatly favoured by students before exams and women before marriage. Across the river Fez there is a new tiled auction yard outside the walls. The smells and sights here are intense: trucks unload raw, bloody skins direct from butchers and slaughterhouses. The great wet bundles are forked over by specialists, bought, packed on to mules and sent down into the medina for the first stage in the long tanning process.

The Jamaï

Next is the **Bab Jamaï**, which leads into the luxurious Palais Jamaï Hotel. This incorporates a few rooms and a magnificent Andalucían garden that belonged to a distinguished Fassi family, the Ulad Jamaï, which had a tradition of government service. The Jamaï brothers, Haj Amaati and Si Mohammed Soreir, served Sultan Moulay Hassan as Grand Vizier and Minister of War. After the death of their master they fell victim to the jealousy of the child-Sultan Abdul Aziz's Turkish mother and her ally the half-black chamberlain, Bou Ahmed. They were imprisoned in Tetouan, their property forfeit and their families persecuted. Haj Amaati died in prison but remained chained to his brother (in high summer) for eleven days. Si Mohammed survived the ordeal but was released only after 14 years. On his deathbed he requested that 'my chains and fetters are to be put back upon my limbs. I desire to appear before God...that I might appeal to Him for the justice my sultan refused me.'

The Vista and the Merenid Tombs

The next gate after the Bab Jamaï is the 13th-century Almohad **Bab Guissa**, above which the road climbs up through the cemetery hill of the same name. Beside the turning down to the ugly Merenides Hotel, a long, wide garden terrace has been established which allows locals as well as rich tourists to enjoy this unsurpassed view over Fez-el-Bali. As you join the colourful mass of kaftans billowing in the breeze of the evening *paseo*, you see below, tucked behind its ribbon of ancient wall, virtually the complete extent of the Karaouiyne district. The zaouia of Moulay Idriss II is immediately recognizable by its high, green-tiled pyramid roof and accompanying tall minaret. Just to the left, and lower, a great expanse of green tiles marks the Karaouiyne Mosque, with its whitewashed minaret. This is crowned with a dome, not the usual Moroccan lantern, faithfully echoing the grand mosque at Kairouan, in Tunisia, founded by Uqba ben Nafi in 683. A lower, conventional minaret can be seen to the right: this is the Trumpeter's tower from which the end of the fast of Ramadan is announced. The city below remains defined by its 12th-century walls, the intense urban network in heady contrast to the hillside olive groves that overlook the medina to the north and south.

The Merenid tombs can be reached only by taking a goat track from the road. Most visitors seem content to enjoy them at a distance, surrounded by a crumbling mass of ruined walls, old quarries, caves and the odd melancholic figure. The tombs were originally established within the extensive walls of an old Merenid kasbah that defended this hilltop. Below it, but outside the city walls, was the medieval leper colony. The prominent arched cube among the tombs was once covered with a green-tiled pyramid roof, while a marble-columned interior court held a simple stone tomb carved with an elegant epitaph in a sea of coloured *zellij* mosaic. In the 14th century this patchwork of enclosed hilltop tombs must have equalled Rabat's Chellah in elegance. Now it is all dust. Well might Alexander have wept at the tomb of Cyrus, the greatest of all the great Persian Kings, when he saw that his mausoleum was neglected and covered in dust and rubbish less than a century after his death.

Bordj Nord

Open Wed–Mon 9–12 and 1–6; closed Tues; adm.

Below the garden terrace viewpoint a series of neat paths takes you down to the star-shaped Bordj Nord. Built in 1582, this was the second of the Saadian fortresses designed as much to cover the city with a threatening field of fire as to protect it. A century and a half later, in the Alaouite period, the elegant lance-shaped corner redoubts were added; in 1964 the weapons collection from the Dar Batha Museum was moved here to form a separate **Museum of Arms** (*Musée d'Armes*). A walk around the cool dark vaults and casements of this immaculately preserved old artillery fortress, however, is worth the price of the ticket by itself. The collection takes you through the whole history of armaments, with cases of prehistoric Stone Age tools, Bronze and Iron Age weapons, casts of rare medieval European devices and a comprehensive display of 18th-, 19th- and 20th-century weapons.

For a foreign visitor it is the vast array of Moroccan weapons stacked in an imposing mass in the three rear casements, which date from the 16th to the 20th centuries, that is most rewarding. They show clearly how far the souvenir swords in the bazaars have evolved from the original very serviceable military sabres with their characteristic 'snake-head' wooden handles and chased-steel hand-guards. This is also true of the daggers, with a practical grip given by their bone, metal and leather handles and the very slight curve of their blades. The *fusils Marocains* with their almost 2m-long barrels (made in Fez, Tetouan or Taghzout) alone live up to one's exotic expectations, with some of their stocks and powder-horn accessories so encrusted with carved ivory, raw coral and silver and gold that they become male jewellery. For the historian the two bronze cannon at the exit provide crucial evidence of Morocco's industrial sophistication in the 16th century, and the self-sufficiency that allowed her to keep both the Portuguese and the Ottoman Empire at bay. The Arabic inscription on the damaged cannon reads 'made on the order of [Sultan] al-Walid ibn Zaydan in 1044 H' (AD 1634), while that on the vast 4.5m-long bronze cannon reads 'made by el Haj el Ghourg on the order of el Ghalib', the Saadian Sultan who ruled from 1557 to 1574.

The Cherarda Kasbah

The Bordj Nord fort overlooks the extensive square-walled Cherarda Kasbah, protected by towers and surrounded on almost all sides by a cemetery. It was built by Moulay Rachid in 1670 to house tribes in the sultan's service, notably the Oudaïa and Cherarda cavalry. It is now divided into hospital and university buildings and is therefore closed to tourists.

At the end of the long kasbah wall the **Bab Segma,** with a single remaining 14th-century octagonal tower, separates the kasbah from Fez Jdid. A kilometre of wall runs west from here to enclose the royal park and palace, and then a left turn before the sports park follows another monumental kilometre stretch of royal wall to arrive back at Place de la Résistance.

Fez ✆ (05–)   ***Where to Stay***

Whatever your budget, stay as close to the heady sights, odours and sounds of the medina for as long as you can. Fez will repay familiarity with a dramatic drop in hassle.

luxury

One of Fez' most luxurious hotels, the **Sheraton Fès,** ✆ 93 09 09, ✆ 62 04 86, with immense marble foyers, big bedrooms and magnificent pools, is tucked away in the New Town suburbs. The **Jnane Palace Fès,** ✆ 65 39 65, is the best of the out-of-town hotels, often used by visiting sheikhs from the Arabian Gulf. It has a splendid mock-Merenid entrance gate, lavish hall, large comfortable leather sofas in the bar, and a very good Moroccan restaurant (advance booking is usually required). The large swimming pool is overlooked by bedrom suites of an almost American standard.

The **Merenides Hotel,** ✆ 64 52 25, ✆ 64 52 29, Av Bordj du Nord, overlooks the old city. It was once sacked by rioters but was rebuilt by order of the government. The **Palais Jamaï,** ✆ 63 43 31, ✆ 63 50 96, has by far the best position, just within the medina ramparts of Bab Jamaï, and all the cachet. Established in 1930 in the enclosed 19th-century palace of a Fassi Vizier, it is the only grand hotel from which you can walk straight out into the medina streets. It also has an extraordinary tiled Andalucían garden, enormous heated pool, tiled *hammam* and Moroccan restaurant. It is featured in many novels, not least Paul Bowles' *The Spider's House.*

expensive

The **Menzel Zalagh,** 10 Rue M. Diouri, ✆ 93 20 33, ✆ 93 24 37, is perched on the edge of the New Town and has splendid views towards medieval Fez. It was recently restored to full working order, with a touch of 1960s style rather than mere swank. The **De Fez**, ✆ 62 50 02, ✆ 62 04 86, Av des F.A.R., with 280 rooms, is centrally placed and has a large pool.

moderate

The **Batha Hotel**, ✆ 74 10 77/✆ 63 64 67, ✆ 74 10 78, occupies an even better position than the Palais Jamaï, beside the Dar Batha Museum on the edge of Fez-el-Bali just above the small but animated Place de l'Istiqlal. Its address is listed as Rue de l'UNESCO, but it is actually at the junction of Av de la Liberté and Rue ed Douh by Place de l'Istiqlal. The double row of tiled bedrooms surrounds a long, open courtyard, and there are fountains, a small but welcome pool and a licensed restaurant and bar in the old block, which once functioned as a British consulate. Book in advance as the hotel's popular.

Hotel Ibis Mousaffir, ✆ 65 19 02, ✆ 65 19 09, is on Av des Almohades just beside the train station on the northern edge of the New Town. It is part of a well-designed national chain of beside-the-station hotels that all have efficiently plumbed bedrooms, pools, bars, licensed restaurants and garden areas. Despite having 83 rooms, it can rapidly get filled up, and is worth booking ahead.

Another useful hotel in this range, right in the middle of the New Town, is the 40-bedroom **De La Paix**, 44 Av Hassan II, ✆ 62 50 72, ✆ 62 68 80.

inexpensive

The **Grand**, ✆ 62 55 11/✆ 93 20 26, at the southern end of Blvd Abdallah Chefchaouni in the New Town, is an 80-room hotel overlooking the gardens of Place Mohammed V. If it's full, try the **Mounia**, 60 Rue Asilah,✆ 62 48 38, ✆ 65 07 73.

Other well-established hotels with restaurants in the centre of the New Town include **Lamdaghri**, 10 Rue Abbas Masaadi, ✆ 62 03 10; **Olympic**, on Blvd Mohammed V, ✆ 62 24 03; and **Amor**, 31 Rue Arabie Saoudite, ✆ 62 27 24.

cheap (in the New Town)

Among the several clean, functional small hotels with some character are the 34-room **Central**, 50 Rue Brahim Roudani, off Blvd Mohammed V, ✆ 62 23 33; the **Excelsior**, Rue Larbi el Kaghat as it meets Blvd Mohammed V, ✆ 65 56 02; and the **Kairouan**, 84 Rue du Soudan (ex d'Espagne), ✆ 62 35 90.

cheap (in the medina)

There are half a dozen very basic to almost squalid hotels around the Bab Bou Jeloud. Busy and with unreliable water supplies, but much quieter since the departure of the bus station, their attraction is their proximity to the main entrance to Fez-el-Bali and the evening café life. In order of preference: **Hôtel du Jardin Public**, 153 Kasbah Bou Jeloud, ✆ 63 30 86—up a small alley and immediately south of the Bou Jeloud Mosque; and **Hotel Kaskade**, 26 Rue Serajine,

✆ 63 39 91 (and its neighbour the **Mauretania** at No.14, which is a last resort), just through the Bab Bou Jeloud, with wide double beds and an old *hammam* on the second floor.

Hotel Erraha, ✆ 63 32 26, is tucked away above the two-corner café and entered from a side alley. On the opposite (northern) side of the Bou Jeloud square is the **National**, ✆ 63 32 48. The **Lamrani**, ✆ 63 44 11, is deeper into the medina on the Talaa Seghira, just before the Bou Inania Medersa.

Outside Fez

If you need a respite from the city, it may be worth bearing in mind a couple of alternatives just outside Fez. The moderately priced **Hotel Fadoua**, ✆ 69 40 50, stands in the centre of the spa of Moulay-Yâkoub, 20km northwest of Fez, and has been recommended. The mini resort of Aïn Chkef, 6km south of the city, has the **Reda**, ✆ 64 09 78, with its own pool and restaurant. It can be reached off the P24 to Immouzer and then on the S315, or with the no.14 bus from Place de Florence, on Av Hassan II in the centre of the New Town.

Fez ✆ (05–)   *Eating Out*

In the daytime, eat in the medina, but in the evening hop into a taxi and explore some of the variety of restaurants in the New Town.

expensive (in the medina)

The only exception to the above rule is the **Palais Jamaï Hotel**, ✆ 63 43 31, which maintains the **Al Fassia** Moroccan restaurant, above the hotel's Andalucían garden in a hall of this former palace. It is watched over by a splendidly imposing head waiter, and most evenings your meal is accompanied by the sounds of classical Andalucían music played by a traditional quintet.

expensive (in the New Town)

The **Restaurant El Ambra**, 47 Route d'Immouzer, ✆ 64 16 87, is one of a half-dozen places that have opened up in the smart quarter of Fassi suburban mansions beside the road to Immouzer. Many are purposely designed for grand marriage and circumcision celebrations; El Ambra is the quietest of them, but still sumptuous enough.

moderate (in the medina)

Dropping down a rank in style there are two more Moroccan restaurants very near the Palais Jamaï that also serve traditional food amid palatial 19th-century interiors and have licences to serve alcohol, but can be dominated by belly-dancing shows to the detriment of their cooking. **Restaurant Firdaous**, 10 Rue Jenifour, ✆ 63 43 43, is just inside the medina through the Bab Guissa (turn right as you approach the Palais Jamaï gates), while for **Les Remparts**, 2 Arset Jiar, ✆ 63 74 15, turn left in front of the hotel gates.

For a grand lunch in the medina most visitors and groups stop at either the **Dar Saada**, 21 Souk el Attarine, ✆ 63 33 43, or the **Palais de Fès**, 16 Rue Boutouil-Karaouiyne, ✆ 63 47 07, a pair of opulent turn-of-the-20th-century mansions. The Palais has by far the best view from its rooftop terrace as it stands just east of the great Karaouiyne Mosque (*see* p.176), but it doubles up as a carpet bazaar. The Dar Saada, in the heart of the medina's richest shopping district, has a licence to serve alcohol. Both are closed in the evening.

The **Palais M'Nebhi**, ✆ 63 38 93, is one of the best and most reclusive addresses in Fez. It is about 450m east of the Bab Bou Jeloud on the northern side of Rue Talaa Seghira. It occupies a beautiful palace built by the famous Menehbi family that was later used by Marshal Lyautey, and also a language school. The current *patron*, Haj Sentissi, serves the best couscous in the medina, which you can eat in the Fez or Meknès salons, at either end of the vast courtyard. It is normally open for lunch only, but has been known to reopen for favoured customers in the evening.

moderate (in the New Town)

Chez Vittorio, 21 Rue Brahim-Redani (sometimes known as Rue Nador), ✆ 62 47 30, is found just south of Av Mohammed es Slaoui, a block east of Place Mohammed V. It is a small, efficiently run Italian restaurant, though both staff and customers are predominantly and animatedly Moroccan. You can choose pasta, pizza or meat dishes from the menu, while picking over some *antipasti* as you sip your wine. They prefer to be paid in cash.

Le Nautilus, 44 Av Hassan II, ✆ 62 50 72, is on the lower floor of the Hôtel de la Paix. It's an efficient place with a good kitchen and a mixed menu (try prawn pil-pil followed by pastilla), only slightly let down by its basement location. Nearby, the **Roi de la Bière**, 59 Blvd Mohammed V, ✆ 62 53 24, is another delightfully aged but dignified place that serves a very reasonable three-course *à la carte* meal.

La Cheminée, 6 Av Lalla-Asmae, ✆ 62 49 02, stands on the avenue that leads directly out of the train station. It offers a simple but effective selection from its *menu du jour*, and the calm unruffled service found in places that do their own thing and do it well.

cheap

In the medina there are many tiny hole-in-the-wall grill-kitchens and café-restaurants. Rue Hormis, deep in the heart of Fez-el-Bali, has the best selection of them. They are found by turning left just before Bab Souk Attarine, coming from Bou Jeloud.

In the area just in from Bab Bou Jeloud there is a good choice of restaurants that are used to feeding budget-conscious backpackers. The **Bouayed**, 26 Rue Serrajine, or the **Des Jeunes**, at No.16, ✆ 63 49 75, are both just in from the gate, stay open late, and are clean, quick and honest. Other recommended places in this area include **La Baraka**, 33 Rue Talaa Seghira, and the **Tariana**, at No.25.

There are few places as relaxing as a table by the waterwheel at the **Nouria** café, ✆ 62 54 22. El Idrissi Hamid, a courteous, English-speaking musician, is the current *patron* of this famous establishment beside Fez Jdid's Bou Jeloud gardens.

The **Mirador**, 1 Dhar Lakhmiss, ✆ 64 56 23, beside the new square and garden terrace built above Bordj Nord and the Merenid tombs, has a delicious array of cakes, ice-creams and cappuccino to accompany the superb view.

Along the great thoroughfares of the New Town, such as Av Hassan II (especially around Place de Florence), Blvd Mohammed V and Av Mohammed es Slaoui, you will find a whole range of cafés. If you are looking for some French colonial vibes, head straight for Place Mohammed V, where you will find the **Café de la Renaissance**, **Le Cristal** and the **Café du Centre** (which all serve alcohol).

Bars in the New Town are mostly concentrated along Av Mohammed es Slaoui but, unless you are a very seasoned male traveller, the mass of beer-drinking men packed within can be too great a challenge. The more cloistered bars found in the major hotels are really your only option. A tour of these would include the **Palais Jamaï** (in order to stroll around its garden), the **Bahia** in Fez Jdid and the **Zalagh**.

Shopping

Fez positively bursts at the seams with ceramics, carpets, metalwork, leather, drums, tambourines, shoes and belts. If you are looking for something a bit special try **Mohammed ben Abdeljalil**'s shop, 35 Rue Talaa Seghira. Do not be content with his street-side stall but ask to be shown the rooms behind, which are laden with objets d'art.

There are a couple of **bookshops** that stock English titles, as well as the news-stands found in the big hotels. The English Bookshop, 68 Av Hassan II, has the largest range, but the Librairie du Centre, 134 Blvd Mohammed V, and the Hôtel de Fez, Av des F.A.R., are also worth a look. Newspapers are sold at all these shops and along Blvd Mohammed V. For **picnics**, the central market is off Blvd Mohammed V, just across the street from the Café Zanzibar.

Riding is possible from the Club Equestre Moulay Idriss, ✆ 62 34 38, at the race-course. **Swimming** is possible in summer at the crowded municipal pool near the stadium off the Av des Sports (*adm*), or at the **campsite**, ✆ 64 15 37.

If you are travelling with children, break your sightseeing with a trip out to **Les Trois Sources**, ✆ 60 65 23, just 4km from the centre of Fez on the P24 road south to Immouzer, where there are three swimming pools watched by lifeguards, together with a playground, table-tennis and billiards tables as well as a range of organized activities and a dancefloor and restaurant.

A mixed **hammam,** with attendant masseur, operates in the Palais Jamaï Hotel. Alternatively, use the *hammam* Aturki in the medina for 5dh; turn right through Bab Bou Jeloud on to Rue Talaa Seghira and then right; it's the first door under the covered arch.

Fez ℗ (05–)   *Entertainment and Nightlife*

Although it hardly counts as a night on the town, you could watch the music show and historical illuminations that cover 12 centuries in 45 minutes and are staged at Bordj Sud every night at 9.30pm. For information, call the Bordj, ℗ 62 93 71, or Apt 65, Place de Florence, ℗ 93 18 93 (*adm*).

There are disco/nightclubs in the **Palais Jamaï**, **Les Merenides**, **Jnane Palace Fès**, **Sofia** and **Zalagh** hotels, though none can be enthusiastically recommended.

Fez ℗ (05–)   *Festivals*

The students' **moussem of Sidi Harazem** is held at the end of April, and the two major city **festivals of Moulay Idriss II and Sidi Ahmed el Bernoussi** are both in September.

For the last few years a **festival of sacred music** has been held in Fez around the end of May and beginning of June, with two or three concerts daily for a week in the garden of the Dar Batha Museum, the Old Méchouar or the governors' palace. Musicians from all over the world may perform, as well as Jewish, Muslim and Christian musicians from Spain and Morocco who share the common inspiration of Andalucía. The French Consulate, 33 Rue el Bahrain, ℗ 62 39 21, has a cultural section that organizes a variety of exhibitions and events throughout the year.

Day Trips from Fez

Moulay-Yâkoub

Moulay-Yâkoub is just 20km northwest of the city, across gently rolling hills. It is a pleasant holiday resort, a favourite sketching-ground of Maghrebi artists and much loved by Moroccan families, who can all indulge in some quiet hypochondria there. It's built on terraces above a hot sulphurous spring which fills a series of natural *hammams* and enclosed pools. In the past it enjoyed a reputation as a haunt of prostitutes and a cure for venereal disease; now the waters are modestly claimed only to cure 'renal and urinary' diseases. There is a small admission charge for the warm sulphurous pool and for the *hammam*, which has separate enclosures for men and women. Swimming trunks are worn in the baths; souk stalls sell a selection of these as well as soap, beads, towels and candles. You can eat at a number of cafés or at the **Restaurant Merhaba**, just above the baths. Opposite the village is the rounded hill of Lalla Chafer, with a few pine trees growing on its slope. Walking up the hill to the café on the summit is all part of the cure, while lower down the hill an all-new spa has been constructed in the last few years.

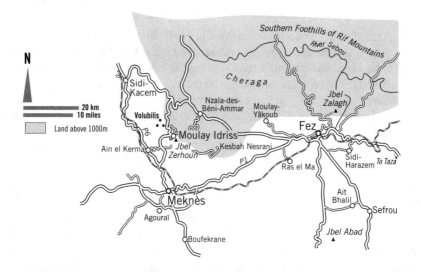

N

20 km
10 miles

Land above 1000m

Southern Foothills of Rif Mountains

River Sebou

Sidi-Kacem

Cheraga

Jbel Zalagh

Nzala-des-Béni-Ammar

Moulay-Yâkoub

Fez

Volubilis

Moulay Idriss

Ain el Kerma

Jbel Zerhoun

Kesbah Nesrani

Sidi-Harazem   To Taza

P1

Ras el Ma

Meknès

Ait Bhalil

Sefrou

Agouraï

Jbel Abad

Boufekrane

Meknès

Meknès is at the centre of a rich agricultural region where olives, grain, vegetables and grapes are successfully grown by the thick-set Berber farmers who seem to characterize this area. Despite its splendid imperial past as the capital city of Sultan Moulay Ismaïl, its present population of around half a million, its army base and its university, Meknès remains more of a large Berber town than a cosmopolitan urban centre. Meknès is divided into three distinct areas: the New Town, with its neat, French-built, tree-lined avenues, cafés, bars and hotels, is to the east of the Boufekrane river valley; the walled medina, its skyline a confusion of green, white and gold minarets, perches on the western hill; to the south of the medina, through the Bab Mansour, stretches the Imperial City, a bewildering, only partially occupied enclosure surrounded by over 25km of massive pisé walls.

Seeing everything Mèknes has to offer would take several days. If you have just one day, start with the Imperial City and then, if you still have time and energy, visit the Dar Jamaï Museum or the medina souks and the Bou Inania Medersa.

History

The origins of Meknès are exclusively local and Berber, in direct contrast to the foreign and Arab birth of Fez. The city originated as a hilltop kasbah that won renown as one of the principal bases of the Khajarite Berbers, who overthrew the rule of the first Arab conquerors in AD 741. By the 10th century it had grown into the principal market of the Meknassa Berber tribe, which dominated the region.

The power of the Meknassa was shattered by the great Almoravid general Youssef ben Tachfine in 1069, when he first united the country, but their name survived in the town of Meknès. It was rebuilt on a generous scale a century later, during the Almohad period, within a rigid square grid of walls. Its neat street plan was focused around the central mosque; Bab El Jdid is a survivor from this period. A later reconstruction under the Merenids is recalled by the exquisite 14th-century Bou Inania Medersa.

A new period in the city's fortunes dawned in 1666 when the ruling Alaouite sultan, Moulay Rachid, appointed his younger brother, one Moulay Ismaïl, to be its governor. He proved to be a loyal and efficient servant who happily involved himself in administration, local trade and the tilling of his own land. After the early, accidental death of his brother in 1672, Moulay Ismaïl succeeded to the throne, which he retained until his death in 1727. Fez and Marrakesh were both embroiled in rebellions against the young monarch, who therefore decided to create a new capital out of the loyal city of Meknès. The existing walled medina was left largely undisturbed, and a brand-new Imperial City built just beyond its southern walls.

A slave army of 50,000 Berbers and Europeans was employed on the enormous project. Dozens of palaces were built for Moulay Ismaïl's court, for his 500 concubines and four wives, and his few favoured children (out of the 800 he sired); gardens, parks, ponds and pavilions were built, improved, knocked down and constantly replaced within the confines of the massive external walls.

The Imperial City also served as the headquarters and garrison for a standing force of 25,000 Abids, the disciplined black slave army which the sultan employed to impose his arbitrary rule. Vast storehouses, stables, exercise fields, enclosures for allied nomadic cavalry and armouries enabled the sultan to dispatch a force quickly at the first sign of dissidence.

Moulay Ismaïl has been presented to history (mostly through the accounts of ex-slaves, missionaries and the snubbed literate population of Fez) as a megalomaniac tyrant. Though his rule was certainly arbitrary, his achievements were sound. He humbled the wild mountain tribes, recaptured Tangier, Mehdiya, Larache and Asilah from foreign powers, and rebuilt mosques, shrines, bridges, kasbahs and whole towns. He attempted to reassert orthodoxy in the confused, cult-ridden life of the country, and was the last sultan to treat the European powers as equals. His offer for the hand of Louis XIV's illegitimate daughter, Marie Anne de Bourbon, should be seen as an overture for an alliance with France against Spain, while in his letters to King James II of England you can read his sound and disinterested advice, arguing in favour of Protestantism.

The Imperial City did not, however, long outlast its founder: the Abid slave regiments grew reckless and greedy without the stern hand of their master, and deposed a succession of his sons. The Lisbon earthquake of 1755 shattered the palace compounds and, while his son Moulay Abdullah and grandson Sidi Mohammed (1757–90) altered and maintained portions of Meknès, they increasingly returned the business of government to either Fez or Marrakesh. It was the French who revived Meknès, for like the great sultan they appreciated the city's strategic position and made it their central army base, building a new town across the river for their regiments.

by rail

The main train station is on Av de la Basse, ✆ 52 00 17/✆ 52 06 89, just off Av des F.A.R., the Fez road. Turn left at the entrance and the centre of the New Town is a 1km walk east, or you could get off at the Meknès el Amir Abdelkader station (ex Lafayette) on Rue Alger, closer to the centre. There are at least eight trains a day from Fez (50mins).

by bus

There are two bus terminals. The most useful and efficient is the **CTM** coach station at 47 Av Mohammed V, at the junction with Av des F.A.R. in the New Town. There are almost hourly departures to Fez (50mins).

Other private coach companies and local buses use the new consolidated terminal outside Bab el Khemis/Bab el Mellah on the western edge of the medina. A shuttle service of buses, nos. 5, 7 and 9, connects the medina and New Town.

by taxi

You will find **grands** and **petits taxis** just west of Place el Hédime in the medina, and on the northern side of the Place Administrative, beside the post office, in the New Town. It is a short 40min/20dh hop to Fez by *grand taxi*.

The **tourist office** is on the Place Administrative, ✆ 52 44 26. They distribute the usual attractive town map leaflets and can arrange for the hire of guides. The building is south of the *place* on the Esplanade de la Foire, inside a big yellow gate.

Banks in the New Town are the BMCE, 98 Av des F.A.R., ✆ 52 03 52, and the Banque du Maroc, 33 Av Mohammed V. There is a branch of the Banque Populaire along Rue Dar Smen near Place el Hédime.

Bab Mansour

The best place to begin exploring either the medina or the Imperial City is Place el Hédime. To get there from the New Town, follow the main road across the valley, Av Moulay Ismaïl, to enter the medina through the Bab Bou Ameir. Then turn right to climb 400m up the busy Rue Rouamzine, turn left by the post office onto Rue Dar Smen; the *place* is at the end of this street.

Bab Mansour separates the central square of the medina, Place el Hédime, from Moulay Ismaïl's vast, enclosed Imperial City. It has come to symbolize Meknès: it is reproduced in countless books, articles, postcards and posters. It is difficult to see it at its best during the day, for the sun shines into your eyes from the east and leaves the gate in shadow. The softer evening light picks out the details, but even then the gate appears ponderous and over-decorated, and the relief too bold. The pillars, a mixture of Ionic and Corinthian columns torn from the classical ruins of Volubilis, appear empty gestures that distract from the overall harmony. It succeeds as architecture in a way that the sultan might have been

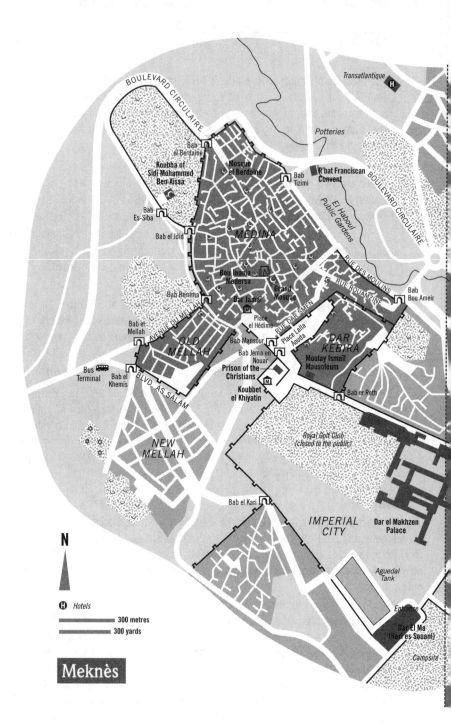

Transatlantique

Potteries

BOULEVARD CIRCULAIRE

Bab
el Berdaine

Koubba of
Sidi Mohammed
Ben Aissa

Mosque
el Berdaine

Bab
Tizimi

R'bat Franciscan
Convent

Bab
Es-Siba

El Haboul
Public Gardens

BOULEVARD CIRCULAIRE

MEDINA

Bab el Jdid

RUE DES MOULINS

Bab Berrima

Bou Inania
Medersa

Grand
Mosque

RUE ROUAMZINE

Bab
Bou Ameir

Dar Jamaï

Bab el
Mellah

AVENUE DU MELLAH

OLD
MELLAH

Place
el Hédime

RUE DAR SMEN

Bab Mansour

Place Lalla
Aouda

DAR
KEBIRA

Bus
Terminal

Bab el
Khemis

Bab Jema en
Nouar

Prison of the
Christians

Koubbet
el Khiyatin

Moulay Ismaïl
Mausoleum

Bab er Reth

BLVD. AS SALAM

NEW
MELLAH

Royal Golf Club
(closed to the public)

Bab el Kari

IMPERIAL
CITY

Dar el Makhzen
Palace

Aguedal
Tank

N

Entrance

Dar El Ma
(Heri es Souani)

H Hotels

Campsite

300 metres

300 yards

Meknès

Place Ifriquia

El Amir Abdelkader Station

AVENUE HASSAN II

AVENUE MOHAMMED V

Rif

(H)

Town Hall

Place Administrative

AVENUE IDRISS II

AVENUE MOULAY ISMAIL

(i)

CTM

ROYALES

AVENUE DES FORCES ARMÉES

Main Train Station

NEW TOWN

Football Stadium

BOULEVARD ABDERRAHMANE BEN ZIDANE

CHARI BIR ANZARANE

River Boufekrane

Bab En Nouar

Méchouar

Jardins de l'Ecole d'Horticulture

Kasbah Hadrach

Campsite

195

content with: powerful, looming, appearing obsessively strong and rigid, its top panel of carved Koranic script a reminder of the strong Muslim orthodoxy of the Alaouite dynasty.

The less obtrusive but altogether more agreeable gate, to the right looking from the square, the **Bab Jema en Nouar**, was built in the same period; it now leads to a school housed in an old mosque and the gate apartments. Both gates were designed by Moulay Ismaïl's court architect, the renegade Christian known as Mansour el Aleuj, and completed in 1732 during the reign of the great sultan's son, Moulay Abdullah.

Place el Hédime

This square was created in the mid-17th century by Moulay Ismaïl, who required a grand entrance before the Imperial City, the traditional area in an Islamic city for the public execution of justice, the issuing of proclamations, the jostle of petitions, the emergence of the royal procession to the grand mosque and the distribution of charity. In modern times it degenerated into a dusty car park, but a few years ago it was transformed once again into an elegant public space complete with new fountains. These are in pleasing harmony with the original 17th-century **enclosed fountain** (on the far side of the square), with its dazzling glimmer of *zellij* mosaic circles.

A **food market** runs along the southern side of the square, screened by a long row of barbers and pottery shops. It is a wonderful place to gather a picnic: choosing from the glistening cones of flavoured olives, pats of goat's cheese, prime fruit and fresh vegetables from the farms that surround Meknès. Here even the dates look polished. At the northwestern corner of the square an alley leads directly to the grand mosque, passing on the left a 14th-century town house, the *Maison Merenide*, which has been turned into a tourist bazaar.

The Imperial City

I have built these buildings—let those who can destroy them.

Sultan Moulay Ismaïl

We have never seen anything equal to it, neither among the modern buildings nor among the ancient.

Temim, a 17th-century French ambassador

The extent and past grandeur of the Imperial City can best be appreciated in a 5km walk broken halfway at the café **Heri es Souani**. Most of the city is in ruins and has been built over by village communities, and the royal palace is not open to the public. The little pavilion of Koubbet el Khiyatin, the nearby underground store rooms, Moulay Ismaïl's mausoleum, the Dar el Ma and the Aguedal Tank are the highlights of the Imperial City, though inevitably the abiding image left at the end of the day is of a bewildering series of massive walls.

The Dar Kebira

The first thing you come to through the Bab Mansour is the large Place Lalla Aouda, the formal processional square of the old Dar Kebira, or enclosed palace quarter, which, like the Place el Hédime, has been renovated with fountains and newly planted trees. None of the palaces has survived, though, and it is now just another residential area of the city.

The Dar Kebira was finished in 1677 and opened by the sultan, who sacrificed a wolf under the full moon at midnight and set its head above the gateway to the palace. According to the chronicler ez-Zayyani, the Dar Kebira contained 24 separate palace compounds, gardens and barracks, and two mosques. Most of these were destroyed by the sultan's son Moulay Abdullah, and the mosques alone have survived. Called the **Lalla Aouda** and **Chaouia**, they face the square, where only eunuchs were permitted to make the call to prayer. The palace museum in the Oudaïa Kasbah at Rabat (*see* p.228) was also originally built as a palace by Moulay Ismaïl, and gives some indication of what must have been the varied splendours of the Dar Kebira. It would have been decorated with columns extracted from Volubilis, and ornamentation looted from the great Saadian palace of El Badia at Marrakesh.

Comparisons with the palace of Moulay Ismaïl's great contemporary, Louis XIV, continue to be made. However, Versailles, with its radial axes of parkland, its draughty uncomfortable interiors and the exterior splendour of its façade, could hardly be further removed from Moulay Ismaïl's secretive, heavily enclosed pavilion gardens. The sultan could not have begun Meknès in any spirit of competition with the French—he is known to have started work ten years before he received the first reports of Versailles. In any case he is much more likely to have looked east to Ottoman Istanbul for his exemplar. What Meknès and Versailles share is a roughly equal consumption of material and human lives.

The Koubbet el Khiyatin

If you go through the Bab Filala at the southwestern corner of Place Lalla Aouda, you will find yourself in a small square that has the pavilion of Koubbet el Khiyatin in the far right corner. This was an audience chamber used for the reception of foreign ambassadors and the interminable bargaining over the ransom of slaves. It literally means 'the hall of the tailors', a poetic Arabic image for the role of an ambassador, who, like a tailor, joins two opposing pieces of cloth (or nations) together with delicate, time-consuming stitch work. The decorated carvings on the walls endlessly repeat in Kufic script '*All jell*'—glory to God. You may notice that the carving is not of the highest quality, for this 17th-century koubba was restored in the 1950s.

Beside the Koubbet is the entrance to the '**prison of the Christians**', a misleading title for a massive vaulted underground network of storerooms, an impressive and mysterious acreage of damp stone lit by skylights. Intriguing bricked-up passages disappear to other decayed sections of the old underground city of cellars. The Christian slaves of Meknès were actually never housed here, but it is known that the sultan moved prisoners here before receiving ambassadors so that the subterranean cries for help would undermine their composure during negotiations.

The right-hand arch of the two ahead leads to the exclusive, walled and guarded **Royal Golf Club**, which has been created out of the central palace garden. Moulay Ismaïl kept a delightful menagerie in this garden: four wild asses from Guinea ran wild, two white dromedaries allowed themselves to be washed in soap every morning, and wounded storks were cared for. Royal Arabian horses that had completed the pilgrimage to Mecca remained unridden and free for the rest of their lives; beads and scrolls from the holy city hung from their necks and any criminal was assured of sanctuary if such a horse allowed him to approach. On its death, each horse was reverently buried in shrouds and a koubba raised over its tomb.

Moulay Ismaïl's Mausoleum

Open July–Aug Mon–Fri 9–5; Sept–June Mon–Fri 8.30–12 and 3–6; adm.

Through the left-hand arch, opposite half a dozen bazaars, is the long white mausoleum of Moulay Ismaïl. The actual prayer-hall of the mosque remains closed to non-Muslims, but the tomb can be approached providing you are respectfully dressed and tip the guardian. The sanctuary was completely restored by King Mohammed V in 1959. As you progress through the three admirably austere courtyards with serene tiled floors and walls, you progressively shed the distractions and the noise of the outside world. The rectangle of blue sky framed by the high walls itself works as a form of meditation on the absolute. At the central fountain court remove your shoes, and enter through the door on the left into a lavishly gilded and decorated Moorish hall with a high-vaulted ceiling capped by a pyramidal koubba. From here you may look onto the marble tomb of the great sultan, flanked by two clocks (the gift of Louis XIV), but do not advance into the room, which is used by pious pilgrims for prayers.

The Dar el Makhzen

Beyond the mausoleum is the **Bab er Reth**, 'the gate of winds', which opens on to a kilometre-long passage below a stretch of massive double walls. The Sultan used to ride along this road in a chariot drawn by his plump concubines. The harem had a precarious status, for Sultan Moulay Ismaïl cared for few of his children (most of his adult sons were exiled to the oasis of the Tafilalt, near Er Rachidia) and even less for his concubines. His official wives were, however, forceful characters. Moulay Ismaïl's first wife, Zidana, who was black, was a fearsome witch who was even allowed out of the harem when escorted by a suitable chaperone. Her ally was his third wife, the English sultana. She had been captured in 1688, aged 15, en route to Barbados with her mother. Moulay Ismaïl returned this surprised mother-in-law to England with presents and a letter for the king.

The wall on the left of the passage is the exterior, defendable perimeter of the Imperial City; that on the right defines a particular palace enclosure, the enormous **Dar el Makhzen**, or chief palace of the sultan, which was finished in 1697 and refurbished by Moulay Hassan in the late 19th century. A right turn at the end of this long walk, below the Water Fort, Bordj el Ma, will take you into the *méchouar*, a colonnaded space where rulers could receive the ovations of their people. The gate on the right is the guarded main entrance to the palace, whilst a stroll to the left, through an enclosed hamlet clustered around a mosque and out through a gate, will allow you to admire the extent and width of the outer walls. To the east, stretching inside these walls, is the **Kasbah Hadrach**, the old barracks of the

Bukharis, the crack guards regiment of the sultan's black slave army. This old kasbah quarter is protected by two gates, Bab en Nouar and Bab Lalla Khadra, next to the mosque of that name.

Beyond the *méchouar*, an arboretum has been established in the pavilioned **Jardins de l'Ecole d'Horticulture** (Ben Halima Park) on the left of the road, while on the right a squatter village nestles beside the royal palace in the ruins of the **Kasbah Bab Merrah**. Storks nest on decaying pisé buttresses and towers, a few cows graze in a paddock that once held a delicate pavilion, and a young cripple shelters in a cardboard hut decorated with pseudo-erotic pictures cut from advertisements in the Western press. Broken faïence tiles are unearthed as the foundations for a new breeze-block wall are dug in the half-shadow of vast soot-blackened arched chambers.

The Dar el Ma

A further 500m walk beside the pisé walls that partly hide these areas brings you to the Dar el Ma, also known as Heri es Souani. This is the most accessible and impressive remnant of the Imperial City, a massive warehouse where silos held provisions for the court and standing army. There is a café selling coffee and cold drinks, surrounded by a garden of olive trees growing on the massive roof (currently closed for restoration). From here you can see miles of walls, modern villages and ruins stretching in every direction, surrounded by open farmland enclosed in turn by distant mountains. To the south a campsite, racecourse, arboretum, military academy and two schools partly fill the enormous enclosed area of the old Aguedal gardens. To the west stretch the four hectares of the **Aguedal Tank** (*Bassin de l'Aguedal*), constructed by Moulay Ismaïl to supply water for the palace gardens and orchards, now often surrounded by picnicking families. Inside the Dar el Ma there are impressive arched chambers and cascades of creepers hanging illuminated from skylights in the roof. In two of the corners, round chambers surround a well where water could be drawn up 50m by machinery worked by circulating mules. A large, roofless area of vaulted rooms—15 rows of 21 broken arches—extends southwest, partly overgrown with fennel, to create a famously impressive vista. It is thought to have been used as a stable, where some of the sultan's thousands of horses were housed in the cool shade.

Most visitors have tired legs by now and are content to walk beside the Aguedal Tank back towards the medina from the Heri es Souani. At the far end of the tank a left turn brings you into the Beni M'Hammed district, and a right turn along the central avenue takes you out of this modern settlement through the **Bab el Kari**. Below this gate is one of the most impressive stretches of external wall, the 'wall of riches'. A road leads from this gate across empty ground west to the new *mellah*, while a right turn climbs up past a taxi rank towards the medina. A left turn along the Blvd As Salam will take you to the most beautiful gate in Meknès, the towered **Bab el Khemis**, or you could continue uphill and go through the **Bab Zine el Abadine** to re-enter Place el Hédime.

The Dar Jamaï Museum

Open Wed–Mon 9–12 and 3–6; closed Tues; adm; © (05) 53 08 63.

The Dar Jamaï, which has an unobtrusive entrance on Place el Hédime, is a 19th-century vizier's palace that now houses a collection of Moroccan arts and crafts (the *Musée Régional d'Ethnographie*). Like every Moroccan museum, it is a disordered presentation of often undated Andalucían-influenced products from urban craftsmen together with the traditional crafts of the Berber tribes of the Middle Atlas.

The palace is an attractive, calm building, and the worn ceramic floors and graceful patina of age greatly contribute to your enjoyment of the exhibits. It belonged to the same brothers who built the Palais Jamaï in Fez. They were powerful officials in the court of Sultan Moulay Hassan and were descended from one of the Arab tribes that had taken service under the Alaouite sultans, the Oulad Jamaï, and become hereditary servants of the government. At the centre of the museum is a mature **Andalucían garden**, well planted with shrubs and often buzzing with birds.

The contrast as you enter through the cool, dark, twisting entrance passage of the palace emphasizes the domestic sanctity of an enclosed Moroccan house. Along this passage are some examples of Andalucían painted wall tiles, their foliate patterns familiar from wood-carvings but rarely seen in this form in Morocco. Even more surprising is the small collection of miniature paintings, all of which were produced here in Meknès.

In the few rooms off the central garden you can see the silk banner used by Sultan Moulay Hassan for his campaigns, dated 1874 to 1887 in the Gregorian calendar, and a small display of brilliantly bound, compact Korans. The collection of elaborate keys is entertaining, and the other items of wrought ironwork, splendid door bosses and supporting hinges show how much the Gothic borrowed from the Moorish taste.

The **vizier's reception room** upstairs is fully furnished, and a useful antidote to the false impression of Moorish domestic style given by the serene interiors of medersas and empty palaces. For here there is a riot of familiar 19th-century clutter—coloured glass, debased workmanship, painted wood and conflicting plasterwork. The display of 19th-century Fez and Meknès ware is more pleasing: these **ceramics** have a gentler line, and warmer, more fluid shapes than seen in today's merely capable, rigid geometricism. The contrast with rural domestic pottery is always strong; though geometric in intent, the gourd-like shapes of the vessels and the black lines on red show Berber design at its most primitive and conservative.

The collection of **Berber jewellery** makes for an interesting comparison with that offered in today's souks, although the universal style of much native Islamic jewellery holds few surprises. The metalwork has a solidity that one hardly expects today, for these were collections of disposable wealth, while nowadays jewellery concentrates on display. For more on this see Jean Besancenot's highly informative *Bijoux Arabes et Berbères du Maroc* (Ed de la Cigogne, Casablanca); he reckons that, traditionally, workmanship used to add less than 25 per cent to the metal's value.

There is a fine mixed collection of Moroccan **carpets and killims** from the indigenous Berber tribes of the High and Middle Atlas. The tendency was to produce woven and embroidered killims rather than a true knotted carpet. The carpet collection also clearly shows why few Moroccan carpets have survived from any period further back than the 19th century: the large, thinly spaced knots tied to inadequate backing will not last more than a century unless the carpets have been used as wall hangings. Consequently, the admirably warm and simple diamond-lozenge original designs are difficult to find today. The Zayan/Zaian carpet is a good example of this, while the carpet from Aït-Bousba opposite shows the origins of the pictogram, or 'message carpet', though it is splendidly random and primitive compared with the over-busy pattern-book designs found in today's bazaars. All the killims here show a natural restraint in embroidery, with designs based on harmonious stripes of colour, interspaced with geometric lozenges, diamonds and triangles. The products from Zemmour and the Beni Mguild tribal confederation are most attractive, and are still being created.

The Medina Souks

If you turn left in front of the museum (while facing it), a 200m walk along Rue Sekakine will take you to **Bab Berrima**, a busy junction of streets. On the left is the old Jewish quarter, the **mellah**. A 300m walk from the Bab Berrima along Souk Bezzarin on the outside of the medina wall—a local shopping street which is a mass display of Tupperware, kitchenware and jeans—will take you to the brick-built **Bab el Jdid**. This translates as 'the new gate', somewhat contrarily since it is the oldest gate in Meknès—with arched vaults dating from the 12th-century Almohad city. In front of the Bab el Jdid there is a good selection of grill-cafés, and a row of tent-makers will probably be busy in their shops cutting canvas and sewing awnings together on their pedal-operated Singers.

Beyond the Bab el Jdid, if you keep to your right the wall that surrounds the vast cemetery of Sidi Aïssa and follow it to the Bab es Siba, 'the gate of dissidence', an avenue on the right leads up to the distinctive green-tiled pyramid roof that covers the venerated **koubba of Sidi Mohammed ben Aïssa**, built by the Sultan Sidi Mohammed (1757–90). You should not approach too closely, nor wander through the cemetery, which is decorated with the domed tombs of many revered Islamic saints.

If, on the other hand, you enter the old town through the Bab el Jdid, a right turn will lead you to the **Souk Seraria**, the blacksmith's souk, populated by an assortment of knife-grinders, charcoal salesmen and tool-makers. On the left you can enter the sultan's *fondouq*, a delightful 18th-century brick courtyard established for the use of armourers.

As the street narrows you enter the centre of the jewellery trade. A right turn lets you out by the Bab Berrima, while a left turn brings you into the covered **Souk Khiatine el Najarine**, the central thoroughfare of the medina, lined with the shops of metalworkers, tinkers and carpenters. You soon pass on the right the **Najarine** ('the carpenters') **Mosque**, which follows a 12th-century Almohad plan even though the visible work is all 18th-century restoration. Beyond the mosque, again on the right, is the **Dlala Kissaria**, one of a number of interior courts lined with carpet and killim booths that stock the products of the Middle Atlas tribes. It is one of the easiest and most accessible places in which to bargain for killims—there is a good range of stock and the merchants are jovial.

A right turn by the Kissaria can take you down the old dyers' street, passing the **Seb-barine Mosque** on your left, to re-emerge in Place el Hédime by the Dar Jamaï Museum.

If, on the other hand, you continue along the main covered thoroughfare, known at this point as **Rue Sebat**, you will enter the richest and most tourist-oriented area of the souk. A hundred metres farther on your right are the ornately decorated gates of the **grand mosque**. The mosque is at the heart of the medina, and has five elaborate entrances; it occupies the same area as the 11th-century Almoravid grand mosque, replaced by the Almohads and then again in the 13th century by the Merenids.

The Bou Inania Medersa

Open July–Aug Mon–Fri 9–5; rest of the year 8.30–12 and 3–6; adm.

The medersa is directly opposite the grand mosque; its entrance is below a cupola in the main street, and protected by enormous bronze decorated doors. It was begun by Sultan Abou Hassan, creator of the Salé medersa, but finished by and named after Sultan Abou Inan, who reigned from 1351 to 1358. The entrance passage leads through a gate in a cedar screen with the Barakat Mohammed symbol carved above, which could be trans- lated as 'the chance for faith'. The tall, rectangular court paved with black and white marble squares surrounds a central pool.

A band of *zellij* mosaic runs beneath bands of Koranic script that are carried upwards by all the decorative materials—carved plaster, glazed tile, marble and carved cedar all conspire together to carry the word of God. Around three sides of the court runs a gallery above which are two storeys of students' rooms. The solid, angular pillars of the gallery are saved from stolidity by columns that reach up towards the tiled cornice, and restrain the tracery design of the plaster walls. The fourth side of the courtyard opens into a spacious prayer- hall tiled in green and yellow, with a carved peacock fan set above the mihrab.

The beauty and sophistication of the Arabic script entwined in the decoration can mislead modern visitors on the depth of the education that was undertaken in a medersa. There was little emphasis on formal literacy: generations of students simply learned to recite the classical Arabic poetry of the Koran. Even centuries ago the language of the Moroccan street, Maghrebi Arabic, not to mention the three Berber dialects, was already far removed from the language of 7th-century Mecca.

The communal life of the *tolba*, the student reciters, is revealed in the ground-floor wash- room with its long shared sink, although the upstairs rooms include an individual and very European-looking WC. Do not miss the view from the roof across the green-tiled grand mosque and prominent minarets of the medina. The double lancet windows of the Touta minaret can be seen almost due west, with the minarets of the Ahmed Chebli and Sidi Kadour el Alaoui mosques to its right.

Leaving the medersa, the rich clothes shops and bazaars of the Kissaria stretch ahead, but a sharp right turn beside the grand mosque will take you down Rue Sabab Socha, passing on the left the **Filala Medersa**, built by Moulay Ismaïl in the 17th century. This is a smaller and cruder version of the Bou Inania, and is not open to the public. From there a right turn down Rue es Zemmour will eventually return you after a few twists and bends to Rue Dar Smen and Place el Hédime.

luxury–expensive

The **Transatlantique**, on Rue El Meriniyine, ✆ 52 50 50–4, 🖂 52 00 57, has a superb view across the river Boufekrane to the skyline of Meknès' medina. The 120 bedrooms are divided between two sections; the traditional rooms in the old portion of the hotel are the same price but of much greater character. It also has two pools, a bar, two restaurants and a tennis court, and a good buffet lunch is served by the pool; for dinner, it's worth reserving a table in the Moroccan restaurant. Don't be put off by the staff's lack of response to telephone calls, it's worth checking out room availability here in person despite what they say.

At a less extravagant level, the **Rif**, on Rue d'Accra, ✆ 52 25 91, 🖂 52 44 28, is an unexceptional, rather worn but pleasant hotel in the centre of the New Town, with a popular bar, the Bahia nightclub and two restaurants.

moderate

Dropping down just a notch in scale and location there are three clean and engaging old hotels in the New Town each with around 30 bedrooms and their own bars and restaurants: the **Palace**, 11 Rue de Ghana, ✆ 51 12 60; the **Volubulis**, 45 Av des F.A.R., ✆ 52 50 82; and the **Majestic**, 19 Av Mohammed V, ✆ 52 03 07, 🖂 52 74 27. Also worth considering are **Bab Mansour**, 38 Rue Emir Abdelkader, ✆ 52 52 39, 🖂 52 83 95, and, directly opposite, at no.27, the **Hotel Akouas**, ✆ 51 59 67, 🖂 51 59 944, both firmly directed at prosperous local businessmen.

inexpensive

There are three comfortable one-star hotels in the New Town still within walking distance of the CTM bus station and the two railway stations: the **Continental**, 92 Av des F.A.R., ✆ 52 50 86, a fine hotel with wide corridors, large bedrooms and an elegant staircase with a fish tank on its banister; the **Excelsior**, 57 Av des F.A.R., ✆ 52 19 00, with 37 tidy rooms; and the nearby **Touring**, 34 Av Allal ben Abdellah, ✆ 52 23 51.

cheap (in the medina)

There are a number of budget hotels in the medina, found along Rue Dar Smen and Rue Rouamzine. The **Maroc Hotel**, 103 Rue Benbrahim, ✆ 53 00 75, just off Rue Rouamzine, is by far the best and often the cheapest. If it's full, the **Regina**, 19 Rue Dar Smen, ✆ 53 02 80, is a perfectly acceptable alternative and also offers free use of its cold showers.

There is a good campsite in the middle of the Imperial City, in a pleasant meadow next to the Heri es Souani arsenal and Aguedal Tank. The **Camping Aguedal/Jnane Ben Hlima**, ✆ 53 07 12, is open all the year and has a kitchen, restaurant, hot showers and a shop.

expensive

The **Al-Ismaili** Moroccan restaurant at the **Hôtel Transatlantique**, Rue el Meriniyine, ✆ 52 50 50, needs to be booked in advance. It can produce a memorable meal, with some of the best food, service and music, and the best view in Meknès.

moderate

The French-influenced restaurants licensed to serve alcohol are all in the New Town, most of them along or just off Av Hassan II. **La Coupole**, on the corner of Rue du Ghana and Av Hassan II, ✆ 52 24 83, is one of the oldest addresses in town, with a capable, reasonably priced Moroccan-French menu and calm, dignified service. Going up in price a bit, **Le Dauphin**, on Av de Paris, ✆ 52 34 23, is the only place in the city to serve consistently fresh fish. For classic, rich, meat-based French cooking head for **La Case**, 8 Blvd Moulay Youssef, ✆ 52 40 19, which is closed on Monday.

For Moroccan cooking there is the **Annexe de Metropolis**, 11 rue Sherif-Idrissi, ✆ 52 56 68, near the covered market just north of the Av Hassan II/Av Mohammed V junction. For a more palatial traditional Moroccan meal you will have to head out of the New Town to the medina. Just in from Bab Tizimi is the **Restaurant Zitouna**, 44 Jamaa Zitouna, ✆ 53 02 81, which occupies a traditional 19th-century Moroccan house.

cheap

In the New Town, for a filling bargain meal head straight for the **Novelty Restaurant**, 12 Rue de Paris, ✆ 52 21 56. Alternatively, on Rue Atlas there are two good addresses: **Pizzeria Le Four** and, directly across the road, the **Restaurant Montana**, ✆ 52 09 68, which runs a close second to the Novelty and has the advantage of a drinks licence.

In the medina there are some delightful café-restaurants by the Bab Berrima and Bab el Jdid that are well placed for a quick lunch, and a good selection along Rue Dar Smen and Rue Rouamzine. The **Café Bab Mansour**, on Place el Hédime, almost opposite its namesake, is particularly good; you can eat couscous and salad and sip tea here.

Sports

There is an efficient *hammam* in the New Town, at 4 Rue Patrice Lumumba off Av Hassan II, with separate male and female sections (*open 7am–9pm*).

Festivals

A *Fantasia* festival is held in the Imperial City in September, the same month as the *moussem* of Moulay Idriss and Sidi Bouzelm.

About 40km west of Fez stand the twin sites of Islamic Moulay Idriss and Roman Volubilis, just 4km apart on the edge of the limestone, olive-covered hills of Jbel Zerhoun.

Getting There

From Fez, your only transport options are hiring a **grand taxi** for the day (ask your hotel receptionist what sort of price you should be paying), and **hire car**. Volubilis is 4km from Moulay Idriss off a loop road, the 3312, to the left of the P28.

Moulay Idriss

Moulay Idriss is the principal and most famous of the villages on Jbel Zerhoun, and a national pilgrimage site as it holds the tomb of Moulay Idriss, the holy founder of the first indigenous Islamic kingdom of Morocco. As an indication of its high status it is governed by its own pasha, and is home to the *caid* of the whole Zerhoun region. It is an astonishingly dramatic site. The two distinct quarters of the town, Tasga and Khiber, are piled up, around and between two massive exposed outcrops of volcanic stone. The landscape around the town—hills where ordered olive groves alternate with rough forests—is in harmony with the spiritual atmosphere, for the Jbel Zerhoun is a centre both of orthodoxy and ecstatic cults.

The First Idrissids

The tomb of Moulay Idriss ibn Abdulla, 'el Akhbar'—the great—is the venerated heart of the town. He was a *sherif*, a descendant of the prophet, who fled to Morocco from Arabia to escape the slaughter ordered by the Abbasid caliphs, who had destroyed his family at the fateful battle of Fakh in AD 786. Accompanied only by his loyal slave Rashid, he journeyed through Egypt and headed west to escape from the area of Abbasid rule. He had arrived at Volubilis (known as Walila in this period) by 788, when he was welcomed by the prominent Arab Auroba tribe as their imam. He was assassinated by a secret agent of the Abbasid caliph in May 791, but the posthumous birth of a male heir in August, from a local Berber concubine, allowed his holy dynasty to continue. The slave Rashid exercised authority until he himself was assassinated (this time by an agent of the Aghlabid dynasty of Tunisia), at which time the 11-year-old Idriss II was proclaimed leader in the mosque at Volubulis. Idriss II later went on to expand his authority greatly and found the city of Fez, in which he was buried. The tombs of both father and son were rediscovered in the 15th century, in the Merenid period, after centuries of neglect. It was a period when Morocco was threatened by strong external enemies, and these new shrines helped provide a focus for a politically expedient orthodox nationalist cult. The present town and sanctuary of Moulay Idriss are mostly 18th century, for Moulay Ismaïl piously and sympathetically restored the shrine, including some of the pillars from Volubilis. The entire town was closed to Jews and Christians until 1912.

Your first experience of the holy town is likely to be of a busy and dusty bus and car park. Above and ahead, a line of stalls leads to the triangular wedge of souks that points towards the sanctuary **mosque of Moulay Idriss**. To the right of the sanctuary stretches the Tasga quarter of the town; the higher Khiber quarter is to the left. The souk stalls are lined with eyebrows of green tiles that contrast well with the rising white mass of the double village beyond. Curious woven reed plates, rosaries, golden scarves, grilled food, religious trinkets and embroidered cloth are displayed for the pilgrims. As you near the sanctuary masses of coloured nougat and enormous green candles predominate. An unmistakable wooden bar halts non-Muslims before the outermost courtyard, while within stretches a whole complex of halls, fountains for washing, prayer-halls and the holy tomb of Morocco's first legitimate Islamic ruler. Pilgrims are allowed to stay in the courtyards, but in summer the chants and collective enthusiasm seldom allow much sleep. To the right of the sanctuary entrance is the royal guesthouse, to the left the offices of the *Habous*, the ministry that administers religious endowments. Most of the olive groves in the region are leased annually by the *Habous* to farmers, the rents being used to maintain the shrine, mosque and schools.

If you go back to the bus park and follow the tarmac road up a steep hill, turn right past the post office and climb some stone steps, you will come to a famous cylindrical **minaret** encased in blue and white Koranic script, built in 1939 from stone and faïence. Later the path splits under the shadow of a great vine, and there is a good view down onto the glazed roofs and white courts of the secretive sanctuary of Moulay Idriss. Both paths lead downhill towards the sanctuary **souk**. The **medina** is small enough to allow you to wander freely along its erratic climbing alleys, their secrecy interrupted by surprising views, lone cafés and a generally friendly populace.

Just above the river is a complete, round, open-air **Roman bath**, the stones worn by use. It's still connected to a hot sulphur spring that oozes up through healing mud, and is particularly good for rheumatism. Farther on, a bridge built by Moulay Ismaïl spans the river Khoumane; on the other side a path climbs up past a few cottages, deteriorating rapidly into a goat track. If you scramble up this slope of rocky undergrowth, you'll reach a ruined 18th-century **pavilion**, with a fine view over the back of the twin rocks and houses of the Tasga and Khiber quarters.

Festivals

The massive national festival is held in September. Five visits to the festival used to be considered, by locals at least, to equal a pilgrimage to Mecca.

Volubilis (Oualili)

Open daily from dawn to dusk; adm 20dh.

The gorgeous ruins of the Roman city of Volubilis, ancient capital of the province of Mauretania Tingitania, sit below the escarpment of Jbel Zerhoun. At dusk it is a magical place and, though I have now trod through the stones for some twenty years, I am constantly surprised by its delicate, melancholic beauty. It is the finest archaeological site in Morocco and fully equal to any of the more famous Roman North African ruins that can be seen in Tunisia, Algeria or Libya. The site's most distinctive feature is an astonishingly well-preserved basilica, though the complete triumphal arch, the columns of a Capitoline temple and a dazzling series of mosaic-floored villas are equally memorable. It is an exposed, largely shadeless site, so try to avoid the midday sun. It is at its best in the morning or evening, when the sun gives a warmer colour to the stones. Volubilis is known locally as Oualili, the Berber for oleander, which covers the riverbed on the southern edge of the town.

History

The physical remains of Volubilis, like so many of the great Roman sites in North Africa, largely date from the golden period of the empire. This stretched from the reign of Trajan to the end of the Severi dynasty (of North African origin)—AD 97–235. The city has, however, a richer and more complex history that symbolically unites the two great Middle Eastern cultures that have had a fundamental influence on Morocco: the Phoenicians and the Arabs.

Excavations into the mound of ruins at the site's centre hint at a past that extends back into a Neolithic culture that came early under Phoenician influence, as ruins found here of an old temple to Baal attest. This inland market town covered 15 hectares and is believed to have served as the western capital of Juba II of Mauretania (25 BC–AD 23). Juba, though of North African blood, was a Roman client-king educated in the household of the Emperor Augustus. His wife was not some native princess but Cleopatra Silene, the child of Mark Anthony and Cleopatra. He became increasingly dependent on Roman support to govern his kingdom, so that in all practical matters it was absorbed into the empire long before Claudius' formal annexation in AD 45. The city stayed loyal to Rome through the testing years of Aedemeon's revolt in northern Morocco (roughly contemporary with that of Boadicea in Britain) and was rewarded with grants of citizenship and a ten-year tax holiday. The actual capital of the province was fixed at Tangier, but the presence of the basilica court house hints that Volubilis may have functioned as the centre of the hinterland.

Volubilis was also the centre of a rich agricultural region (over 50 villas have been found in the immediate area) which exported corn, wild beasts and oil to the coast. It was, however, on the vulnerable southeastern edge of the province, and was defended by a ring of five forts at the modern hamlets of Sidi Said, Bled el Gaada, Sidi Moussa, Tocolosida and Aïn Schkor. There was no road east to the city of Oujda, then ruled as part of Mauretania Caesarensis (Roman western Algeria), for the sternly independent Baquates tribe occupied the area around Fez and Taza. Increased frontier tension at the end of the 2nd century is evident in the decision during the reign of the Emperor Marcus Aurelius to construct a 2.5km circuit of city walls, pierced by eight gates and buttressed by forty towers. This period also witnessed the peak of prosperity, with a population estimated at over 20,000.

The near collapse of central government by the end of the period of military anarchy (235–84)—when over 30 generals had seized control of the Imperial throne in a debilitating succession of coups—resulted in the fall of the city to tribal attack in around 280, a disaster evidenced by the hidden caches of coins and bronze statuary found by archaeologists beneath some of Volubilis' villas. This partial collapse of the frontier (Banasa and Thamusida, north of Rabat, had also fallen at this time) was confirmed during the reign of the Emperor Diocletian (284–305) for, although a Roman army was based in Tangier in the 290s under the command of a co-emperor, it was decided that it was too expensive to undertake the reconquest of much of Morocco. The province was reduced to just the northern hub of the ports of Lixus-Tangier and Ceuta, and henceforth governed as if it was part of Spain.

After the initial trauma of the sack, a reduced form of urban life seems to have continued in Volubulis, boosted by refugees escaping the heavy taxes and persecutions of the late Roman Empire. Records from the Arab conquest speak of an independent trading community, now known as Oualila, ruled by a council of Christian tribal chiefs. The location of this city was downhill, beside the oleander-strewn banks of the river Khourman. A wall fenced off the old Roman town centre, which was used as a cemetery. A new intact *hammam*, built over a Roman bathhouse by the riverbank, provides a lone standing testament to this era.

It was to this city that Moulay Idriss fled at the end of the 8th century, and here that his son Idriss II was first proclaimed imam. Idriss II's foundation of Fez deliberately removed the capital from this ancient town with its traditions of oligarchy and religious pluralism. The new capital quickly drained the old of vitality, and by the 11th century Volubilis was a deserted shell.

The city was only reduced to ruin in the 18th century by Moulay Ismaïl's architects, who used its stones to build the Imperial City of Meknès, and by the Lisbon earthquake of 1755. Fortunately, an English antiquarian, John Windus, had sketched the site in 1722. These drawings were of great use to the French archaeologists who began work here in 1915, their digging assisted by Marshal Lyautey's loan of thousands of German prisoners of war.

The Olive Presses

The arch by the ticket office is the old southeastern gate of the Roman city. There is an open-air collection of sculpture and inscriptions next to the office, and a shaded café which sometimes serves lunch. From here a path leads across a largely unexcavated area of the city to cross a stream, the river Fertassa. Beyond this stream, on the left, squats the first of many classical stone olive presses with their associated drains, storage and separation tanks. The construction of a replica press here is a delightful addition to understanding the site.

The extraction of olive oil was of primary importance to Volubilis, as it still is to the villages of Jbel Zerhoun, where techniques have remained unchanged. The olive flesh and stones are first crushed by a large millstone, then shovelled into woven grass-reed sacks that look like a deflated tyre. These are then packed on top of each other on a pole (or poles) and compressed by a heavy cross beam which is gradually tightened. Liquid oozes out from the sacks and is caught by a circular drain which feeds off into a number of tanks where the oil, watery fluids and solid vegetable matter separate naturally. It is an easy matter to add more water and float the olive oil off into jars for export or domestic use.

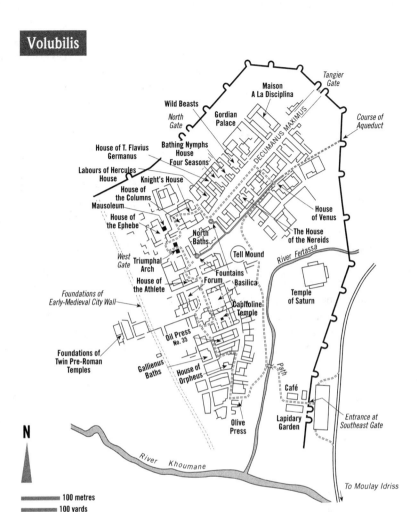

Olive oil was an essential part of ancient urban life: it was a basic ingredient of cooking; used for bathing and medicines; and was the preferred fuel for lamps. The residue from the presses was put to good use—it was either fed to livestock, or the dried cakes were used as fuel to power the bathhouses. Throughout the city you will find that even the grandest houses had their own olive press. Commerce and manufacture were forbidden to the Roman senatorial class, but anything remotely agricultural, even making bricks, could be done to your heart's content without losing status. It is refreshing to imagine this grand provincial capital surrounded by piles of crushed olives, and the back doors of mansions reeking of discarded black tarry oil. The river Fertassa, joined by the river Khoumane from Moulay Idriss, flowed outside the southern city walls and served as a combined moat and sewer.

The House of Orpheus

The House of Orpheus stands by a conspicuous clump of three cypress trees. This is the largest house in the southern part of the city, named like all the mansions of Volubilis after the subject of their principal mosaic. It is a palatial building divided, in the eastern tradition, into public and private quarters, each with its own entrance.

The first, private entrance leads to a room with a **dolphin mosaic** on the floor. The diamond lozenges, interlocking circles and airy curls which surround the central figure echo traditional carpet designs. There is also a **kitchen** with its niche for statuettes and lamps dedicated to the household gods, the *genius*, the *lar* and the *penates*. The *genius* can be thought of as a guardian angel, the *lar* as a representative of dead ancestors, and the *penates* as twin benevolent spirits who stopped food and drink going off and looked after the sanctity of the family hearth. To the right of the kitchen is an intimate paved bath with its adjacent boiler room.

The second entrance leads directly into the **atrium**, a lavish open-air court decorated with a mosaic floor showing the sea goddess Amphitrite pulled by a seahorse and surrounded by sea creatures. The courtyard is surrounded by the main living rooms, a similar arrangement to contemporary Moroccan houses. The large southern room, the *triclinium* or dining room, has the magnificent **Orpheus mosaic**. The U-shaped plain area of flooring would have been covered by couches, leaving the central circular panel free to be admired from a number of angles. It shows Orpheus playing his harp, encircled by a ring of trees which, like the mammals and birds, are seduced by his music—even the sphinx and griffins look tranquil. It is enclosed by a disciplined decorative pattern with two delightful infills that show a pair of mallards feeding from an urn, and a pair of Barbary partridges at a bird table. Orpheus (amongst other musical triumphs) descended to hell in an attempt to rescue his wife Eurydice and 'to the music of his strings he sang and all the bloodless spirits wept to hear…and Sisyphus sat rapt upon his stone. Then first by that sad singing overwhelmed, the Furies' cheeks it's said were wet with tears' (Ovid).

Next door, to the left of the path, lie the ruins of the **Gallienus Baths**, an extensive *hammam*, notable now only for one section of broken and faded mosaic amongst a series of gaping holes. These public baths were redecorated by order of the Emperor Gallienus (AD 260–68), who turned them into the most lavish in the whole city. Gallienus is otherwise known for his military reforms. He divided the army between reserve forces and highly trained mounted regiments, who could rush to any trouble on the border.

The Forum, Basilica and Capitoline Temple

Passing another, smaller public bath on the right, the path climbs a flight of steps to enter the paved public square of the city, the **forum**. This formal centre was usually ringed with market courtyards, official temples and the offices of civic government. On the western side, the *macellum*, a small butcher's souk, has been identified. Archaeologists have also discovered that it was built over a number of ancient temples. The southern face of the forum is dominated by the long arcaded outer wall of the **basilica**, the Roman courthouse, which was completed in the early 3rd century AD. It is one of the finest examples in North Africa of one of the most determinedly Roman of all civic buildings. The walls are substantial enough for the original shape of the building to be easily imagined, though you will have to fill the central nave with two double rows of columns. These ran down the entire interior length to frame the two apses at either end of the building. In the centre of each of the two apses would sit a presiding Roman magistrate, usually the governor and his deputy, surrounded by his legal staff and secretaries. The administration of justice was a very public affair, and the citizens of Volubilis would freely wander in and out of the forum to listen to part of a case, view a prominent litigant or assess the character of a new Roman official. The plan of the building may call to mind that of a church, and rightly so, for the first State-built churches of the 4th century took the basilica, not the existing religious architecture of the temples, as their direct model. In front of the basilica stand various plinths that bore monuments to commemorate officials, generals and emperors.

The raised **Capitoline temple**, with its elegant Corinthian columns, stands to the right of the basilica. Now very obvious, it would have been less so when the area was enclosed in an arcaded courtyard. Within this enclosed court an altar can be seen from which thirteen steps advance up to the terrace of the temple, which, like the ancient temple in Rome, was dedicated to the trinity of gods, to Jupiter, Juno and Minerva. There were two classes of Roman gods, those who protected the State and those who protected the family. The Capitoline triad were the chief divinities of the State. A council would assemble below the Capitol to declare war, generals appeared before setting out to battle, and after victory they would return here to offer crowns of gold and booty. Juno and Minerva, like the Virgin Mary, were appealed to on all manner of occasions, but in their Capitoline role they watched over the health and population of the whole province.

At sunset the view through these pillars east to Moulay Idriss is triumphantly photogenic. This would have been the usual orientation for a temple, but instead it stares mysteriously at the back of the basilica. It makes little sense, unless the whole complex was built over a pre-existing shrine.

The **House of the Athlete**, labelled '*Maison au Desultor*', stands at the northwestern corner of the forum. It contains a crude mosaic of a sportsman who has won a cup for vaulting over a grey horse. Beyond this stand the ruins of some fashionable shops and, opposite on the right, one of two public fountains that surround the ruins of the city's third and largest public bath, which covered an area of 1500 square metres. This, the **north baths**, and the fountains were probably built on the orders of the Emperor Hadrian, and fed by an aqueduct that channelled fresh spring water from the Zerhoun hills.

The Triumphal Arch

The path now leads across the principal avenue to the magnificent triumphal arch, raised in AD 217 by the governor Marcus Aurelius Sebastenus in honour of the Emperor Caracalla and his mother Julia Domna, whose defaced medallion bust can be seen on the right. Julia Domna, a Syrian intellectual and a princess in her own right, accompanied her husband, the Emperor Septimius Severus, on his campaign in Britain from 208 to 211, where she became known as the 'mother of the camp'. After Septimius' death at York she was later the unhappy witness of the fratricidal murder of her son Geta, who had tried to take refuge in his mother's lap from his brother and co-emperor Caracalla's murderous rage. For all this, the family may have been genuinely popular in Volubilis, for they were North African by origin and had achieved a remarkable legal reform by extending Roman citizenship to all provincials. By the time the arch was finished, however, Caracalla and Julia Domna had already been murdered by an usurper. The arch remains an impressive monument, built from local Zerhoun stone and with little evidence of the reconstruction by French archaeologists in 1933. It was originally capped with a bronze six-horse chariot and nymphs who cascaded water into carved marble bowls below. It carried an inscription which thanked the province for this symbol of loyalty and remitted all outstanding debts to the Imperial exchequer, though there was a broad hint that the emperor would be happy to accept a free gift of soldiers and elephants.

From the arch, the broad **Decumanus Maximus** leads to the Tangier gate. This central street was faced with a columned arcade which would have been lined with small shops and craft stalls. Tucked discreetly behind this screen were the large residences of officials, landlords and merchants. Just south of the arch is a house that is sometimes pointed out to visitors as a brothel, though the penis carved on to a stone lintel that now stands alone in a room was probably nothing more than a good-luck sign.

The Grand Houses

The **House of the Ephebe**, named after the fine bronze head found here (now in the Archaeological Museum in Rabat), is immediately north of the arch. It has an impressive interior courtyard with a central pool, around which are arranged public rooms ornamented with mosaics. The most elegant of them, second on your right, has Bacchus being drawn in his chariot by leopards. On the northern side of the house there is an old mausoleum which seems to have been incorporated into the house as a cellar. Next door to the west is the **House of the Columns**, which sports a circular pool in the atrium, beds of geraniums and a famous spiral, fluted column which was carved in the early 3rd century AD.

At a back dining room in the next-door house, known as the *Maison au Cavalier*—the **Knight's House**—there is a mosaic of a lascivious Bacchus, aided by Eros, discovering Ariadne, neglected by Theseus, asleep on the shore at Naxos. The figures are crude but the god's prurient eyes are alive and the flesh glistens with colour. Ariadne subsequently bore Bacchus six children, and her bridal chaplet was placed in the stars, where it forms the Corona Borealis or Cretan Crown.

Next along, staying on the left side of the road, is the **Labours of Hercules House**, named after the crude mosaic found in the dining room. Here, in oval frames, are strip-cartoon images from the life of Hercules—as a child strangling snakes; the capture of Cerberus; the Cretan Bull; cleaning the Augean stables; the Stymphalian birds; wrestling with Antaeus; the Erymanthian boar; the Lernean hydra; Hippolyta's girdle; and slaying the Nemean lion. It is thought the mosaic might have been made in the reign of the Emperor Commodus, who had a Hercules obsession, but Hercules was always a popular hero in Morocco due to his identification with the Phoenician Melkarth and the number of his achievements that occurred here. Another room has Jupiter and his boyfriend Ganymede in the centre, with the four seasons depicted in the corners. There are the usual private quarters behind the public rooms, with bath and frescoed panels painted to imitate marble. The arches in front of the house provided space for eight shops. The house was entered from a side street, guarded by a porter's lodge.

Beyond is a row of five smaller but still grand houses. The first held an inscription that has identified it as the **House of T. Flavius Germanus**; the second has a well-preserved and amusing mosaic of Dionysis and the four seasons; the third, marked by one crude pillar, is known as the **Bathing Nymphs House** (*Maison des Bains des Nymphes*) after a mosaic which shows three nymphs undressing and dancing beside the Hippocrene spring, over-looked by Pegasus, an ancient cult tree, and a horned wild-man (presumably Actaeon half-metamorphosed into a deer). Directly behind this house is the northern gate, which opens out into the extensive western cemetery, while opposite, across the street, is the **House of the Nereids**. If the restorations have been completed, the poolside mosaic here is well worth a look, as is the disturbing mosaic of four wild beasts—a bull-baiting scene, a lion, a lioness and a leopard eating heads.

Back on the left-hand side of the main street, beyond the smaller houses, is the **Gordian Palace**. With its imposing exterior of a dozen Ionic columns, this is believed to have been the governor's seasonal residence, rebuilt during the reign of Gordian III (AD 238–44). Two houses were combined to give a total of 74 rooms, including courtyards with pools and bath-houses. Inscriptions found in the palace record a series of agreements between the Roman governor and the chief of the Baquates tribe. The frequency of new treaties in the 3rd century suggests a troubled frontier. The last pact, made just a few years before the fall of the city, refers wishfully to a '*Foederata et ducturna pax*', a federated and lasting peace. To those in the know, the wording of the treaty—which treated the Baquates kingdom almost as an equal entity to the Roman Empire—must have spelt trouble. Though the palace is strong in atmosphere, its decoration is restricted to a few columns and some simple geometric mosaics. The large villa complex next door known as the **Maison a la Disciplina** is the most recent to have been excavated. It is believed to have served as a place of detention.

A single cypress tree about 100m east of the Decumanus Maximus marks the **House of Venus**. Renowned for its mosaics, this was also where the superb bronze busts of Juba II and Cato (now in the Rabat Archaeological Museum) were discovered, buried in a protec-tive bed of sand. The house is currently undergoing stabilization and is not accessible to the public, although a platform has been built to one side to allow a good view of the two most famous mosaics.

The currently closed central courtyard has an I-shaped pool, decorated with a damaged mosaic of a series of racing chariots drawn by rival teams of peacocks, geese and ducks, which includes accurate period details of a hippodrome. The large dining room straight ahead used to house a mosaic of Venus being carried through the waves (now displayed in Tangier). From the raised platform one can see the naked Hylos captured by nymphs, a colourful composition dominated by rippling muscles and erotic curves; the two side panels show scenes of guilty *erotes* being chastized. Hylos was an Argonaut who joined Jason's crew as the darling squire of Hercules. He went ashore but was seized by two nymphs, Dryope and Pegae, who dragged him away to live with them in an underwater grotto. The next-door mosaic shows chaste Diana with a nymph surprised by Actaeon at her bath, her bow hanging from the branches of a cult tree. Actaeon is already sprouting horns, for the goddess—in revenge for being surprised—changed him into a stag, and he was then chased and devoured by his own hounds.

Returning back to the forum, you get a brief look at pre-Roman Volubilis as you pass an ancient mound composed of fragments of past temples and burial chambers. Across the river Fertassa are the foundations of the **Temple of 'Saturn'**, where over 600 carved stone offerings have been discovered. This was established centuries before the Roman period as the Phoenician temple of Baal, a Semitic horned male deity of the mountains and streams, whose rites and worship continued unchanged under the Roman label of Saturn.

Moulay Idriss and Volubilis ⓒ (05–)   ***Eating Out***

This area is almost perfect for a picnic, taken either in the olive groves of Jbel Zerhoun or by the tree-shaded, ruin-skirted river Khoumane, which trickles just south of Volubilis. Provisions can be bought in Moulay Idriss. Aside from the café inside the Volubilis site entrance, the café-restaurants in Moulay Idriss and the licensed restaurant at the **Volubilis Hotel**, ⓒ 54 44 08, ◉ 54 43 69 (*expensive*), overlooking the Roman ruins, there is one exceptional local address: **El Baraka de Zerhoun**, 22 Aïn Smen-Khiber, ⓒ 54 41 84, ◉ 54 48 40 (*moderate*), is on the left of the tarmac hill road that climbs directly through Moulay Idriss. It is a delightful restaurant that offers meals that can consist of bowls of local Zerhoun olives, hot pastries, an excellent spiced vegetable salad and local *tagine*. It has no drinks licence.

Rabat

The Atlantic coast was known by the French as 'Maroc Utile'—useful Morocco. The industrial, commercial and political heartland of the country is concentrated in the three neighbouring coastal cities of Rabat, Kénitra and Casablanca; the fertile coastal provinces of the Rharb, Chaouïa and Doukkala have long been prized as the grain-bowl of the nation. For a visitor the comparatively prosperous and Western-influenced Atlantic coast serves as an excellent bridge to the more striking and aggressive culture of the interior.

Rabat has been the political capital of Morocco since 1912. It wears the well-ordered urban architecture of the 20th century: broad tree-lined avenues, a central park, apartment blocks and suburban quarters for the ministries, officialdom and foreign diplomats. The conurbation now has a population of over a million and an impressive air of activity by day. Brisk men armed with briefcases stride to their appointments along the avenues of the city centre. The main streets are lined with newsagents, bookshops, cinemas and cafés, but this familiar core of a modern capital city also contains striking monuments from the past.

The twin cities of Rabat and Salé, on opposite banks of the Bou Regreg estuary, have a long history. Rabat, the city on the southern bank, has known greater extremes of fortune, while its northern twin has had a steadier but less glamorous history. Half an hour's walk from the city centre, Salé is now really a suburb of Rabat, but it still retains its own traditional identity.

The 12th-century city walls still dominate 21st-century Rabat. The more intimate achievements of the Merenid dynasty can be found in the 13th-century medina of Salé and in Rabat's royal necropolis—the walled garden of the Chellah. The Rabat Kasbah, in its strategic position above the estuary, has been at the heart of the city's long Islamic history. It has a celebrated Almohad gate, an Andalucían urban interior and a garden palace from the 17th century now transformed into a delightful museum. For rarer insights into the Phoenician and classical achievements there are the Archaeology Museum and the ruins of Sala Colonia inside the Chellah walls, to reward you with haunting views and art of the highest order.

History

All the civilizations of Morocco have been drawn to the safe harbour of the estuary of the Bou Regreg, where the river has cut access to the sea through a forbidding line of Atlantic cliffs. For Rabat the wheel of fortune has in 2,500 years twice turned to elevate it as an imperial capital, and twice as a maritime trading power; in between these glories it has been reduced to a humble village.

Ancient Sala Colonia and the Orthodox Rabat

Like Tangier and other cities of the Moroccan coast, Rabat was first Phoenician, then Roman. It was the southernmost urban centre of the Roman province and, as Sala Colonia, given the privileges of a *colonia* or self-governing city by Trajan. Though Roman rule was withdrawn in the 3rd century, it remained a trading centre, identifying with the Muslim Kharijite heresy in the mid-8th century. Protected by the powerful Berber Berghouata confederacy, it survived until the 10th century, when a garrison of orthodox Arabs established a *rabat*, a religious community of warriors, on the site of the present Kasbah. The Almoravids took up the struggle against the heretic Berghouata and lost their first two leaders to it, but their deaths were avenged by Youssef ben Tachfine, celebrated founder of the Almoravid Empire.

The Imperial Capital

The first Almohad sultans, in the 12th century, found the site useful as a combined military and naval base, but it was not until the reign of Yaacoub el Mansour, the third Sultan, that it was decided to turn Rabat into an imperial capital. He raised the vast grand mosque of Hassan, the series of impressive gateways, and built the enormous and still-surviving extent of city walls for his Rabat el Fath, the Rabat of Victory. Work stopped the day Yaacoub died; his successors neglected this empty but magnificent encampment on the Atlantic coast, and chose to rule from Seville or Marrakesh. The Almohad walls of Rabat were only to be occupied fully in the 20th century. In the 14th century the Merenid sultans, with their exquisite taste, selected the backdrop of the near-empty city as the site for their royal necropolis. They enclosed the Roman ruins of Sala Colonia in high walls pierced by a magnificent gate that hid a complex of fine gardens, delicate mosques and sanctuaries, the Chellah. Commercial life was then concentrated in Salé—Leo Africanus, who passed through Rabat in 1500, reported that it sheltered a scattering of a mere hundred houses.

The Pirate Republic

Recovery came in the early 17th century when Muslim refugees, expelled from Andalucía by Philip III of Spain, were offered the empty city of Rabat by the Saadian Sultan Zaidan. Because the original Almohad walls enclosed far too large an area, the Andalucíans built the dividing wall that still separates the medina from the New Town. The principal business of Rabat and its sister city of Salé then became organized piracy and, due to the collapse of Saadian authority, from 1627 the two cities were able to establish themselves as an independent entity, the Republic of the Bou Regreg. The Republic was governed by an elected council or *divan* of sixteen members, which met in Salé. Each year the *divan* in turn elected a *caid* and an admiral.

Jan Jansz, a German renegade who took the name Murad Reis, was the first and most successful pirate admiral of Salé. In one of his raids he took 237 captives from the village of Baltimore outside Cork in Ireland, before proceeding to attack fishing fleets off Iceland. Five years later, in 1636, he raided the south coast of England, and then sent his captives across France by land to Marseille, where they were shipped to the slave markets of

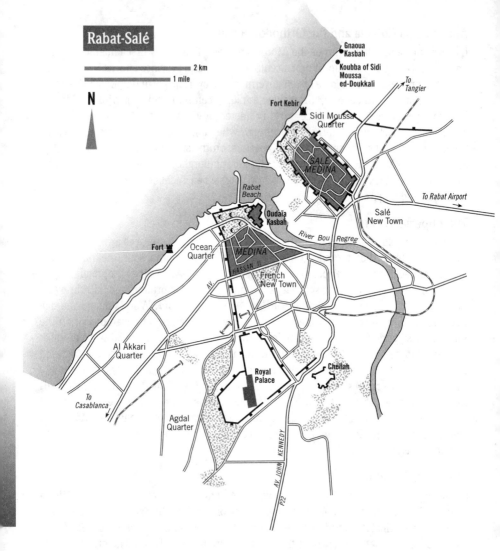

Algiers. In 1640 he was back in northern waters again, and St Michael's Mount in Cornwall lost 60 villagers to the 'Sallee Rovers'.

The European renegades were usually employed only in the navigation and the technical handling of the corsair ships. It was the Andalucían refugees under their captain who acted as the fighting force. They spoke a lingua franca that was a mixture of French, Italian, Spanish and Portuguese. On return to Salé, 10 per cent of the prize money was awarded to the *divan*, which increasingly became an oligarchy of successful captains and merchants. The Republic of the Bou Regreg was never a homogenous entity, and only constant external pressure from the European powers at sea and rival Muslim warlords by land kept the inhabitants from pursuing faction fights and civil wars to their full conclusion. The sand bar across the estuary and the savage cliffs prevented any European fleet from seriously threatening the pirate craft, although a subtle mixture of bombardment, blockade and bribes from the English and Dutch led to the release of some slaves and a variety of 'protection' arrangements with some of the European powers.

The golden days of anarchy, profit and adventure ended when Sultan Moulay Rachid took possession of Rabat in 1666. The sultan assumed a controlling 60 per cent stake in the corsair business and profits nose-dived for the other shareholders.

New Rabat

The period after Sultan Moulay Ismaïl's death in 1727 saw a rapid decline in Moroccan trade and widespread destruction by warring heirs to the throne. Locally this conflict was intensified by rivalry between Rabat and Salé. During the wise rule of Sultan Sidi Mohammed (from 1757) an attempt was made to discourage the remaining pirate activity, even before the French bombardment of Rabat in 1765. After this attack the Sultan allowed a French consul to settle in Rabat, established a new administrative palace on its present site—safely out of range of European cannon—and encouraged the town to develop its now renowned carpet trade, as well as building two new mosques and laying out a park. Unofficial coastal piracy and wrecking continued, though, until the navy of the Austrian Empire took savage revenge for the loss of one ship in 1829 by shelling all the coastal cities of Morocco.

Rabat enjoyed reasonable prosperity as one of the towns under the firm control of the government during the 19th century, though it was increasingly superseded as a trading centre by Casablanca, with its large harbour. Rabat's future was radically altered in 1912 by France, who, wary of the old cities of the interior, selected Rabat as the new political centre for the administration of the country. The fiction that the French Resident administered Morocco for the sultan was vigorously maintained, and Sultan Moulay Youssef was duly installed in the palace of Rabat.

French rule from 1912 to 1956, while rapidly developing a glittering new town, made few changes to the traditional pattern of life in the old city. The Protectorate was a colonial regime interested in ruling a conquered Islamic nation with the minimum of expense. This necessarily involved ruling through traditional power structures, and avoiding any unnecessary social, moral or political interference. As part of this policy the native quarters were left as sanctums of traditional custom, while separate modern quarters for Europeans were built outside them. This policy, defensible on aesthetic grounds as well as that of convenient security, was initiated in Rabat by the first French Resident, Marshal Lyautey. After Independence, Mohammed V and his son, the late King Hassan II, developed the palace of Rabat from a mere symbol into the actual seat of national authority.

Orientation

Rabat and Salé have spread enormously in recent decades, but all the places of interest remain in walking distance of each other. Rabat itself could hardly be more convenient for the traveller. Av Hassan II conveniently divides the medina from the new city: to the east it leads to the Pont Moulay Hassan, the bridge across the

Bou Regreg to Salé, and to the west (having passed through the Almohad walls) it takes you to the main bus station and the road to Casablanca. Av Hassan II is crossed by Av Mohammed V, which leads you north right through the medina, or south, as Av Yacoub al Mansour, past the Royal Palace to the Chellah.

The pavements of Av Mohammed V are the heart of the city, and here you can find the impressive exteriors of the post office, the train station and the major banks. Cinemas, cafés, hotels and restaurants are also all concentrated on this boulevard or on the side streets that connect it to the parallel Av Allal ben Abdallah to the east.

Rabat © (07–)   ### Getting There and Around

by air

International flights use Casablanca rather than Rabat's small airport. Six buses a day leave from outside the Hotel Terminus by the central train station on Av Mohammed V direct to Casablanca's Mohammed V International Airport. It's also possible to get there with a change of trains at Casablanca. Taxis are an expensive option, costing around 400dh. The RAM ticket office, © 70 97 10, is opposite the train station on Av Mohammed V (*open Mon–Sat 8.30–12.15 and 2.30–7*); Air France at 281 Av Mohammed V, © 70 70 66.

by rail

Travelling by train to and from Rabat is recommended: it's no more expensive than buses, is punctual, reliable and takes you straight to the city centre. The elegant white Rabat-Ville station, complete with cafés, lockers, electronic departure boards and newsstands, is at the intersection of Av Mohammed V and Av Moulay Youssef. Other nearby stations include Rabat Agdal, 2km southwest of the centre, and Rabat-Salé, the other side of the estuary. There are frequent (almost hourly) departures for Casablanca (50mins on the direct, 90mins on the stop-a-lot), five daily trains for Fez (via Meknès) and seven for Marrakesh (via Casablanca). There are a café-restaurant and baggage lockers in the station.

by bus

Local buses can be picked up on Av Hassan II. **Nos.6 or 12** take you to the Bab Fez at Salé; **nos.1, 2 and 4** go south along Av Allal ben Abdallah; for Chellah, get off at Bab Zaer, where you pass through the outer walls; **no.30** runs from the centre to the main bus depot at Place Zerktouni, which is otherwise a tedious 2km walk along Av Hassan II from the Bab Al Had (ticket 3dh, or *petit taxi* for 10dh). At the depot it is worth getting a CTM ticket at booths 14 or 15. Other services have elastic departure routines and Arabic timetables. CTM services from Rabat include Marrakesh (three buses a day), Fez via Meknès (four buses a day) and Casablanca (every two hours).

by taxi

Petits taxis, which normally keep to their meters, are found next to the train station, along Av Hassan II and opposite the Kasbah. **Grands taxis** for crossing over to Salé or long-haul destinations are found along Av Hassan II. For a place to Casablanca or Bouknadel (Plage des Nations), go to the taxi rank outside the bus depot at Place Zerktouni. It's a quicker, more pleasant trip which should cost you only a few dirhams more than the bus ticket.

by car

Driving in Rabat's one-way system is confusing. It is easier to park your car along Av Hassan II and walk. **Car hire** agencies in the city are Avis, 7 Zankat (Rue) Abou Faris El Marini, ✆ 76 79 59; Hertz, 291 Av Mohammed V, ✆ 76 92 27; and InterRent-Europcar, on Place Mohammed V, ✆ 70 44 16.

Rabat ✆ (07–) **Tourist Information**

The **tourist office** is on the angle of Av Allal Abtal and Rue Oued Fez, ✆ 77 51 71, with a branch in Rue Patrice Lumumba, ✆ 77 22 54, in the New Town. The central **post office** (PTT) is on Av Mohammed V at the junction with Rue Soekarno (*open Mon–Fri 8.30–12 and 2–6.45*). International telephone calls are best made from the numerous private booths.

Central **banks** include the BMCE, 260 Av Mohammed V, and at the train station; Banque Populaire, 64 Av Allal Ben Abdallah; and Banque du Maroc, 277 Av Mohammed V.

There is a late-opening **pharmacy** on Rue Moulay Sliman, and the Pharmacie de Chellah on Place de Melilla, ✆ 72 47 23. Others are listed in newspapers or on ✆ 72 61 50. The **Hospital Avicienne**, on Av Ibn Sina, offers emergency medical assistance.

Dial ✆ 15 for fire or medical **emergency** services, and ✆ 19 for the **police**, whose main station is on Rue Soekarno.

embassies and consulates

British: 17 Blvd de la Tour Hassan, ✆ 72 09 05 (also caters for Irish and New Zealand citizens).

Canadian: 13 Jaafar As Sadik, ✆ 67 28 80 (also Australians).

Dutch: 40 Rue de Tunis, ✆ 73 35 12.

United States: 2 Av de Marrakesh, ✆ 76 22 65.

religious services

In addition to the large number of mosques in Rabat, open to Muslims only, there are several churches and synagogues: Synagogue Talmud Torah, 9 Rue Moulay Ismaïl, and Synagogue Berdugo, at El Aloul Buenos, Rue dar El Beida. For details of services call ✆ 72 54 04. For details of services in the Catholic Cathedral of St Pierre in the New Town, call ✆ 72 23 01; for the Church of St Francis of Assisi, ✆ 72 43 80; for the Church of St Peter in the Agdal, ✆ 77 04 50. French Protestant services are conducted at the Temple, 44 Av Allal ben Abdallah, ✆ 72 38 48.

The Medina

The Rabat medina was built by the Moriscos, those Spanish inhabitants of Muslim descent who were expelled by Philip III in 1607. They built the **Andalucían wall** (*Rempart des Andalous*), a long rampart reinforced by rectangular towers that enclosed the northerly fortifiable portion from the excessive 5km perimeter wall constructed in the Almohad era. The Andalucían wall stands on the northern side of Av Hassan II, its flat top furnished with narrow gun slits in keeping with its 17th-century origins and in contrast to the comparatively light-hearted crenellations that decorate the medieval Almohad walls to the west.

Two gates pierce the western Almohad wall of the medina: the northern Bab Al Alou and the southern **Bab Al Had**. The latter was the principal entrance and is protected by a pair of protruding five-sided towers cut with gun ports. The handsome entrance gate is formed from three superimposed horseshoe arches and was rebuilt by Sultan Moulay Sliman in 1814. It was decorated with the heads of the executed until the early 20th century. Since the hole was punched through the walls by the nearby Av Hassan II it has functioned as an entrance into the vegetable market that stretches beyond this gate. In its shadow, a row of clerks armed with typewriters sits ready to assist the less literate through the formal paths of bureaucracy. Around the market are ranged all the cheaper pensions, as well as a tempting assortment of grill-cafés that provide some of the best cooking in the city.

Just behind the bustling market area, with its artisans' stalls, bazaars and intimate little cafés, are the tranquil residential quarters of an Andalucían town. Houses of stone are barred by old stained and riveted doors, their walls half-plastered and painted with lime with details picked out in azure or ochre yellow. Each quarter has a local mosque for daily prayers, a communal bakery, a fountain and usually a bath-house. Its ordered 17th-century Andalucían foundation has given the medina a regulated street pattern. It is easy to explore, in contrast to the tortuous mystery of the medieval medina in Fez.

Beginning in the southwest, at the crossing of the Rue Souika and Rue Sidi Fatah, is the **mosque of Sultan Moulay Sliman**, which he founded in 1812. Farther along Rue Souika, past intriguing displays of domestic goods—mostly bolts of cloth and kitchen ware—is the **grand mosque**, entirely rebuilt in the late 19th century, although it was founded by the Merenids. Opposite the mosque, on the right-hand side of the road that leads down to the Bab Chellah, there is a 14th-century **fountain** that is the sole surviving remnant of the Merenid mosque. The three broken arches with their fading decoration were placed here around 1370; they now provide an impressive façade for an Arab and Islamic bookshop.

The market booths around a grand mosque traditionally hold more expensive merchandise (their rents help in the upkeep of the mosque). The covered **Souk es Sebat** was once a famous centre for Morocco work: the intricate gold-stamped leatherwork which can still be found amongst the glittering array of embroidered slippers, filigree belts and ornamental hats. There are a number of specialist courtyards off the main market. A reconstructed arch leads into Rue des Consuls. Across this medina thoroughfare, a street passes through

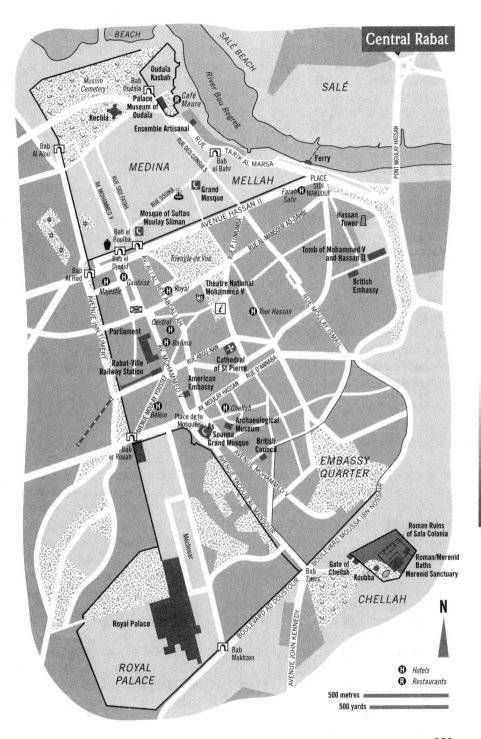

Central Rabat

BEACH

SALÉ BEACH

River Bou Regreg

SALÉ

PONT MOULAY HASSAN

Muslim Cemetery

Oudaïa Kasbah

Bab Oudaïa

Palace Museum of Oudaïa

R Café Maure

Kechla

Ensemble Artisanal

Bab Al Alou

MEDINA

RUE DES CONSULS

RUE

TARIK AL MARSA

Bab el Bahr

Ferry

RUE SIDI FATAH

AV. MOHAMMED V

RUE SOUIKA

Grand Mosque

MELLAH

Farah Safir H

PLACE SIDI MAKLOUF

Mosque of Sultan Moulay Sliman

AVENUE HASSAN II

RUE P. LUMUMBA

RUE AL-MANSOUR AD-DAHBI

Hassan Tower

Bab el Bouiba

Bab el Djedid

Triangle de Vue

Tomb of Mohammed V and Hassan II

Bab Al Had

Majestic H

H Gauloise

H Royal

Theatre National Mohammed V

H Tour Hassan

British Embassy

RUE MOULAY ISMAÏL

AVENUE IBN TUMERT

AV. ALLAL BEN ABDALLAH

Central

H Balima

Parliament

AV. MOHAMMED V

Rabat-Ville Railway Station

RUE ABOU-NAN

Cathedral of St Pierre

RUE D'ANNABA

American Embassy

AV. MOULAY HASSAN

AVENUE MOULAY YOUSSEF

H Bélère

Place de la Mosquée

H Chellah

As Sounna Grand Mosque

Archaeological Museum

British Council

EMBASSY QUARTER

Bab er Rouah

AVENUE MOHAMMED V

AVENUE YACOUB AL MANSOUR

Mechouar

BOULEVARD MOUSSA IBN NOSSAIR

Roman Ruins of Sala Colonia

Gate of Chellah

Bab Zaers

Koubba

Roman/Merenid Baths Merenid Sanctuary

CHELLAH

AVENUE JOHN KENNEDY

BOULEVARD AD DOUSTOUR

Royal Palace

Bab Makhzen

ROYAL PALACE

N

H Hotels

R Restaurants

500 metres

500 yards

223

a small square colonized by fishermen and cheap grill-cafés to twist down past pavements dressed with the pathetic objects of the flea market and pop out through the low walls of the **Bab el Bahr**, the old port gate, to meet the thundering traffic on the coastal highway. From this gate an alley leads south up to the **shrine of Lalla Qadiya**, where returning pilgrims from Mecca spend their first night home in prayer. Here a charming trader has set up a tea shop in the street which has a fine view up the estuary. Follow this alley into the old *mellah* (Jewish quarter), or a short walk upstream along the main road will take you to the boat crossing to Salé.

Rue des Consuls

This is where the larger carpet dealers and bazaars are found. Between the French bombardment of 1765 and the Protectorate of 1912, all European consuls and merchants were obliged to live on this street. No.62 was the house of the consul Louis Chenier, father of the celebrated French poet André Chenier. There is a series of splendid old *fondouqs*: No.109, the Fondouq ben Aicha, is the grandest; No.93 is the Tailleurs' Courtyard; No.141 the Kissariat Moline; Nos.31–2 are the Fondouq Ben Aïssa; and at 232 Rue Souka is Fondouq Daouia.

A right-hand turn on to the main coast road, Rue Tarik Al Marsa, takes you to the **National Artisan Museum** (*Musée National de l'Artisanat: open Wed–Mon 9–12 and 3–6; closed Tues; adm*), with a display of traditional crafts in two old shops. On the other side of the road, arranged around a modern courtyard and beside a private beach club, is the **Ensemble Artisanal**, which can be useful for carpet-pricing research; their own prices are fixed high.

The Souk el Ghezel

At the end of the Rue des Consuls in front of the Kasbah is the Souk el Ghezel, now no more than a tree-shaded car park with a whitewashed koubba at its heart. This was the wool market for the carpet-weavers of Rabat, a space that was also convenient for the auction of Christian captives from the 16th to the 18th centuries, when speculation over the size of the eventual ransom played a large role in the bidding. The wool market hasn't moved far: it can be found about 140m to the west, spread down half of the length of Blvd Al Alou. The shops in this area are home to the best joiners, wood-carvers and painters in the medina, as well as to a number of profusely stocked antique-bazaars.

The square whitewashed **Kechla**, also known as Château Neuf, was built by Sultan Moulay Rachid in the 17th century to keep a check on the Andalucían population of the Kasbah and medina, and has served as a prison, slave pen, arsenal and garrison in its day. It is surrounded by an extensive Muslim cemetery; these hug the coast in both Salé and Rabat. An underground tunnel connects the Kechla to the Kasbah, but neither this secret entrance nor the Kechla fortress itself is open. The cemetery is enlivened once a year by the *moussem* of Lalla Kasba, when young girls pray for help in finding a good husband. At the western end of the boulevard is a collection of shops such as Himmi's, which can provide everything on hire for the great day: tents fit for *caids*, vast couscous pots, and a fantastic assortment of bridal litters that range from traditional painted boxes to peacock and conch-shell floats of glittering glass.

Rue Sidi Fatah

There is no need to carry on west to the Bab Al Alou—it is not one of the city's great gateways. About 150m down the Rue Sidi Fatah, near the Mosque el Qoubba, are the 'new' baths, Hammam el Jedid, a 14th-century Merenid building whose income is partly devoted to the maintenance of the Merenid tombs at Chellah. Farther down Rue Sidi Fatah a splendid high porch shelters the gates to the mosque and tomb of Moulay Mekki, an 18th-century saint. The painted geometric design of the porch includes wreaths of flowers, a very rare detail in the strictly image-less religious art of Morocco. It hints at Ottoman influence and has now faded into a charmingly harmonious fusion of light blue and green. The mosque's elegant octagonal minaret is decorated with small arches and stalactites under the windows. Beyond it there is also the **zaouia of Sidi ben Aissa**, on the right before the Rue Souika.

The *Mellah*

This, the old Jewish quarter of the medina, can be entered through its own gate in the Andalucían wall, opposite Place du Mellah. After 50m, a right turn off Rue Ouqqasa (the southern continuation of Rue des Consuls) leads to the central passage of the *mellah* with its many dead-end alleys extending off from both sides. The *mellah* is now very low-rent, where it has not crumbled completely, and the cramped, claustrophobic atmosphere is intensified by the street vegetable and meat stalls with their accumulated refuse.

Somewhere within this area are over a dozen synagogues, all now closed—some carefully locked and preserved, some the haunt of squatters. It is not, though, a particularly old *mellah*: the Jews of Rabat were constantly being moved around by different sultans, and this cramped but defensible quarter was allocated to the community by Moulay Sliman only in 1808. At the far extremity of the *mellah* is the **mausoleum of Sidi Makhlouf**, a Jew who converted to Islam. He was venerated for his piety and spectacular miracles, not least of which was parting the waters of the Bou Regreg to enable a student, stranded in Salé, to visit him.

The Oudaïa Kasbah

The Oudaïa Kasbah is at the heart of the military history of Rabat. This was the site of the original *rabat* from which generations of cavalry issued to bring the heretic Berber tribes into obedience to successive sultans. It has also been a government bastion against a recurring enemy that came to destroy by sea. Garrisons of Almoravid, Almohad, Merenid, Andalucían and Alaouite troops have stood on guard here ready to repel raiding fleets, which from the Vikings of the 11th century through to the marines of 20th-century France have all come from Western Europe.

The Kasbah walls are consequently 10ft thick and 30ft high. Built by the Almohads, they have been constantly reinforced, most noticeably by the Andalucían refugees and the Alaouite Sultans in the 17th and 18th centuries.

The name Oudaïa is a comparatively recent innovation. The Oudaïas were one of the bedouin Arab tribes that entered southern Morocco in the 13th century. They became

Battery

Semaphore Terrace

Carpet Factory

Mosque

Rue Jemaa

Almohad Wall

River Bou Regreg

Bab Oudaïa

Rue Bazzo

Café Maure

Palace Museum of Oudaïa and Andaluciian Garden

0   25   50   75   100 m

clients of the Alaouite sherifs from the Tafilalt, and were an important source of strength in the meteoric rise of Moulay Rachid to the throne. Moulay Ismaïl sent part of the tribe to the Rabat Kasbah to keep an eye on the Andalucíans and to campaign against the Zaer, a truculent Berber hill tribe.

Bab Oudaïa

The approach to the Bab Oudaïa is up a broad stairway from the Souk el Ghezel to the Kasbah. The gate was constructed in the late 12th century by the Almohad Sultan Yaacoub el Mansour. Though capable of defence it has an obvious ceremonial purpose and this side of the Kasbah is not a first line of defence: the city walls screen the land to the west and the coast to the north. Instead, the Bab Oudaïa overlooks the medina, and formed the entrance to the original Almohad palace complex in the Kasbah. The sultan's gate had a role in Moorish society not far removed from an ancient forum. Here petitioners would wait, assemblies and meetings take place and justice be seen to be dispensed.

The Bab Oudaïa is one of the accepted masterpieces of Moorish architecture. The puritanism and self-confidence of the Almohad creed, rather than restricting artistic expression, encouraged a triumphant return to first principles. The powerful impression that you receive from the gate is not achieved by either great size, expensive materials or lavish decoration but by an instinctive sense of balance, proportion and inner tension. At one level you have the simple, clear, strong form of a **horseshoe arch** cut through a stone wall and flanked by two rectangular towers. At a second level the veneer of **exuberant decoration** seems to float out from the stone in an abstraction of pure form. The traditional Islamic decorative design has been cut into the same strong ochre-rose stone as the gatehouse, the bold-cut reliefs casting dark, contrasting shadows against the evening glow of burnt gold. Two bands surmount a **false circular arch**, with the corner spaces balanced by two stylized scallop-shell palmettes surrounded by bevelled serpentine forms. The false outer arch is decorated with a distinctive band of *darj w ktarf*, that ubiquitous leaf-like profile of interlocking arches. The superior bands each continue the shell motif, one with a calligraphic layer and the upper band with a shell-studded relief line of stalactite arches.

The genius of the whole is in the subtle relation of decoration to form. The decorative arch discreetly indicates with its diffuse edge the circumference of a circle whose diameter is exactly half the width of the square formed by the top lintel that includes the two flanking towers. A few minutes spent absorbing this tension, pursuing the clean form defined by the decorative skin, is to enter into a form of meditation.

The gatehouse is composed of two halls, with the inner gate set at a right angle to its more celebrated brother. It is often used for exhibitions and may at other times be closed, but at such times an arch to the right serves as the entrance to the kasbah. The Bab Oudaïa is one of the few spots in Rabat where young men importune you to be your guide. This must be a hard task, as the Kasbah is small, safe and easy to find your way around.

Inside the Kasbah

The Kasbah interior is a delightful whitewashed Andalucían village built by the refugees from Hornachos, who also fortified the gatehouse roof in their feud with their fellow Andalucían refugees in the medina. The central street, the Rue Jemaa, passes the Kasbah **mosque**, La Jamaa el Atiq, founded by Abdel Moumen in 1150, and the oldest in Rabat. The minaret was restored in 1700 and the mosque repaired by Ahmed el Inglizi, an English renegade who worked for Sultan Sidi Mohammed (1757–90). Farther on is the **semaphore terrace** (*plateforme du sémaphore*), a signal station that now provides an intriguing view over the entrance to the Bou Regreg estuary and across to Salé. A storehouse on the right built by the mad Sultan Moulay el Yazid at the end of the 18th century now houses a **carpet factory**. Below the platform there are further defensive walls and a round tower refortified in 1776 by Sidi Mohammed after the French bombardment. The chief defence of Rabat-Salé remained the estuary sand bar, which sealed the harbour from any deep-keeled sailing vessels. The Atlantic swell, the savage cliffs and outlying rocks made naval bombardments in the age of sail a difficult operation.

It is possible to climb down to the batteries, where you will find **Le Coulille** bar (*closes at 8pm in summer*) in the Borj des Suboefis, ✆ (07) 73 88 44. It no longer serves food, but you can consume cold beer on the terrace or in the killim-strewn bar area. The beach below is sandy and, although it can become quite crowded in summer, the Atlantic current keeps the water reasonably clean and provides some gentle surfing.

The Palace Museum of Oudaïa and the Andalucían Garden

Open Wed–Mon 8.30–12 and 3–6; closed Tues and national holidays; adm museum, garden free.

The Palace Museum, which is ranged in an assortment of rooms around the Andalucían Garden, can be approached from either of two archways below the Bab Oudaïa, and also from the Kasbah. Rue Bazzo, the second turning on the right from the central Rue Jemaa in the Kasbah, takes you downhill by a beautiful twisting path to the museum. You pass by the **Café Maure**, enclosed in a secretive terrace between the museum garden and the estuary ramparts. It is a delightful place, with tiled benches and rush mats, where you can sip a restful mint tea and consume plates of sticky cakes.

Sultan Moulay Ismaïl built this palace between 1672 and 1694. It is a walled enclosure within the Kasbah area, the delightful garden it contains cut through by a number of traditional pebble-paved paths. The museum is housed in two rooms on the western side of the garden as well as in the **palace apartments**. At the heart of the palace stands a cool courtyard paved in terracotta and green tiles, filled by the sound of a central marble fountain gently trickling into a basin. This is enclosed within a whitewashed arcade to form a heavenly vision of Moorish taste.

The two raised alcoves on each side have been used to display the two traditions of ceramic design. On one side there are pots painted in pale green, yellow and washed blue, their basic geometric patterns enlivened with floral motifs. On the other side the pure-blue-on-white design sticks to a sterner geometric scheme of interconnecting circles and stars. The latter is sometimes considered to have come exclusively from Fez, the former from coastal towns such as Rabat, Tetouan and Safi. In fact they both seem to have come from Andalucía, and to have coexisted in every urban centre of pottery production. Glazed coloured ceramic tiles (seen in *zellij* mosaics throughout Morocco) date from the 13th century, while the tradition of painted pottery seems to have been created by the influx of skilled Andalucían refugees in the late 15th century.

The reception room overlooking the garden has been furnished in the traditional style with a cascade of colours from the carpets, embroidered cushions and curtain hangings—the rich reds with purple, and greens with gold beloved by Moroccan women. You may recognize the four distinctive marble capitals of the columns which are copied from those in the 14th-century Attarine Medersa in Fez. To the east a passage leads to the two domed chambers of the *hammam*, their marble floors lit by small glass skylights set into the dome. The former kitchen area beyond, used for occasional exhibitions, leads back into the gardens.

The two galleries on the western side of the garden contain the best collection of Moroccan crafts in the country. There is enough here to keep you busily sketching for hours: costumes, armour, jewellery, pottery and musical instruments of the different tribal groups of Morocco are all displayed and labelled in slightly dusty glass cases amongst blown-up photographs. Aside from the blue robes of the Saharan tribes, the star of the collection is a black tent of the Middle Atlas nomads, complete with all its woven blankets, killims and cooking pots. Folk art rather than fine art, the simple geometric decoration of the pottery from the Berber tribes seems closer to the warrior culture of Greece in 800 BC than the urban Moroccan tradition, while the jewellery throws up strong analogies with the torcs and brooches of Celtic Britain.

The Hassan Mosque

Open daily 8am–dusk; adm free; daily guard ceremony at 5pm.

For eight centuries the unfinished Hassan Tower has loomed above Rabat. It is the minaret of the Almohad grand mosque, the truncated pillars of which stretch out in a great rectangular field below. The mosque had fallen into disrepair and was a bramble-covered ruin when Leo Africanus visited Rabat in 1500, but it was not until the great earthquake of 1755 (the same one that shattered Lisbon) that the arches and pillars of the mosque were thrown down. More recently, on the southern edge of the site a white **mausoleum**, **mosque** and **library** have been built on a raised terrace to the memory of King Mohammed V.

The Hassan Tower

Poised on the high escarpment above the river the tower looks particularly magnificent as you approach Rabat by the bridge from Salé. It has great solidity, a lordly purpose and, in its unfinished state, a noble flaw that does not distract from the beauty of its proportions or the decoration of boldly carved tracery.

The tower was built between 1195 and 1199 by the Almohad Sultan Yaacoub el Mansour as the centrally aligned northern pivot of his grand mosque. It was to be the conclusion of a building programme that included the Koutoubia in Marrakesh and the Giralda in Seville. The floor of the mosque was raised and levelled from the surrounding ground so that the tower has two heights: 50m from the natural level of ground on its northern wall and 44m from the raised mosque floor of the southern wall. Each face of the tower is different, with a subtle movement of relief arches and interlaced decoration that is based on two classic designs brought to Almohad Morocco from the sophisticated culture of Andalucía. Inside, a ramp rather than a staircase ascends through six chambers that become more ornately decorated the farther you climb. This ramp deliberately echoes the Samarra Mosque in Iraq, which was acknowledged to be the biggest in the world. It was built in AD 850 and allowed the caliph to ride up to the summit on horseback on an external ascending ramp and call his army to Friday prayers. Behind the tower there is a staircase that leads down to a tomb for the unknown warrior, and a small additional mosque dedicated jointly to all the many previous ruling dynasties of Morocco.

The Mosque Ruins

The ruins of the Hassan Mosque and that of Samarra in Iraq are still among the largest in the world. Yaacoub el Mansour, who ruled over the entire western half of the Islamic world, with an empire that stretched from Spain to Libya, deliberately attempted to build a mosque that would vie with the finest efforts of the great cities of the East. The rectangular plan of the mosque measures 183m by 139m, and was crossed by a forest of aisles: 21 longitudinal spans and 28 laterals that multiply into 312 marble columns and 112 stouter arch-bearing pillars. Three arcaded courts open to the sky broke this massive roofline. The open court nearest the tower, the *sahn* or washing area, had rows of fountains that played into marble basins and were fed from eleven huge cisterns hidden beneath the floor. There were four doors in this northern wall and six on the eastern and western sides. The central 'nave' leading up to the mihrab was designed to be significantly wider, to draw the worshippers' attention to the direction for prayer. It is just possible now to imagine the splendour of the interior, by ignoring the irritating modern paving and transforming the truncated remnants into the shifting vistas of columns, flooded with arcaded pools of harsh sunlight and the mass of genuflecting warriors that filled it for just a few years.

The Mausoleum

King Mohammed V's tomb has a traditional and distinctive green-tiled pyramidal roof capped with a triplet of golden spheres. A broad ornate staircase leads up to it from the southern end of the old mosque. Royal guards in scarlet with a white burnous patrol the arcade of Italian white marble, with its four arches leading to the balcony of the royal koubba. The sarcophagus is a block of white onyx from the mountains of the Hindu Kush set in a sea of polished black marble. A scholar mutters verses from the Koran in one corner, or dozes. Heraldic banners from all the provinces and towns of Morocco are suspended in serried ranks under the balcony, and a bronze chandelier, which weighs one ton, hangs from the roof. The decoration of the ascending ceiling must be the last word in gilded ornate. The king's sarcophagus has been accompanied by that of his youngest son, the genial Prince Moulay Abdullah, since his death in 1983.

The mausoleum was designed by a Vietnamese architect, Vo Toan, and finished in 1971. Aesthetically it must be considered something of a disaster. It is impressive only in the lavish use of luxurious materials, which expresses the Moroccan people's great regard for the king who led them in their struggle for Independence. He has already assumed an almost holy status, and it is traditional in Morocco that the interiors of saints' shrines should be decorated as richly as a community can afford. On a lower level of the terrace a mosque has been constructed, its three handsome doors and mihrab arranged on the same axis as the ancient mosque. The colonnade of finely sculpted white marble from Carrara stands atop a library dedicated to every aspect of the reigning Alaouite dynasty.

The New Town
The Boulevards

The major French-designed public buildings of Rabat are all found along or around the Avenue Mohammed V, the grand boulevard that connects the medina with the royal palace. Their architecture combines Egyptian, classical and Moorish elements to create an impression of order and stability. The PTT ministerial building contains a small **postal museum**, mainly a stamp collection, which is open during office hours. Rue al Mansour ad Dahbi leads off to the **Theatre National Mohammed V**, opposite which is the **Triangle de Vue**, a pleasant, restful urban garden created in 1920. The northern corner contains the walls of a ruined 18th-century mosque and a number of tombs.

Farther down Avenue Mohammed V is the terracotta-coloured and U-shaped **parliament building** (Chambre des Représentants). Opposite the station, Rue Abou-Nan leads to Place Sahat al Golan and the striking Catholic **Cathedral of St Pierre**. Two palisade-like towers emerge from a totally white nave; the windows and lintels have been decorated with geometric shapes in brick in a deliberately Islamic borrowing.

The Walls and the Bab er Rouah

The 5km **Almohad wall** encloses the Kasbah, medina, palace and New Town, and has five city gates surviving in some form: the Bab Al Alou, Bab Al Had, Bab er Rouah, Bab Makhzen and Bab Zaers. The section between the Bab Al Had and the Bab er Rouah on Rue Ibn Tumert provides a pleasant 1km walk; the ochre battlements are decorated with flowering plants and clusters of palm trees.

The **Bab er Rouah**, 'the gate of the winds', was built in the same era as the Bab Oudaïa, and is the only true surviving Almohad structure that is comparable with it. Set above Place An Nasr, isolated from the traffic flow, the two massive surrounding stone bastions still allow you to envisage its central defensive role. The stone carving in this exposed position is still carefully balanced and controlled, with a ring of concentric engaged arches rippling out from the gate and enclosed by an ancient scroll of the Koran in Kufic script. The eastern face of the gate has an even lighter cut of stone with a delicate bed of floral and vegetable tracery supporting a palmette. The blend of elegant fantasy, tension of design and the gate's purpose in defence are reinforced by the interior chambers. Four rooms with elegant cupolas inevitably force visitors into a series of dizzying turns. The rooms are open periodically for exhibitions and for the moment are as close to a national gallery of art as there is in Morocco. If they are open at all the hours will be 8.30–12 and 2–8.

Going back into the city from the gate you face the **As Sounna Grand Mosque**, the minaret of which dominates the skyline of the New Town. It was built by Sidi Mohammed in the 18th century and has been the victim of frequent restorations.

The Royal Palace

The southeastern corner of the Almohad defences was selected as the site for a new palace in the 18th century, and a park was enclosed behind the grand mosque. Constantly altered and improved, the palace was almost entirely rebuilt by the late King Hassan, who also extended the grounds behind the main block to include a private golf course, enclosed by a new stretch of the city wall. Many of the chief offices of state are housed within the walls and it is very much a working palace. You can go into the grounds, but don't wander off the central avenue.

Through the ornamental northern gate, on the left, is the **Lycée Moulay Youssef** and a small suburb for past and present employees of the king. On the right are the stables, an exercise paddock and the princes' school, and then the open *méchouar*, or assembly place. The building on the right is the Ministry of the Habous (responsible for religious foundations). The outer wings of the main block contain the house of the president of the council and cabinet offices. A mosque, the supreme court, an oratory and the central

mausoleum of Moulay Hassan coexist with the various royal apartments. The mosque on the left, **Ahl Fas**, is used for the official Friday royal prayers when the king as imam rides the short distance from the palace in a carriage and returns riding on a horse, his brow shaded from the sun by a crimson parasol of state. This procession, a weekly ritual for past sultans, is now rarely performed, and the 12.30pm cavalcade will be advertised well in advance.

The southern gate leads into the Blvd Ad Doustour. If you turn left, the southern Almohad wall leads to Bab Zaers, from where you can return to the New Town or take the turning right to go into the Chellah.

The Archaeological Museum (Musée Archéologique)

Open Wed–Mon 9–11.30 and 2.30–5.30; closed Tues; adm.

This small but excellent museum is the major attraction of the New Town. To reach it, take the Rue Moulay Abdul Al Aziz from the As Sounna Grand Mosque and turn right on to Rue al Brihi. The museum is the low, modern building on the corner.

The **central hall** contains a large marble statue that was discovered at Sala and has been identified with King Juba II or his son Ptolemy. The handsome marble torso beside it was recovered from Volubilis and considered to be from the 2nd century AD. Around the walls are the results of the excavations at the microlithic site of Taforalt, and Neolithic child burials from Skhirate and Harhoura from about 4000 BC.

The **first floor** has a chronological collection of artefacts extracted from Sala Colonia, in four cases. The first contains bronze fragments of sculptures, a little bust of Juba II, an ivory cylinder with four carved scenes and a representation of Apollo; the second contains ceramic shards and coins from the excavations; the third holds funerary objects from the classical period; and the fourth contains objects from Islamic Chellah. The next exhibits demonstrate the often overlooked survival of the classical sites into recent history, with Christian and Jewish cult objects and relics of Islamic occupation up to the 14th century.

Recent archaeological digs reflected in the museum have concentrated on old Islamic sites. Finds from two towns opposite the Spanish coast, Ksar-es-Seghir and Balyounesh (between Tangier and Ceuta), show the high state of Islamic civilization that these foundations of Ommayad Córdoba enjoyed from the 10th century. There is also pottery from Sijilmassa (south of Er Rachidia), from the 8th century, and fragments from the medieval sugar mill at Chichaoua (between Marrakesh and Essaouira). Going back down to the central hall, a small open-air courtyard on one side is lined with a random selection of carved stones from different epochs.

The greatest treasures of the museum are its **bronzes**, displayed in a special side hall (*no photography allowed*). The finest pieces are the 1st-century AD **bust of Cato the Younger**, probably modelled from the death mask of the orator, who preferred to die free under the Republic than live under an emperor, and the **bust of the young Berber man** with his hair bound by a fillet, which is another sculpture thought to be King Juba II, who married Cleopatra Selene, daughter of Anthony and Cleopatra.

The **Lustral Dionysius** is a superb full-length statue, a Roman copy of the original carved by the Greek master Praxiteles. The fisherman casting his net and the rider with his missing leg are further 1st- or 2nd-century Roman works. The bronze guard dog from Volubilis was discovered in 1916, and probably made during the reign of Hadrian in the 2nd century. In the glass cases further small bronzes can be seen—a horse and rider from Volubilis, a snake discovered in Banasa, a head of Oceanus from Lixus, and figurines of Eros and Bacchus. There are fine marble heads of Diana and of a Berber youth. In the extensive collection of classical objects, the military diploma given by the Emperor Domitian to the cavalryman Domitius, found at Banasa, adds a striking personal touch.

Five Phoenician standing stones are on show, their crude symbolic carving looking out of place in this treasure house of humanistic art. They do, however, convey the Semitic devotion to an abstract divinity, which has been a much stronger influence in Morocco than the buried remnants of Greece and Rome. One of them was discovered in the ancient mound of the temple the Romans equated with Saturn at Volubilis.

Chellah

Open daily 8.30–6.30; adm.

One of the most beautiful of Morocco's many striking historical ruins, Chellah is not distinguished architecturally but has a wistful atmosphere of antiquity. The walled enclosure has bred strange beliefs—such as those of the buried treasure of Sultan Yaacoub, guarded by a prince of the Jinn, and of a fleeting visit from the Prophet Mohammed—but the factual narrative is fanciful enough. Freshwater springs flow out from this hill less than 500m from the brackish estuary of the Bou Regreg, and human settlement probably always clustered on this slope even before the Phoenicians founded Sala. This city, after a millennium of existence, was reduced to a ruined mound in the 10th century, but continued to be used as a revered burial ground. The first Merenid Sultan, Abou Yusuf Yaqub, chose to build a tomb and mosque here, burying his wife, before joining her in his own grave in 1286. Later, the Merenid sultans enclosed it for the use of their own dead. Now their shrines are also reduced to picturesque ruin, and Roman Sala Colonia has been re-exposed by excavation. A lush growth of jungle garden is established beside the path that leads down to the sacred spring, the Merenid tombs and along to the corner tower that looks over the meandering turns of the Bou Regreg river.

The Walls

The Merenid Sultan Abou Said Uthman (1310–31) began the walls, which were finished by his successor, Abou Hassan, in 1339 and further embellished by Abou Inan (1348–59). The Zippoun Berber tribe were appointed as the hereditary protectors of Chellah, a duty which they continued for centuries after the fall of the dynasty.

The simple arch of the gate is enclosed by half-octagonal towers, their lean, twisted battlements supported by a delicate tracery of dripping stalactites. The Kufic script on the gate reads, 'I take refuge in Allah, against Satan, the stoned one', a useful invocation for the biers of dead sultans to pass under. The gate enforces a double twist before you enter the Chellah through a more orthodox Islamic horseshoe arch decorated with flanking shell motifs. On the left there is a café inside a disused guard-house, and street-sellers and snake-charmers sometimes gather here. A stairway descends steeply through the well-watered, luxuriant gardens, a confused mass of palm, bamboo, banana, hibiscus, fig and the drooping handkerchief leaves of the datura.

The Roman Ruins of Sala Colonia

To the left are the excavations of the Roman city, which have at last been opened for inspection. They occupy the northern half of the enclosure and border the Merenid necropolis. It is a confusing site because of the different levels of terraces. The heart of the excavation is the broad main street; look out for the foundations of the triumphal arch that crossed the thoroughfare. Immediately south of this are the intriguing remains of a bath complex with an elegant circular hall. The rest of the complex survives as the *hammam* restored by the Merenid Sultan Abou Inan (not yet accessible).

Immediately above the arch stood the temple to Jupiter, though less than half of the 45m by 28m ground plan survives. This once overlooked the forum (the irregular plaza) at the end of the main street. Fragments of columns can be found which once enclosed this space with a shaded colonnade. Look around the inscriptions for there is one here dedicated to the Emperor Constantine (AD 306–37). This late date came as some surprise for it was believed Sala had fallen, like the other Roman cities in Morocco, to the barbarians in AD 280. The Limes frontier stood just south of the city, connecting the Ouad Akrach to the Atlantic, watched over by a fort on the Sidi Khalifa cemetery. The city was defended by walls from AD 144, but somehow survived as an isolated coastal outpost of Empire until the 5th century.

The Sacred Pool

A group of koubbas surrounds a walled pool. Stubs of gutted candles can be found within. The venerated saints, though wrapped in Islamic green shrouds and familiar whitewashed shrines, belong to pre-Islamic cults of great antiquity. The pool is surrounded by old brick vaults, and drains out through a gravel stream that runs through an enclosing grove of drooping banana plants. Sacred black eels swim up to lurk in shaded recesses of the pool; infertile women peel boiled eggs (sold by two boys who sleep on the floor of the shrine above) to offer to them. The scene is so strongly archetypal, such a graphic pagan survival in the shadow of ruined cities and royal tombs, that you instinctively check twice to discover if you are dreaming. That barren women should offer eggs, the universal symbol of fertility, to be devoured by phallic eels as emissaries of an ancient deity calls any visitor to compose a few lines of verse.

The Merenid Sanctuary

The sanctuary is easily recognized: its two minarets, of the mosque and zaouia, are invariably topped with a ponderously balanced pair of storks adding to their nest. Enter into the *sahn*, the small introductory courtyard, and proceed into the ruined **prayer-hall**. This and the adjoining tomb were the first structures built by Abou Yusuf Yaqub, in 1284. The mihrab is straight ahead, by the four columns of the pillared **mosque**. The ruined

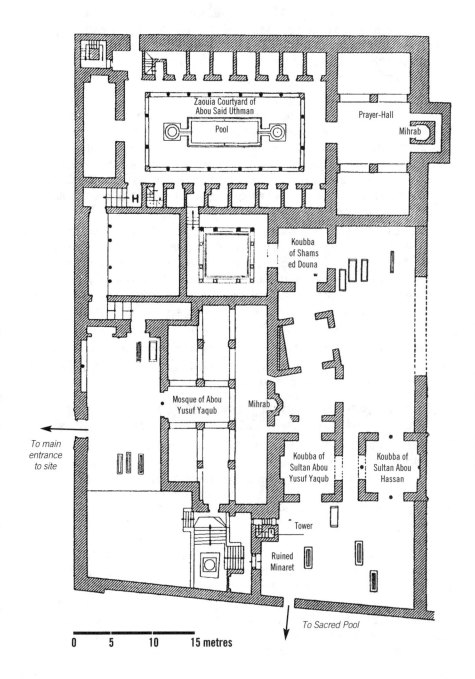

Zaouia Courtyard of
Abou Said Uthman

Pool

Prayer-Hall

Mihrab

Koubba
of Shams
ed Douna

Mosque of Abou
Yusuf Yaqub

Mihrab

To main
entrance
to site

Koubba of
Sultan Abou
Yusuf Yaqub

Koubba of
Sultan Abou
Hassan

Tower

Ruined
Minaret

To Sacred Pool

0   5   10   15 metres

minaret is conspicuous to your right, near a pool. Pass either side of the mihrab to enter the necropolis.

This larger complex was designed by Sultan Abou Hassan (1331–48). Leo Africanus counted 32 Merenid graves here in 1500, but the number that can be distinguished today is very much less. The grave of the 'Black Sultan', Abou Hassan, lies against the outer wall to the right, within a koubba decorated with arches and tracery. The facing koubba is that of Sultan Yaqub, known locally as the 'Commander of the Jinn'.

The **tomb of Shams ed Douna**, 'the Light of Dawn', can be seen in the southeastern corner (bottom left as you stand by the mihrab) under a recess. Her long tombstone has been carved with verses celebrating the magnificence of her funeral. A Christian convert to Islam, she was a concubine of Abou Hassan and mother of Abou Inan, who eventually deposed his father. Abou Hassan was chased into the High Atlas and died an exile in the winter of the following year, but was buried decently, as you can see, in the Chellah in 1352 by his son. Abou Inan would himself choose to be buried on the heights overlooking Fez.

The sanctuary also contained a **zaouia**, a religious college which, though damaged, is in a better state than the mosque. The minaret is on the left, with the wash basins and latrines directly below. The court lined with cells faces a central rectangular pool with two sunken white marble shells for water jets that drained into the pool. The bases of the thin white marble columns can be seen with some surviving mosaic tilework. A much smaller prayer-hall faces the mihrab, with a passage behind that allowed pilgrims to make the seven circuits that were believed by some to be equal to the pilgrimage to Mecca.

The beautiful soft red glow of the sanctuary wall shields a tranquil and formal **garden** formed by a double line of orange trees, fed with water from the sacred spring. From here you can look out over the walls to inspect tidy and fertile vegetable plots.

Salé

Salé has long maintained a separate identity from Rabat. Its great period of prosperity was under the Merenid sultans, who rebuilt the walls and constructed the medersa and several other buildings. These medieval achievements still seem to express the spirit of the town, which consciously maintains a low-key and pious Islamic identity in contrast to the secular and political bustle of its neighbour.

History

The very name of Salé proclaims a past different from that of its neighbour. Local traditions assert that the citizens of the ancient city of Sala Colonia settled the headland of Salé after their venerable home had been destroyed by the orthodox *rabat* garrison stationed in what is now known as the Oudaïa Kasbah of Rabat. Salé grew into a prosperous port city, until one terrible night Alfonso X of Castile descended like a wolf on the fold, attacking during the feast night of Aid es Seghir in 1260. The booty the Castilians captured was immense, the city was sacked and most of its citizens were killed or enslaved. Abou Yusuf Yaqub, the

brother of the founder of the Merenid dynasty, hurried to the rescue of the city and reached Salé in one heroic day's ride from Taza. He was too late to rescue the city but succeeded in expelling the raiders, and in an emotional scene vowed to rebuild it. His actions helped establish the Merenids as credible rulers of Morocco, and Salé consequently became a cornerstone of Merenid pride.

The sacked city was rebuilt with an energy and elegance which still marks its identity. While Rabat shrank to a village raided by the Portuguese in the 16th century, Salé according to Leo Africanus had 'all the ornaments, qualities and conditions necessary to make a city civil, and this in such perfection that it was visited by several generations of Christian merchants'.

Old Salé maintained a troubled supremacy over the Andalucían settlements in Rabat in the dazzling days of the pirate Republic of the Bou Regreg, from 1629 to 1666, but then stagnated. The Alaouite sultans who came to power from 1668 preferred to live and build in Rabat.

There is hardly anywhere to stay in Salé, so most visitors base themselves in Rabat. A fishing boat will take you from the wharf below the Rabat medina across the Bou Regreg for a dirham. The Jaich el Malaki, also known by its old name of Avenue de la Plage, leads straight up from the Salé wharf to the medina through the Bab Bou Haja. *Grands taxis* (*petits taxis* are restricted to either Rabat or Salé) or buses (nos.6 and 10 ply the route from Rabat's Avenue Hassan II) will drop you farther along at the Bab Fez.

The Medina

Three streets, Boulevard Touil, Rue de la Grande Mosquée and the central Rue Souika/Kechachin, provide sinuous crossings of the length of the old town, an under-visited network of twisting and irregular streets. The streets wind past the white façades of houses that have little ornamentation other than strongly reinforced doors. The medina is entirely enclosed by walls and roughly rectangular in shape, 800m wide and 1,500m long; the northern coastal third is occupied by a large cemetery. Outside the walls Salé has grown greatly to the north and west, in a fairly dismal style, since Independence.

Bab Mrisa

This unmistakable massive arch is flanked by two elegant towers and decorated with floral tracery and sculpted inscriptions. It was built by Sultan Abou Yusuf Yaqub between 1260 and 1270, after the Castilian sacking of the city, in a similar style to the Almohad gates of Rabat. A reinforced canal led from the estuary through this water-gate into a basin within the city walls. Here the fleet moored in complete safety, surrounded by arsenals and dockyards.

The *Mellah*

The Jews were given this area after the canal had become hopelessly silted. They were moved again, over the road to the north, when Moulay Ismaïl required this corner for a garrison of Abids, but expanded back again before the exodus after Independence.

The Souks

The **Bab Fez** is a natural point of entrance, with taxis, train and bus station clustered outside it. Stalls of grilled kebabs, and tables full of nuts, sweets and fruit are clustered in and around the portals. There is a health centre immediately on the left through the gate, and the second left turning after it, Rue Dar Reghai, takes you in a natural flow of pedestrians to the heart of the town. The stalls along the way are full of products for the local rather than the tourist market, for Salé has remained largely aloof from the world of hassles and quick sales. A number of tempting kitchens exist along this street and its extension, Rue Souika. Here, as well as absorbing the colour and sounds, you can also taste the medina.

On the right is the **tomb and mosque of Sidi Ahmed Hadji**, a respected 17th-century marabout, venerated with gifts of tall green candles.

The triangular **Souk el Kebir**, partly shaded by trees, is the main market in Salé. Piles of secondhand clothes are sorted through at the back whilst carpenters, leather-workers and slipper-makers create a delightful cacophony of sound and activity.

Christian slaves captured by the 'Sallee Rovers' of Rabat and Salé were often sold here. In spite of the many salacious-Orientalist tales that have circulated ever since, Christian women were commonly treated with a certain care and respect. Whether or not these rules were always adhered to is of course another matter, but in theory any proof of sexual interference from the captors gave automatic liberty to the captive, and married women— or those who, despite beatings, refused to embrace Islam—were occasionally returned. Barbary piracy was a business activity, which had its code of conduct.

To the left of the Souk el Kebir, just before some gates, a right-hand turn leads to Rue Haddadine, the blacksmiths' and tinkers' street that leads directly north to cross Rue Bab Sebta. To your left Rue Kechachine takes you on west past the workshops of the sculptors in wood and stone, and joiners' shops turning out headboards for beds and footboards for the wall benches that are found in most Moroccan homes.

Taking the left turn from the Souk el Kebir takes you to the **Kissaria**, a small pocket of alleys where the most skilled artisans have their stalls. The **Souk el Ghezel**, the wool market, is an open space lined by shops where early in the morning, under the protection of canvas and a few trees, bales of wool are weighed from tripod stands and gently haggled over.

The adjacent **Souk el Merzouk** is the quarter for the tailors, cloth merchants and embroiderers, whose young assistants create long trails of twisting silk. After the fountain on the right, look out for the door of the **Fondouq Askour**, the hospital and school founded by the Merenid Sultan Abou Inan in the 14th century. The courtyard is functional but the door is covered in a cascade of carved stalactites.

The Medersa and Grand Mosque

The main mosque is 300m on down Rue de la Grande Mosquée. Tailors' shops with their array of kaftans give way to the larger walled houses of the merchants, decorated with their Andalucían, rather classically proportioned doorways. A charming small white-washed square has stairs leading up to the grand mosque and, on the left just past an 18th-century fountain, a gate into the medersa. The mosque was built in the reign of the Almohad Abou Yaacoub Youssef (1163–84). The clear lines of the doorways and the simple elegance of the carving contrast with the gates of the Merenid medersa built by the Black Sultan, Abou Hassan, in 1341 (*ask for the custodian; adm*). Here there is rich cedar- and plaster-carving, vivid paintwork and an overhanging roof over the arch.

The building is much smaller than the great medersas of Fez, though the details are as lavish and exciting. In the central court a gallery of columns, decorated with contrasting designs and coloured faïence mosaics, leads your eye up to the area of delicately carved cream plaster that gives way to the crowning walls and hanging gallery of sombre carved cedar. The prayer-hall has a finely painted ceiling and the **mihrab** has some fine carved decoration. The courtyard is designed to sit in rather than pace around. A few minutes can be spent spotting the recurring motifs of Islamic decoration drawn entirely from the natural world—flowers, fruit and shells. These are found at every level and worked into each material by bands of the cursive Arabic script of the Koran.

The foundation stone introduces the one distracting secular tone, 'Look at my admirable portal, rejoice in my chosen company, in the remarkable style of my construction and my marvellous interior. The workers here have accomplished an artful creation with the beauty of youth...' Arabic poetry does not always translate well. The courtyard pillars would perhaps present a more serene interior if their distracting decoration were removed. Two galleries of cells can be explored, and do not miss the opportunity to get out on the roof with its view over the rooftops of the Salé medina across the estuary to Rabat.

The Zaouia of Sidi Abdallah ben Hassoun

Through an arcade just to the left of the grand mosque is the door of the zaouia of Sidi Ahmed el Tijani decorated with geometric mosaics and carved plaster. At the back of the mosque is the zaouia of Sidi Abdallah ben Hassoun. A window allows you to look into the mausoleum, which was rebuilt in the 19th century. Each year on the afternoon of Mouloud, the Prophet Mohammed's birthday, a collection of large candles and complicated wax lanterns is escorted through the town in a great procession guarded by the guild of boatmen dressed as Turks or corsairs, and the saint's descendants and devotees carrying filigree and silk-decorated candles. The entire retinue deposit their offerings at the shrine, where they remain until the new year. Sixteen days later, Sidi Abdallah, Salé's patron saint, is venerated by all the religious brotherhoods, who sing chants, psalms and mystical exercises in his honour.

Sidi Abdallah came from the south of Morocco but moved to Salé in order to avoid the distractions of tribal politics. He was respected during his lifetime and attracted many pupils before his death in 1604. The Sidi was adopted by sailors and travellers, who continue to visit the shrine for auguries to indicate the safety of their voyage.

The Cemetery

The cemetery extends west from Sidi Abdallah's shrine and a dirt track winds out across the large expanse of graves to the **Northwest Fort**, Borj Nord-Ouest, an 18th-century redoubt containing a number of bronze English and Spanish cannon. At the end of the bastion there is a good view across the estuary to Rabat. The track passes a number of simple whitewashed koubbas. The shrine nearest the fort is that of **Sidi ben Achir**, an Andalucían scholar and mystic who died in 1362. He has a great reputation for curing the sick and the mad, and in 1846 Sultan Abder Rahman built a series of lodgings for pilgrims to stay in as they await their cure. The reputation of the saint has not diminished, particularly among women. The old ladies will be upset if you walk too close, perhaps for your own benefit—the saint also has the power to wreck Christian ships along this coast.

Beyond the Walls

The Koubba of Sidi Moussa ed-Doukkali

The cliffs along the coast at Salé do indeed look evil to shipping. The Boulevard Circulaire that runs along the edge of the cemetery takes you out through the Bab Chafaa, from where the road continues above the sea. Patient men with long bamboo fishing poles perch above these high and dangerous cliffs.

A 3km walk beside the shore will take you to the **koubba of Sidi Moussa ed-Doukkali**, which Moulay Ismaïl carefully restored. This Sidi is greatly loved by the poor, who hold an enormous celebration in August in his honour. He voluntarily chose an ascetic life, grubbing along this shore for edible roots and sorting driftwood and debris to sell in order to buy fresh bread for the poor. He was also a skilled magician, and humbled the arrogant rich by miraculously flying to Mecca each year for the pilgrimage. Today the shore is lined with refuse, while shantytowns extend inland from the road.

The Gnaoua Kasbah

Just beyond the koubba is the kasbah of the Gnaoua, a pisé fortress built by Moulay Ismaïl to house his Abid troops—black Africans from Guinea, as the name still proclaims. The wind and the salt spray have etched weird patterns into the walls, and graffiti left by the Abid regiments or renegades with their captives can still be seen etched into the less eroded sections.

Oulja Pottery

A rich deposit of clay has been discovered on the northern bank of the Bou Regreg estuary and there are now two dozen kilns at work in the pottery hamlet of Oulja, a 2km *petit taxi* ride from Salé. Though Rabat-Salé was a pottery-producing centre in the 17th, 18th and 19th centuries, nothing has been made on a wheel here for over a century. This craft centre follows some of the traditional influences that can be seen in the Palace Museum of Oudaïa, as well as striking out in new directions.

Rabat ✆ (07–)   **Where to Stay**

Bedrooms fill up quickly throughout the year in Rabat and it is advisable to find a room early in the day or book in advance. Rabat is a fairly hassle-free city to walk around and so there is no need to buy the protective shelter of a top-class hotel. Anywhere clean and central should do for all but the most luxury-addicted travellers.

luxury

The **Farah Safir**, ✆ 73 47 47, 🖂 72 21 55, has everything you could ask for from a modern, international hotel, with a superb position on Place Sidi Maklouf, overlooking the estuary, medina and the Hassan Tower. Perched on the roof is a bar and a small but very welcome plunge pool.

First place has, however, been taken by the newly restored **La Tour Hassan Méridien**, 26 Rue Chellah, ✆ 70 42 01/✆ 73 25 31, 🖂 72 54 08/🖂 73 18 66 (or make reservations in the UK: ✆ 0800 40 40 40, or in the USA: toll free ✆ 1 800 543 4300). This dignified old hotel (founded in 1914) occupies a central streetside position in the heart of the city. It has an elegant enclosed garden courtyard, the Moroccan **La Maison Arabe** restaurant, the **Pasha** bar, and the contented hum of a busy social and business centre.

The **Chellah**, 2 Rue d'Ifni, ✆ 70 10 51, ✉ 70 63 54, is an unexceptional hotel, well placed near the grand mosque and the Archaeological Museum, but it looks a little faded. It and the **Bélère**, 33 Av Moulay Youssef, ✆ 70 96 89, ✉ 70 98 01, are very popular with Western travellers. In this price range, the **Dawliz Rabat-Salé**, Av du Prince Heritier Sidi Mohammed, ✆ 88 32 77/✆ 88 32 81, ✉ 88 32 79, on the banks of the Bou Regreg river, is much to be preferred. It's a romantic situation, with a pool and only 43 rooms, but bring some insect repellent if you wish to enjoy a drink at dusk.

Out from the centre of town but well placed for coach-borne groups is the 200-room **Hyatt Regency**, ✆ 77 12 34, ✉ 77 24 92, in the suburb of Souissi-Rabat.

moderate

There is a good selection of moderately priced hotels (with bars and restaurants) that get most of their business from locals, not tourists. Good choices are the bustling **Terminus**, 384 Av Mohammed V, ✆ 70 06 16/✆ 70 52 67, ✉ 70 19 26, near the railway station, or the fading grandeur of the **Balima**, on Av Mohammed V and Rue de Jakarta, ✆ 70 86 25/✆ 70 74 50, opposite the Parliament. Once the smartest hotel in town, it now has an aged interior, but retains all its external dignity and is usually one of the last in Rabat to fill up. The foyer and café gardens are still at the centre of Rabat social life. For twice the standard rate, you can take one of the faded suites on the top floor with balconies that give an alarming view over the city. These rooms must be full of the ghosts of *caids*, French senators and assorted power politicians who stayed here while petitioning the Resident or his successors, the Alaouite kings.

Two smaller and slightly cheaper personal favourites are the **Grand Hotel**, 19 Rue Patrice Lumumba, ✆ 72 72 85, and the **Bou-Regreg** (ex Rex) **Hotel**, on the corner of Rue Nador and Av Hassan II, ✆ 72 41 10.

inexpensive

The two most comfortable and amusing hotels in the New Town are also the cheapest. The **Hôtel Majestic**, 121 Av Hassan II, ✆ 72 29 97, has a piano in the foyer and faded furniture. Immediately to the left of the prominent Balima Hotel, the **Central Hotel**, 2 Rue Al Basra, ✆ 70 73 56, with 34 large comfortable rooms, fills up slightly later in the day and is run by an efficient but remorseless matron. If these are full, try the **Gaulois**, 1 Rue de Hims, ✆ 72 30 22.

cheap

There is no particular charm, short of the perennial bonus of economy, in staying in unclassified medina hotels in Rabat. They are mostly found within 200m of the market area by the Bab Al Had. **Hôtel Marrakesh**, 10 Rue Sebbahi, ✆ 72 77 03, (the third turning off Av Mohammed V in the medina) has clean rooms with towels, with a small extra charge for a shower. The gaudy **El Alam** and indifferent

Regina are nearby if it is full. The second turning, Rue Souk Semara, has another nest of hotels: the **France**, at no.46, ✆ 72 34 57, and the **Voyageurs**, at no.8, ✆ 72 37 20, as well as the **Algers** and **du Marché**. The Voyageurs is the best run, but the France might be preferable as it has a roof terrace as well as a surprisingly large number of small dank rooms and well-used double beds. **Hôtel Darna**, 24 Blvd Bab el Alou, ✆ 73 67 87, is on the northern edge of the medina. It's the most expensive in this category but has a wonderfully secluded position close to the Kasbah and the beach.

Rabat ✆ (07–)   ***Eating Out***

Rabat is not a city famed for its restaurants, but if you have the money and something to celebrate there are a few alternatives.

expensive

The **Koutoubia**, 2 Rue Pierre Parent, ✆ 72 01 25, with its gaily painted interior and separate bar, is one of the oldest restaurants in Rabat. It has been living off its reputation for decades, but can still throw some memorable evenings. For traditional Moroccan cooking the best evening is to be had at the **Dinarjat**, 6 Rue Belgnaoui, ✆ 70 42 39/✆ 72 23 42, opposite the Oudaïa Kasbah. From the car park on Av El-Alou, a flunky will lead you deep into the medina. Abandon yourself to the mystery, and take cash.

Two restaurants vie for laurels over the best seafood in town: **Le Goéland**, 9 Rue Moulay Ali Cherif, ✆ 76 88 85, and **Le Vert Galant**, in the Agdal Quarter, ✆ 77 42 47, but I imagine that you would rather eat your fish overlooking the sea. Try the **Restaurant de la Plage**, ✆ 70 75 86/✆ 72 31 48, or the **Restaurant Borj Eddar** (Chez Rhefir), ✆ 70 15 00, ✆ 73 74 90, which stand beside each other on the beach opposite the Oudaïa Kasbah. At a pinch the latter (which occupies part of an old coastal battery) is to be preferred, particularly if you can get a table outside. **Restaurant La Caravelle**, on a terrace in the Kasbah itself, ✆ 73 38 76, used to have a good reputation, but the cook is often off duty and it has degenerated into a beer bar.

To sample traditional Jewish Moroccan cooking, head for **Zerda (Chez Michel)**, 7 Rue Patrice Lumumba, ✆ 73 09 12. It's worth booking as there are only 20 places to be filled and it has a strong local following. Music is a strong feature—western, jazz, traditional oudh or rai, depending on who is playing.

moderate

The greatest concentration of bistro-like French restaurants licensed to serve alcohol is just south of the train station on or off Av Moulay Youssef. If you choose the *menu du jour* this can work out very reasonably at around 50dh, though you can spend much more. Choose from the **Restaurant Brasserie Français**, 3 Av Moulay Youssef, with its downstairs bar and upstairs restaurant; **Café-Restaurant de la Paix** at No.1; or just round the corner on Rue Hattim the small, well-regarded upstairs dining room of the **Restaurant La Clef**, ✆ 70 19 72, above the bar **Marocain et Français**. Excellent crêpes are served at **Au Crép'uscule**, 10 Zankhat Laghouat, ✆ 73 24 38.

For Italian or Spanish food pop behind the Balima Hotel to eat pizza and pasta at **La Mamma**, 1 Rue de Tanta, ✆ 70 73 29, or paella and tapas at **La Bamba** at No.3. A more exotic experience (for Morocco) can be found at the **Yucatan**, 7 Rue Al Osquofiah (formerly Rue de L'Evêche), ✆ 72 05 57, which provides fairly standard Mexican dishes. There is one good place to eat reasonably cheap Moroccan food and drink alcohol at the same time—**Saadi**, 87 Av Allal ben Abdallah, ✆ 76 99 03. Despite its history and grand demeanour, the **Balima Hotel** provides food that's filling but only very ordinary so, unless you are a bulk consumer, it's best to be satisfied with just sipping a drink in the courtyard.

cheap

As ever in Morocco, some of the most rewarding eating is to be found not in a formal restaurant but in the cheap café-restaurants scattered around the market area in from the Bab Al Had. These you can sniff out for yourself, but there are in addition a few specific café-restaurants nearby that are worth finding.

The **El Bahia** is built into the Andalucían walls of the medina, approached along Av Hassan II, halfway between the entrances to Rue Sidi Fatah and Av Mohammed V. Take the cheap fixed menu or order a chicken or *kefta tagine* in the upstairs Moorish dining room or in the courtyard. The **CTM café**, on the corner of Zankat Bayreuth and Av Hassan II, stays open late, serving good cheap Moroccan food on tables around the animated oblong bar. The caged birds, when in the mood, can produce extraordinary volumes of sound.

cafés and bars

No visit to Rabat is complete without a visit to the **Café Maure**, tucked between the Palace Museum of Oudaïa and the estuary. Amongst the cafés strung along Av Mohammed V, **Le Petit Poucet** rates highly, and an evening spent 'people watching' in the café and bar of the **Balima Hotel** remains one of the city's chief entertainments.

Just behind the Balima on Rue Tanta there is a more intense drinking scene in either the **Baghdad Bar** or **La Dolce Vita**. The glass-fronted lobby of the **Terminus Hotel**, near the train station, is another good observation post for street life. Just up from here, along Av Moulay Youssef, there is a string of busy bars: that of the d'Orsay Hotel as well as the ground floor of restaurants such as the Français, de la Paix and Marocain et Français. On Place des Alaouites, opposite the train station and beneath the 'Siemens' sign, there is the wood-lined **Henry's Bar**, with the elliptical hall of the Italian Restaurant next door—which has long since become another café-bar, lined with clichéd views of a dozen great cities.

Rabat ✆ *(07–)* | **Shopping**

The shops and stalls of the medina sell all the traditional **Moroccan crafts**—the best streets are Rue des Consuls and the Souk es Sebat. **Flowers** are sold in the market in the medina, and in a square on Av Moulay Hassan. Sunday is the busiest day for the **vegetable market** in the medina.

As befits a capital city, the New Town is conspicuous for its large number of **bookshops**. There are two English-language bookshops—an American one, 4 Rue Tanger, with a good shelf on Islam and Morocco; and an English one, 7 Rue Ayamama, with a similiar stock supplemented by some secondhand editions. There are also two useful English-speaking cultural centres in Rabat: the **George Washington Library**, 35 Avenue Fas, has American papers and journals available in its lounge; and the **British Council**, 36 Rue Tanger, ✆ 76 08 36, operates a small library and reading room (*open Tues–Fri 9.30–12 and 2.30–5.45, and Mon afternoon*). **French–Moroccan phrasebooks** are available from the bookshop at 38 Av Allal ben Abdallah. The train station news-stand usually has a good selection of **international newspapers and magazines** in English, French and other languages, normally a day after publication.

There are only a handful of **galleries** in Morocco that show the works of contemporary artists. **L'Atelier**, 16 Rue Annaba, ✆ 72 26 68, is run by the pre-eminent dealer and exhibitor Mme Demasier, who has drawn an impressive range of pan-Arab and Islamic art to her elegant gallery. The **Gallery Marsam**, 6 Rue Oskofiah, ✆ 70 92 57, deals purely in prints, but has a good stock of fine limited editions which enables you to see the work of many of Morocco's leading artists. **Antiquités Lyre**, 38 Av Mohammed V, and **Galerie le Mamoir**, 7 Rue Baitlahm, have the same management and one or two good things amongst piles of international junk. The prolific French painter of Moroccan scenes, Henri Pilot, can often be seen at work in one or other gallery.

Sports

The Royal Dar es Salaam **golf club**, a quarter of an hour's drive from central Rabat, is one of the world's top 50 golf courses. The 45-hole complex was designed by Robert Trent Jones on a 1,000-acre woodland site. Four hundred groundsmen maintain three courses: the 9-hole green course, the 18-hole blue, and the red, an 18-hole championship course for those with a handicap of at least 18. There are also two **tennis courts**, a **swimming pool** and a luxurious clubhouse where you can eat a three-course lunch with wine for under £10.

Entertainment and Nightlife

The **Theatre National Mohammed V**, on Rue Cairo, is the home of one of Morocco's three classical orchestras that conserve the traditions of Andalucía. It also puts on a range of visiting Arab stars and Western classical orchestras. French, American and good-quality Maghrebi films can be seen at the **Cinema Martignan**, on Av Mohammed V, and at **Salle du 7ème Art**, on Av Allal ben Abdallah. American films are shown in the same building as the American bookshop (4 Rue Tanger), but check with the shop for the schedule.

The distinctive feature of Rabat's street life is that the city has a mad flurry of *paseo* life at dusk but begins to close down at 8 in the evening and is shut by 10. As in other new and earnest political capitals, such as Ottawa, Canberra and Washington, the demand for sleazy joints and raffish bars does not seem to be strong amongst the administrators of government.

Dancing and floor-shows are sometimes staged at the **Tour Hassan Hôtel** (*open from 10.30pm; adm*), and Club Five in the **Farah Safir Hotel**. There is a distinctly down-market disco, **L'Arc en Ciel**, at the back of the Balima, as well as the conspiratorial **Baghdad Nightclub**, which has belly-dancing shows after 10pm, though they are not as exciting as its black-studded door promises. The Place de Melilla/Av Patrice Lumumba, on the eastern corner of the Parc du Triangle de Vue, is another area for music bars and discos, such as **Jefferson's**. A welcome new addition is the unstuffy **Amnesia**, on Rue Monastio, © 70 18 60.

Festivals

In August there is the *moussem* **of Dar Zhirou** and the *fête des cires* on Mouloud in Salé. Rabat sometimes hosts a two-week **film festival** in December, below the law courts in the New Town.

Day Trips from Rabat

Bouknadel Jardins Exotiques and Plage des Nations

It's a 1km drive off the Rabat–Kénitra highway to the most attractive and tranquil beach on this area of coast—the **Plage des Nations**. Coming from Rabat, stay on the old P2 road—not the new motorway—and it is 18km north of Salé. The beach's name is due to its status as a haunt of Rabat's diplomatic community, and it still retains a certain cachet, with the expensive **Hôtel Firdaous** sitting perfectly alone on the Atlantic shore. Its unchanged late-1960s interior is beginning to look rather classic. All the rooms face the sea, there are two pools, two restaurants, bars and a piano, and the staff are friendly to day visitors, who may use the facilities for a small charge. The beach is open to all and a few cafés are established here in summer. To get to the beach from Salé, there is a no.28 bus that leaves about every 20 minutes from Bab Mrisa and drops you beside the road for the beach or gardens. A place in a *grand taxi* will cost around 10dh, and take you right to the beach.

The **Musée Dar Belghazi** (© *(07) 82 21 78*, ● *(07) 82 21 79; open daily 8am–9pm; adm 50dh*) stands close to the Plage des Nations turning, near the 17km milestone to Salé. This private museum, opened in 1995, was created by an architect, antique dealer and decorator with an eye for the more sumptuous elements of Moroccan culture: rich embroideries, metal gilt, splendid coffers and cascades of jewellery. The exhibits change as they are sold or lent to various other exhibitions and museums.

The **Bouknadel Jardins Exotiques** (*open daily 9–6.30; adm*), with their tattered sign-post, are on the western side of the road, 12km from Rabat. Even if you are not wild about plants, the cool, shaded, intimate bamboo benches, the flowers, smells and tranquillity

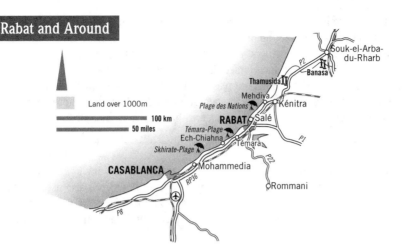

make this a whimsical and restful place. The gardens were created by the ingenious horticulturist and ecologist M. François in the 1950s, and at their peak held over 1,500 species. His verse thoughts on ecological principles and on his love for Morocco are found at the entrance, before a mass of hibiscus and red-hot pokers. The garden originally contained a zoo and an aquarium but the cages are thankfully now empty, leaving a delightfully profuse series of gardens inhabited by birds, turtles and frogs. The site extends in a long, thin belt of four hectares between the road and the coastal dunes. There are three sections: an indigenous collection of Moroccan flora, a formal Islamic Andalucían garden and a collection of exotica from all over the world. The lush ecosystems of America, Japan, China, the Pacific, the Caribbean and southeast Asia have all been skilfully re-created in delightful confusion on this dry, sandy coastal plain. The network of bamboo bridges, stone walkways, root passages, ruined temples and pagodas is magnificently eclectic, definitely bizarre and saved from being kitsch by rapid weathering and luxurious overgrowth. There are special coloured and timed routes of up to one hour, but it's hard to imagine that anybody would allow themselves to be organized in such a way. On the way back to Rabat you will pass a number of nurseries, as well as local sculptors hacking the bright yellow sandstone into architectural embellishments.

Mohammedia

Mohammedia does a surprising double act. It is on the one hand the centre of Morocco's oil business, with a refinery and an oil terminal on the western side of town, and on the other a swish summer beach resort with a 3km seafront promenade, casino, racecourse, a pretty kasbah quarter, a yacht marina and a terrific golf course. The yellow sands of the beach have so far remained untouched by pollution from the oil tankers, and from June to September the town is full of families from Casablanca on holiday. The beach gets emptier and more enticing the farther north you go. If you are a golfer looking for a relaxed resort, without tourists and with a strongly Moroccan flavour, Mohammedia is made for you.

Though the oil terminal was opened only in 1960, Mohammedia has a long history as a port. It was known as Fedala to the medieval merchants of Europe. Their common trading pitch was taken over by the Portuguese, who briefly occupied the place at the turn of the 15th century. Local opposition soon forced them out, though they have left a memorial—the kasbah looks indigenous enough but was actually built by the Portuguese. It has been restored in recent years and now contains a pretty residential quarter whose neat pavements and window boxes are at happy variance with the usual medina street scene.

Mohammedia ✆ *(03–)*   ***Getting There***

Mohammedia is most easily approached by **train** (seven a day from Rabat). The station looks out over a small square on Av Hassan II which is also used by taxis and buses. This is directly behind the kasbah, and a 500m walk north along Av Abderrahmane Sarghini and Blvd Moulay Youssef will lead you directly down to the beach.

Mohammedia ✆ *(03–)*   ***Eating Out***

The best restaurants are congregated at the western end of town near the port. **Restaurant du Port** (formerly Chez Irene), 1 Rue du Port, ✆ 32 24 66, naturally by the harbour, is easily the most famous place to eat in town; you can gorge on fresh fish simply grilled on charcoal in the garden courtyard. Equally popular are the **Sans Pareil**, ✆ 32 28 55, on Rue Farhat Hached, and the **Frégate**, Rue Oued-Zem, ✆ 32 44 47.

Casablanca

This city is a surprise for those who have been fed with picturesque images of Marrakesh and Fez. For it is a modern city, with a skyline dominated by towering office blocks, and sprawling suburbs ringed in the approved metropolitan style by a motorway ringroad. The streets are jammed with cars and the five-storey apartment block is the dominant housing form. The pavements are filled with elegant besuited figures and women dressed in international styles such as you would find in any southern European city.

Casablanca dominates the national economy: it is the chief port, the financial, industrial, commercial and manufacturing centre of the kingdom. This was all achieved within the 20th century—from a town of 20,000 in 1900, the Casablanca conurbation is now home to 3,500,000. In North Africa, only Cairo can compete with Casa in growth, verve and vibrancy, but it is this city facing out to the Atlantic that seems the more orientated to the international pattern of trade and sympathetic to Western influences. At times, as you cruise down a palm-fringed, car-packed boulevard to catch glimpses of the sun setting in a western ocean, you could be forgiven for thinking yourself in California. The French administration must be credited with much of this achievement. They carefully planned the new Atlantic face of Morocco in their own image, while allowing the xenophobic cities of the interior to wither into mere historical monuments.

Nothing to Do With Casablanca

No scene of the film *Casablanca* was shot in Morocco, nor does the finished film bear much relation to the city of the past or the present. The film was released in the winter of 1942 and was lucky to gain from the enormous free publicity generated by the Casablanca landings and the Allied conference here. It was also fortunate in a last-minute change of cast: Ronald Reagan and Ann Sheridan were replaced by Humphrey Bogart and Ingrid Bergman, and as an inspired afterthought the director Michael Curtiz added Dooley Wilson singing 'As Time Goes By'.

If Casa is a source of fascination to the political observer and speculation for the businessman, it has tended to be dismissed by far too many travellers. A pleasant day can be spent taking a taxi out to the vast Mosque of Hassan II, the only working mosque in Morocco open to non-Muslims; or a stroll through the grand streets of the French-built New Town and the stone arcades of the suburban Nouvelle Medina, Morocco's most elegant and hassle-free souk. No one with an eye for colour or street theatre should miss a stroll through the packed streets of the Ancienne Medina. It is true that as a mere 18th-century construction it cannot stand comparison with any of the medieval cities, but if you have spent any time in Morocco there is an almost unearthly satisfaction in walking through a medina without so much as a whiff of a bazaar, carpet shop or a guide. Casa also has some fabulous fish restaurants, while its humbler bars and cafés offer the opportunity to dive through the external distractions of tourism and meet some of the people of Morocco on common ground. My abiding image of the city is of two old women walking hand in hand down a street, one typically French, one unmistakably Moroccan. This could and should happen anywhere, but only in Casablanca did it feel commonplace.

History

The smart western residential suburb, Anfa, was the site of a Phoenician trading station founded in the 6th century BC. It became the capital of the great Berghouata confederacy of Berber tribes who, under the banner of the Khajarite heresy, resisted the authority of the early Islamic states. The Almohad Sultan Abdel Moumen finally broke the resistance of the Berghouata and destroyed Anfa in 1149. The port remained in use for the export of corn, but by the 15th century it also housed a flotilla of corsairs who raided the Portuguese coast so effectively that the kings of Portugal were forced to send an armada of 50 ships against this threat in 1468, and again in 1515.

In 1575 the Portuguese commander of El-Jadida closed the corsair base for ever by building a fort at Anfa which also served to guard the northern approach road to El-Jadida. This citadel remained in European hands until the Lisbon earthquake of 1755 shattered both the walls of Anfa and the treasury of Portugal.

Sultan Sidi Mohammed reclaimed Anfa, and built the present medina to the east of the ruins in 1770. The walls, fortifications and grand mosque of the medina all date from this

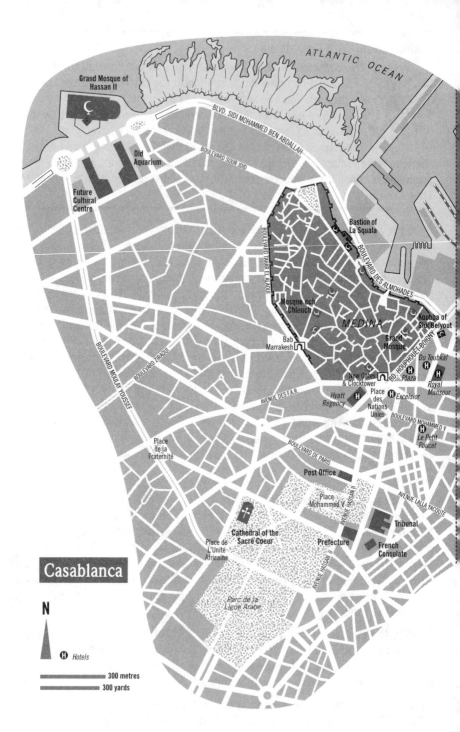

ATLANTIC OCEAN

Grand Mosque of
Hassan II

BLVD. SIDI MOHAMMED BEN ABDALLAH

Old
Aquarium

BOULEVARD SOUR JDID

Future
Cultural
Centre

Bastion of
La Squala

BOULEVARD DES ALMOHADES

BOULEVARD FAHR EL ALAOUI

Mosque ech
Chleuch

MEDINA

Koubba of
Sidi Belyout

Bab
Marrakesh

Grand
Mosque

Du Toubkal

New Gates
& Clocktower

BD. HOUPHOUET-BOIGNY

Plaza

BOULEVARD ZIRAOUI

BOULEVARD MOULAY YOUSSEF

Place
des
Nations
Unies

Hyatt
Regency

Excelsior

Royal
Mansour

AVENUE DES F.A.R.

BOULEVARD MOHAMMED V

Le Petit
Poucet

Place
de la
Fraternité

BOULEVARD DE PARIS

AVENUE LALLA YACOUTE

Post Office

Place
Mohammed V

AVENUE HASSAN II

Place de
L'Unité
Africaine

Cathedral of the
Sacré Coeur

Prefecture

Tribunal

French
Consulate

AVENUE HASSAN II

Casablanca

Parc de la
Ligue Arabe

N

Hotels

300 metres
300 yards

250

period. From the previous era only the Portuguese name for their fort, Casa Branca, 'white house', remained in use, although strangely it would be neither the Arabic translation, Dar el-Beida, nor the French equivalent of Maison-Blanche, but the Spanish version, Casa Blanca, that would pass into general usage.

Sultan Moulay Sliman closed the port as part of his policy of isolating Morocco from Europe, but it was reopened by his successor in 1830. The tempo of trade increased with exports of wool and corn to Britain, whose merchants sold tea, teapots, clothes and paraffin candles through the city in return. In 1907 the town exploded in anger against the predominant influence of the Europeans, and nine French port workers were killed in the streets. This, however, furnished a useful pretext for the subsequent landings by the French army in Morocco. The energetic French Resident-Governor from 1912 to 1925, Marshal Lyautey, began the process of urban planning and port extension that soon produced its own tempo of commercial dynamism and growth. Morocco's mercantile élite from Fez were quick to move to the coast, and join in the colonial city's development and property boom.

A generation later the new city was at the forefront of agitation against French colonial rule. Casablanca still is the centre of contemporary political protest. In Western minds it is linked to three rather spurious events—the landings, the conference and the film. The Casablanca landings of November 1942 had no military significance, as the result had already been pre-arranged between the supposed opponents, the American and Vichy French generals. Seasick American troops were in fact landed with great confusion at Safi, Mehdiya and Fédala (Mohammedia), but not Casablanca. The Casablanca conference was held two months later in January 1943. It had no significance for Morocco: Roosevelt and Churchill spent their days planning the invasion of Sicily from a suburban villa in Anfa.

Orientation

A few years ago King Hassan II swapped the names of the two principal centres of the city, Place Mohammed V and Place des Nations Unies, around. This change is still by no means recognized by every citizen, taxi driver, directory or map-maker. It's as well to be aware of the potential misunderstandings this can lead to and, at the risk of things becoming over-bracketed but in an attempt to minimize confusion, both are used in this guide.

Casablanca ✆ (02–) **Getting There and Around**

by air

Many international flights to Morocco, and most domestic flights, use the Airport Mohammed V, 30km out of town on the main P7 route to Marrakesh. By far the easiest way to get there is on the direct **train** link that takes you from either the Port or Voyageurs railway stations in Casablanca to the main airport concourse in half an hour. There are 12 trains a day, running from 6am. CTM also run a connecting **bus** service that takes you direct from the airport to the central CTM station. In addition there is a *grand taxi* rank, though the taxi fare, at around 200dh, compares badly with a train ticket of 35dh.

by rail

Arriving by train you can get off at the port station, Casa Gare du Port, or Casa Gare des Voyageurs. The **Gare du Port** is admirably sited by the main coast road and fronts on to Blvd Houphouët-Boigny (formerly Blvd Mohammed el Hansali, and still shown as such on many maps), which leads 500m straight to Place des Nations Unies (formerly Place Mohammed V). This is the hub of the city and of its major avenues, as well as the main entrance to the medina. The **Gare des Voyageurs** leaves you with a half-hour walk or a taxi ride into the centre of town. Most, but not all, trains from Rabat (1hr) arrive at the Gare du Port. There are 18 a day, the last one leaving Casablanca at 8.30pm.

by bus

The CTM station, with its café and separate luggage check-in, is on Rue Vidal, which runs parallel to and between the central thoroughfares of Av des F.A.R. and Rue Allal ben Abdallah. There are 11 buses a day for Rabat (1hr40mins), which makes it slower and less frequent than the train.

by car and taxi

Walking around the city centre is one of the major charms of Casablanca. It is only worth catching a taxi for a trip out to the Grand Mosque of Hassan II, the Nouvelle Medina or the Gare des Voyageurs. *Petits taxis* can be caught on Place Mohammed V and the Av des F.A.R. They usually have meters, but if the meter is switched off the fare, per person, should be around 10dh for the Gare des Voyageurs or the Nouvelle Medina.

If at all possible try not to **drive** in Casablanca, which has few street signs, competitive traffic, packs of scooter-riders and the usual indomitable Moroccan pedestrians who maintain a courageous indifference to cars.

Casablanca ✆ (02–) **Tourist Information**

The **tourist board (ONMT)**, 55 Rue Omar Slaoui, ✆ 27 11 77, and the **tourist office**, 98 Blvd Mohammed V, ✆ 22 15 24, both supply city maps and booklets.

The **main post office** is at the junction of Blvd de Paris and Av Hassan II (*open Mon–Fri 8.30–12*). There is a smaller branch at 116 Av Mohammed V. There are plenty of **banks**: Banque Populaire, 101 Blvd Mohammed Zerktouni; BMCI, 26 Place Mohammed V; and SGMB, 2 Av des F.A.R., are some of the most convenient.

The Grand Mosque of Hassan II

The 200m-high minaret of this vast new mosque—the second largest in the world, surpassed only by that in Mecca—floats above the skyline of Casablanca, the sun glancing off its façade of pale marble and glazed tile and from the three gilded balls at its summit. The tower is aligned to the points of the compass, not the direction of prayer, and so it is offset from the enormous rectangular 22-acre prayer hall, three times the size of St Paul's Cathedral. Vast titanium and steel doors guard the glimmering interior, a palatial expanse of polished marble floor, granite columns, carved stone and plaster Moorish arches with more than 70 cedar-panelled cupolas, which is lit by vast Venetian chandeliers of pale-green crystal. The roof is richly carved, painted and gilded and the size of a football pitch, but can slide open automatically to flood the hall with sunlight. As well as the cool marble ablution fountains beneath the prayer-hall, on important feast days the water rill in the middle of the mosque flows too. A mezzanine level, wrapped in a carved wooden screen, seems to float on a floor of coloured tiles and provides a reserved area for female worshippers.

Perhaps the most astonishing aspect of the mosque is its position. It has been built out from the natural shoreline on a reclaimed embankment. This is in deliberate fulfilment of a Koranic verse, 'the throne of God was built on the water'. It is also a careful piece of symbolism: the wedding of late 20th-century Morocco to its new but ever more influential

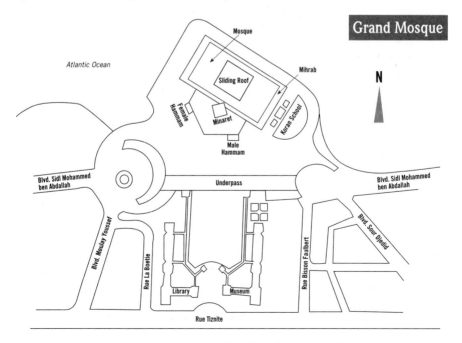

Atlantic identity. Moroccan culture has long been concentrated in the cities of the interior and has virtually ignored the Atlantic coast, which is still littered with the monumental evidence of medieval invaders, colonists and foreign merchants. For a long time the Arabs felt insecure about the Atlantic (known to them as the Sea of Obscurity), a coastline that was the final refuge of weak tribes driven from the good grazing of the interior. Only the most desperate stooped to the dishonourable occupation of living from the sea. This vast mosque is an attempt to correct a long cultural imbalance, its towering minaret a beacon to draw the faithful seawards.

The mosque is one of the late king's most extraordinary, extravagant but ultimately successful building projects. Its cost has been estimated at $800 million, entirely funded by donations from the people of Morocco, as the ubiquitous certificates displayed in every café, hotel, shop and home proudly attest. The immense plaza opposite is being enclosed by an arcade of shops and cafés that will eventually incorporate a cultural complex with a museum, school and medersa. As well as the existing approaches there is to be a new processional avenue opened to the west of the medina. It will be interesting to see if this will eventually shift the focus of the city, for at the moment the area around the mosque remains determinedly low-rent. About 3,000 people use the mosque on a normal Friday, and it only reaches its 20,000 capacity at the great festivals. This is the only working mosque in Morocco open to non-Muslims, but at a price (currently 100dh). There are four escorted tours a day (*Sat–Thurs 9, 10 and 11am and 2pm*).

The Old Town (Ancienne Medina)

There is an enormous and continual charm in exploring the old medina of Casablanca, where the crumbling 18th-, 19th- and early 20th-century houses conjure up an almost Neapolitan vision of street animation. Noon and mid-afternoon are the worst times to explore here. Owing to the late date of the medina's construction, it is relatively easy to pick your own route through the streets, which are comparatively wide, well labelled and without the labyrinthine intensity of Fez or Marrakesh. It is also quite without carpet shops and bazaars (which are all neatly laid out by the southern exterior wall) and so is empty of guides and multilingual commission men. Instead the narrow streets are packed with street stalls with exuberant displays of vegetables, fruit, groceries, cooked food, Tupperware and clothes.

The old Jewish quarter, the *mellah*, stood just to the north of Place des Nations Unies (old Place Mohammed V). A dusty car park a few years ago, the old back entrance to the medina here has now been completely reconstructed, with an ornamental clock tower (the third in a succession of such towers to stand here) in front of the elegant walls and a gate worthy of Anfa's Almohad period. The area behind it is filled with an open-air market selling T-shirts, tourist bric-a-brac and freshly squeezed orange juice.

On the northeastern side of the medina is the 18th-century **bastion of La Squala**. This prominent artillery terrace is dominated by a handsome gatehouse, from where the battery commander once directed the range and elevation of cannon fire that last opposed a European fleet in the mid-19th century. Today there are only four cast-iron cannon, their muzzles pointing towards the rattling masts of the yacht harbour, while on either side the white houses of Casa stand suspended above the sand-yellow city walls. The postern gate, which once led directly to the old port but now gives access to the wallside gardens, is usually locked.

Opposite the Gare du Port sits the **koubba of Sidi Belyout** (a name derived from Abou el Louyou, 'father of the lions', the title of a great commander of a *jihad*), set reclusively amid a stand of trees within whitewashed walls. Non-Muslims are not allowed to enter, but you can peer through the gateway and admire the constant succession of Casa babies brought by their mothers to pay their respects to one of the principal patrons of the city.

The New Town

The 500m length of Blvd Mohammed V is lined with some delightful Art Deco apartments and hotels, as are the two parallel streets, Rue Allal ben Abdallah and Av Houmane el Fetouaki. The **market square**, a splendid Moorish courtyard, is your principal objective. The arcaded interior is lined with a dazzling display of the full range of Moroccan fruit, vegetables, meat, shellfish and flowers. It is a wonderful vision of the freshest and ripest products of the land, with one or two tourist stalls for visitors. The surrounding streets have a large choice of bars, cafés and licensed restaurants. Stop to have a coffee in the cool arcade, or a drink in the unreconstructed 1920s interior of **Le Petit Poucet**, 86 Blvd Mohammed V. This is the ideal place to imagine the lost world of French North Africa immortalized by Albert Camus. It was the favourite haunt of Antoine de Saint-Exupéry, the pioneer poet of flight and philosopher of aviation. Though better known for *The Little Prince*, his classic work *Wind, Sand and Stars* is partly based on the heroic days of flying mail across the Western Sahara (*see* **Further Reading**, p.267).

Place Mohammed V (Formerly Known as Place des Nations Unies)

Heading south from Place des Nations Unies, the broad Av Hassan II leads towards Place Mohammed V, which was formerly the Place des Nations Unies, the dry administrative heart of Casablanca. In the 1920s Henri Prost and Robert Marrast were employed as the architects for most of the official buildings that surround the square. They helped define the neo-Moorish style of French colonial architecture, which remains very influential. They took details hitherto reserved for the interior of a Moorish house and used them to create an impressive monumental exterior. Behind the traditional decorative elements— the green-tiled roofs, horseshoe-arch arcades, interior courtyards and the free use of *zellij* mosaic—the functional subdivision of the building into corridors and offices followed Western traditions. The central fountain operates on Fridays and weekends; to its east rises the mass of the **Palais de Justice** or Tribunal. Next door, tucked into the corner, is the **French Consulate** with a statue of Marshal Lyautey to the fore, neatly protected by a high fence. The **Prefecture** to the south is easily recognizable, with its famous modernist clock tower striking a jarring note amid the principles of the neo-Moorish style. The post office and the Banque du Maroc sit very solidly on the northern face of the square.

To the south of the *place* stretches the flat expanse of the **Parc de la Ligue Arabe**, with neat promenades and a number of elegant cafés such as La Pergola du Parc, in the half-shade along Blvd Moulay Youssef. On the western edge is the School of Fine Arts, across the street from the old **Cathedral of the Sacré Cœur**, designed by Paul Tornon in 1930. The ferro-concrete nave washed with a creamy yellow is being converted by the municipality into a cultural centre. It is a striking structure, the exterior dominated by three rows of descending buttresses and gargoyles. The long narrow apertures are filled with a geometric arrangement of glass that deliberately recalls the marquetry and *zellij* mosaic traditional to a religious building in Morocco.

The Nouvelle Medina (Habous Quarter)

Created as a showpiece of colonial paternalism, this new quarter for Muslims was built to the southeast of the then European city centre. It was directly modelled on the surviving 18th-century quarters of Casablanca, and on the elegant town of Essaouira to the south. A few of the inhabitants of the shantytown slums were transferred to these elegant narrow streets, with wider connecting roads lined with stone arcades.

The Nouvelle Medina now has Casablanca's largest concentration of bazaars and craft shops. It is the cleanest, most ordered **souk** in Morocco, lacking vitality but with a fine selection of all the national crafts. The most attractive arcades are in the area north of the railway and south of Blvd Victor Hugo. The high walls of the royal palace, which enclose a secretive and elegant garden, line the boulevard to the north. A street surmounted by three picturesque arches leads to Place Moulay Youssef, with a central garden and a mosque built by the present king's great-grandfather in 1938. Two arcaded and arched streets on the left of the square lead to the larger Place de la Mosquée, with well-kept shaded gardens and the mosque of Mohammed V on its southern side. To the north are the imposingly high outer walls of the **Mahakma du Pasha**, the combined residence of the Pasha of Casablanca and tribunal of the Islamic courts, finished in 1952 by the French. It is for the moment closed to visitors, which is a pity, as the interior is a maze of courts decorated in traditional Moorish style with carved plaster and wood.

A bridge, the **Sidi Jdid**, leads south across the railway line to the main residential area of Nouvelle Medina. The vegetable and spice market of the **Balilida Quarter** is off the Rue du Rharb, a delightfully animated court full of the competing colours and odours of the souk. A terrace that runs parallel to the market above, the Rue Taroudannt, contains the stalls of herbalists and enchanters. Hedgehogs and turtles are sold live, and there are curtains of dried animal and bird skins from which to make charms and love potions. Madame Chrifa Dukkalia, who runs one of the stalls, will tell your fortune from her pack of henna-stained cards. The small cones of green dried leaves from the henna tree are sold as the base for the henna paste used throughout Morocco for decorating hands and feet, and for invigorating and dyeing hair.

Casablanca ℗ (02–)   **Where to Stay**

Casablanca has a number of moderately priced hotels, solidly built during the Protectorate, which are concentrated in the city centre. They have spacious, comfortable bedrooms and are largely undamaged by improvements. There is not much interest or economy to be enjoyed by staying in the medina. If this is your first night in Morocco, give yourself a bit of extra comfort while you slowly adjust. This is especially relevant for Americans and Canadians who have just flown in.

luxury

The **Hyatt Regency**, ✆ 26 12 34, 🖅 22 01 80, stands behind sound-proof windows right in the centre on Place des Nations Unies (ex Mohammed V). There are in addition several other luxury hotels along Av des F.A.R., of which the **Royal Mansour** at No.27, ✆ 31 30 11/✆ 31 21 12, 🖅 31 25 83, is rated the best, with its opulent polished-marble interior, pseudo-Moorish style and swanky doormen.

expensive

The **Hotel Toubkal**, 9 Rue Sidi Belyout (2nd left off Av des F.A.R. from Place des Nations Unies and directly opposite the Royal Mansour), ✆ 31 14 14, 🖅 31 22 87/ 🖅 31 11 46, has an unexceptional exterior but reveals itself to be a model of calm efficiency within. With just 68 rooms, some with trelliswork balconies, it is a more intimate alternative to the vast hotels, and less than half the price. There is also a small bar, a restaurant and a popular nightclub within the building.

The **Sheraton**, 100 Av des F.A.R., ✆ 31 78 78, 🖅 31 51 37, is a centrally placed and reliably efficient 300-room hotel with a swimming pool and car parking. The **Holiday Inn Crowne Plaza**, Rond Pont Hassan II, ✆ 29 49 49, 🖅 29 30 29, is the smallest of the five-star hotels. The **Safir**, 160 Av des F.A.R., ✆ 31 12 12, 🖅 31 65 14, is part of a reliable chain of Moroccan hotels.

moderate

The **Ibis Moussafir**, ✆ 40 19 84, 🖅 40 07 99, just beside the Gare des Voyageurs on Blvd Bahmad, is away from the centre of town but is part of an efficient and attractive national chain and has its own garden, bar and restaurant. In the city centre, similar facilities are offered by the older **Plaza**, 18 Blvd Houphouët-Boigny (ex Mohammed el Hansali), ✆ 29 78 22, on the tree-lined street leading from the Gare du Port.

cheap

For something dignified, colonial and dead central, with a comfortable touch of shabbyness, head for the **Excelsior**, 2 Rue el Amraoui Brahim (ex-Rue Nolly), ✆ 20 00 48, which looks on to Place des Nations Unies; or the small **Hotel de Foucauld**, 52 Rue Araïbi Jilali (ex-Rue de Foucauld), ✆ 22 26 66.

Casablanca ✆ (02–)   **Eating Out**

expensive

Casablanca has the reputation of having some of the best cooking in Morocco, led by André Halbert's celebrated **Restaurant A Ma Bretagne**, ✆ 36 21 12/✆ 39 79 79, 🖅 94 41 55 (*closed Sun*), generally considered to be the best French restaurant in Africa. It occupies an unusual modernist building with a stunning view over the sea. Prices are worthy of a *Maître Cuisinier de France*, but remain a bargain by European standards.

For a reasonably priced French fish restaurant walk 150m past the Gare du Port along Blvd Moulay Abderrahman, turn left at the dock gates and after another 150m walk through another set of dock gates to the restaurant ahead of you. **Le Port de Pêche**, ✆ 31 85 61, has a large busy upstairs dining room with napkins and waiters in matching red, a full seafood menu and a happy mix of Moroccan families, Franco-Maroc businessmen and travellers.

Alternatively, head for the bustling, friendly atmosphere of the **Taverne du Dauphin**, 115 Blvd Houphouët-Boigny, ✆ 22 12 00/✆ 27 79 79. Fish seldom tastes this good, particularly the grilled prawns. For more French cooking head for **La Braserade**, 68 Rue el Araar (ex Gay-Lussac), ✆ 29 84 28 (*closed Mon*), or carry on to the nearby Spanish **La Corrida**, at No.59, ✆ 27 81 55 (*closed Sun*).

For a traditional meal of Moroccan cooking, both **Al Mounia**, 95 Rue du Prince Moualy Abdullah, ✆ 22 26 69 (*closed Sun*), and **Imilchil**, 27 Rue Vizir Tazi, ✆ 22 09 99, are reliably decorative and not too expensive. The food in the Al Mounia is probably the best Moroccan fare in town.

cheap

For a considerably less extravagant meal, try **L'Etoile Marocaine**, 107 Rue Allal Ben Abdallah, ✆ 31 41 00, a small restaurant decorated in the Moorish taste and serving traditional food (but no alcohol) at a reasonable price. **Le Petit Poucet**, 86 Blvd Mohammed V, ✆ 27 54 20, was one of the smartest centres of urban life in Casablanca before the Second World War. It has a reasonably priced restaurant, but for a cheaper meal use the snack bar next door. Another good cheap address on this street, not licensed to serve alcohol, is **Le Buffet** at No.99. Of the cheap snack bars around the market, the **Brasserie Sphinx**, a block south on Av Houmane el Fetouaki on the corner opposite Rue Ibn Batouta, is one of the most tranquil.

pâtisseries and glaciers

The most famous Moroccan pâtisserie in Casablanca is **Bennis**, 2 Rue Fikh el Gabbas. Along Blvd Mohammed V you will find **Trianon** at No.37 and **La Normande** at No.213. Blvd du 11 Janvier boasts the two finest ice-cream shops, **Glacier Gloria** and **L'Igloo**, where the most exotic combinations of fruit, sherbets, ice-creams, whipped cream, flavoured milks, juices, teas and coffees can be ordered. The Boulevard is just east of Place Mohammed V (old Place des Nations Unies).

Shopping

The market off Blvd Mohammed V and the streets of the Nouvelle Medina make a memorable shopping trip: for antiques and decorative pieces get a taxi to **Le Riad des Antiquaires** on the corner of Av Lalla Yacout and Rue Mustapha el-Maami.

There are a number of well-established commercial **art galleries** in Casa that have exhibitions of Moroccan artists, decorative art from other Islamic countries and works from France and Belgium: **Galerie d'Art Moderne**, 5 Rue Manaziz, the **Galerie Alif**, 46 Rue Omar Slaoui, and **Galerie Bassamat**, 2 Rue Pierre Curie.

1100BC	Phoenician merchants from the Near East establish a network of coastal ports trading with the indigenous Berber tribes, ruled from 550 BC by Carthage.
202 BC	Control passes to the Mauretanian kings.
44–303	A period of growing influence leads to the outright annexation of 'Mauretania Tingitania' by the Roman Empire.
303–682	The northernmost ports of Tangier and Ceuta pass from Roman to Vandal then Byzantine rule.
682	Uqba ben Nafi brings Islam to Morocco, just 50 years after the death of the Prophet Mohammed.
705–40	The Caliphate: the Arab Empire extends west to Morocco, allowing for the conquest of Spain in 711, but is expelled after the Tangier Mutiny of 740.
789–921	Moulay Idriss and his posthumous son, Idriss II, found Fez and establish the first independent Moroccan kingdom.
1042–1147	Almoravid Empire: Morocco is united by a fundamentalist reform group drawn from the nomadic Berber tribes of the Sahara, and in 1071 their leader Youssef ben Tachfine founds Marrakesh.
1147–1248	Almohad Empire: a second Islamic reform, drawn from the Berber tribes of the High Atlas, brings Morocco to its glittering zenith.
1248–1554	The Merenid dynasty rules from Fez, its glorious first century recalled by a number of supremely elegant mosques and medersas.
1554–1668	The Saadian dynasty: the growing power of Portugal in the 15th century is repelled at the Battle of the Three Kings in 1578.
1668–1727	Anarchic 17th-century Morocco is re-united under the first Alaouite sultans: Moulay Rachid and Moulay Ismaïl.
1822–73	Relentless growth of European influence, partly checked by the energetic reign of Moulay Hassan (1873–94).
1912	Treaty of Fez. French and Spanish Protectorates formally established.

Chronology

1912–56	France introduces technical, industrial and medical improvements and subdues all areas of tribal dissidence.
1956	Independence: Mohammed V leads the struggle and re-establishes royal authority.
1961–99	Reign of Hassan II. After the coup attempts of the early 1970s, the king becomes popular due to his re-occupation of the Western Sahara.
1999	Mohammed VI leads his people towards new expectations from the government.

Abassids. The 2nd dynasty of caliphs who ruled the Muslim world from AD 750–1258.

Abd (sing.), **abid** (plural). A slave. By inference a black slave, and used to distinguish the black regiments from the tribal ones in the sultan's army.

Agadir. Principal city and port of southwestern Morocco. Literally the fortified communal hilltop granaries of the Berber tribes, also known as *ighrem*, *igherm* or *irherm*.

Aid. The holy day or feast, as in Aid es Seghir at the end of Ramadan.

Aïn (sing.), **aïoun** (plural). Spring or water hole.

Aït. Child of, as used in the creation of a tribal identity, such as Aït-Atta.

Aït-Atta. Berber tribe from Jbel Sarhro who dominated the south from the 16th century to 1934.

Akbar. 'The Great', as in Allah Akbar.

Alaouite. The present ruling dynasty of Morocco who, from their base in the Tafilalt Oasis, replaced the Saadian sultans in 1666.

Ali. Cousin and son-in-law of the Prophet through his marriage to Fatima, and father of Hassan and Hussein. Ali succeeded Othmann as 4th caliph in AD 656 but his reign was punctuated by disputes which split Islam into the Sunni, Shiite and Kharijite camps.

Almohad. 'The unitarians'. An Islamic reform movement founded by Ibn Tumert in the High Atlas which replaced Almoravid rule over Morocco. The Almohad Empire, AD 1147–1248, was a peak period of Moroccan history.

Almoravid. 'The warrior monks'. An Islamic reform movement founded by Ibn Yaasin in the Sahara which, under his successors Abu Bekr and Youssef ben Tachfine, controlled an empire that stretched from Spain to West Africa (AD 1060–1147).

Arabesque. General adjective describing the architecture and the calligraphic, floral and geometrical decoration of Islam.

Argan. Hard oil-producing thorn tree that grows only in southwestern Morocco.

Asif. River that flows throughout the year.

Averroes/Ibn Rushd. Muslim scholar born in Córdoba in 1126 who originally enjoyed the patronage of the Almohad sultans. His translation of Aristotle and philosophical works was of great influence to the Christian universities, though the orthodox of both Islam and Christendom condemned his rationalism.

Azrou. Rock, and the name of a town in the Middle Atlas.

Bab. Gate.

Beni. The sons of, often used in the description of a tribe, such as the Beni-Merin.

Berghawata/Berghouata. Heretical Berber tribal group who occupied the coastal region from Salé to Casablanca until conquered in the 12th century by the Almohads.

Bit. Room.

Cadi. Judge of Muslim law.

Caftan/Kaftan. Formal outer garment, though it increasingly refers to an embroidered cotton robe.

Caid. Magistrate who in the lawless areas was often a tribal chief recognized by the sultan. Now the chief magistrate of a commune.

Caliph. The successor of the Prophet to the rule of the Muslim community.

Caravanserai. Defensive lodgings on a caravan route.

Chleuh. One of the three Berber tribal groupings who occupy the western High Atlas, the Sous and the Anti-Atlas. They are also known as Soussi or Masmuda and speak a dialect known as Tachelhait.

Cursive. The familiar style of flowing rounded Arabic script.

Dakhla. An entrance to a gorge and the name of a town of the Western Sahara, known under Spanish rule until 1976 as Villa Cisneros.

Dar. House, building or palace. City quarters are often named after the most distinctive house of the quarter, like Dar Sejene in Meknès.

Daya. Lake.

Dirham. The Ommayad caliphs based the first Muslim silver coinage on the Byzantine drachmae. The name and style was in turn copied by Moroccan mints.

Drâa. Arm. The river Drâa flows south from Ouarzazate into the Sahara.

Emir. 'He who commands'. Originally the military deputies of the caliph, and transformed into a title of sovereignty.

Erg. Dunes or region of dunes in a desert.

Fantasia. A display of horsemanship featuring small charges, dramatic halts and musket firing.

Fassi. An inhabitant of Fez. It can also refer to the rich merchant class in Morocco.

Fatima. Only surviving daughter of the Prophet, wife of Ali and mother of Hassan and Hussein. The central female cult figure of Islam. The Hand of Fatima is an ancient good-luck talisman.

Fiqh. The Islamic legal code. There are four traditional codes acknowledged by the orthodox Muslim: the Malekite, Hanefite, Chafiite and Hanbalite. The Malekite is favoured in Morocco.

Foggara/Khettara. Underground irrigation canal.

Fondouq/Fondouk. A courtyard surrounded by rooms which takes on a great range of functions.

Gandoura. A simple cotton tunic with sleeves and plain collar, mostly worn by men.

Garum. Peculiar fish paste made of salt and mashed tuna intestines, beloved by the ancient Romans and manufactured for centuries on the Moroccan Atlantic coast.

Gnaoua/Gnawa/Gnaiwaya. Black religious brotherhood from West Africa and also the name of their spirit music.

Habous. Religious foundations.

Hadj. A pilgrimage to Mecca. The honorific title for those who have made the journey is *Hadji.*

Haik. Large cloth used by women to cover themselves in the street.

Hammada. Flat pebbly plateau of the Sahara.

Islamic and Moroccan Terms

Hammam. Steam or Turkish baths.

Haratine. Black serf caste in the south, having no tribal loyalties but often attached in a share-cropping arrangement to a nomadic warrior group.

Harmattan. Hot dry winds which blow from the Sahara.

Hassan II. King of Morocco 1960–99. Born in 1929, he was educated in Rabat and Bordeaux, where he read law. He accompanied his father into exile from 1953 to 1955 and on Independence was put in command of the new royal army.

Hegira. The Islamic era which began with the flight of the Prophet from Mecca to Medina in July 622. The Muslim calendar is based on a lunar rather than a solar year, and each year is therefore 11 days shorter than each Gregorian year.

Hilali. A nomadic bedouin tribe that with the Sulaym left the Arabian peninsula in the 11th century to advance west along the North African coast.

Ibn Battuta. Travel writer who was born in Tangier in 1304 and died at Fez in 1377. Trained as a *cadi*, he travelled, worked and married throughout the Muslim world from Timbuktu to China.

Ibn Khaldoun. Celebrated historian and sociologist who was born in Tunis in 1332, his parents having fled from Andalucía. He obtained positions in a number of Muslim courts and lived in Fez before settling in Egypt as the Malekite Mufti of Cairo.

Idriss I/Moulay Idriss. Great-grandson of the Prophet and founder of the first Muslim kingdom of Morocco in 788. His tomb at Moulay Idriss is the pre-eminent national shrine.

Idriss II. Posthumous son of Idriss I. Creator of the city of Fez, where his tomb is venerated. His descendants, the Idrissids, have been a numerous and influential clan throughout Moroccan history.

Ighrem. *See* **Agadir**.

Imam. Leader of prayers and by implication also a political leader.

Islam. 'Submission to God'. Mohammed is the best known and the last of a long line of prophets who taught submission to God, giving rules for the conduct of life and threatening unbelievers with divine punishment.

Istaqlal. Independence party founded by Allal al Fasi in 1934, which took a leading role in the civil resistance to the French Protectorate. It held a strong position in post-Independence government from 1956 to 1962.

Jbel/Djebel. Mountain. The Djeballa are a specific group of Arabic-speaking tribes that occupy the western Rif. It is also a city dweller's label of contempt for the unsophisticated, the hill-billies.

Jdid/Djedid. New. As in Fez Jdid, new Fez, the 14th-century royal extension to the city.

Jellaba. Large cotton or wool outer garment with sleeves and a hood.

Jihad. Holy war against the enemies of Islam.

Kaaba. A meteorite venerated from antiquity in Mecca and situated on the spot where, according to tradition, Abraham erected his altar. Muslims pray towards the Kaaba and circle it seven times before kissing it as the culmination of the Hadj.

Kasbah. The citadel of a town or a rural fortress.

Khaima. Grand tent of a tribal leader, now much reproduced for use at fêtes and as restaurants.

Khettara. *See* **Foggara**.

Killim. A woven carpet.

Kohl. Ground powder of the metallic-looking sulphur of antimony. Applied to the eyes, it stimulates an attractive watery sheen that is useful protection against soot and dust.

Koran. The word of God dictated to the Prophet Mohammed by the archangel Gabriel in Arabic.

Kouba. Women's room.

Koubba. Dome. By extension a koubba is the shrine of a saint's tomb which is usually covered by a small white cupola. They often form the object of a pilgrimage and are at the centre of female spiritual activity.

Ksar (sing.), **ksour** (plural). An Arabic noun derived from 'Caesar' that describes a fortified village.

Kufic. Angular style of Arabic script, named after the city of Kufa in Iraq, which is chiefly used in stone and plaster carving.

Leo Africanus. Born in Granada in 1483, El Hassan ibn Mohammed el Fasi was enslaved by Christians, but when recognized as an intellectual was presented to the pope. He was freed, baptized and awarded a pension by Pope Leo V, who encouraged him to write his famous description of North Africa. Having completed the great work, he died a Muslim in Tunis in 1554.

Litham. Veil.

Lyautey, Marshal Hubert. One of the most important commanders of the French Colonial Army, he served in Madagascar and Indo-China before taking charge of the absorption of eastern Morocco from Algeria. As Resident-General from 1912 to 1926 he set the shape and objectives of the French Protectorate.

Maghreb. 'The land of the setting sun or furthest west', containing the three nations of Tunisia, Algeria and Morocco.

Makhzen. Government, or government district.

Maksoura/Maqsara. Wooden screens in a mosque that protect rulers from assassination.

Malekite. The most widely practised school of judicial practice and Koranic interpretation in North Africa. It was formulated by Malik ibn Anas, a judge from Medina who died in 795.

Marabout. Holy warrior, ascetic or the chief of a religious brotherhood who has won the respect of the people. His tomb may be covered by a dome.

Mauritania. The two Roman provinces of Mauretania Caesariensis and Mauretania Tingitania, whose boundaries approximate those of modern Morocco and Algeria. It now refers to the Saharan country south of Morocco on the Atlantic coast.

Mecca. Sacred town of the Muslims, 8km inland from the Red Sea, on the old caravan route from Syria to Yemen. Mosques are all oriented towards Mecca, 45° east and 12.5° south from Fez.

Méchouar. A square adjoining a palace in which the population can assemble to pay homage to the ruler.

Medersa. Residential schools for the study of the Koran and religious law. They were introduced into Morocco in the 12th century, though the earliest surviving buildings date from the 14th.

Medina. Walled city or old city, in distinction to the new European-style quarter. Named after the city to which Mohammed fled to avoid persecution in Mecca.

Mellah. The Jewish quarter. The name derives from the word *melh*, meaning salt, as the Jewish community used to perform the task of salting the severed heads of the sultan's enemies in order to preserve them.

Mendoub. Agent or representative of the sultan, as found in Tangier from 1927 to 1956.

Merenids. Dynasty who originated from the Beni-Merin nomadic tribe who dominated the eastern plains of Morocco and replaced the Almohads in 1248.

Midha. Fountain for ritual washing before prayer.

Mihrab. A niche in a place of prayer which indicates the direction of Mecca.

Minaret. The tower of a mosque used for calling the faithful to prayer. The pinnacle is crowned with domes representing the daily prayers, and a blue or green flag flying indicates Friday, the Muslim sabbath.

Minbar. A pulpit-like staircase in mosques used for the noonday Friday sermon, the *khutba*.

Minzah. In a palace, a garden pavilion, especially one enjoying a fine view.

Mohammed. The Prophet, the last in the succession of Abraham, Noah, Moses and Jesus who have called man to worship the one God.

Mohammed V. The popular monarch who led the struggle for Moroccan Independence and was exiled by the French. After Independence in 1956 he initiated a new era by ruling as King Mohammed V.

Mohammed VI. King of Morocco, who succeeded his father Hassan II in 1999, aged 36.

Mosque. The place of prostration, the place of reunion, the place of prayer.

Moukarnas/muqarnas. Stalactite-like decorations chiefly of carved wood, stone or plaster.

Moulay. Honorific title, approximately 'lord'. Used in Morocco by the descendants of the Prophet.

Mouloud. The great feast day celebrating Mohammed's birthday on the 12th day of the Muslim month of Rabi at-Tani.

Moussem. Originally an annual popular pilgrimage to the tomb of a saint, but now by extension any festival or outdoor entertainment.

Msalla. Prayer area; open-air mosque.

Muezzin. The call to prayer, also the prayer caller.

Oasis. An island of life in the desert supported by a water-gathering system.

Omayyads. The first dynasty of caliphs who ruled the Islamic world from 660 to 750 and were descended from Muawiya, the governor of Syria, who was proclaimed caliph after the assassination of Ali.

Oued. River.

Pasha. Provincial governor, or the governor of a city.

Pisé. Packed wet clay, naturally baked by the sun. Widely used throughout Morocco for the construction of walls, kasbahs and roads.

Protectorate. Period of French colonial rule of Morocco (1912–56). Administered by the Resident-General under the pretence that the sultan had contracted his authority to France by the 1912 Treaty of Fez.

Rabat/r'bat. A *r'bat* is a fortified monastery. Rabat is a city founded by the Almohads on the site of an old *r'bat*; it has been the capital of Morocco since 1912.

Ramadan. Muslim month of fasting in the ninth lunar month of the year. No food, drink or sex is allowed during the hours of daylight. Travellers, the sick, the old, the pregnant and pre-pubescent children are exempt.

Reguibat. A desert Berber tribe.

Rehamna. An Arab tribe that dominated the arid plains north of Marrakesh from the 16th century.

Resident-General. The French rulers of Morocco from 1912 to 1956: Lyautey, Steeg, Saint, Ponsot, Peyrouton, Nogues, Puaux, Labonne, Juin, Lacoste, Grandval, Boyer de la Tour and Dubois.

Rharb/Gharb. West. The Rharb is the fertile coastal region between Larache and Kénitra.

Rogui. A pretender to the sultanate.

Roumi. Roman, Christian, foreigner.

Saadian. Moroccan dynasty which replaced the Wattasid sultans in the 15th century and repulsed the Portuguese. They originated as sheikhs from the Drâa Valley and established their first capital at Taroudannt.

Sabil. Public drinking fountain.

Sanhaja. One of the three great groupings of the Berber people occupying the Sahara and parts of the Middle and High Atlas. Their dialect is known as Tamazight.

Sebka. Decorative repetition of interlaced arches, as were often used on the stone gates and walls of the Almohads.

Sebkha. Lake or lagoon.

Seguia. Irrigation canal.

Sheikh. Leader of a religious brotherhood.

Sherif/Shorfa. Descendant of the Prophet.

Sidi. Male honorific title, always used to denote a saint but also more widely used.

Souk. Market.

Sufi. General description for mystical Islamic brotherhoods.

Sultan. Ruler. A word of Turkish origin which implies a single, paramount ruler.

Sunni. The orthodox Muslims, and the prevalent Moroccan form of Islam. The dispute between the schismatic Shiites and Sunni has never been of importance in Morocco.

Tagine. Traditional Moroccan stew.

Taibia. Brotherhood.

Targui (sing.), **Tuareg** (plural). The Sanhajan Berber tribe that occupy the central Sahara and dominated the caravan routes. They alone have retained a Berber alphabet, known as Tifinagh, and speak a Berber dialect known as Temajegh.

Tizi. A mountain pass.

Ulema. The council of professors of Islamic law who since the 12th century have been consulted by sultans for the approval of new laws. They must also formally approve the accession of each new ruler.

Vizier. Chief minister of an Islamic ruler.

Wadi. Dry riverbed.

Wahabbi. Puritanical reforming Muslim sect from Arabia who were active from the 18th century.

Wattasid. Cousins of the Merenid sultans who first became hereditary viziers and from 1472 ruled directly until replaced in 1554 by the Saadians.

Zaouia/zawiya (sing.), **zouawi** (plural). The sanctuary or college of students that often collects around the tomb or sanctuary of a marabout.

Zellij. Geometrical mosaic pattern made from chipped glazed tiles, usually seen on the lower portion of a wall.

Zenata. One of the three great divisions of the Berber people, whose homeland is the northeast, the Rif and the eastern plains. Their dialect is known as Riffi or Tarifit.

Travelling Companions

Bidwell, Margaret and Robin, *Morocco, The Travellers' Companion* (IB Tauris, 1992), a wide-ranging anthology of travel writing.

Rabinow, Paul, *Reflections on Fieldwork in Morocco*, an almost painfully honest account of an anthropologist's attempt to find a Moroccan friend he can trust.

Rogerson, Barnaby, *The Traveller's History of North Africa* (Windrush Press, 1998), the only one-volume history in English of the Maghreb from the Stone Age to the present day.

History

Abun-Nasr, Jamil M, *History of the Maghreb in the Islamic Period* (Cambridge, 1987).

Africanus, Leo, *A Description of Africa, 1600*.

Barbour, Nevill, *Morocco* (London, 1965).

Blunt, Wilfrid, *Black Sunrise, The Life and Times of Moulai Ismaïl, Emperor of Morocco, 1646–1727* (Methuen, 1950).

Bovill, EV, *The Golden Trade of the Moors* (OUP).

Dunn, Ross E, *Resistance in the Desert, 1881–1912* (Croom Helm, 1977).

Forbes, Rosita, *El Raisuni, The Sultan of the Mountains* (Thornton Butterworth, 1924).

Hodges, Tony, *Western Sahara, Roots of a Desert War* (Croom Helm, 1983).

Ibn Battuta, *Travels in Africa and Asia, 1324–54* (RKP).

El Idrisi, *Description of Africa and Spain* (1866).

Julien, CE, *History of North Africa* (London, 1970).

Le Tourneau, R, *Fez in the Age of the Merenids* (Norman, Okla, 1961).

Lewis, Bernard, *The Jews of Islam* (Princeton, 1984).

Maxwell, Gavin, *Lords of the Atlas, The Rise and Fall of the House of Glaoui 1893–1956* (Longmans, 1966, rep Century, 1983).

Meakin, Budget, *The Moorish Empire, The Land of the Moors*, and *The Moors* (London, 1899, 1901, 1902).

Montagne, R, *The Berbers* (London, 1973).

Perkins, KJ, *Quaids, Captains and Colons in the Maghreb* (New York, 1981).

Porch, Douglas, *The Conquest of Morocco* (Cape, 1983); and *The Conquest of the Sahara* (Cape, 1985).

Thompson, V, Adloff, R, *The Western Saharans, Background to Conflict* (Croom Helm, 1980).

Woolman, David, *Rebels in the Rif* (OUP).

Anthropology

Chimenti, Elisa, *Tales and Legends of Morocco* (New York, 1943), folk tales collected by the daughter of a royal surgeon.

Crapanzo, Vincent, *Tuhami, a Portrait of a Moroccan* (Univ. of Chicago), an academic study of an illiterate artisan.

Deshen, Shlomo, *The Mellah Society* (Chicago Univ., 1989), pre-colonial Jewish life.

Dwyer, Kevin, *Moroccan Dialogues* (Johns Hopkins, 1982), interviews from the Sous Valley.

Gellner, Ernest, *Saints of the Atlas* (Weidenfeld & Nicolson, 1969), celebrated study of a holy dynasty in the High Atlas.

Mernissi, Fatima, *Doing Daily Battle: Interviews with Moroccan Women* (Women's Press, 1988); *Beyond the Veil: Male-Female Dynamics in Modern Muslim Society* (Al Saqi, 1985), and

Islam and Democracy: Fear of the Modern World (Virago, 1993), a hard-hitting assault on Muslim political culture in the wake of the Gulf War.

Munson, Henry, *The House of Si Abd Allah*, conversations with a family outside Tangier.

Peets, Leonara, *Women of Marrakesh, 1930–79* (Hurst), acute social observations by a long-resident Estonian doctor.

Waterbury, John, *North for the Trade* (Berkeley 1972).

Westermarck, Edward, *Ritual and Belief in Morocco* (London, 2 vols, 1926); and *Wit and Wisdom in Morocco* (London, 1930).

Travel Writing

Bowles, Paul, *Their Heads Are Green*, and *Points in Time* (Peter Owen).

Canetti, Elias, *The Voices of Marrakesh* (M Boyars); if you read just one book, make it this one.

Cunnighame Graham, RB, *Moghreb el Acksa* (London, 1898, rep Century).

Harris, Walter, *Morocco That Was* (London, 1921, rep Eland Books). *The Land of an African Sultan* (London, 1889), and *Tafilet* (Blackwood, Edinburgh, 1895) remain out of print.

Landau, Ron, *Kasbahs of Southern Morocco* (Faber & Faber, 1969).

Lewis, Wyndham, *Journey into Barbary*, first published as *Filibusters in Barbary* (London, 1932, rep Penguin).

Saint-Exupéry, Antoine de, *Wind, Sand and Stars* (Heinemann, 1939, rep Penguin), the pioneer poet of flight flying mail across the Sahara.

Wharton, Edith, *Morocco* (Travellers Library, 1927, rep Century).

Moroccan Fiction Translated into English

Maghrebi fiction is at its best in novella or short-story form. It is distinguished by its fast narrative and plots, its violence and recurring theme of betrayal by friends and lovers.

Five Eyes (Black Sparrow Press) is a collection of short stories by Abdesalam Boulaich, Mohammed Choukri, Larbi Layachi, Mohammed Mrabet and Ahmed Yacoubi, translated by Paul Bowles.

Ben Jalloun, Tahar, *The Sand Child* (H Hamilton), *Sacred Night* (Quartet), *With Downcast Eyes* (Little, Brown, USA), three novels by one of Morocco's most fêted and literate of novelists, a long-time resident of Paris.

Choukri, Mohammed, *For Bread Alone, an Autobiography* (Peter Owen, 1973), a celebrated description of a harrowing childhood on the outer edge of society.

Chraibi, Driss, *Heirs to the Past* (Heinemann), *Mother Comes of Age* (Three Continents Press), *The Butts* (Forest Books), three novels, of which the first is a classic not matched by its successors.

Layachi, Larbi, *A Life Full of Holes* (Grove Press, under Driss Charhadi penname), *Yesterday and Today* (Black Sparrow Press, 1985), *The Jealous Lover* (Tombouctou Books, California, 1986).

Further Reading

Mrabet, Mohammed, *Love With a Few Hairs* (Arena, 1986), *M'Hashish* (Peter Owen, 1988), *The Beach Café* and *The Voice* (Black Sparrow Press, USA, 1980), *The Chest* (Tombouctou Books, California, 1983), *Marriage With Papers* (Tombouctou Books, California, 1988), *Look and Move On* (Peter Owen, 1989), all translated by Paul Bowles. Start with the 1960s collection of ten tales, *M'Hashish*, which could be translated as 'bombed out of your mind'.

Serhane, Abselhake, *Messaouda* (Carcanet), rites of passage for a young boy growing up in Azrou and for Morocco shedding the paternalism of the French Protectorate.

Western Fiction Set in Morocco

Barea, Arturo, *The Forging of a Rebel* (Flamingo, 3 vols). Vol 2, *The Track*, deals with the Rif war.

Bowles, Paul, *The Sheltering Sky* (Granada), set in the Algerian Sahara; *Let it Come Down* (Arena, 1985), on Tangier; *The Spider's House* (Arena), and *Collected Stories, 1939–1976* (Black Sparrow Press, USA 1986), the most complete collection; though there is a host of rivals such as *The Delicate Prey* (1950), *A Hundred Camels in the Courtyard* (1962), *The Time of Friendship* (1967), *Things Gone and Things Still Here* (1977), *A Little Stone* (1950), *Call at Corazon* (1980).

Burgess, Anthony, *Enderby* (Penguin), scenes from Tangier clublife.

Burroughs, William, *Naked Lunch* (Paladin), to those who know them the silhouettes of Tangier and Gibraltar emerge through the dazzling, distorted static of this fantasy.

Busi, Aldo, *Sodomies in Eleven Point* (Faber, 1992), in the words of the blurb, 'a journey of the heart and soul through Literature, Life and Homosexuality'. Morocco and its men on pp.37–129.

Chirbes, Rafael, *Mimoun* (Serpent's Tail, 1992), the tale of the breakdown of a young Spaniard in Sefrou, in which every object, each moment is rendered mysterious.

Freud, Esther, *Hideous Kinky* (Hamish Hamilton, 1992/Penguin, 1993), a warm evocation of the joys of Morocco, as seen in the life of an English hippy mother by her five-year-old daughter.

Gray, Pat, *Mr Narrator* (Dedalus 1989), an unpublicized modern classic that 'portrays with documentary accuracy a Morocco...colonized by surrealism'.

Grenier, Richard, *The Marrakesh One-Two* (Macdonald, 1984), a comic adventure that takes its humour from the clash between Western and Muslim culture.

Gysin, Brian, *The Process* (Abacus), kif-induced adventures in 1960s Tangier and the Sahara.

Hughes, Richard, *In the Lap of the Atlas* (Chatto), set in a fictional Telouèt.

Malouf, Amin, *Leo the African* (Quartet), historical novel on the 15th-century life of Leo Africanus.

Maugham, Robin, *The Wrong People* (David Griffin, 1967), gay adventures among the smart British expatriate set of Tangier.

Journals, Letters, Diaries from Tangier

Bowles, Paul, *Without Stopping* (Peter Owen, 1972), an autobiography nicknamed *Without Telling*, a failing not much corrected in the unauthorized biography by C Sawyer-Lauccano, *An Invisible Spectator* (Bloomsbury, 1989).

Other Bowles-iana include *Paul Bowles by His Friends*, ed. G Pulsifer (Peter Owen); Bowles' slim *A Tangier Journal, 1987–89* (Peter Owen, 1990); and Jane Bowles' *In and Out in the World, Letters 1935–70* (Black Sparrow, 1985).

The Tangier scene has been well covered in: **Green, Michelle**, *The Dream at the End of the World: Paul Bowles and the Literary Renegades of Tangier* (Bloomsbury), and **Finlayson, Ian**, *Tangier, City of the Dream* (Harper Collins, 1992).

Entertaining memoirs include **Croft-Cooke, Rupert**, *The Caves of Hercules* (London, 1974); **Edge, David**, *Harem*; **Herbert, David**, *Second Son* (Peter Owen, 1972) and *Engaging Eccentrics* (Peter Owen, 1990); **Stewart, Angus**, *Tangier, A Writer's Notebook* (London, 1977); and *Joe Orton's Diaries* (London, 1986).

Art and Architecture

Besancot, Jean, *Costumes et Types du Maroc* (Paris, 1942), and *Bijoux Arabes et Berbères du Maroc* (Casablanca, 1954, rep. KPI, London).

Burkhardt, Titus, *Art of Islam, Language and Meaning,* and *Moorish Culture in Spain*.

Damluji, Salma, *Zillij: The Art of Moroccan Ceramics* (Garnet, UK), expensive but definitive examination of the Ceramic tradition.

Dennis, Lisl and Landt, *Living in Morocco* (Thames & Hudson), illustrated handbook on using traditional crafts in modern interiors.

Hurbert, Claude, *Islamic Ornamental Design* (Faber & Faber, 1980).

Jacques-Meunie, DJ, *Greniers Citadelles au Maroc* (Paris, 1951), *Architectures et Habitats du Dadès* (Paris, 1962), *Sites et Forteresses de l'Atlas,* (Paris, 1951).

Khatabi, A, and Sigilmassa, M, *The Splendours of Islamic Calligraphy* (Thames & Hudson, 1976); *Matisse in Morocco: The Paintings and Drawings, 1912–13* (Nat. Gallery of Art, Washington DC).

Parker, RB, *Islamic Monuments in Morocco* (Baraka Press, USA).

Wade, D, *Pattern in Islamic Art* (London, 1976).

Islam

The Koran, trans. NJ Dawood (Penguin, 1956), or *The Koran* (OUP) are the most easily available of the various rival texts.

Burkhardt, Titus, *An Introduction to Sufi Doctrine*.

Guillaume, Alfred, *Islam* (Penguin).

Nigosian, Solomon, *Islam: The Way of Submission* (Crucible, 1987).

Flowers, Birds and Animals

Bergier, P and F, *A Birdwatcher's Guide to Morocco* (Prion Press), a practical site guide for the committed birder.

Haltenorth, T and Diller, H, *A Field Guide to the Mammals of Africa* (Collins).

Heinzel, Fitter and Parslow, *The Birds of Britain and Europe with North Africa and the Middle East* (Collins).

Hollom, Porter, Christensen and Willis, *Birds of the Middle East and North Africa* (Poyser), the best field guide (used in conjunction with *The Birds of Britain and Europe with North Africa and the Middle East*).

Huxley, Anthony and Polunin, Oleg, *Flowers of the Mediterranean* (Chatto & Windus), the classic well-thumbed travelling companion.

Raine, Peter, *Rough Guide to Mediterranean Wildlife,* fine general coverage plus a detailed country chapter.

Cooking

Benkirane, Fettouma, *Secrets of Moroccan Cooking,* and *Moroccan Cooking: The Best Recipes* (Sochepress).

Carrier, Robert, *Taste of Morocco* (Arrow, London), an illustrated labour of love concentrating on the palace traditions.

Guinaudeau, Z, *Fez, Traditional Moroccan Cooking* (Rabat, 1957).

Roden, Claudia, *The Book of Jewish Food* (Viking, 1997), a fascinating exploration of Jewish culinary tradition, including a section on Morocco.

Wolfert, Paula, *Good Food from Morocco* (John Murray, 1962), all the secrets of traditional home cooking.

The official language of Morocco is Arabic, though 40 per cent of the population speak one of the three Berber dialects as their first language. Moroccans have a natural linguistic ability, and in the cities they will typically speak Arabic, possibly know one of the Berber dialects, learn French or Spanish at school and also juggle with a little English, Dutch or German. In all but the most rural areas you will be understood speaking French. Despite an official Arabicization policy, French remains the language of higher education, technology, government and big business. Spanish is understood and spoken in Spain's old colonial possessions in the far north and south, the Rif and the Western Sahara. Hotel porters, guides and hustlers can usually be relied on to know some English. In short, it is easy to travel and communicate in Morocco without learning Arabic. However, if you can learn a few phrases or greetings you will not only give great pleasure but will also earn goodwill useful in any transaction or relationship.

Moroccan Arabic Pronunciation: Classical Arabic and modern Arabic as spoken in Cairo or Mecca are very different from the official language of Morocco—Maghrebi Arabic. It is a very guttural language, but this does not mean that it should be hard sounding. As a general rule, hard consonants should be pronounced as far back in the throat as possible, thereby softening them slightly. In particular:

'q'	should be quite like a 'k', softened by being vocalized from farther back in the throat
'gh'	should sound like a purring 'gr', again from the back of the throat, a hardened French 'r'
'kh'	like a Gaelic 'ch', pronounced from the back of the throat, as in the Scottish 'loch'
'j'	again a softer sound, like the French pronunciation of the letter, as in 'Frère Jacques'
'ai'	should sound like the letter 'i' as you would pronounce it when reciting the alphabet
'ay'	should sound like the letter 'a' as in the recited alphabet

English	*French*	*Arabic*
Basic		
Yes, No	*Oui, Non*	*Eeyeh/Waha, La*
Please	*S'il vous plaît*	*Minfadlik*
Thank you	*Merci*	*Shokran/Barakalayfik*
Good, Bad	*Bon, Mauvais*	*Mizeyen, Meshee mizeyen*
Meetings, Greetings, Conversation		
Sir, Madam	*Monsieur, Madame*	*Si/Sidi, Lalla*
Hello	*Bonjour*	*Labes (informal), Salam Alaykoom*
How are you?	*Comment allez-vous?*	*Ooach khbar'ek?*
Fine	*Ça va bien*	*Labes*
Good morning	*Bonjour*	*Sbah l'khir*
Good evening	*Bonsoir*	*Msa l'khir*
Goodbye	*Au revoir*	*B'slemah*
Good night	*Bonne nuit*	*Leela saieeda*
My name is ...	*Je m'appelle ...*	*Ismee ...*
How do you say ... in Arabic?	*Comment dit-on ... en Arabe?*	*Keef tkoobal ... Arbia?*
I don't understand	*Je ne comprends pas*	*Ma fhemshi*
I don't know	*Je ne sais pas*	*Ma arafshi*
Help!	*Au secours!*	*Ateqq!*
Excuse me, Sorry	*Excusez-moi, Pardon*	*Smeh lee, Asif*
Never mind/such is life	*C'est la vie*	*Maalesh*
No problem	*Pas de problème*	*Mush mushkillah*
Travelling and Directions		
Train	*train*	*tren*
Bus	*autobus*	*l'kar/tobis*
Car	*voiture*	*tomobeel, sayara*
When is the first/ last/next ...?	*A quelle heure part le premier/dernier/prochain...?*	*Waqtash ... loowel/l'akher/lee minbad?*
Where is ...?	*Où se trouve ...?*	*Fayn kayn ...?*
... a hotel	*... un hôtel*	*... otel/fondouk*
... a campsite	*... un camping*	*... mookhaiyem*

... a restaurant	*... un restaurant*	*... restaurant*
... a lavatory	*... un W.C.*	*... vaysay*
... the bus station	*... la gare d'autobus*	*... mahata d'lkeeran*
... the train station	*... la gare*	*... mahata d'ltren*
... a bank	*... une banque*	*... bank*
... a post office	*... une poste*	*... bousta/barid*
ticket	*billet*	*bitaka/beeyay*
left, right	*à gauche, à droite*	*al leeser, al leemin*

At a Hotel

I want a room	*Je voudrais une chambre*	*B'gheet beet*
Do you have a room?	*Est-ce que vous avez une chambre?*	*Wesh andik wahid beet?*
Can I look at it?	*Est-ce qu'on peut la voir?*	*Wesh yimkin nshoof?*

At a Restaurant

What do you have to eat?/to drink?	*Qu'est ce que vous avez à manger?/à boire?*	*Ashnoo kane f'l-makla? /f'l musharoubat?*
What is this?	*Qu'est ce que c'est?*	*Shnoo hada?*
big, small	*grand, petit*	*kbir, sghrir*
glass, plate	*verre, assiette*	*kess, t'b-sil*
knife, fork, spoon	*couteau, fourchette, cuillère*	*moos, forsheta, malka*
bread, eggs	*pain, œufs*	*l'hobs, beda*
salt, pepper, sugar	*sel, poivre, sucre*	*l'melha, lebzar, azoukar*
The bill please	*L'addition, s'il vous plaît*	*L'h'seb minfadlik*

Vegetables/Salads/Fruit · Légumes/Salades/Fruits · Ikhoudra/chalada/Fekiha

olives	*olives*	*zitoun*
rice	*riz*	*rouz*
potatoes (chips)	*pommes de terre (frites)*	*btata (btata mklya)*
tomatoes, onions	*tomates, oignons*	*matesha, l'basla*
mixed salad	*salade Marocaine*	*chalada*
oranges, grapes, bananas	*oranges, raisins, bananes*	*leetcheen, l'a'arib, banane*
peaches, apricots	*pêches, abricots*	*l'khoukh, mishmash*
almonds, dates, figs	*amandes, dattes, figues*	*louze, tmer, kermus*

Meat/Poultry/Fish · Viande/Volaille/Poisson · L'hem/L'hout

beef, mutton	*bœuf, mouton*	*l'habra, l'houli/kabch*
chicken	*poulet*	*djaj*
sardines	*sardines*	*sardile*

Numbers · *Nombres*

1, 2, 3, 4, 5,	*un, deux, trois, quatre, cinq*	*wahed, jooj, tlata, arba, khamsa*
6, 7, 8, 9,	*six, sept, huit, neuf*	*setta, seba, tmenia, tse'ud*
10, 20, 50	*dix, vingt, cinquante*	*achra, achrin, khamsin*
100, 1000	*cent, mille*	*mia, alef*

Buying and Bargaining

How much is that?	*C'est combien?*	*Bsh hal hadeek?*
Too expensive	*Trop cher*	*Ghalee bzef*
Do you have ...?	*Est-ce que vous avez des ...?*	*Wesh andik ...?*
larger, smaller, cheaper	*plus grand, plus petit, moins cher*	*kebira, seghira, rkhaysa*
This is no good	*Ça ne va pas*	*Hadee meshee mizeyen*
I don't want any	*Je n'en veux pas*	*Mabgheet shee*
Okay!	*Okay!*	*Wakha!*

Language

Note: Page numbers in *italics* indicate maps. **Bold** references indicate main references.

Also Available from Cadogan Guides...

Country Guides

Antarctica
Central Asia
China: The Silk Routes
Egypt
France: Southwest France;
    Dordogne, Lot & Bordeaux
France: Southwest France;
    Gascony & the Pyrenees
France: Brittany
France: The Loire
France: The South of France
France: Provence
France: Côte d'Azur
Germany: Bavaria
Greece: The Peloponnese
Holland
Holland: Amsterdam & the Randstad
India
India: South India
India: Goa
Ireland
Ireland: Southwest Ireland
Ireland: Northern Ireland
Italy
Italy: The Bay of Naples and Southern Italy
Italy: Bologna and Emilia Romagna
Italy: Italian Riviera
Italy: Lombardy, Milan and the Italian Lakes
Italy: Rome and the Heart of Italy
Italy: Sardinia
Italy: Tuscany, Umbria and the Marches
Italy: Tuscany
Italy: Umbria
Italy: Venetia and the Dolomites
Japan
Morocco
Portugal
Portugal: The Algarve
Scotland
Scotland: Highlands and Islands
South Africa, Swaziland and Lesotho
Spain
Spain: Southern Spain
Spain: Northern Spain
Syria & Lebanon
Tunisia
Turkey
Yucatán and Southern Mexico
Zimbabwe, Botswana and Namibia

City Guides

Amsterdam
Barcelona
Brussels, Bruges, Ghent & Antwerp
Bruges
Edinburgh
Florence, Siena, Pisa & Lucca
Italy: Three Cities—Rome, Florence, Venice
Italy: Three Cities—Venice, Padua, Verona
Italy: Three Cities—Rome, Naples, Sorrento
Italy: Three Cities—Rome, Padua, Assisi
Japan: Three Cities—Tokyo, Kyoto and
    Ancient Nara
Morocco: Three Cities—Marrakesh, Fez, Rabat
Spain: Three Cities—Granada, Seville,
    Cordoba
Spain: Three Cities—Madrid, Barcelona, Seville
London
London–Paris
London–Brussels
Madrid
Manhattan
Moscow & St Petersburg
Paris
Prague
Rome
St Petersburg
Venice

Island Guides

Caribbean and Bahamas
Jamaica & the Caymans

Greek Islands
Greek Islands By Air
Crete
Mykonos, Santorini & the Cyclades
Rhodes & the Dodecanese
Corfu & the Ionian Islands

Madeira & Porto Santo
Malta
Sardinia
Sicily

Plus...

Bugs, Bites & Bowels
London Markets
Take the Kids Travelling
Take the Kids London
Take the Kids Paris and Disneyland
Take the Kids Amsterdam

Available from good bookshops or via, in the UK, **Grantham Book Services**, Isaac Newton Way, Alma Park Industrial Estate, Grantham NG31 9SD, ℗ (01476) 541 080, ✉ (01476) 541 061; and in North America from **The Globe Pequot Press**, 246 Goose Lane, PO Box 480, Guilford, Connecticut 06437–0480, ℗ (800) 243 0495, ✉ (800) 820 2329.

The Best of Morocco

HOLIDAYS FOR THE INDEPENDENT TRAVELLER

No other company (anywhere) can offer you the variety, flexibility and unparalleled advantage of over 30 years' knowledge and experience. We have the most comprehensive programme of holidays you will find. Our holidays are mostly tailor-made, based on 4- and 5-star hotels for independent travellers to all the major cities (Marrakech, Taroudant, Rabat, Fes, Meknes, Essaouira, Tangier and Casablanca) as well as many of the remoter places in the Sahara Desert and the High and Anti Atlas Mountains.

Our brochure was awarded 'Best brochure on Morocco' by the Ministry of Tourism in Rabat and was shortlisted among the best holiday brochures in the Observer/Guardian Travel Awards 1999. We also have an extremely comprehensive and frequently updated website.

In addition to the 60 hotels featured in our brochure, we arrange fly-drive with self-drive or chauffeur-driven cars, weekend breaks, camel-trekking in the Sahara, horse-trekking in the Atlas Mountains, golf holidays in Marrakech, El Jadida, Tangier and Rabat, skiing in the High Atlas and walking/trekking holidays from 3 to 7 days in the High Atlas.

Our holidays are based on scheduled flights with British Airways from Gatwick or Royal Air Maroc from Heathrow and Stansted airports. We are fully Bonded with the Civil Aviation Authority (Licence No. 2640).

We have our own office in Marrakech who will help you during your visit to Morocco and can even help you buy your own villa or house in the old part of Marrakech.

Contact us for further information.

The Best of Morocco Ltd
Seend, Wiltshire SN12 6NZ
England

Tel: 01380-828533   Fax: 01380-828630
morocco@morocco-travel.com
www.morocco-travel.com